CIVIL WAR
MONUMENTS
and the
MILITARIZATION
OF AMERICA

CIVIL WAR AMERICA

Peter S. Carmichael, Caroline E. Janney,
and Aaron Sheehan-Dean, editors

This landmark series interprets broadly the history and culture
of the Civil War era through the long nineteenth century and
beyond. Drawing on diverse approaches and methods, the
series publishes historical works that explore all aspects of
the war, biographies of leading commanders, and tactical and
campaign studies, along with select editions of primary sources.
Together, these books shed new light on an era that remains
central to our understanding of American and world history.

CIVIL WAR MONUMENTS

—— and the ——

MILITARIZATION OF AMERICA

Thomas J. Brown

THE UNIVERSITY OF NORTH CAROLINA PRESS

Chapel Hill

Publication of this book was supported in part
by a generous grant from the Watson-Brown Foundation.

© 2019 The University of North Carolina Press

Designed by Jamison Cockerham
Set in Arno, Scala Sans, Sorts Mill Goudy, American Scribe, and Brothers
by Tseng Information Systems, Inc.

Manufactured in the United States of America

The University of North Carolina Press has been a
member of the Green Press Initiative since 2003.

Cover illustration: Gen. William T. Sherman statue in Grand Army Plaza,
Central Park, New York. Photograph by Albert Knapp / Alamy Stock Photo.

LIBRARY OF CONGRESS CATALOGING-IN-PUBLICATION DATA
Names: Brown, Thomas J., 1960– author.
Title: Civil War monuments and the militarization
of America / Thomas J. Brown.
Description: Chapel Hill : The University of North Carolina Press, [2019] |
Series: Civil War America | Includes bibliographical references and index
Identifiers: LCCN 2019020029| ISBN 9781469653730 (cloth : alk. paper) |
ISBN 9781469653747 (pbk : alk. paper) | ISBN 9781469653754 (ebook)
Subjects: LCSH: United States — History — Civil War, 1861–1865 —
Monuments. | War memorials — United States — History. |
Soldiers' monuments — United States — History. | Militarization —
United States — History. | Militarization — United States — Public
opinion. | Political culture — United States — History.
Classification: LCC E641 .B885 2019 | DDC 973.7/6 — dc23
LC record available at https://lccn.loc.gov/2019020029

For Veronica, and in remembrance of Lucian

Contents

Illustrations

CIVIL WAR MONUMENTS
and the
MILITARIZATION OF AMERICA

FIGURE I.1. William Walcutt, *Pulling Down the Statue of George III at Bowling Green, New York, July 9, 1776* (1857). Courtesy of Lafayette College Art Collection.

Introduction

BEYOND THE
ICONOCLASTIC
REPUBLIC

American memory began in iconoclasm. After the public reading of the Declaration of Independence ordered by George Washington upon arrival of
the document in New York City on July 9, 1776, a crowd surged to Bowling
Green and tore down the equestrian statue of George III dedicated six years
earlier. This symbolic regicide was a profoundly antimilitary protest. Since
antiquity, the equestrian monument had been an emblem of imperial authority precisely because it depicted the sovereign as a military commander.
Even if a monarch like George III was hardly prepared to lead troops in the
field, the king's statue in lower Manhattan complemented the adjacent garrison that enforced his royal authority. American commemoration developed
in accordance with the hostility toward standing armies central to the Revolution. Through the first half of the nineteenth century, the most prominent
outdoor monuments to Washington in the nation's capital, New York, and
Baltimore showed the general giving up his authority at the end of the war
and dramatizing a radical disjuncture of military and political governance.
Americans often observed that public monuments were less compatible
with democracy than other modes of remembrance, especially print.[1]

The Civil War monuments installed by communities across the North
and South from the 1860s into the 1930s transformed the civic landscape and
the place of the military in national life. The United States became a lead-

ing contributor to the transatlantic canon of war memorials. This highly decentralized process yielded many different commemorations, but prevailing patterns emerged. The introduction of the common-soldier monument responded to the crisis of Civil War death without immediately relinquishing antebellum reservations about martial institutions. Early tributes to military and civilian leaders also expanded creatively on prewar precedents. As the shock of the carnage faded, however, a second proliferation of monuments assumed a different cast. Often dedicated to veterans, these memorials identified soldiers as exemplars of a robust, disciplined citizenry. Commander statues idealized hierarchical leadership. Celebrations of victory shifted emphasis from regeneration to affirmation. Civil War monuments reshaped remembrance of the Revolution and helped to divert American conceptions of World War I from the anguished meditations of the Allied Powers. Cultural form invigorated ideology in the metamorphosis of the country from an iconoclastic republic to a militarized nation.

This militarization included symbolic and practical dimensions. The establishment of the American war memorial shaped the broader evolution of public monuments in the United States and the development of other patriotic practices. Art historian Dell Upton has recently underscored the pervasive legacy of Civil War commemoration by observing that even monuments to the mid-twentieth-century civil rights movement, a heroic demonstration of democracy grounded in doctrines of nonviolence, routinely turn to martial iconography as emblematic of citizenship.[2] Contrary to the hopes of the iconoclastic republic, military monuments became an authoritative representation of the nation. That shift not only correlated with but preceded and facilitated policy developments. Civil War monuments, which became more belligerent during a period of international peace, modeled the forcible imposition of labor and racial order amid late-nineteenth-century struggles over the prerogatives of industrial capitalism and white supremacism. Veneration of soldiers also advanced military measures like the consolidation of a veterans' welfare state and the restructuring of an expanded army.

As a dominant vehicle of Civil War memory the public monument contrasted sharply with the principal commemorative institution of the iconoclastic republic, the Fourth of July. That anniversary did not celebrate battlefield achievement but the self-realization of a political community. Annual rites of observance in the early nineteenth century subordinated military dimensions to a civilian framework. Militia units participated in parades, but the soldiers marched alongside trade groups, civic and benevolent organizations, ethnic societies, and other fellow citizens. Orations and after-dinner toasts were more essential to the occasion than drill, and many of the national heroes honored by the speakers never wore a uniform, including Benjamin Franklin, Sam and John Adams, Thomas Jefferson, and Patrick Henry. Although cannon salutes were commonplace, the less regulated and more spectacular fireworks displays better typified the carnival of liberty.[3]

Even this national festival exaggerated the everyday influence of the armed forces in the antebellum polity. Military service commanded much less public respect than the skilled craftsmanship of artisans and mechanics or the productive husbandry of yeomen farmers, Jefferson's "chosen people of God, if ever he had a chosen people." Continued opposition to standing armies restricted the full-time "regular army" to an authorized force of about 18,000 and an enrolled strength of 16,000 in 1860, when the population was more than 31 million.[4] Mostly assigned to frontier outposts, officers often left the tedious service for civilian life; the poorly paid rank and file came largely from the northeastern underclass. State militias were equally indicative of public attitudes. Although the notion that every man owed military duty lingered in the theoretical concept of the "enrolled militia" comprised of all adult males in a jurisdiction, extensive exemptions from service punctured this fantasy in the early republic. Satirists frequently targeted the pompous and evidently pointless militia. Massachusetts legislation of 1840 led a shift to reliance on volunteer companies, which survived primarily as a transitional form of civil police amid anxieties about rioting in rapidly growing cities divided by class and ethnicity. New York abandoned the pretense of compulsory service six years later. Many rural states did not maintain any militia system by the late antebellum period. Alexis de Tocqueville recognized the bankruptcy of the republican militia ideal when he reported that "in America, the use of conscription is unknown, and men are induced to enlist by bounties." He observed that "the notions and habits of the people of the United States are so opposed to compulsory enlistment, that I do not imagine that it can ever be sanctioned by the laws."[5]

Distrust of the military guided Jacksonian mobilization for the Mexican War. Congress expanded the regular army and added to it a set of regiments that served for the duration of the war rather than a standard five-year term. Recruitment drew on southern and western enthusiasm for territorial acquisition but also the usual urban basis for the regular army. Beyond the resulting temporary regulars, Congress authorized a larger set of volunteer regiments to be organized within the states. To head these units governors appointed officers likely to recruit successfully or fulfill other political objectives. President James K. Polk, who disdained career officers as an elite isolated from common people, prioritized Democratic partisanship in his appointment of volunteer generals. Field commanders' assertion of discipline was a constant negotiation, in which desertion was an important bargaining tool for the rambunctious rank and file. Serving the same identifying purpose as prison stripes, the uniform of the regular army inspired so little respect that volunteers in one Massachusetts company went on strike rather than don the standard-issue blue tunics with brass buttons after their distinctive gray uniforms had worn out. The paramilitary excursions into Latin America that followed the imperial conquest suggested that the filibuster was more popular than the soldier as a model of late antebellum manhood.[6]

Widespread reservations about the army were ironically consistent with the frequent election of former military commanders to high political office. As different as George Washington and Andrew Jackson were in temperament and ideology, both volunteer generals updated the Roman story of Cincinnatus, who proved virtue by sacrificing personal interests to defend the republic. Antebellum Americans did not suppose that military service created virtue, as turn-of-the-century Americans would argue. The plow left behind by the prototypical volunteer implanted the moral excellence merely ratified by the sword. The drinking, cursing, gambling, whoring, and rigid hierarchy of army life were specters of corruption often blamed for the ruin of innocent youth. Field command offered scope for manifestation of leadership, variously based on social privilege or charisma, but few civilians considered military professionalism particularly admirable. Shrewd generals like Jackson disdained conventions of high rank. Many factors contributed to the election of Zachary Taylor in 1848 and the defeat of Winfield Scott in 1852, but it was fitting that "Old Rough and Ready" won the presidency while "Old Fuss and Feathers," the most thoroughly professional soldier in the antebellum United States, lost decisively to one of Polk's inept commanders of Mexican War volunteers.

The epic mobilization for the Civil War did not cause permanent changes in the relationship between the military and the polity. The quasi-conscription system hesitantly adopted by the federal government, designed less to compel service than to stimulate municipal bounties that would attract volunteers, apparently confirmed Tocqueville's judgment that Americans would not accept obligatory military enlistment. Even the readily avoidable Union draft sparked rioting on an unprecedented scale.[7] Civilians continued to debate the value of specialized military training and regard camp life as a moral hazard. Assertions of lasting uplift usually depended on religion and close contact with home. The gulf between the institutional cultures of the regular army and the vastly larger U.S. Volunteers narrowed only partly. Commanders at every level still negotiated their claims to authority over volunteers; in exasperation they often resorted to physical coercion. Thomas Wentworth Higginson, who typified the northeastern elites most enamored with martial regimentation, sighed late in the war that the prototypical American soldier "is more ready than any other to comply with a reasonable order, but he does it because it is reasonable, not because it is an order." Characteristically unwilling to salute or otherwise cultivate habits of obedience, volunteers rejected the premise of the regular army that strict division between officers and the rank and file was crucial to development of an effective bond. Savvy officers instead inspired respect by leveraging extra-military relationships with enlisted men, which were sometimes ideological, sometimes neighborly, and sometimes quasi-paternal. Higginson recognized the ascendancy of political engagement and sociability over military norms when he observed that "the discipline of our soldiers has been generally that of a town-meeting or an engine-company, rather than an army." The situation was similar in the Confederacy. Volunteers expressed their sense of entitlement to withhold service in the readiness with which they deserted, if only for a short term.[8]

William Conant Church, a starker example of bourgeois northeastern affinity for military order, ruefully testified to the postwar survival of deeply ingrained national values. Brief experience as a volunteer Union officer anchored Church's career as one of the few civilians to promote the military as a template for American society. He launched the *Army and Navy Journal* in 1863 with hopes that "for the future we are a military people." Within a few years of Appomattox, however, Church was complaining that the "prejudice against military men and military measures which is an inheritance from our colonial days revived the moment the smoke had cleared away from the battlefields."[9]

The transformation sought by Church did not take place in the war but through commemoration of the war. As his frustration indicated, the shift was not immediate or inevitable. Martial ideals prevailed only occasionally in Civil War monuments before the intensive organization of Union veterans in conjunction with the pension legislation of the late 1870s. The Grand Army of the Republic and similar societies pioneered a polity in which veterans enjoyed unprecedented material entitlements and successfully claimed authority as arbiters of patriotism. White southern veterans began to assume comparable stature shortly afterward, with the vital aid of the United Daughters of the Confederacy. Civil War monuments were a prime manifestation of these privileges.

The soldier's replacement of the farmer as the paradigmatic American citizen created a social metaphor conducive to Gilded Age reinforcement of class and racial hierarchy, and the proliferation of monuments continued to accelerate long after Civil War survivors' political influence peaked. War memorials illustrated the values of the men who were coming to be known as captains of industry. Esteem for the soldier as a champion of discipline, brute force, and self-sacrifice offered a model for labor relations that working-class admirers of Civil War monuments could not fail to notice. The origins of the soldier memorial in democratic recognition of ordinary Americans established a lasting leverage for didacticism that turned against workers' interests. Old-stock ethnic bias often helped explain monument supporters' compromises in a period of massive immigration and anxiety about social fragmentation and political radicalism. Obeisance to the Lost Cause in the white South strengthened the recoil from the egalitarian potential of Reconstruction.

The trend toward memorial militarization did not proceed without resistance. Some critics decried the pattern. Peaceable early works remained in place, though often obscured by changes in public understanding of their designs. The slow gestation of projects occasionally resulted in old-fashioned reassertions that patriotic virtue was anterior to military service rather than its product. The revival of Lincoln commemoration in the early twentieth century prompted tributes to his humane intellect as well as salutes to the federal commander-in-chief. Other complex monuments presented artists as alternatives to the warriors ostensibly honored. Civil War remembrance offered selective preparation for engagement with French and British reflections on World War I, and a few internationalists challenged the American zeal for combat.[10]

The intersection of race and military monuments illustrated several strategies of contestation. Initial proposals for celebration of emancipation featured many visions of freedom, but the transformation of slave into soldier soon emerged as the main memorial argument for black citizenship. African Americans and their allies accordingly sought to realize the logic of the martial ideal and claim recognition of black service in the Union army. They achieved little success, however, for the militarization of American memory was thoroughly entwined with white supremacism.[11] The mid-twentieth-century civil rights movement, including the desegregation of the armed services, weakened that link. Monuments to black Union soldiers were among the most conspicuous types of Civil War memorials multiplying at the turn of the millennium. But the belated, marginal integration of commemorative militarism was not enough to undo its racial implications. In the early twenty-first century, protest against militarized white supremacism led to the most important resurgence of American iconoclasm since the overthrow of the equestrian monument to George III in 1776. Several dozen communities removed Confederate monuments from places of honor, including statues of martial paragon Robert E. Lee and tributes to rank-and-file soldiers who gave their lives in response to the call of the state.

Civil War Monuments and the Militarization of America is structured around the development of three overlapping but distinct categories of memorials. Most innovative was the recognition of ordinary citizens, the topic of the first two chapters. Vastly exceeding the scattered precedents in the United States and Europe, the outpouring included a variety of memorial halls, obelisks, allegorical figures, and soldier statues. Monuments to exemplary Union and Confederate manhood prompted a complementary set of monuments to exemplary Union and Confederate womanhood. A second group of Civil War memorials entered into the denser international tradition of tributes to public leaders. The war was the last great subject for the equestrian monument, for centuries the most prestigious sculptural commission. Portrait statues of orators, another ancient motif, also explored the sources of power in the sectional crisis. The third field of Civil War memorials reconsidered the equally venerable lineage of victory monuments. Americans built their first triumphal arches and reimagined the figure of Nike, the classical embodiment of success. Across all of these genres, democratic postwar creativity gradually gave way to more violent, hierarchical, self-aggrandizing representations of social and political order.

This organization of chapters sets up the relationship between theme and chronology in the book. The sections on common-soldier monuments, leadership monuments, and victory monuments each chart competing models of martial commemoration from the eve of the Civil War to the eve of World War I. Changing ideas about the military undergirded crucial differences between American mobilization in the secession crisis and American intervention in the European crisis, including the elimination of the U.S. Volunteers, the coordination of the army and state militias, the introduction of more systematic conscription, the disappearance of "political generals," the reliance on a general staff, the training of reserve officers, and the fundamental confidence that military victory was the best path to long-term peace rather than an unavoidable legal necessity. The fifth chapter moves forward chronologically to examine the intersection of Civil War commemoration and Great War commemoration, a dialogue that ended with the broad decline in the prestige of public monuments during the 1930s. The epilogue examines the influence of Civil War memorials during that relative lull and the revival of the public monument later in the twentieth century. Recent controversies over Confederate remembrance close the book at a point of dramatically renewed interest in Civil War commemoration.

My emphasis on form highlights but does not isolate the designs of Civil War memorials. Although sculptural and architectural statements were central to the debates I trace, public monuments offer a valuable focus for study because they are sites for negotiation of historical interpretation. The relationships between artists and the many other constituencies interested in Civil War monuments varied across the thousands of initiatives. A leading student of French memorials of World War I has observed that "to concentrate on the statuary alone is tantamount to deciphering a long sentence by focusing on a single word," and exemplary scholarship on war memorials has combined analysis of sponsors' identities and fund-raising strategies, the location selected for a work, its design and inscriptions, and the long-term uses of the memorial space.[12] One general application of that principle in this book is my treatment of monuments in battlefield parks. The advent of the battlefield park was important context for the civic memorials on which I concentrate, and I attach considerable significance to the transference of some monument designs from battlefield parks to towns. I do not, however, attempt to survey memorial development within those specialized environments.[13]

My definition of genres facilitates quantitative identification of broad trends as well as intensive analysis of particular monuments.[14] Focus on the common-soldier statue, for example, reveals change over time in the successive idealization of the picket guard, the standard-bearer, and the warrior in combat. Examination of the primary types of memorials provides context for close consideration of revealing examples within each category. I pause over dozens of monuments, from the tribute to fallen comrades installed by the Thirty-Second Indiana Volunteer Infantry Regiment near Rowlett's Station, Kentucky, in the first year of the Civil War through the Confederate memorial moving glacially toward completion on Stone Mountain, Georgia, at the onset of World War II. Certainly many of the works discussed in the book would sustain more detailed treatment, and I would be pleased if this synthesis stimulated such studies.

As the book braids together many local stories, it also embeds several sketches of artists' career trajectories. Civil War commemoration was central to the economics and creative opportunities of sculpture and a recurrent impetus for architecture during the late nineteenth and early twentieth centuries. My chronicle spotlights differences between the Civil War monuments that Augustus Saint-Gaudens conceptualized as a rising young sculptor, including his Farragut Monument (1877–81), Shaw Memorial (1881–97), and standing Lincoln (1884–87), and the works he began as one of the most celebrated artists in the country, his Logan equestrian (1894–97), Sherman group (1892–1903), and seated Lincoln (1897–1906). As the immigrant shoemaker's son more fully adopted the outlook of the metropolitan elite, his interests turned from problems of artistic and political representation toward questions about the exercise of power. The leading master of the Civil War monument encapsulated a transformation of American culture. Other prominent artists with important roles in my narrative include J. Q. A. Ward, Daniel Chester French, Frederick Law Olmsted, and Gutzon Borglum. I am equally attentive to New England Granite Works, Smith Granite Company, and similar commercial innovators in the lower-budget market.

Civil War Monuments and the Militarization of America reframes a rich recent literature on Civil War memory. This scholarship has treated the Union and the Confederacy as the basic categories of analysis and explored the extent to which the political rupture over slavery resolved in sectional reconciliation and white supremacism.[15] In my approach, the divide between North and South is less fundamental than the transformations that reached both sides. Union and Confederate remembrance differed in important ways, but the twinned development of evolutionary ideology and militarism shaped monuments across the country. My arguments draw both from scholarship that has emphasized the prevalence of a conciliatory mode in Civil War memory and scholarship that has highlighted the persistence of sectional antagonisms. Some tributes to soldiers of both sides, often installed in sites that attracted nationwide audiences, contributed to the emergence of a notion that military service is honorable regardless of the cause in which it is rendered. Most communities instead sought to praise only those who fought for right. That tension has made the Civil War monument a crucial vantage point for political conceptualization of the American soldier.

This study of monuments builds directly on scholarship that has examined other ways in which recognition of Civil War soldiers transformed citizenship. The invention of the military cemetery paralleled the war memorial in inscribing commemoration of the fallen in the national landscape, and like their calendrical counterpart Memorial Day, both institutions turned from specific remembrance of the Civil War to a flexible framework for valorization of military exploits.[16] In stressing the shift of public attention from the fallen soldier to the former soldier during the 1880s, I join many historians in debt to outstanding studies of the Grand Army of the Republic and the United Confederate Veterans.[17] Much of the subsequent scholarship has traced the expansion of pensions, health care, and housing for veterans.[18] The proliferation of soldier monuments established a group counterpart to these individual entitlements. Like the military cemeteries and welfare legislation, monuments contributed to the redefinition of the state. Civil War memorials in some major cities, including the nation's capital, were central to the organization of government art commissions and the growth of urban planning. More fundamentally, the martial conception of citizenship provided momentum for reorganization and expansion of the army. This process largely took place in hundreds of local monument campaigns, but I also examine the military's institutional interests in the public image of the Civil War commander.

Emphasis on the broad domestic basis of militarization complements recent explanations focused on cultures of professionalism in the army and navy, gender ideology, and the acceleration of American imperialism.[19] Neither the restructuring of the armed forces nor the demand for more resources simply responded to international situations. Although policymakers treated the Spanish-American War as the consequence of a diplomatic crisis that thrust new responsibilities on the United States, fresh bellicose tendencies had been evident in Civil War monuments for more than a decade before 1898. These monuments show that the turning point in the rise of a martial ideal took place in a period of relative international peace. That ideal was crucial to the success of the movement to "reform" the army.

The Civil War monument took shape in a tenaciously narrative era of American sculpture. Statues alluded to incidents in the careers of particular heroes and to generic wartime situations and plotlines popularized by stories, songs, and prints. This book accordingly benefits from the scholarship on the literature of the Civil War, which is much more fully developed than the work on monuments. Thoughtful commentators have examined the conflicts between family and nation in domestic ideology, the volunteer ethos as an alternative to the culture of the regular army, and the gendered displacement of civilian war stories by more exclusively martial tales. The explication of literary tropes suggests possibilities for the reading of public monuments.[20]

Such cross-fertilization notwithstanding, architectural and sculptural commemoration developed within frameworks distinctive to those arts. Classicized building styles and figurative sculpture responded to more rigorously self-referential traditions than even an age-old plot device like the politically divided household. And although publication was a collaborative process by which authors might speak for substantial constituencies, the more collective enterprise of the public monument involved a different political dynamic with a narrower range of possible outcomes. War memorials did not often recognize the alienated outsiders who were the heroes and heroines of so many novels. The tensions between monuments and print are a recurrent motif of this book. The relationships of monuments to cinema and digital media are among its endpoints.

In highlighting the transatlantic vocabulary of monuments and culminating in the response to World War I, I aim to situate Civil War memory in a wider frame of reference than most works on the topic. The ordeal fostered a communal creativity in institutions of mourning comparable to the artistry of suffering that Paul Fussell has described in the literature of the Western Front, though the extent to which fresh forms initially sustained antebellum ideologies parallels Jay Winter's conclusion that even profound war trauma need not necessarily overturn long-standing social attitudes. I have pursued in detail the international comparisons of war memorials that Annette Becker recommended a quarter century ago and that Ken Inglis has modeled in his contextualization of Australian monuments. This book engages what George Mosse's *Fallen Soldiers* (1990) called the Myth of the War Experience. In the American formulation defined by the Civil War, the fallen soldier was only one icon in complex relations with other emblematic figures like the veteran, the supportive woman, the commander, the political leader, and the personification of victory.[21] My focus on the late nineteenth century as the watershed of remembrance underscores that the changes in thinking about citizen-soldiers that Mosse traced from the French Revolution to World War II have not always resulted from changes in the nature of warfare.

By the sesquicentennial anniversary of the iconoclasm of 1776, Americans had installed thousands of Civil War monuments in their communities. These works were the centerpiece for a martial memory that now reached back to the War of Independence and was in the midst of extensive supplementation to mark the intervention in Europe. An urban legend had recently grown up around the dozens of Civil War monuments that adapted the ancient equestrian form so objectionable during the Revolution. Supposedly the number of the horse's legs lifted in the air indicated whether the rider was killed in battle, wounded, or fortunate enough to survive without injury.[22]

The inaccuracy of this folklore poses a warning for interpretation of Civil War monuments. Their importance is not in a code to be deciphered. The historian's goal is instead to explain how people in specific situations came to see significance in the monuments. As the popular rumor about equestrian statues illustrates, that social process of making meaning has incorporated contributions from many different sources. Scholarship may be antithetical to the mythmaking that animated belief in a master key to statuary poses, but research on commemoration can bring empowerment rather than merely disenchantment. Like other facets of American political history, Civil War monuments include inspiring achievements as well as tragic tendencies. Understanding of the national record should inform our continual revisiting of the civic landscape.

The EMERGENCE of the SOLDIER MONUMENT

"In raising this monument to-day, we are doing no new thing, but what has been endorsed by the sentiments and customs of all nations," declared John M. Stowe at the dedication of the monument to the Civil War dead of Sullivan, New Hampshire, in July 1867. Many orators at parallel ceremonies made the same observation. "At no time has man been so ungrateful, so recreant to a noble and lofty nature, as to deny to the fallen brave suitable marks of respect and admiration," Joshua H. Hudson echoed three weeks later in Cheraw, South Carolina. Edmund de Schweinitz told his audience at an academy in Nazareth, Pennsylvania, in June 1868 that memorials to the war dead were an "intuitive impulse of the heart." The speakers provided scant evidence for these claims. The most often cited precedent was the stone placed on the burial mound of the Spartans who blocked the Persians at Thermopylae. Hudson opened his speech with a translation of its famous epitaph, "Stranger! Tell the Spartans we lie here in obedience to their laws."[1] Other orators mentioned memorials of the Napoleonic wars. The eagerness to situate the new soldier monuments within a Western tradition typified American pride that the Civil War constituted a national epic as grand as the histories of ancient Greece and Rome or the upheavals of postrevolutionary Europe. The effort to establish a lineage also reflected recognition that commemoration thrives through evocation of previous commemorations as well as direct remembrance of historical events.

The assertions of continuity were especially tenuous because Jeffersonian republicans had conspicuously sought to prevent American emulation of European war memorials. Republicans identified military power as dangerous to democracy, and they regarded public monuments as idolatrous anachronisms unsuitable to an enlightened citizenry in the age of print. Federalist attempts to build admiration for a British-style officer class that began with the 1787 unveiling of the Richard Montgomery memorial at Trinity Church in New York faded after the 1808 installation of the Tripoli Monument at the Washington Naval Yard. The Tammany Society's campaign to consecrate a monument in Brooklyn to the martyrs of Revolutionary prison ships epitomized republican countermemory not only in its depiction of ordinary citizens as victims of war but also in the abandonment of the project after the cornerstone-laying ceremony. The multiple controversies over representation of George Washington on the landscape, including the impasse over the National Mall monument that remained a stone stump throughout the Civil War, testified to the persistence of the republican critique of military memorials.[2]

The antebellum United States offered few precursors to the monuments placed where Civil War soldiers lay buried, like Cheraw, or the monuments put up by communities and institutions from which soldiers went to the war, like Sullivan and Nazareth Hall. Lexington, Massachusetts, installed an obelisk on the town green in 1799 inscribed with the names of local residents who had died in the opening engagement of the Revolutionary War nearly a quarter-century earlier. Almost four more decades passed before Danvers erected an obelisk in 1835 to its casualties of the initial skirmish and Concord dedicated a obelisk in 1837 at the former site of "the rude bridge that arched the flood," where "once the embattled farmers stood, / And fired the shot heard round the world." Ralph Waldo Emerson's popular "Concord Hymn" described the "votive stone" as a metaphorical replacement for "the ruined bridge" long ago swept downstream by Time. That relentless flow lent a chill to the pastoral nostalgia with which Emerson expressed hope "that memory may their deed redeem, / When, like our sires, our sons are gone." Aesthetics of landscape appreciation thoroughly overwhelmed military narratives at the most touristed battlefields of the Revolution and the War of 1812, along the Hudson River and around Niagara Falls. The quest for the sublime and the picturesque fostered interest in ruined fortifications, but not in commissioning memorials. Construction of Maximilian Godefroy's Battle Monument (1815–25) at the same time as Robert Mills's Washington Monument (1815–29) was unusual enough to earn Baltimore the nickname "The Monumental City" in the 1820s.[3]

Even the most famous Revolutionary War monument betrayed diffidence toward soldiers. The promoters of the Bunker Hill Monument Association aimed at its founding in 1823 to honor both "the civil and military heroes of New England." The artist whose plan they adopted, Horatio Greenough, emphasized that the towering granite shaft did not single out for recognition the men killed at the site, who had been buried in unmarked trenches like almost all fallen rank-and-file soldiers until the Civil War. Downplaying the ancient funerary associations of the obelisk, Greenough favored it for the "singular aptitude in its form and character to call attention to a spot memorable in history." The directors of the association chose the design as "the most simple, appropriate, imposing, and as most congenial to republican institutions." Distanced from the dead of the battle, the monument completed in 1843 was also unsatisfactory to many aged survivors, who saw the project as a grandiose obfuscation of the public disregard for veterans manifested by anemic federal pensions. Such charges of hypocrisy pervaded Herman Melville's *Israel Potter: His Fifty Years of Exile* (1855), beginning with the satirical dedication of the novel "To His Highness, The Bunker-Hill Monument." The ironic contrast between the humble book and the lofty stature of the "Great Biographer . . . of the anonymous privates of June 17, 1775," renewed the republican tradition of hostility toward public monuments.[4]

War memorials were part of a significant uptick in American production of monuments after the outbreak of the Mexican War. Continental imperialism contributed to this trend, along with economic prosperity, international ideas about urban planning, and the continued popularization of historical imagination, including its mobilization in sectional politics. Some initiatives would offer templates for Civil War commemoration. Kentucky brought home the remains of its officers and soldiers who had died at the battle of Buena Vista, notably including Lt. Col. Henry Clay Jr., and interred them with ceremony in July 1847. The next year the legislature appropriated $15,000 for a monument at the Frankfort burial site, which was dedicated in June 1850. The federal government collected the remains of 750 of the almost 14,000 Americans who had died in the war and reinterred them in a mass grave in Mexico City, marked with a small obelisk. The South Carolina legislature fashioned a monument to the dead of the Palmetto Regiment in 1856 by purchasing a twenty-five-foot-high cast-iron and copper palmetto tree that a local artisan had speculatively placed on the construction site for a new statehouse. Pennsylvania authorized a monument to its Mexican War dead in 1858, though the project made little progress until after the Civil War. Several Revolutionary War battlefields received new monuments during the 1850s, especially in secessionist South Carolina. A few Massachusetts towns pioneered broader community monuments to local soldiers. Chelmsford commissioned an elaborate shaft in 1859 dedicated to all residents who served their country in the Revolutionary War and inscribed with the names of the dead and circumstances of their deaths. When Lexington proposed a more ambitious minuteman monument the next year, however, *Harper's Weekly* skeptically observed that "the truth is that the genius of our people does not incline them to monuments or commemorative statues."[5]

Civil War monuments did not spring unmediated from northern and southern experience of the war, but neither did antebellum practices preordain commemorative patterns. Contrary to the reassurances of dedication orators, the building of memorials to rank-and-file soldiers only began to become commonplace in the 1860s.[6] The latitude for experimentation remained wide for much of the following decade. The celerity with which Americans turned to built memorials, a stark contrast with remembrance of the Revolution, reflected varying and sometimes competing responses to the shocking challenges of death in Civil War.

WARTIME MONUMENTS

Many communities and institutions generated suggestions for soldier monuments during the Civil War, but few proposals made material progress before 1865. Uncertainty about the resolution of the conflict and the ultimate death toll, as well as the demands of the war on northern and southern resources, induced most potential sponsors to delay action. Promoters of the first completed monuments shared an eagerness to reject inherited commemorative practices and offer models for a reformed society. Projects begun in the midst of the war emerged disproportionately from Union initiatives to increase armed manpower, initiatives that posed fundamental questions about the relationship between citizens and the state. Although dedicated to men who died in a common cause, these memorials revealed divisions within the

The Emergence of the Soldier Monument

North—including tension between soldiers and civilians—that would continue to influence commemoration in the early postwar era.

No group carried into the war a more thoughtful determination to build new forms of military memory than the regiment that dedicated the first soldier monument of the war, the Thirty-Second Indiana Volunteer Infantry. The commander who so meticulously shaped the unit, Col. August Willich, was steeped in German remembrance of the Wars of Liberation, which featured the most widespread system of memorials to common soldiers in the Western world in the mid-nineteenth century. Willich grew up in the household of Friedrich Schleiermacher and trained at the Royal Military Academy under Karl von Clausewitz. During his nineteen-year career in the Prussian army, he became a leader of the antimonarchical intellectuals in the officer corps. In a pamphlet that explained his decision to leave the army in 1847, he charged that the Crown had supplanted the people's army that arose in resistance to Napoléon with a mere instrument of royal and state sovereignty. War memorials vividly illustrated this pattern. Although some church tablets celebrated the regeneration of local communities, most monuments affirmed allegiance rather than voluntarism. The inscription on the Kreuzberg Monument in Berlin (1821), for example, characterized it as a gift "from the king to the people who, at his call, nobly sacrificed their blood and chattels to the fatherland." Young radicals active in the *Turnverein* gymnastics associations mocked and sometimes vandalized such monuments. As a leader of the 1848 revolution Willich sought to mold his command into a model for republican society, and he continued that effort in the Civil War with the added benefit of his experiences as editor of a socialist newspaper in Cincinnati.[7]

The initial combat experience of the Thirty-Second Indiana in the battle of Rowlett's Station provided Willich an opportunity to exemplify commemoration in mid-December 1861. After impressively repelling an attack by Terry's Texas Rangers, the regiment turned attention to the thirteen men it had lost. The survivors dug individual graves for their comrades near the camp at Munfordville, Kentucky. A stonecutter in the unit who had studied at the Royal Academy of Fine Arts in Dresden, a center of the 1848 revolution, carved a limestone stele embellished with a relief of an eagle, cannons and cannonballs, an American flag, and an oak branch and olive sprig. The German-language inscription declared that the men "gave their lives for the free institutions of the Republic" and listed the name, birth date, and birth place of each fallen soldier. In addition to reflecting Willich's commitment to realization of the full humanity of each individual, the monument offered a communal resource. According to one newspaper account, the funeral ceremony of the rigorously nonreligious unit "looked novel indeed to those used to Christian burials," but Willich delivered a eulogy that elicited tears and hurrahs from his men. While the dead were lowered into their graves, the regimental band played the "Marseillaise," after which each survivor in the companies of the dead men stepped forward, pulled a sprig of evergreen from his hat, and dropped it in fraternal benediction into a grave. The regiment continued to assemble regularly at the site while stationed in the area. On a cold Sunday morning in February 1862, they "showed our respect for our fallen comrades by presenting arms and the sound of music," after which Willich spoke for an hour and a half on the historical and scientific bases of socialism.[8] Willich and his regiment, many of whom were active in the Turnverein movement in Ohio or Indiana before the war, had replied in form and ritual to the monarchical German legacy of war memorials.

The first community Civil War monument offered a parallel confutation of American military remembrance. Dedicated in the Kensington section of Berlin, Connecticut, in late July 1863, the joint project of artist Nelson Augustus Moore and Congregational minister Elias Brewster Hillard expressed the same viewpoint as their next collaboration, *The Last Men of the Revolution* (1864). That book fit squarely within the vein of republican remembrance mined by Melville in *Israel Potter*. The starting point and chief novelty of the work was the contribution of Moore, one of Connecticut's leading photographers, who made portraits of what he understood to be the last seven surviving soldiers of the Revolution. Pension records were both a source of information and an impetus for the project, which originated in the publicity that surrounded legislation to increase the pensions of Revolutionary veterans. Hillard's written profiles highlighted how little the centenarians had previously received, and his reports of their reminiscences supplied a late capstone to the genre of Revolutionary narratives that had arisen from pension applications. The soldier monument designed by Moore and placed near Hillard's church in Kensington shared the emphasis on individual identity that animated their book and the many *carte-de-visite* photographs of departing soldiers produced by Moore's studio in Hartford. Inscribed on the brownstone obelisk was the name of each Kensington soldier who died in the war and the date and place of his death, as well as a couplet of consolatory poetry. The orator at the dedication ceremony was the chairman of the committee on pensions in the U.S. Senate.[9] An alternative to the grander obelisk on Bunker Hill, the monument expressed a community regard for the wel-

FIGURE 1.1. Hazen Brigade Monument, Murfreesboro, Tennessee, 1863.
*Report of Lieutenant Colonel E. B. Whitman, Superintendent of National Cemeteries,
Department of the Cumberland, May 10, 1869.* Courtesy of the National Archives.

fare of each citizen comparable to the fraternal bonds underlying the monument of the Thirty-Second Indiana Regiment.

The farthest-reaching institutional result of the impulses illustrated by these first wartime monuments was the creation of military cemeteries with separate headstones for each soldier, identified whenever possible. The small lot of the Thirty-Second Indiana near Rowlett's Station anticipated national military cemeteries established during the war by field commanders at Stones River and elsewhere, by the War Department at Arlington and elsewhere, and by multistate cooperation at Gettysburg and Antietam. This democratic innovation would provide prominent sites for Civil War monuments. Even before Gen. George H. Thomas set up the Murfreesboro cemetery, an encamped brigade built a funerary mastaba near the graves of the unit's soldiers killed in the battle along the Stones River during the last days of 1862. The inscription also listed men who had died at the Battle of Shiloh in April 1862. Thomas similarly called for a monument to overlook the cemetery he founded after the Battle of Chattanooga in late 1863. The state commissioners in control of the Soldiers' National Cemetery at Gettysburg held a design competition for a central monument in the spring of 1864 and awarded the commission in July.[10]

The national cemetery was not the only new form of burial that prompted soldier monuments. Leaders of the rural cemetery movement quickly recognized opportunities to add to its influence. Spring Grove Cemetery in Cincinnati donated a lot to Ohio for men who died in local military hospitals, and the state soon bought two additional lots. Spring Grove commissioned Randolph Rogers to make a statue as the principal feature of a memorial there, consistent with the established interest of rural cemeteries in the promotion of public monuments.[11] The obelisk unveiled at Mount Hope Cemetery in Bangor, Maine, in June 1864, with vice-president Hannibal Hamlin in attendance, showed that the institutional ambitions of rural cemeteries need not depend on the availability of soldiers' bodies. The project originated when Maj. Stephen Decatur Carpenter died at Stones River without family ownership of a plot for the remains brought home to Bangor. Mount Hope donated a lot for Carpenter and any other fallen soldier who might need it, but only one additional officer and a chaplain would ever be interred there, as the remains of rank-and-file soldiers rarely returned home. The monument nevertheless bore the names of all fifty-five Bangor men who had died in the war before completion of the obelisk, which functioned as a community memorial rather than a grave marker exclusive to the officers buried below.[12]

Union initiatives to increase the size of the army in 1863 posed challenges to the ideal of individual dignity honored in these earliest Civil War monuments. Hostility toward conscription quickened efforts to encourage volunteers and insistence on the compatibility of a draft with democratic liberty. Newton, Massachusetts, took its first action toward a monument in an August 1863 town meeting that centered on the extension of municipal support to the families of drafted men.[13] The township of Bristol in northeast Ohio, a strongly Republican area that experienced some resistance to conscription, endorsed the policy in the draped urn dedicated ceremoniously in October 1863. The community began work on the monument in direct response to the fourteenth local death of the war, a grisly Cleveland railroad accident that claimed the life of a lieutenant on detached assignment to conduct drafted men to his regiment. The first soldier whose name was inscribed on the list of the Bristol fallen, he personified the argument that the specific mission in which he gave his life was consistent with the fundamental principles of the United States.[14]

Not all monuments expressed enthusiasm for the new federal measures. Around the same time that Bristol dedicated its urn, the Somerville Light Infantry gave its Massachusetts hometown an obelisk surmounted by a sculpted eagle. Dispatched to Washington in April 1861 with the rest of the Fifth Massachusetts Regiment in response to Lincoln's initial mobilization of 75,000 state militia, the unit returned home after Bull Run with the loss of two men. Forty percent of the soldiers in that three-month company did not serve in the military again during the war. When Lincoln called for 300,000 fresh three-year volunteers after the collapse of the Peninsula campaign, three members of the Light Infantry determined to raise a company in Somerville with the aid of a $125 local bounty. That company did not fill until after the War Department requisitioned an additional 300,000 militia, this time for nine months under the Militia Act of 1862, to be produced by state conscription if insufficient volunteers stepped forward. Gov. John Andrew again called out the Fifth Massachusetts. Somerville raised its bounty to $200 and provided the full company necessary to avoid a draft. That unit returned from the North Carolina coast in late June 1863, only to attract special attention in yet another call for 300,000 three-year volunteers, with deficiencies to be remedied by the first federal draft under the Enrollment Act. Announcing a $402 bounty, Andrew exclaimed that "the expiration of the terms of enlistment of our nine months' troops, affords an opportunity for a renewed display of patriotic zeal and devotion." None of the veterans took up that opportunity by the late September deadline. To the governor's plea that "the voice of our brothers' *blood* cries to us from the ground," the Somerville Light Infantry replied with a stone shaft "IN MEMORY OF ALL FROM THIS TOWN WHO HAVE FALLEN IN THE SERVICE OF THEIR COUNTRY." The funding, the inscription explained, came from the remaining balance of a pool donated by local citizens in support of the company at the outset of the war.[15]

The monument entered boldly into wartime debates over the scope and structure of military duty. The Somerville Light Infantry claimed the legacy of the minutemen, noting on the inscription that the company entered federal service on the eighty-fifth anniversary of Lexington and Concord. The militia unit asserted authority to speak for the town by applying the unused

FIGURE 1.2. John N. Hyde and William J. Peirce, *Erected by the Somerville Light Infantry*, engraving published in *Report of the School Committee, Selectmen, Treasurer, and Collector of Taxes of the Town of Somerville, for the Year Ending March 1, 1864.* Courtesy of the Somerville Public Library.

fund to the monument and by honoring all the local fallen, only a small pro-portion of whom had any affiliation with the Light Infantry. The elaborate squaring of financial accounts also underscored that the men of the com-pany had fulfilled their civic obligations, notwithstanding any anxieties over the refusal of three-month men or nine-month men to reenlist in three-year regiments. The commissioning of a public monument by this group at this moment implied that individual consciences and circumstances defined the standards of citizenship, not federal exhortations or mandates. The Somer-ville Light Infantry had originated in an antebellum transformation of the Massachusetts militia that started with abandonment of mandatory service and embrace of voluntarism. The company aptly represented its community in championing an alternative to compulsory military duty. Faced with chal-lenging quotas, the town continued to increase bounties and cast a wider search for recruits to avoid local conscription as much as possible. Praise for the willing sacrifices of the fallen depended on respect for individual will.[16]

The shaft and eagle that the Fifty-Eighth Indiana Infantry placed on the Gibson County courthouse lawn in Princeton began with volunteers' an-tipathy toward a different Union manpower initiative of 1863, the crackdown on deserters. Lincoln announced on March 10 that soldiers absent without leave would be welcome to return by April 1 without consequences other than forfeiture of pay but that holdouts beyond the amnesty period would be arrested and punished. The formation of the Invalid Corps, later the Veteran Reserve Corps, added force to the threat. Richard Hembree of the Fifty-Eighth Indiana, who had deserted in the fall of 1862, was arrested in May 1863 and sentenced to be shot. According to the regiment chaplain, "no event occurred during our entire service up to this time, that stirred the sympa-thies and feelings of the men so much as did this announcement." The regi-ment commander, an attorney in civilian life, prepared an appeal endorsed by all of the commissioned officers of the unit. He argued that previous lack of punishment for deserters had established a policy that the government could not fairly change so abruptly and harshly. He also emphasized that administration opponents in Democratic southern Indiana warmly encour-aged desertion. After Lincoln ended the two-month ordeal by pardoning Hembree without comment in mid-July, the regiment commander sought to restore morale by focusing his unit on a monument to fallen comrades. Although garrison duty at Murfreesboro had made the Fifty-Eighth Indiana familiar with the Hazen Brigade mastaba, the regiment decided to raise its monument at Princeton in remembrance of the site where the men mus-tered into service and in admonition to the community. The soldiers refused to accept civilian contributions. The expression of group solidarity reflected alienation from military discipline and from the home front. The construction contract called for the monument to be ready by the scheduled return of the regiment in late 1864. Perhaps because the unit cohesion had grown so strong, however, enough men reenlisted in early 1864 for the Fifty-Eighth Indiana to continue as a veteran regiment. The unveiling instead took place on July 4, 1865.[17]

The monument at Princeton underscored the extent to which works initiated in the midst of the war resulted from the efforts of military units like the Thirty-Second Indiana, the Hazen Brigade, the Somerville Light Infantry, and the Fifty-Eighth Indiana. Nationwide publicity greeted the climax to this pattern, the two shafts installed at Bull Run in June 1865 under the supervision of James McCallum of the Sixteenth Massachusetts Light Artillery Battery.[18] The theme of soldiers mourning fellow soldiers would engage the interest of sculptors when communities and cultural institutions began to follow the lead of Kensington, Newton, Bristol, and rural cemeteries like Spring Grove and Mount Hope with postwar monuments. Decisions to sponsor such monuments situated wartime political debates over military obligations within cultural responses to the circumstances of death in the Civil War.

GRAVESTONES AND CENOTAPHS

The end of the war unleashed scores of commemorative projects. Unitarian minister Frederic A. Whitney remarked at a dedication ceremony in July 1866 that "every newspaper tells you that somewhere else through these States United . . . another monument has risen to mark the great struggle." The wave of activity reflected the sweeping significance of the Union triumph, including emancipation, and the immense number of northern and southern lives the war had ended. The initiatives also illustrated the self-conscious creativity with which mid-nineteenth-century Americans approached the problem of death. Presented at Evergreen Cemetery in Brighton, Massachusetts, founded in 1850, which had turned its planned Chapel Grove into Monumental Grove upon commissioning an obelisk for fallen local soldiers, Whitney's observation that the Civil War had "inaugurated a new era in monumental art" grew from his argument that the previous watershed was the opening of Mount Auburn Cemetery in 1831.[19] The society that invented the rural cemetery was now developing the soldier monument. The innovation intersected with other responses to the war, including national cemeteries,

The Emergence of the Soldier Monument

memorial halls, and Memorial Day. These emerging cultural forms acknowledged community obligations to the dead and their families.

The disposition of soldiers' remains framed much of the planning for monuments in the first years after the war. The establishment of seventy-four national military cemeteries prompted collective monuments as well as hundreds of thousands of individual headstones. In September 1866 the War Department placed a granite sarcophagus atop 2,111 unidentified Union soldiers at Arlington National Cemetery, the confiscated home of Robert E. Lee. The commissioners of the Soldiers' National Cemetery at Gettysburg unveiled a central monument in 1869, and the state of Illinois paid for a statuary group installed at the Mound City National Cemetery in 1874. Private supporters contributed obelisks to the national cemeteries at Hampton Roads, Virginia (1868), and Beaufort, South Carolina (1870).[20] White southern women's voluntary organizations usually called Ladies' Memorial Associations headed arrangements for burial plots and monuments for the Confederate dead. At least twenty-six such societies formed in Virginia by the fall of 1868.[21] Almost all southern memorials completed during the first years after the war ornamented cemetery sections set aside for soldiers' remains gathered from nearby battlefields or interred by local hospitals. The most spectacular project was the ninety-foot-high pyramid built atop the remains of approximately 18,000 Confederate soldiers at Hollywood Cemetery in Richmond in 1869.

The unavailability of fallen soldiers' bodies influenced the development of Civil War monuments as much as the tangible presence of human remains. Relatively few of the dead rank and file returned home. The federal government reported that it had consolidated 309,225 Union soldiers, or about two-thirds of the federal dead, at national cemeteries by 1871. Herculean efforts had proposed identifications for 54 percent of the bodies. Doubtless others were never found.[22] The negation of familial bereavement was even more disturbing to Victorian Americans than the sheer number of deaths. The record of proceedings at the December 1866 dedication of a memorial for twenty-one residents of Bolton, Massachusetts, noted that "the mortal remains of none of them came back here for interment with kindred dust." The town clerk reported that "some of them, it is known, received only such rites of sepulture as could be hurriedly given amid the confusion after the fight, or as the hospital train, wending on its melancholy ways, surrounded by guerillas and other perils of the time, delayed for a moment by the roadside." The community sought to fill the ritual void caused by the war: "Now, for the first time, at this comparatively distant period, the wives, the

FIGURE 1.3. Charles H. Dimmock, Monument to Confederate Dead,
Hollywood Cemetery, Richmond, 1867–69.
Photograph by E. S. Lumpkin & Company. Courtesy of the Library of Congress.

children, the parents, the dear friends, the brothers and sisters of these fallen
soldiers join in something like funeral obsequies."[23]

New England, and especially Massachusetts, dominated the early commissioning of community monuments, which were far more numerous than
monuments installed at soldiers' burial plots during the 1860s. The regional
pattern resulted from several factors. Long before the state became a Republican stronghold, the intensely Federalist and Whig political culture of
Massachusetts fostered an unmatched tradition of public commemoration.

The Emergence of the Soldier Monument

Remembrance of the Civil War built on the foundations of Plymouth Rock and the Bunker Hill monument. The distinctive Unitarianism that informed the creation of Mount Auburn Cemetery continued to influence responses to death. And as Newton had demonstrated during the war, recruitment of soldiers through the town system of government provided a well-developed structure for addressing local casualties. Nathaniel Banks observed at the Fitchburg dedication in 1868 that "the municipal organizations of the country" had been "the engine of war."[24] Many towns followed the unveiling of a monument with publication of a report that included not only the proceedings of the dedication ceremony but also a record of wartime meetings and resolutions, troop quotas and enlistments, expenditures for recruitment and support of soldiers, and other related information. Funded largely from public treasuries, the monuments represented a final statement of community responsibility for the conduct of the war.[25]

"We are all pretty well aware that the facts which make to us the interest of this day are in a great degree personal and local here," remarked Ralph Waldo Emerson as he began the oration at the dedication of the Concord monument in April 1867. He noted that the chosen date was "doubly our calendar day," anniversary of both the Revolutionary battle in 1775 and the departure of the volunteers in 1861. Speakers routinely traced town histories from the colonial period to the present. Their purpose was to identify Union martyrs as the products of local institutions and also to identify the community as sufficiently intimate to conduct a ceremony comparable to a funeral. The sage of Concord spoke as a neighbor when he concluded that "a gloom gathers on this assembly, composed as it is of kindred men and women, for, in many houses, the nearest and dearest is gone from their hearthstone." Moral conviction served the purpose of friendly consolation in his assurance that the shared gloom was "tinged with the light of heaven. A duty so severe has been discharged, and with such immense results of good, that though the cannon volleys have a sound of funeral echoes, they can hear through them the benedictions of their country and mankind."[26]

Early monuments shared several strategies of remembrance. The listing of fallen soldiers' names was so essential that some communities considered nothing else necessary. Bolton was one example of a town whose memorial consisted of a large marble tablet inscribed with the names of the local dead. Similar lists were fundamental to almost all memorials of any kind except in a few large jurisdictions. The state of Rhode Island recorded the names of its 1,727 dead on bronze tablets at the base of a large monument unveiled in Providence in 1871.[27] In contrast, collective monuments at national or Confederate cemeteries ordinarily could not feature such lists because the sites included large numbers of unidentified remains. This centrality in one context and impossibility in the other setting underscored the symbolic interchangeability of names and bodies. Fewer bodies meant more names, and more bodies meant fewer names.[28]

Nearly unanimous judgment considered the inclusion of any other names inappropriate. Harvard Memorial Hall, dedicated to "graduates and students who have given or risked their lives for the country," was one of few early projects even to broach the possible listing of survivors' names. Future military historian John Codman Ropes objected that "the indiscriminate and equal commemoration of men whose labors and sufferings and perils in the late conflict have been so various in magnitude, cannot but give occasion to the most unfortunate jealousies and criticisms."[29] Phillips Brooks distinguished the dead from the survivors with exceptional candor and eloquence at Andover in 1873. Although glad to recall scenes of soldiers returning home, the minister stressed that their names were not written on the town tablets. "It is the lives that stopped at loyalty and freedom that have left the strongest emphasis upon those words," he reasoned. The list of the dead "signifies the total manhood they gave. It was not only their deeds, their strength—it was themselves they consecrated; and a man is always more precious than his work."[30] The memorial was not as much a reminder of service as of loss.

The list of names unveiled at North Brookfield in 1870 dramatized this commitment to comprehensiveness, particularity, and impartiality. Former volunteer general Francis A. Walker was more insistent than most orators that the town monument was primarily an instrument to inculcate a duty of armed service and secondarily "a token of personal remembrance, personal affection and personal gratitude" toward each of the fallen. He nevertheless devoted a substantial part of his address to William F. Hill, who did not die in a battle, hospital, or Confederate prison, like the other thirty men identified on the monument. Hill was a nineteen-year-old laborer when he enlisted in July 1862 in the recruitment drive that followed the failure of the Peninsula campaign. He later reported that "a man got him drunk and had him sworn in before he knew what he was about." After Hill survived the battle of Antietam, he fell out of the ranks during a march and deserted. He returned home to North Brookfield, where he lived openly with his aged father and invalid sister until arrested in Lincoln's crackdown on deserters. On August 28, 1863, a Union firing squad killed Hill in a prolonged and grisly execution. Local veterans unanimously endorsed the inclusion of his name on the monument that was, in the words of the main inscription, "ERECTED / BY

THE TOWN OF / NORTH BROOKFIELD / IN HONOR OF HER / SOL-
DIERS WHO LOST THEIR / LIVES IN DEFENCE / OF THE COUNTRY /
AGAINST THE REBELLION." Walker told the audience that he heartily approved this decision even though he had drawn and signed the order for
Hill's court-martial. In retrospect, he conceded, enforcement of a uniform
duty had failed to consider individual situations adequately.[31] Walker's admiration for army discipline notwithstanding, his tribute to the deserter shared
in a postwar determination to recognize each life the nation had taken.

This pattern was consistent with the widespread tendency to list the
dead in order of rank or otherwise mark those with commissions. Like the
identification of soldiers' regiments or companies, the practice invited the interpretation that monuments valued the national at the expense of the local
and treated the army as a model for the community. But volunteers' rank correlated significantly with social status and largely mirrored the local order
rather than advancing an alternative. In the broader context of early inscriptions, the details mainly differentiated individuals within a homogenous set.
Other information served the same purpose. Monuments at North Bran-
field, Connecticut (1866), Barnstable, Massachusetts (1866), Jackson Township, Iowa (1866), and other locations listed the age of each soldier at the
time of his death. Quincy, Massachusetts (1868), organized its roster into
lists of men who died from disease, from wounds, in battle, or in prison; the
intent was not to elevate one experience above another but to avoid the conflation of 111 names into a single mass. Early monument inscriptions supplemented names with the date and place of death only slightly less often
than with ranks and regiments. Many dedication orations recited the circumstances in which each man died. Publications issued in conjunction with
proceedings appended additional individual information.

Place names became a symbol for this specificity. Large cities like
Newark (1869) and Pittsburgh (1871) inscribed monuments with sites of
suffering rather than lists of individuals. Smaller community memorials
highlighted both kinds of names. "Donelson and Shiloh, Murfreesboro and
Chickamauga, Corinth and Atlanta, Fredericksburg and Chancellorsville,"
chanted one orator. "I dare not add one word of mine to the recollections
clinging in the heart of each one of you about those suggestive and momen-
tous sounds."[32] Battlefields comprised most of the resonant place names, but
inscriptions and orators also referred regularly to Confederate prisons, especially Andersonville, "that modern Golgotha."[33]

The conjunction of place and memory directly supported sponsors'
goals for civic monuments. They hoped their projects would similarly con-

catenate local remembrances of the war. "This monument will have its own history," declared a Boston alderman in 1867 at the cemetery lot that the city set aside for indigent soldiers and sailors. He argued that the obelisk "becomes a part of the war" by joining with and absorbing residents' mental images of volunteers' departures, Sanitary Commission fairs, public assemblies, and parades of returning legions.[34] Inaugural ceremonies aimed to leave an equally permanent, sometimes painful impression. The 1868 procession in Lewiston, Maine, ended with the formation of a square around the monument. The audience joined in prayer, watched the unveiling, and heard a speech. The city government marched around the monument while a band played. The local newspaper reported that "the guard was then removed, and the crowd surged up about the monument, many of whom were deeply afflicted as they recognized the name of some dear friend or relative whose death in his country's cause is here recorded." New Orleans newspapers echoed that at the Greenwood Cemetery dedication "many were those who lingered here, even for hours afterwards, filled with sad thoughts, weeping over lost sons and lost hopes."[35]

Dedication orators experimenting with variations on the individual eulogy envisioned the monument as a site of communication between death and life. They described obelisks "pointing toward that Heaven whither it is humbly hoped and believed that our patriotic fellow citizens in whose memory this has been erected have been called" and imagined paradise as "a memorial hall of vaster proportions."[36] Congressional representative Aaron Stevens typified adaptation of the rhetorical vision trope that Daniel Webster had identified with Plymouth Rock in 1820. The former Union officer argued that the monument in Peterborough, New Hampshire, crystallized "something in the mysterious veil which separates the mortal from the immortal." He exclaimed repeatedly that "I see them now!" in camp, on march, in battle, in hospitals, in prisons, and in their final hours. Other orators professed to hear the voices of the dead at monuments. Alexander McKenzie of Cambridge, Massachusetts, was one of many to speak directly to the spirits "who may be hovering invisible above us, watching with eager interest the services of this hour." "O patriots, heroes, martyrs!" the Congregational minister implored. "Tell us ye are content!"[37] Joshua Chamberlain stressed in his early dedication addresses that a soldier monument was an emblem of the expectation of resurrection.[38]

The compound nature of monuments shaped decisions about their placement. Only a minority of the more than 300 memorials dedicated by 1874 marked the sites of substantial collections of soldiers' graves. Some

The Emergence of the Soldier Monument

other sponsors also chose to install their monuments in cemeteries. "True, the mortal remains of the brave dead moulder not beneath it," conceded the chair of the monument committee for Cherryfield, Maine. He suggested a parallel between the selected location at Pine Grove Cemetery and the final resting places of the town dead: "The turf above their heads is made green by the dews that weep under the soft skies of Virginia and the Carolinas, and by the still waters of Georgia and Louisiana." But more than twice as many communities elected not to install their monument in a cemetery. At Concord, Massachusetts, a town proud of its Sleepy Hollow Cemetery, committee chair Ebenezer Rockwood Hoar explained that "the Monument is a *cenotaph*, and marks no place of burial; so that it need not seek its place in a cemetery."[39]

Installation of many monuments on a New England common marked a new stage in the development of a public space that originated with the town system. The common was usually next to the first church and often where the militia mustered. The placement expressed a hope for how the monument would function in the community. "Standing not as a thing apart to be visited and admired — not as a stern *memento mori* — but in the midst of your daily village life, this noble shaft is in your sight as you go to the shop, the post-office, or the bank," observed Henry Dwight Sedgwick at Stockbridge. "It will greet you with a daily welcome. It will be a standard of duty always before you, cheering you when by the faithful measure of your conscience you have come up to its high demand, and warning you by its shadow upon the same truthful dial, when you have fallen away from its severe requirement of that devotion to the right which does not shrink when called to the sacrifice of life itself." Children would learn from it as they toddled to school, and the names of the dead would be preserved "not by the flattering lips of the historian, but by the common consent of the community in which they lived."[40]

Beyond this ambition to enrich the everyday landscape of their communities, monument promoters soon saw a close relationship between their projects and the annual observance of Memorial Day that emerged across the North and South in the first years after the war. Decoration of soldiers' graves with flowers readily suggested more permanent tributes. "The shaft is in the stone," prophesied Henry Timrod in the ode he composed for the inaugural observance of Memorial Day at Magnolia Cemetery in Charleston, South Carolina, in 1866. The impulse was even stronger in communities that looked to monuments as the principal object to wreathe on what was generally known as Decoration Day. Waltham, Massachusetts, installed its monument in time for unveiling in May 1868 on the first observance coordinated across the North by the Grand Army of the Republic. Schoolmaster and minister L. P. Frost pointed out the common origins of soldier monuments and Memorial Day in the rural cemetery movement. "This monument is an emblem of life, not death; of resurrection, not burial," he emphasized. He invited his listeners to "come, then, and visit it in early spring, when nature is arrayed in beauty. Come in the early morning, when the birds sing and the air is perfumed with the breath of flowers. Never come in the hour of sadness, or when grief oppresses the mind."[41] Memorial Day gatherings also became occasions for planning monuments. Even before completion, long-term projects linked observances across the years.

Timrod's ode hinted at a tension between Memorial Day and soldier monuments. He worried that the regenerative beauty of the day would be lost "when some cannon-moulded pile / Shall overlook this bay." Not everyone was as pessimistic about the aesthetic potential of Civil War memorials. Before considering possible designs, however, sponsors first had to decide whether to commission a monument or something that might have uses in addition to public remembrance. The utilitarian memorials of the early postwar era were in some ways an even more innovative cultural form than soldier monuments, but as their proponents stressed, the projects built upon foundational American ideas about democratic commemoration.

MEMORIAL HALLS

Despite the flurry of obelisks and statues dedicated in the first years after the war, reservations about the public monument as a cultural form persisted and even intensified. Wayland, Massachusetts, reasserted the superiority of the printing press, reporting that the town had discussed plans for a monument to the local dead before realizing that "a much better memorial, in many respects," would be a book that narrated the experience of each soldier.[42] Other initiatives preferred to honor the Union dead by continuing to fight directly for the cause they had served. The Soldiers' Memorial Society, organized in Boston in the spring of 1865, disdained "simply whitewashing the sepulchres of martyrs" and pledged that "our monuments to our brothers who have served the country shall be in the hospitals, schools, and other beneficent institutions to which we can contribute in the region where they fought for us."[43] Wartime promoters of a monument for the site where Confederates had buried Robert Gould Shaw and his black troops in an unmarked trench decided instead to fund the Shaw Memorial School in

The Emergence of the Soldier Monument

Charleston to advance the African American citizenship epitomized by the Fifty-Fourth Massachusetts. Parallel initiatives in northern localities treated the call for remembrance of the dead as an opportunity to strengthen democratic institutions. Sponsors of memorial halls described military service not as a transformative departure from civilian life but as proof of the community cultivation of engaged, informed citizens.

New England, and especially Massachusetts, dominated the commissioning of utilitarian memorials even more than monuments. The town system prompted strong interest in the construction of municipal buildings that might serve as memorials. Regional leadership in the development of educational institutions, especially colleges and public libraries, further shaped reflections on the end of the war. New England was also the heartland of nineteenth-century pacifism. Amasa Walker, a longtime officer of the American Peace Society and the father of Francis A. Walker, was an early promoter of memorial halls as an alternative to military monuments.[44]

The most elaborate commemorative structure dedicated in the North or the South during the decade after the war, Harvard Memorial Hall presented a clear vision of the postbellum United States and an example for smaller-scale community projects. As elsewhere, the undertaking proceeded from substantial wartime discussion. The death of Shaw at Battery Wagner in July 1863 electrified the suggestion of a former Harvard president at the annual alumni dinner two nights earlier that the graduates should raise a monument on the college grounds after the war. An essay in the *Atlantic* soon called instead for a memorial hall suitable for alumni dinners and commencements, a proposal that reflected the increasing importance of the graduates in oversight and financial support of the school as the state relinquished its role.[45] A month after Appomattox, an open meeting of alumni debated the merits of a monument and a memorial hall. Advocates of a monument pointed out that the plan for a dining hall would "subject the Alumni to a charge of Yankee shrewdness." The allegation especially stung because the main practical purpose of the facility was to host commencement gatherings for alumni encouraged to fund the expanding ambitions of the university, which contrasted with the more limited memorial chapels, libraries, and classroom facilities that Beloit, Bowdoin, Colby, and Wesleyan built after the war. William R. Ware and Henry Van Brunt's design for a dining hall and academic theater flanking a memorial transept candidly announced the aim of Harvard to emulate the national leadership of Oxford and Cambridge. The building signaled the reorganization of higher education and the deepening of class identity that marked the postwar United States.[46]

FIGURE 1.4. William R. Ware and Henry Van Brunt, Harvard Memorial Hall, 1865–77. Photograph by G. W. Patch, c. 1879. Courtesy of Harvard University Archives.

Harvard Memorial Hall also emerged from broader ideological investments in useful memorials. U.S. Sanitary Commission veteran Edward Everett Hale, designated to serve as chief spokesman for a memorial hall in the debate with proponents of a monument, was at the same time playing a key role in formation of the Soldiers' Memorial Society. Another leader of that organization was former Union officer Charles Greely Loring, whose father chaired the committee of fifty that alumni appointed for Harvard Memorial Hall. Perhaps the most vigorous early proponent of the project was Charles Eliot Norton, then editor of the *North American Review* and actively involved in founding the *Nation*. He and George W. Curtis had taken to cultivating Ashfield, Massachusetts, as an ideal New England village, and in 1867 they would persuade the town to install a fountain surmounted by an urn as the community Civil War memorial because they "thought that the useful should be combined with the ornamental and the patriotic in monumental projects." Initial liaison to the architects interested in the Harvard project, Norton was fully in sympathy with the argument of Russell Sturgis Jr. that colleges could avoid allegations of institutional selfishness in memorial buildings through "evidences of lavish expense of money, all well

The Emergence of the Soldier Monument

spent indeed, but also *freely* spent, of beauty sought for itself, and ornament loved for its own sake, and used to dignify the building."[47]

Enthusiasm for useful memorials reflected concern that monuments tended to elevate the soldier into a singularly exemplary citizen. Norton maintained that Harvard Memorial Hall should focus on "the sacrifice of life for a cause wholly disconnected with ordinary warfare, and above it." With a Ruskinian attachment to the medieval cathedral as a model of community-building, Norton hoped the Harvard project would transmute rather than preserve remembrance of individual martyrs or the sectional conflict; he thought "it is a work on which the labor, the wealth, and the genius of a half-century may well be expended."[48] William Dean Howells extended the collegiate pattern to municipalities shortly after he settled into Cambridge as editor of the *Atlantic.* "We are not a military people (though we certainly know how to fight upon occasion)," he observed in May 1866. "The pride which we felt in our army as a body, and in the men merely as soldiers, was an exultation which has already in a great part subsided." Proliferation of soldier monuments would consequently "misrepresent us and our age to posterity." Howells suggested a variety of projects that might cultivate war remembrance as an uplifting "aesthetic sensation," including public gardens, fountains, chapels, libraries, schoolhouses, and town halls.[49]

Many Massachusetts towns built memorials during the next few years that followed lines Howells recommended. He conspicuously did not suggest that a suitable memorial hall could primarily serve ex-soldiers, and no town adopted such a plan. When Boston veterans pressed for a memorial hall in which they might display relics, hang portraits of fallen comrades, and hold meetings, the city council responded that longtime civic forum Faneuil Hall was the only authentic locus of community memory of the war. "To no other structure could such associations be imparted by any official action," the council declared. Memorial town halls situated soldiers' experiences and sacrifices within a broader field of civic action. "Where, I ask, is a more suitable place to put our memorial of those names, than where men must gather for successive generations, to exercise the prerogative of the citizen?" argued one dedication orator.[50] Other municipalities identified military service with local democracy by installing ornate tablets in town halls not specifically designated as memorial halls.

Commentators often associated commemorative goals with the educational elements of multipurpose town halls. The municipal offices and schoolhouse dedicated on the first day of 1875 at Oakham, a rare memorial building promoted by and partly for veterans, offered space for meetings of a local group called the Soldiers' Union that initiated the project. But the principal orator stressed that the public building was superior to a monument because "youth shall be educated with better advantages than they have had, with this hall above in which lectures, lyceums, public meetings, and the transactions of town business shall continue through life the education begun in the rooms below." He added, "How much more appropriate and touching, more expressive and beautiful, is this than a shaft of stone however elaborate, for it not only points upward, but it steps upward. It not only helps us to remember the dead, but plants in us the virtues for which they died."[51]

Memorial libraries best typified early antimonumental remembrance of the war. They illustrated the municipal basis for the commemorative predominance of Massachusetts, as libraries proliferated across the state after the legislature authorized towns to spend funds for that purpose in 1851. Massachusetts would account for about two-fifths of the purpose-built libraries completed in the United States over the rest of the century. Andover, Framingham, Lancaster, North Reading, and Northampton opened freestanding libraries as town memorials to the Civil War dead between 1868 and 1875. The genre was sufficiently distinct that William R. Ware set it as the program for a round of student projects in the architectural department at the Massachusetts Institute of Technology. Several other towns put up memorial town halls that included libraries or schoolrooms; some refurbished existing town halls to add memorial library rooms. The memorial hall in Shelby County, Ohio (1877), featured an opera house, municipal offices, and space for the fire department as well as a library.[52]

Public libraries highlighted several facets of the critique of monuments. The institutions shared in the celebration of print as the successor to built memorials, a vision that identified literary appeal rather than military power as the acme of distinction. Unitarian minister Christopher T. Thayer noted at the Lancaster dedication that the local Union dead, "for their worthy and glorious deeds, are placed side by side with, and share the immortality of, those who by their writings have been made, so far as on earth they could be, immortal." Henri Labrouste's dramatic use of cast iron and glass at the Bibliothèque Sainte-Geneviève in Paris, one of the most celebrated architectural works of the mid-nineteenth century, underscored the modernity of libraries. Most important, public libraries earned recognition as foundational for a government that depended on an educated citizenry. "If these Andover soldiers were indeed the best fruits of our institutions, the best specimens of our character, then all that can educate that character is the best memorial of them," observed Phillips Brooks.[53]

The memorial town hall and library at Lexington particularly epito-mized the postwar reinvigoration of republican remembrance because the project subsumed a late antebellum campaign for a military monument. Fresh from his leadership role in the preservation of Mount Vernon as a sym-bol of intersectional comity, Edward Everett agreed to head fund-raising for a minuteman monument in 1860 as "a national work on a spot of national renown." After the Civil War, the widow of a vice president of the Lexing-ton Monument Association redirected the project by offering a large dona-tion for a memorial hall. Embellishments of the interior included statues of a minuteman and a Union soldier, but the civic and educational purposes of the building controlled the tribute to martial virtue. Dedication orator George B. Loring argued that the Invalides in Paris and Nelson's Column in London "were low and mean, when compared with this structure, which in-vites an intelligent people within its walls, and perpetuates the memory of a war fought for the freedom and elevation of mankind."[54]

The dedication of Harvard Memorial Hall in June 1874 provided a cap-stone to the collegiate and municipal projects that followed the alumni's re-jection of a monument in 1865. The orator of the day was Charles Francis Adams Sr., who looked back at the Civil War but also personified the diplo-macy that had avoided a possible war with England. He framed his speech around the irony that Harvard should consecrate such an elaborate war memorial even though its curriculum encompassed almost all topics except the art of war. He pointedly did not suggest that the university incorporate military instruction, a response of some colleges to the Civil War. "Not be-cause any and all these young men embarked in military enterprises do we award them permanent remembrance here," declared the champion of inter-national arbitration. The school instead honored sacrifices "to reinstate the rule of law," a situation unlikely to present itself to the United States again.[55]

The president of the alumni association, Adams spoke for a community that idolized orators rather than soldiers. Exterior decoration of the polygo-nal academic theater featured rondel busts of great orators from different nations. Daniel Webster was the American representative. Former aboli-tionist and colonial historian John Gorham Palfrey protested that university president Charles William Eliot should have used the busts to honor Samuel Adams, James Otis Jr., and other graduates who had devoted their talents to "that cause of freedom to which Harvard College had consecrated them."[56] Beneath their disagreement over slavery politics, however, Palfrey and Eliot shared an antimilitarist nationalism forged in struggles with Andrew Jack-son and opposition to the Mexican War. Harvard Memorial Hall and similar buildings around New England indicated that an updated Whig historicism offered a potent framework for Civil War commemoration.

Monuments multiplied more rapidly than memorial halls for several reasons. Useful projects tended to be much more expensive. Public libraries in Andover and Northampton each cost roughly $60,000, or about the same amount that New York City and the state of Michigan spent on monuments. Harvard Memorial Hall cost almost $400,000. Leicester converted three rooms in the town hall into a memorial library for $6,000, which the *Springfield Republican* saluted as "a very good model for towns of limited means wishing to perpetuate their soldiers' names."[57] But many communities aimed to spend considerably less. Influential rural cemeteries also helped to popularize the commissioning of monuments. Whether intended for placement in a cemetery or a town, monuments offered more potential than municipal buildings for ritual use, most notably in observance of Memorial Day. Proponents of monuments argued that the alternatives failed to function as a cenotaph. "The solemnity which always surrounds death is an essential element in producing the moral impression, which our Memorial is designed to make. Let us not weaken it," argued the chief critic of the Harvard plan for a dining room to accommodate alumni festivities. "Is it a Memorial Hall after all?" he asked. "It is a Dining Hall, called a Memorial Hall. But does calling it a Memorial Hall make it a Memorial Hall?"[58] Promoters of monuments favored forms more indicative of death.

Obelisks and other shafts accounted for about two-thirds of the monuments installed during the decade after the war. As Russell Sturgis Jr. pointed out in August 1865, the obelisk was a "simple and not necessarily expensive kind of monument which is often used for a private tombstone, and which will answer as well for many other occasions." He considered the form especially suitable for a Civil War monument because it was "an emblem of eternity" and also because "the Egyptian idea of this monument was the idea of an excellent place for inscriptions," which suited monument sponsors' determination to list the names of local martyrs. The precedent of Revolutionary War monuments at Bunker Hill, Savannah, and other sites may have added in some cases to the historical connotations of obelisks. Ebenezer Rockwood Hoar provided a classical gloss on the Concord obelisk designed by Hammatt Billings, noting that it resembled Tacitus's account of the representation of the goddess Aphrodite at a sacrificial temple in Cyprus. Other towns

FIGURE 1.5. Martin Milmore, Sphinx, Mount Auburn Cemetery, Cambridge, Massachusetts, 1871–72. Courtesy of the Library of Congress.

with budgets sufficient to afford statuary also chose to commission shafts by well-known architects. Waltham hired George Meachem for an obelisk that in the view of the dedication orator "rises higher and higher until its top passes the empyrean."[59] Carved drapery effects added to the solemnity of obelisks in several locations.

The most popular ornamentation for a shaft was the addition of an American eagle on top. *Harper's Weekly* helped to keep this design before a wide readership by printing illustrations of six such monuments between 1865 and 1870.[60] A. B. Mullett, supervising architect of the U.S. Treasury, provided a design of an eagle strangling a serpent for installation atop a granite column in the first statewide soldier monument, unveiled in Wilmington, Delaware, in 1871. The casting of the bronze ensemble from condemned cannons appropriated by Congress reinforced the nationalist imagery.

Few early monuments consisted solely of allegorical figures. Several instances resulted from extraordinary individual control over a project. The most idiosyncratic and recondite example was the sphinx donated to Mount Auburn Cemetery by its longtime president Jacob Bigelow in 1872. The combination of a woman's face and a lion's body extended previous Egyptian Revival elements of the prototypical rural cemetery and depicted the redefinition of gender and race as the postwar hallmark of a nation prepared "BY THE UPRISING OF A GREAT PEOPLE / BY THE BLOOD OF FALLEN HEROES," to take its place among the major civilizations of world history.[61] Admiral David Dixon Porter commanded similar authority over the Naval Monument installed at the base of Capitol Hill in Washington, which Porter recruited Franklin Simmons to execute as Bigelow had hired Martin Milmore.

Sculptors probably would have preferred more allegorical monuments. Beseeched to make a memorial for Saint Johnsbury, Vermont, while on a visit to his home state several years after he joined the circle of American expatriate sculptors in Italy, Larkin Mead delivered in August 1868 an image of Liberty closely related to the ideal statues that had launched his career. But most monument sponsors who agreed with Mead's brother-in-law William Dean Howells that Union principles "should be represented in every memorial work of the time" also agreed with the editor that "we should be sorry to have this done by the dreary means of conventional allegory." Purely ideal imagery was "too much in the line of cemeterial art," observed a critic of the Naval Monument. The Ladies Memorial Association of Savannah, which spent more than $20,000 on a monument that was among the most expensive in the South when dedicated in Forsyth Park in 1875, removed its two allegorical statues only four years later and instead placed a statue of a soldier on top. The allegorical figures went to soldiers' lots in cemeteries.[62]

The most ambitious attempt to describe the importance of the Civil War through allegory reflected foreign commemorative impulses. A leading scholar of the United States and an active Union supporter, Edouard Laboulaye proposed the gift of a monument to liberty in the summer of 1865 with keen awareness that monuments in his native Paris had often served as instruments of imperial rule. He lent his influence in France and contacts in America to a revision of Frédéric Auguste Bartholdi's failed proposal to create a modern version of the Colossus of Rhodes at the Suez Canal partly because a gargantuan allegorical lighthouse in New York harbor presented an antimonarchical contrast to the monuments that ordered vistas on the Haussmannized streets of Paris. The radically superhuman scale of the project also reflected the Catholic scholar's interest in the religious foundations of political liberty, a theme more closely keyed to debates in mid-nineteenth-century France than mid-nineteenth-century America. Although the majestic statue of liberty trampling on a broken chain and enlightening the world that Bartholdi advocated on his first transatlantic visit in 1871 was a powerful representation of the triumphant Union, the initiative differed sharply from most American strategies for commemorating the war.[63]

SOLDIER STATUES

Postwar statuary centered on the figure of the soldier. In April 1866 the monument committee for Urbana, Ohio, wrote to native son John Quincy Adams Ward, now established in New York as one of the leading sculptors in the country, with a statement of priorities that many communities shared. "We want all the names of our fallen soldiers of the County engraved upon the monument and as far as practical the battles in which they fell," Ward's former neighbors stipulated. After noting that decorative tablets might complement the list of names, the committee envisioned, "then if our money will reach, a Bronze Soldier Statue on the top with accoutrements and uniform."[64] The Urbana sponsors expressed a groundswell, not the imitation of a widely publicized model. Spring Grove Cemetery had commissioned Randolph Rogers to produce a soldier statue three years earlier, but the Cincinnati work did not correspond well with postwar interest in images directly related to the roll of the dead. Men of lesser artistic standing more directly answered the popular demand. James G. Batterson and Martin Milmore independently developed a visual formula that drew upon familiar narratives about Civil War soldiers and death. Other artists arrived at similar solutions. Ward's contribution, for Central Park rather than his hometown, helped to redirect the genre at its unveiling in 1874. The fifty soldier statues commissioned in the first decade after the war would eventually lead to a thousand more, but the ubiquity of the icon disguised the debates involved in its codification.

The statue that Rogers titled *The Sentinel (Soldier of the Line)* reflected its wartime origin and the sculptor's feisty patriotism. Commissioned in mid-March 1863, the centerpiece for the state-owned soldiers' lots in Spring Grove paralleled the monuments with which Newton, Massachusetts, and Bristol, Ohio, sought to stimulate mobilization. Rogers supported the Union with characteristic fervor from his studio in Rome. When an English visitor asked if the working model for *The Sentinel* depicted Stonewall Jackson, the sculptor replied, "No, Madam, it is the man who shot Stonewall Jackson," notwithstanding the well-known circumstances of the Confederate's death by friendly fire.[65] The expatriate failed to appreciate, however, that northerners regarded themselves as peaceable people drawn into a defensive war,

FIGURE 1.6. Randolph Rogers, model of *The Sentinel (Soldier of the Line)*, 1863–65.
Courtesy of Bentley Historical Library, University of Michigan.

rather than as warriors advancing with rifles raised. He also did not comprehend the desperation with which Americans tried to preserve an ideal of individuality despite the immensity and profound impersonality of the army. The "soldier of the line" epitomized the disposable anonymity they feared. No community ordered a similar work during the decade after the war, except for the monuments for Providence (1871) and Worcester (1874) in which Rogers recycled the pose. Along with his monument in Detroit (1872), these ensembles helped to establish a commemorative template for large cities. At the top stood allegorical figures who variously represented America Militant or Victory or Michigania, consistent with the principle that the levels of a monument advanced upward from the real to the ideal, but the centers of attention in these works were the statues of soldiers and sailors that stood in the middle register.

Rogers teamed with Batterson on an ensemble for the Soldiers' National Cemetery at Gettysburg that drew more effectively on the popular culture of wartime death. Batterson, a Hartford stone and monument supplier and Republican party activist, won the contract in July 1864, shortly after he collaborated with Rogers on Samuel Colt's grand funerary monument in Hartford.[66] The composition for the spot where Lincoln had delivered the Gettysburg Address consisted of a sixty-foot column topped by a statue of Liberty, surrounded by four lower figures in two male-female pairs. Batterson's firm sent models of these figures to Rogers, who was responsible for supervising the production of marble versions in Italy. Classically robed History recorded the recollections of War, an aging, bearded veteran with a hawk nose and deep-set eyes who resembled photographs of John Brown in the year before his execution. The visual allusion touched on soldiers' favorite musical resource for addressing the wartime specter of death, "John Brown's Body," which offered assurance that principled, dignified acceptance of death could lead to an individualized afterlife that transcended "mouldering in the grave."

Well before the dedication of the Gettysburg monument in 1869, Batterson began to sell single-figure monuments that presented a more direct antithesis to Rogers's *Sentinel*. The bronze statue dedicated in Deerfield, Massachusetts, in September 1867 stood atop a truncated obelisk in an exaggerated contrapposto stance. The soldier held his rifle with both hands at the end of the barrel, the stock resting on the ground. A long cloak hung loosely from his shoulders. He was not an aggressive or even an alert figure. He was clearly contemplative, his head tilted sharply downward. By the time

FIGURE 1.7. Randolph Rogers, Worcester Civil War Monument, 1871–74.
Courtesy of the Library of Congress.

of the unveiling in Deerfield, twenty-three-year-old Boston sculptor Martin
Milmore was completing a similar statue for Roxbury, Massachusetts, which
had purchased a lot in the Forest Hills rural cemetery upon recovering the
bodies of eight local soldiers from the Antietam battlefield in 1862. Milmore's soldier was young and beardless, but the Deerfield and Roxbury figures suggested the same narrative. A visitor to Milmore's foundry in late 1867

The Emergence of the Soldier Monument

reported that "our artist has found him after the din of battle, fatigued, de-jected; wandering alone, he comes upon new made graves of his fallen com-rades and there he stops a moment to muse." Another profile of the sculptor written in the same year confirmed that the statue depicted a soldier "resting on his gun, and contemplating the graves of his comrades."[67] Shortly after the Roxbury unveiling on Memorial Day in 1868, Milmore sold the model to North Brookfield, Massachusetts (1870), and the New Hampshire towns of Claremont (1869), Peterborough (1870), and Amherst (1871). Batterson supplied downward-looking soldier statues to at least ten additional munici-pal or institutional customers within eight years of the Deerfield dedication. Thomas D. Jones provided such a cavalry officer to Urbana, Ohio (1871). W. W. Lummus designed an infantryman for West Roxbury, Massachusetts (1871), that according to the official description represented "a soldier lean-ing in a pensive attitude upon his musket, as if contemplating in sorrow the loss of his comrades."[68] Henry Lovie's statue for Springfield, Ohio (1870), was in a "mourn arms" position, holding the butt of the rifle with the muzzle pointed downward.

These monuments seized on a motif with strong currency during and shortly after the war. Winslow Homer chose it for his painting *Trooper Medi-tating beside a Grave* (1865). Walt Whitman chose it for his poem "As Toil-some I Wander'd Virginia's Woods" (1865), in which the speaker happens across the hasty tree-side grave of an unknown soldier inscribed "Bold, cau-tious, true, and my loving comrade." Like that epitaph, the monumental image of soldier as mourner called attention to the wartime possibilities of what Whitman described in *Democratic Vistas* (1867) as "adhesive love," or "the personal and passionate attachment of man to man." The draped obelisk installed in Woodland Cemetery in Cleveland by survivors of the Twenty-Third Ohio Volunteer Infantry in 1865 and the urn placed in the Soldiers' Na-tional Cemetery at Gettysburg by the survivors of the First Minnesota Vol-unteer Infantry in 1867 extended the line of regimental monuments begun by the Thirty-Second Indiana in 1861. But like Homer's painting, early post-war statues also invited the speculation that the soldier contemplated a grave that was as anonymous as the marker in Whitman's poem. The scene was in this sense a variation on the ancient theme of "Et in Arcadia ego." The land-scape of the Civil War was an upside-down Arcadia in which death was espe-cially present. Even here, however, mortality impressed its meanings most vividly in sudden individual encounters.

Whether the monumental soldier was mourning or meditating, his role as representative of sensibility inverted the convention that women were the

FIGURE 1.8. Batterson Monumental Works (Carl Conrads and George
Keller), monument to "Lamented Sons and Soldiers / Who for Their
Country and for Freedom / Laid Down Their Lives in the War / of the Great
Rebellion," Deerfield, Massachusetts, 1866–67. Courtesy of Alamy.com.

FIGURE 1.9. Martin Milmore, plaster cast of Roxbury Monument,
Forest Hills Cemetery, Boston, 1867. Courtesy of the Library of Congress.

caretakers of the dead. Batterson underscored the blurring of gender norms
in his Green-Wood Cemetery ensemble for New York City, mostly executed
by 1869 although not completed until 1876. In addition to a set of soldier
statues like those he sold singly to smaller communities, Batterson included
a relief panel that depicted a woman overcome with grief. The juxtaposition
suggested that the contemplative soldier shared the same emotions as the
widow. Local sculptors Cyrus and Darius Cobb wrote that their statue in
Cambridge, Massachusetts (1870), showed a soldier buffeted between public
and private identities as he looked back "on the fearful strife through which
he has passed, the awful baptism by which his country has been purified. . . .

The Emergence of the Soldier Monument   47

And then the thoughts of his fallen comrades sweep through his mind, and with a tighter clasp of the gun on which he rests, and which has been his inseparable companion during those years of bloodshed, he uncovers his head, and with unfolded arms contemplates, with a mingling of solemnity, sternness, and tender memory, the scenes which these thoughts conjure before his mental eye." The mid-Victorian ideal of manliness required a readiness to incorporate some normatively female traits, but the break with social custom also reassured communities that their response to the emergency of the war was heartfelt.[69]

Soldier statues corresponded with additional cultural narratives of death in the Civil War. Picket duty was a popular motif. A report on Milmore's monument for Woburn, Massachusetts (1869), noted that "the attitude is easy, and not any of the 'positions of the soldier,' sometimes copied in statues of this kind, but rather suggestive of a soldier on picket." The sponsors' description of the statue that the South Carolina Monument Association ordered in 1873 described the figure as "a picket 'in for' a night's duty," with bayonet fixed and a cloak to ward off the midnight chill.[70] As songs like "All Quiet Along the Potomac To-Night" (1861) emphasized, the picket was an especially representative figure because he was an isolated individual, immersed in thoughts about his family at home, and exceptionally vulnerable to unseen attack. When Joshua Chamberlain sought in a dedication address to conjure "pictures of a soldier's hardships" that were "harder things to bear than battles," his first specific example was "picket duty in cold and wet, where neither fire nor light nor shelter must be had, amidst lurking perils and harrowing responsibilities."[71]

The picket who guarded his sleeping comrades associated the soldier statue standing in an authentic or imaginary cemetery with a text that monument sponsors sought to realize in three dimensions, Theodore O'Hara's "The Bivouac of the Dead." Written around 1850, the poem was widely identified with the Frankfort monument to Henry Clay Jr. and other Kentuckians killed at Buena Vista. Ceremonies for the dedication of Civil War monuments routinely featured recitation of the opening of O'Hara's lament:

> The muffled drum's sad roll has beat
>> The soldier's last tattoo;
> No more on life's parade shall meet
>> That brave and fallen few.
> On Fame's eternal camping-ground

Their silent tents are spread,
And Glory guards with solemn round
The bivouac of the dead.

Quartermaster Gen. Montgomery Meigs ordered tablets featuring a quotation from "The Bivouac of the Dead" for display in national military cemeteries. In conjunction with the dedication of Antietam National Cemetery on the fifth anniversary of the battle in September 1867, the trustees asked Batterson to make a colossal statue of a soldier "standing guard over the remains of the loyal dead."[72]

The mourning and meditating soldier, the picket, and the guard at the bivouac of the dead all indicated that versions of what historian Alice Fahs has called "the sentimental soldier" continued to thrive several years after the war. The widely marketed soldier statue expressed tensions Fahs identifies between mobilization for war and insistence on the priority of private relationships. Monuments were collective undertakings and existed to inform the civic order. Speakers at dedication ceremonies often addressed current political issues. The sectional conflict sometimes entered into monument designs, as when a Wilmington, North Carolina, newspaper pleaded, "Let not those sacred graves be desecrated by the erection over them of marble from the Northern land—better, far better and far more appropriate would it be to place there the roughest hewn post of Carolina wood."[73] More emphatically, however, the depictions embodied ideals of personal intimacy shared across both sections. A report on the statue in Columbia, South Carolina, observed that "although we do not recognize its special resemblance to any one we have known, yet it recalls many faces." Alluding to one of the most popular songs of the war, the writer added that "tears swell as we recall the fact that this figure is typical of the brave and fallen youth who was 'somebody's darling.'"[74]

Harbinger of a more assertive approach, the Seventh Regiment Memorial designed for Central Park by J. Q. A. Ward and Richard Morris Hunt ironically began with the sentimental trope of soldiers mourning for comrades. But this commission to honor war casualties differed from the regimental monuments that contributed to the popular image of the graveside soldier. The Seventh Regiment was not a component of the Union army, except for a period of six weeks in the spring of 1861 and a few scattered intervals afterward. The unit of the New York militia had established itself long before the Civil War as a prominent social organization of the Manhattan elite.

Supporters of the regiment believed that its wartime record—more than 500 members served as Union officers—had permanently refuted antebellum charges of dandyism and sympathy with slaveholders. The group looked ahead to the postwar era with a sense of vindicated leadership. Its plan for commemoration of the Civil War partly resembled the initiatives that led to monuments for the Independent Corps of Cadets in Mount Auburn Cemetery (1867), the Washington Light Infantry in Charleston (1870), and the Washington Grays in Philadelphia (1872). The importance of Central Park as a model for the reconstructed nation, however, made the Seventh Regiment Memorial comparable in potential impact to Harvard Memorial Hall. Where the college building linked class privilege to postwar reorganization of higher education, the Seventh Regiment Memorial asserted social entitlement justified by martial virtues.

The Seventh Regiment Memorial emerged not only from memory of the Civil War or the longer history of the Seventh but also from debates over the design and purpose of Central Park. Richard Morris Hunt, the first American to study at the École des Beaux-Arts, initiated the controversy in the spring of 1865 by exhibiting a plan of formal gates for the southern entrances of the park. He had submitted the drawings to the park commissioners two years earlier, while he was also completing the first of his summer cottages for Gilded Age tycoons in Newport, Rhode Island. The show at the National Academy of Design prompted Central Park landscape architects Frederick Law Olmsted and Calvert Vaux and their allies in the art press to denounce Hunt's proposal as "barren spawn of French imperialism" that would ruin the casual transition between city and park essential to their hopes for a democratic pastoral landscape.[75] The park commissioners' authorization of a Seventh Regiment monument at the entrance to be called the Warriors' Gate in February 1867 offered the architect a chance to revive his floundering campaign. He and Ward sketched plans for a memorial that would integrate architecture and sculptural groups in the first American showcase for the beaux arts style and a step toward the broader gateway plan. Olmsted and Vaux and their supporters continued to resist successfully, however, and Hunt and Ward had to settle for a single statue installed along the western walk of the park. The thwarted scheme nonetheless revealed the potential for military commemoration to serve as a fulcrum for overthrowing antebellum ideals of social democracy.

Ward's statue shared with its more sentimental contemporaries an emphasis on the distinctiveness of volunteers, though it proposed to describe a civilian leadership corps. One critic stressed that the figure was "not that

The Emergence of the Soldier Monument

of the mere routine soldier of a regular army." Another commentator agreed that the figure depicted "the ideal citizen soldier—the man of culture, refinement and social position." A third newspaper report praised the sculpture as "a model of *physique*," a distinction increasingly pursued by the urban upper classes, but it also found that "delicate lines" in the hands and face suggested "the tender culture of the brave soldiers of the well-beloved Seventh."[76] Although the statue illustrated the uniform of a private, New York governor and former U.S. secretary of the treasury John Adams Dix stressed in his June 1874 dedication address that the number of Union officers who began in the Seventh proved that "there was scarcely a man in your ranks who was not capable of leading other men." The superintendent of the parks department noted that the young men "who made the Seventh Regiment famous for its superb appearance in civic parades" typified "the heroic manhood that can one day build cities or railways or whiten the sea with sails."[77] Recognition of the Seventh Regiment in the most visionary urban space in the nation identified the American future with the consolidating metropolitan bourgeoisie.

Military discipline symbolized the social order preferred by privileged men who expected to hold positions of command. The statue Ward exhibited in his studio in 1869 was among the first to be widely publicized as a soldier in the stance of "parade rest." After a visit with the sculptor, the *New York Times* explained that "the attitude is what is known as 'parade rest,' or in European armies as 'standing at ease.'" Artists and viewers elsewhere did not always share an enthusiasm for drill positions. The Cobb brothers emphasized that their soldier in Cambridge, Massachusetts, "is not at 'parade rest,' as many unacquainted with military tactics have supposed. He is at ease, taking such position as suits him best; and the beholder is at liberty to place him where his fancies may dictate." Only two months before reporting on Ward's work, the *Times* published an oration that described a similar bronze in Salem, New York, differentiated mainly by its down-turned head, in purely metaphorical terms as "a soldier at ease with ordered rifle; facing southward to the fields of their victory; waiting the last command 'attention!' So sleep our dead, at rest, arms forever ordered, awaiting the last summons, which shall bid them come forth to the new and better life."[78] The Seventh Regiment Memorial, in contrast, looked from its prescribed ready position toward the future of the institutions it represented.

In that respect Ward's statue corresponded well with Olmsted and Vaux's view of the park, for the landscape architects eagerly sought to distinguish their masterpiece from the precedent of rural cemeteries. The park

FIGURE 1.10. John Quincy Adams Ward and Richard Morris Hunt,
Seventh Regiment Memorial, Central Park, 1868–74.
Courtesy of the Public Design Commission of the City of New York.

commissioners mandated that the monument was not to be "of sepulchral character." Looking back at the most memorable event in the brief collective service of the Seventh, its grand parade down Broadway and rapid passage to Washington in response to Lincoln's first call for troops in April 1861, Olmsted and Vaux remarked to the sculptor that "the typical idea represented by the Regiment seems to have been '*Vigilance*.' When the war commenced it was found to be *on Guard*, prepared for immediate action." Praise of Ward's statue for its "alert and active expression, and suggesting at once the idea of readiness for emergency and peril," contrasted diametrically with viewers' empathy elsewhere for statues of contemplative, vulnerable soldiers. The Seventh Regiment Memorial even failed to list the names of the fifty-eight men of the unit who died in the war. The dedication ceremony recognized that the tribute also honored survivors of the war, particularly those who had become officers, and even current members of the unit who had not fought in the war.[79]

Completion of the monument for Antietam National Cemetery presaged the trajectory of the competition between the ideas that Batterson and Milmore advanced at Deerfield and Roxbury and the ideas that Ward advanced in Central Park. After the trustees agreed in 1867 to commission Batterson to supply a colossal guardian of the dead, controversies over the burial of Confederate remains prevented the cemetery from moving forward with a contract until 1871. Batterson's firm quarried and carved the mammoth figure and its base over the next three years. Constructed from two granite blocks that were thirty and seventy tons when excavated, the soldier was slightly over twenty-one feet tall. The massive base added twenty-five feet in height. Batterson billed the work as the largest stone figure outside of Egypt. As the cemetery trustees were not ready to complete payment on the $35,000 project, the entrepreneur exhibited it at the Philadelphia centennial exposition. Art critic Earl Shinn's catalog of the fair recognized that the project honored not only the dead of Antietam but also the 500 employees of the New England Granite Company who had "succeeded in conquering the stubbornness of this mossy stone, and making it bend before them into the desired shape by the power of ingenious machinery." As the Seventh Regiment Memorial portrayed the urban elite, the Antietam monument stood in for the industrial working class. The soldier was "hard and firm though alert." His features included none of the refinement viewers saw in Ward's representative man. "Something rocky, rude and large-grained is obvious still in this stalwart American," observed Shinn. His moustache was "of barbaric proportions." He decidedly was not the personification of sensibility

FIGURE 1.11. New England Granite Works (Carl Conrads and George Keller), *The American Volunteer*, 1867–80. Photographed at Centennial Exhibition, 1876. Courtesy of the Free Library of Philadelphia.

that Batterson had pioneered in the immediate aftermath of the war. Shinn characterized the "monster" as the antithesis of the sentimental soldier. "His heart is of granite too," the critic pointed out.[80]

TOWARD REGIMENTATION

Dedications of soldier monuments decreased sharply after the first few years of the 1870s. The number of monuments unveiled in New England between 1870 and 1874 fell by a third from the total installed during 1863–69 and then again by a half between 1875 and 1879.[81] Even in the last five years the regional total remained a third of the national total. The only region to accelerate its production of soldier monuments during the 1870s was the lower South, which rose to the same pace as the Midwest. Even more striking than the slowdown in the proliferation of soldier monuments, however, was the evaporation of such alternatives as educational buildings and tributes to Abraham Lincoln. The soldier monument had become the dominant vehicle of Civil War commemoration, its influence manifest in observances of the centennial of the American Revolution.

The grip of the Civil War dead on the public imagination loosened by the mid-1870s. "The time for natural tears has passed," declared Charles Devens at the dedication of the Boston monument in 1877. "To every heart the years have brought their new store of joys and sorrows, since these men made their great sacrifice for country." Parents and widows may have disagreed with the orator's insistence that "there is no sorrow that cannot find its recompense in the added grandeur and dignity of the whole country," but pervasive fascination with the extinguishing of so many lives under such appalling circumstances gradually receded. Former Confederate officer John Tyler Morgan echoed Devens two years later at the installation of a monument on a mound in Winchester, Virginia, that contained the remains of 829 unknown dead, exemplars of the fate often regarded during the war as one of its saddest features. "It is not because these men have died that we are paying them honors," Morgan maintained. "All men are born to die; and the greater number die while they are toiling as earnestly in the performance of duty as were those who are in these graves. It is the cause in which they died that claims our reverence, and in that grand association, their honors even increase as their personal identity is lost." The transition was intermittent. At the 1881 unveiling of a monument atop the huge Confederate burial mound in Metairie Cemetery in New Orleans, orator Fitzhugh Lee recited the full text of "Somebody's Darling."[82] But an overall decline in engagement with the individuality of the dead reshaped commemoration and contributed to a slowing spread of initiatives.

Fading emphasis on the claims of intimacy coincided with shifts in the political context for Civil War monuments. The transition was more straightforward in the South, where national military cemeteries tended to contain the possible influence of Union memory while Confederate memory expanded in resistance to Reconstruction. The establishment of the South Carolina Monument Association in 1869 was part of a network of institutions designed to reverse Republican victories at the polls. The dedication of the association's monument a decade later at the "redeemed" statehouse effectively marked the overthrow of biracial democracy, and Democrats "with a feeling of sureness that they were a free people let themselves loose in a mighty jubilation."[83] The unveiling of the soldier monument in Augusta, Georgia, in October 1878 was a similar celebration. It was not difficult to foresee the rise of more Confederate monuments across the South as Democrats sought to consolidate political control of the region.

The commemorative dimension to the end of Reconstruction was more complex for the North. The idea that Union soldiers might best be remembered through a thorough rebuilding of the South lost traction even before the Republican Party retreated fully from Reconstruction. The Soldiers' Memorial Society, founded as an explicit alternative to civic monuments, ceased operations shortly after issuing its sixth annual report in 1870. The New England branch of the American Freedman's Union Commission, which bought land for the Shaw Memorial School in Charleston with funds collected for a monument, turned the school over to the city when the branch folded in 1874.[84] These withdrawals marked a waning of white northern attention to southern freedpeople and a sense that progress in public education depended on government action rather than grassroots philanthropy.

The building of memorial halls in northern communities also declined sharply. Canton, Massachusetts, was at least the eighteenth New England municipality to complete a memorial hall when it opened its town house and public library in 1879. Only a few towns followed this model in the next decades. Public libraries continued to depend heavily on private benefactions, but those gifts increasingly honored donors or their family members rather than Civil War soldiers.[85] College construction ended more decisively with the dedication of the classroom building at Bowdoin in 1882. Columbia, Dartmouth, and Yale, all of which had announced plans in 1865 to build memorial halls, let the initiatives lapse.[86] Critics of memorial buildings had argued that new governmental and educational facilities did not respond sympathetically to public grief, but the commemorative form was more inextricably embedded in the immediate postwar period than the monumental cenotaph.

The exhaustion of nonmilitary themes in Union monuments paralleled this shift away from memorial institutions. As outstanding scholarship has demonstrated, a surge of enthusiasm for celebrating the landmark of emancipation quickly resolved into a variety of projects to honor Lincoln. Howells recalled in May 1866 that a year earlier "each city was about to celebrate him by a statue in its public square; every village would have his bust or a funeral tablet." Five of the twelve largest cities in the country—New York, Philadelphia, Brooklyn, San Francisco, and Washington—unveiled statues of Lincoln by 1871. Congress commissioned a statue for the Capitol, and private fund-raising campaigns claimed national significance for additional monuments in Springfield, Illinois, and Washington, DC. All of these tributes recognized emancipation as central to Lincoln's legacy. The most substantive effort to define the meaning of emancipation, however, was Harriet Hosmer's proposal to place a slave-to-soldier cycle of statues at the heart of a multitiered ensemble. The soldier monument effectively monopolized the public visualization of freedom. When whites denied African Americans access to this form of representation, the black presence in Civil War monuments defaulted to the genuflecting figure in Thomas Ball's design for the Freedmen's Memorial to Abraham Lincoln, dedicated in Washington in 1876. As Kirk Savage has observed, that composition was an "act of completion" that imposed closure on the emblematic abolitionist challenge, "Am I not a man and a brother?" The replication of Ball's work in Boston in 1879 confirmed its status as a definitive remembrance of emancipation.[87]

Sculptors' portraits of Lincoln varied somewhat but achieved little amplitude in interpretation of the Union cause. The most elaborate contextualization, the tomb in Springfield, situated Lincoln squarely in an adaptation of the metropolitan soldiers monument, varied by the introduction of three-figure groups from each branch of the armed services rather than single representatives of the infantry, artillery, cavalry, and navy. Lincoln's potential as a monumental personification of the Union cause was waning well before the dedication at Oak Ridge Cemetery in October 1874, an event that achieved the intended level of festivity mostly by tying it to an annual meeting of the survivors of the Army of the Tennessee.[88] Citizens of Davenport, Iowa, formed a Lincoln Monument Association in 1865 that accumulated only $700 by 1871, when the association accepted a pledge of $1,300 conditioned on transformation of the project into a county soldier monument. Other donations raised the fund to $8,000, and the sponsors unveiled a soldier statue in 1881.[89]

Display of Larkin Mead's naval group for the Lincoln tomb at the Philadelphia centennial exposition in 1876 — along with the Antietam statue, Peter Rothermel's monumental painting of Pickett's charge, and related works — suggested the extent to which remembrance of the Civil War entered into remembrance of the Revolution. Congress took over the long-stymied Washington Monument in 1876 and placed it under the control of a commission like those that had recently completed Washington statues to Winfield Scott and John Rawlins, in which War Department administration of the Office of Public Buildings and Grounds ensured military supervision. Congress also appropriated $100,000 to make good on its 1781 pledge to raise a victory monument in Yorktown, Virginia, a promise that state representatives had long prodded the federal government to fulfill. Saratoga, New York, another site where the absence of a monument had drawn notice for decades, laid a cornerstone in 1877. The Monmouth Battle Monument Association received $20,000 from Congress and $10,000 from New Jersey after raising $10,000 in donations.[90] The designs for all of these monuments owed a significant debt to the Civil War soldier monuments unveiled in major cities during the past decade.

The Statue of Liberty illustrated both the broad influence and the narrowing possibilities of Civil War commemoration. Bartholdi would indicate in the mid-1880s that Laboulaye had linked the project to the centennial of the Revolution upon proposing the monument in August 1865, but its American impetus was clearly the Civil War triumph of liberalism as a source of hope for France and the rest of the world. Only when Bartholdi visited the United States in 1871 and learned about debates over Reconstruction did he understand that a postwar celebration of liberty might be a politically awkward gift. Congress had authorized the centennial exposition shortly before Bartholdi sailed, and Laboulaye's contact, John C. Forney (a prominent Philadelphia newspaper editor before he became one of Lincoln's agents on Capitol Hill), had assumed a leading role in promotion of the observance in his hometown. Laboulaye and Bartholdi repositioned their initiative as a commemoration of the Revolution, and the 1876 fair featured an exhibition of the colossal right hand and torch. But as the monuments for Yorktown, Saratoga, and Monmouth would soon demonstrate, Americans increasingly looked upon independence as primarily a military achievement rather than an inspirational political movement. Forney realized as early as 1875 that his

　　　　　　　　　　　　　　　　The Emergence of the Soldier Monument

fellow citizens would appreciate the statue dedicated in 1886 mostly on the understanding that "all the nations may see by day the figure of Liberty welcoming them to United States, and follow her shining welcome in the darkest hours of their despair."[91]

The centennial observance of the skirmish at Concord best measured how much remembrance of the Revolution had changed since the dedication of the obelisk made famous by Emerson in 1837. Principal orator George W. Curtis emphasized to an audience that included President Ulysses S. Grant, Vice President Henry Wilson, and much of the cabinet and congressional leadership that "we who stand here to-day have a sympathy with the men at the old North Bridge, which those who proceeded us here at earlier celebrations could not know." The commemoration centered on a monument initiated by a bequest from Ebenezer Hubbard, who had long expressed displeasure that the town placed the 1837 obelisk on the side of the stream occupied by the British in 1775 even though it was the first American shot that gave Concord a claim to greater importance than the earlier confrontation at Lexington. Hubbard left enough money for a comparable obelisk on the American side, along with funds to replace the bridge that had washed away decades ago. A town committee instead resolved that the new monument should be a statue of a minuteman. Concord compensated for the funding shortfall by arranging for federal donation of condemned brass cannons to the enterprise and accepting a donation of unpaid services from an untested young local sculptor, Daniel Chester French. The town resolved from the outset to inscribe the opening stanza of the "Concord Hymn" on the pedestal and placed a copy of the proceedings from the 1867 dedication of the monument to the Civil War dead in the cornerstone of the centennial tribute.[92]

Local precedents notwithstanding, French's *The Minute Man* had less in common with the 1837 or 1867 obelisks than with J. Q. A. Ward's sentinel in Central Park. The month that French spent as a pupil in Ward's studio shortly after completion of the Seventh Regiment design was an important episode in the younger artist's training. The two sculptors exemplified an American naturalism wary of the domestic sentimentality that shaped early soldier statues. Ward and French both aimed to highlight the readiness of the volunteer rather than the meditation of the soldier on picket duty or beside a grave. The sculptors sought to share the easy independence that they attributed to their subjects. Critics who found that the Seventh Regiment Memorial "is modeled broadly and freely, and is strikingly simple and unaffected in composition," would have seen the same merits in *The Minute*

FIGURE 1.12.
Daniel Chester French,
The Minute Man, Concord,
Massachusetts, 1871–75.
Courtesy of the Library
of Congress.

BY THE RUDE BRIDGE THAT
ARCHED THE FLOOD,
THEIR FLAG TO APRIL'S
BREEZE UNFURLED,
HERE ONCE THE EMBATTLED
FARMERS STOOD,
AND FIRED THE SHOT HEARD
ROUND THE WORLD.

Man. Ward's manner usually earned him the distinction achieved by French's work "that the statue wins praise alike from the scholar and the laborer, the cultivated and the untrained taste."[93]

That combination of critical and popular acclaim, a fundamental ambition of civic monuments, had become conspicuously elusive for Civil War monuments by the mid-1870s. Even Ward's admirers conceded that the Seventh Regiment Memorial would "not increase greatly his fame as an artist." A journalist called the Antietam statue "an enormous pile of unexceptional granite shapen by American hands into the similitude of an American soldier of to-day, eloquent to contemporary eyes, but little apt favorably to affect connoisseurs of the more remote future impliedly addressed by the selection of an unchangeable material." To those observers the work would "speak poorly for the notions of grace and beauty prevalent among those who chiseled and set up this votive offering to gunpowder." James Jackson Jarves had predicted after the installation of the Green-Wood Cemetery ensemble in 1869 that "soon there will be seen in high place and in low, huge effigies, in bronze and stone, of volunteers on guard at corners of columns, obelisks, and shafts of every conceivable degree of disproportion, misapplication, and inappropriate ornamentation, dedicated to the heroes of our late contest." *American Architect and Building News* made denunciation of Civil War monuments a standard feature almost as soon as W. P. P. Longfellow established the Boston journal in 1876. The next year a review declared that Milmore's monument on Boston Common, which followed the metropolitan pattern established by Rogers at Detroit, Providence, and Worcester, committed "the unpardonable sin" that "it is commonplace" and showed "no touch of grace or poetic feeling." Even more disturbing, continued the journal, was the lack of public outcry over such mediocrity. The sentiments animating Civil War monuments were "of such a nature that criticism in regard to their artistic merits or demerits is, to a certain extent, disarmed."[94]

Cultural elites Jarves and Longfellow spoke for only one faction interested in Civil War commemoration. When the Ladies Memorial Association of Macon, Georgia, installed a $4,500 marble memorial near the county courthouse in 1879 that featured a stock soldier carved in Italy for the regional leader Muldoon Monument Company, a newspaper approved that "the position of the soldier is that of 'Rest.' How typical the design. How appropriate to those who repose beneath the sod." An orator at the 1882 dedication of a standard figure sold by New England Granite Works to Easton, Massachusetts, assured his audience that it "will compare favorably with any soldiers' monument." Two years later the *Manchester Union* described

FIGURE 1.13. L. Prang and Co., *Army and Navy Monument on Boston Common*, lithograph, 1877. Courtesy of the Library of Congress.

the similar $2,000 granite statue in Londonderry, New Hampshire, as "in the graceful position of 'parade rest.'" Community satisfaction remained an important reason for the popularity of replicated poses, although over time sponsors came to emphasize that "the monument represents a soldier upon duty—alert and watchful."[95]

The aesthetes were not wrong, however, in arguing that inertia partly explained the regimentation of Civil War memorials by the early 1880s. The statues variously read as mourning or meditating or drilling or vigilant soldiers now defined initial expectations for a community commemoration. As the diminished numbers and consolidating interpretations of those monuments indicated, the impetus behind the development of the genre had waned since the end of the war, although not as much as the forces that had produced educational buildings or Lincoln memorials. Many projects would assume the familiar shape when new pressures prompted another surge of monuments, but the clearest expression of the transition would be the emergence of new idealizations of the Civil War soldier.

MODELS *of* CITIZENSHIP

In the early 1880s the production of Civil War monuments reversed its recent decline throughout the North and entered a new phase. The number
of common-soldier memorials installed in the antebellum nonslaveholding
states during the five years ending in 1890 was well over double the number erected in the five years ending in 1880 and, at least outside New England, higher than the number dedicated by 1870. The establishment of the
trade monthly *Monumental News* in 1889 reflected a justified optimism about
the further growth of the industry and particularly its Civil War sector. Production of Confederate memorials began to increase dramatically shortly
afterward. The number of common-soldier monuments unveiled across the
country during the first fifteen years of the twentieth century was almost
double that of the previous fifteen years.

As the distribution and continuation of this surge indicates, the re-
covery of the economy after 1879 was only a secondary explanation for the
pattern. More important was the mobilization of Union veterans touched

off by George E. Lemon's founding of the *National Tribune* newspaper in 1877 and the lobbying campaign for expanded federal pensions that proved its strength in the Arrears Act of 1879. Membership in the Grand Army of the Republic (GAR), stagnant before the financial panic and in moderate decline during the first years of the depression, multiplied more than tenfold between 1876 and 1884. Additional 30 percent growth across the next three years put the membership above 350,000.[1] The proliferation of southern monuments similarly followed a reorganization of Confederate memory marked by the establishment of the United Confederate Veterans (UCV) in 1889, the monthly *Confederate Veteran* in 1892, and the United Daughters of the Confederacy (UDC) in 1894. Civil War monuments of the late nineteenth and early twentieth centuries partly continued the early postwar commemorative impulse but largely reflected fresh sponsorship with altered objectives.

The hallmark of this transition was a shift in the soldiers to whom communities dedicated monuments. Inscriptions of the early postwar era overwhelmingly tended to focus on the war dead, even for monuments installed in town centers rather than cemeteries. This pattern began to change in the North during the 1880s, and by the first decade of the twentieth century, local monuments in both sections usually honored Civil War soldiers whether they died in the war or survived it. Lists of names that had once served as substitutes for missing bodies instead recorded all enlistments from a town or county, and sometimes a large city. Other dedicatory patterns underscored the switch in emphasis from the dead to the soldier. A handful of monuments installed before the Spanish-American War honored Civil War soldiers alongside local participants in other wars; dozens of communities adopted this approach afterward, although the Civil War remained the dominant historical framework for imagining military life. By the early twentieth century, northern and southern sponsors not infrequently dedicated monuments directly to veterans rather than to all soldiers who served in the war, perhaps inadvertently excluding the dead but firmly recognizing the distinctive peacetime role of ex-soldiers. The GAR installed a monument to itself on Pennsylvania Avenue in Washington in 1909.

The exaltation of the Civil War soldier made the figure a vital resource for a variety of groups that shared veterans' interests in the promotion of martial ideals. Debates over current army and navy policy reverberated through Civil War memory. The national battlefield parks administered by the War Department, a key outlet for veterans' organizational efforts, also influenced community monuments. State militia units complemented veterans as embodiments of voluntary service and sometimes followed the lead of the Seventh Regiment in commissioning memorials. Economic and cultural polemicists often identified the soldier as an exemplar of discipline and daring. The intensified admiration for a form of citizenship monopolized by men had significant consequences for gender politics.

The new monuments were central to the soldier's displacement of the farmer as the primary personification of American ideals. The memorial unveiled in 1897 in Pawtucket, Rhode Island, the most elaborate Civil War variation on Daniel Chester French's *The Minute Man*, showed how far the country now stood from Ralph Waldo Emerson's embattled yeomen. The project began in 1886 when a local GAR post called for a memorial. Prominent women chartered the Ladies Soldiers Memorial Association to lead fund-raising efforts. Representatives of the wealth generated by one of the longest and most intensively industrialized areas of the country, the matrons raised much of the money by holding an industrial and art exposition. Designed by W. Granville Hastings, in-house sculptor for the Gorham Manufacturing Company based in nearby Providence, the monument was itself a display of local industry. The work featured two unusual side-panel reliefs that depicted one robed woman writing on a tablet and another contemplating a fern leaf. In addition to underscoring the enhanced public visibility of women illustrated by the association, the classical images of intellectual activity modeled for Wilkinson Park visitors the experience of studying an artwork that updated the Cincinnatus story. Unlike the Roman patrician whose virtue preceded military service, the raw young farmer fundamentally changed by accepting a sword from Hastings's allegorical female figure of liberty. Agricultural life was not a moral reservoir in late-nineteenth-century New England. Instead the youth matured at war. The monument identified military experience as a path of advancement from the simple society signified by the farmer's plow. This idealization of the soldier served the army and navy of an increasingly bellicose United States and also institutions that drew on martial analogies, especially factories and schools.[2]

Veterans' increased influence in monument promotion added to art critics' discontent with the designs of Civil War monuments. The development of battlefield parks sharpened those aspersions. William S. Rosecrans, who had commanded Union forces at Chickamauga, argued for the precedent-setting creation of the Chickamauga and Chattanooga National Military Park as a place "where the organizations who choose to do so can put up monuments to the heroism displayed on those fields, without criticism."[3] Commentators nevertheless routinely condemned the state-funded

FIGURE 2.1.
Gorham
Manufacturing
Company (W. Granville
Hastings), *Liberty
Arming the Patriot*,
Pawtucket, 1896–97.
Courtesy of Rhode
Island Historical
Preservation &
Heritage Commission.

commissions, heavily dominated by veterans, who placed large numbers of monuments in the federal parks by the early twentieth century. *Monumental News* complained that many of these commissions were "not such as to command the respect of the intelligent citizen."[4] Community monuments also caused friction between veterans and the art world. The most spectacular clash was a lawsuit filed by ex-soldiers in Jersey City to prevent installation of a monument selected in a juried competition administered by the recently established National Sculpture Society. Dedicated in 1899 after court dismissal of the suit, Philip Martiny's work featured a seated Athena-like figure wearing a battle helmet and holding a large sword and an olive branch. The chairman of the monument committee, county clerk John G. Fisher, scoffed that "the veterans know nothing about art, of course, and they felt that the monument should represent something terrific. They thought there ought to be a soldier shooting another through the heart, or a horseman whacking out another's brains with a saber." Like the significant overlap between monument designs for battlefield parks and municipalities, however, Fisher's active membership in the GAR, which the aggrieved Jersey City veterans regarded as "an exclusive and unrepresentative body," indicated that commemorative entities could often negotiate differences.[5]

Veterans and artists and critics and entrepreneurs and other men and women interested in Civil War memory found enough common ground to forge revealing patterns in the many monuments installed across the North and South during the late nineteenth and early twentieth centuries. The initial preference of the GAR post in Pawtucket for a memorial building illustrated one such pattern. Like the fund-raising committee there, most sponsors turned to commemorative statuary, which unlike the outcome in Jersey City usually involved depiction of the Civil War soldier. The continued proliferation of sentinel statues masked the extent of efforts to find alternatives. Figures of soldiers carrying flags, engaged in battle, or on the march presented new visions of American citizenship, as did the memorials dedicated to women's wartime contributions. Martial imagery provided a flexible and powerful vocabulary for monument promoters to assert forms of national identity as resolutions to class, ethnic, and gender tensions.

MEMORIAL HALLS REVISITED

In the serial installment of Henry James's *The Bostonians* published in September 1885, the novelist sent his main characters on a visit to Harvard Memorial Hall that dramatized the intertwining of private and public life

James had set in previous books at the Colosseum and the Louvre. The next year, art critic Sylvester R. Koehler published one of the most thorough responses to the widely shared view that "in the United States, at least, monumental art has almost fallen into contempt." While skeptical about Harvard's combination of a memorial transept with a dining room and a theater, Koehler concluded that "it is nevertheless clear that in the memorial hall we have found the solution of the problem."[6] These appreciations for the potential of the commemorative form coincided with the onset of a reversal in its characteristic design. After the mid-1880s memorial halls increasingly became facilities for veterans rather than public libraries or other educational structures. Even buildings that served the entire community shared the martial values of less expensive and more ubiquitous soldier statues.

The most politically salient memorial to Civil War veterans was the immense building that Congress authorized for the Pension Bureau in 1881 to handle the workload multiplied by the Arrears Act, which permitted retroactive payments for claims filed by July 1880 and invited submission of ex parte affidavits to supplement military records in determining whether an injury resulted from Union service. The Pension Bureau received more petitions in 1880 than in the five previous years combined. Expenditures doubled the total for 1878 and consumed more than one-fifth of the federal budget.[7] A flipside to Republicans' insistence on a protective tariff for industry, the expansion of Civil War pensions remained a lively political issue and stimulus to veterans' organizational efforts through the passage of the Dependent Pension Act of 1890, which offered a pension to every Union veteran unable to perform manual labor regardless of financial need or the reason for his limitation, in many cases simply age. By 1893 the Pension Bureau spent 42 percent of the federal budget. But GAR membership began to decline after passage of the Dependent Pension Act, a reflection not merely of mortality but also the controversies in which *Nation* editor E. L. Godkin, *Harper's Weekly* columnist Carl Schurz, and other Mugwumps criticized the pension lobby as unworthy of veterans' reputation for selflessness.[8] The state-building characterized by benefit payments contributed only partially to popular recognition of military service as an entitlement to unique privileges of citizenship.

The ornamentation of the Pension Building completed in 1887 exposed tensions between the vision of military service that animated the former volunteers who dominated the GAR and the perspective of building architect Montgomery Meigs, the soul of the regular army. The longtime quartermaster general demonstrated his political savvy and eagerness to define the

FIGURE 2.2. Montgomery Meigs and Caspar Buberl, Pension Building and detail of frieze, Washington, DC, 1881–87. Courtesy of the Library of Congress.

war's legacy by circumventing the ordinary channels for design of federal buildings and securing a personal commission in the authorizing legislation for the Interior Department structure. From the outset Meigs planned to encircle the Pension Building with a memorial frieze. He recruited sculptor Caspar Buberl to fashion a set of twenty-eight terra cotta panels, two to four feet in length and uniformly three feet in height, which provided sixty-nine feet of reliefs on six themes available for repetition in varying combinations around the 1,200-foot perimeter.[9] The panels fit together in this way because all depicted the army at march, except for an unavoidable acknowledgment of the navy. Although economical, the decorative strategy and Buberl's execution represented Union soldiers as interchangeable, barely differentiated

Models of Citizenship

bits in a vast file, like the 15 million red bricks that distinguished the building from so much government architecture. The Gate of the Quartermaster, one of the four entrances, highlighted not only Meigs's administration but also the army connection between the wartime vanguard of the federal bureaucracy and its postwar successor.[10]

The Pension Building, which hosted its first presidential inaugural ball in 1885 even before installation of the roof, may have foreshadowed the long-term growth of the American state, but the GAR halls opened in communities across the country better illustrated Civil War veterans' changing relationship with the nation in the last two decades of the nineteenth century. Individuals belonged to the GAR as members of a chartered post, and local meetings were the lifeblood of the fraternal society. In the membership boom of the 1880s, active posts increasingly sought buildings that would provide meeting space as well as banquet facilities, lounges, and venues for display of war relics and circulation of war chronicles. Frederick W. Lander Post #5 in Lynn, Massachusetts, one of the largest posts in the country with more than 1,000 active members in 1886, dedicated a headquarters that year at a cost of $37,000 outfitted with "every convenience that can add to the comfort of the comrades" and storefronts to supplement the rental income that the post derived from an auditorium built four years earlier.[11]

Veterans' eagerness for accommodations led them to make claims on public resources. Toledo, Ohio, offered a prototype. An association formed in 1879 resolved to combine a war memorial with a militia armory, a building type spreading across the country since the great railroad strike two years earlier. Lucas County donated an unexpended bounty fund, and the city contributed a prime site near the courthouse. After a subscription campaign failed to generate the remaining funds necessary for the estimated $65,000 outlay, the city council took over the project and paid for it with municipal bonds. The building dedicated in 1886 included an arsenal, a drill hall, reception rooms, a library of military history, relic cases, and meeting space to be shared by the GAR, regimental associations, and the veterans' groups dominated by former officers, such as the Military Order of the Loyal Legion and the alumni societies of the various Union armies.[12] The combined purposes underscored the extent to which veterans' groups reproduced the male sociability associated with the volunteer militia. An architectural critic made a similar point when he described Louis Comfort Tiffany's work with Stanford White and Francis Davis Millet for the posh Veterans' Room and Library of the privately financed Seventh Regiment Armory in New York, opened in 1880, as "the veteran idea embodied in iron."[13]

FIGURE 2.3. David W. Gibbs, Soldiers Memorial Building, Toledo, 1883–86. Lithograph by Locke & Trowbridge. Courtesy of the Ohio History Connection.

Public funding of veterans' rooms reversed the ways earlier memorial halls had situated military service within a broader ideal of engaged and informed citizenship. The new municipal commemorations singled out the fraternally secret proceedings of GAR posts as an official representation of local ties to the nation. After the Illinois legislature donated one-fourth of Dearborn Park as a site for a memorial hall to be shared by the GAR posts headquartered in Cook County, the veterans transferred those land rights to the Chicago Public Library in exchange for an opulent memorial hall in the library opened on the park in 1897. The GAR spokesman argued that neither the city nor the state had "ever erected a memorial building or monumental structure of any importance," and the library accommodation did differ significantly from the memorial hall that Illinois, like other states, had dedicated in its new capitol in 1884.[14] Both rooms displayed Civil War flags, other relics, and artwork, but the GAR hall invested veterans with ownership rights to a site of municipal remembrance.

Nonveterans did not always defer to veterans' assertions of unique representative status. The public library opened in 1890 in Petersham, Massa-

Models of Citizenship

chusetts, which featured tablets with names of local men who served in the Revolutionary and Union armies, was one of several to continue the conception of a memorial hall that honored soldiers without creating civic privileges for ex-soldiers. A GAR officer grumbled that the tribute was "more useful than sentimental" and reported that veterans in another town considered recognition through a similar library rather than a monument "not at all agreeable."[15] Fidelity to the early postwar pattern produced litigation in Brockton, Massachusetts, as several residents sued to prevent the city from leasing space in a proposed memorial library to a GAR post at nominal rent. The Supreme Judicial Court ruled that the accommodation for the veterans was not a public purpose sufficient to sustain exercise of the power of taxation. Brockton instead incorporated a memorial rotunda, featuring marble tablets inscribed with the names of the local dead, in the city hall for which the municipality laid the cornerstone on Memorial Day in 1892. Lunette paintings of the departure for war and return home and the decoration of graves emphasized the close ties between soldiers and civilians rather than enshrining division in a post room.[16]

Such commemorations were contending against a clear trend by the 1890s. Despite the court decision in the Brockton case, Lowell opened a memorial library in 1893 that set aside much of the second floor for the local GAR, whose relics included the bloodstained jackets worn by early Union martyrs Luther Ladd and Addison Whitney during the passage through Baltimore in April 1861. Detroit covered more than four-fifths of the cost of a castle-like structure leased to GAR posts without rent for thirty years after it opened in 1900. Three years later Winnebago County, Illinois, dedicated a memorial hall at Rockford outfitted for veterans with banquet facilities, game and card rooms, meeting space, and an auditorium.[17] Ohio enacted legislation in 1902 that authorized counties to issue municipal bonds to build memorial halls and authorized county commissioners to permit occupancy by veterans' groups and historical societies. Impressive auditoriums soon opened in Columbus (1906), Cincinnati (1908), Lima (1908), Dayton (1910), and Greenville (1912).[18] Communities in other states that completed notable taxpayer-funded GAR halls in the next few years included Melrose, Massachusetts (1912); Hardwick, Vermont (1912); Wichita (1913) and Topeka, Kansas (1914); and Waterloo, Iowa (1915).

Ironically, the increasing grandeur of these projects correlated with a decline in the GAR's political influence as a result of the backlash against the Dependent Pension Act and the waning of the veteran generation in the early twentieth century. GAR membership fell more than 40 percent from its 1890 peak to 1905, when the surgeon-general of the organization reported that about 60,000 former Union soldiers were dying each year.[19] Veterans were instrumental in reinvigorating Civil War commemoration in the 1880s and turning attention from the Union dead to all former servicemen, but the triumph of the citizen-soldier as embodiment of the polity did not rely solely on the votes of a large demographic cohort. The martial ideal also served the purposes of an industrial order coalescing in American society at the same time that old soldiers were fading away.

The most spectacular of the new public buildings designed to support and showcase veterans' organizations, the Soldiers and Sailors Memorial Hall dedicated in Pittsburgh in 1910, illustrated the civic values best personified by Andrew Carnegie, who had avoided wartime conscription by hiring a substitute while laying foundations for his postwar fortune.[20] Although Allegheny County dedicated an imposing monument to its Union dead on a North Side hill in 1871, veterans' groups began agitating twenty years later for further commemoration. Upon enactment of 1895 legislation that authorized municipal funding for a monument endorsed by a popular vote, a local official told the veterans not to expect approval of another shaft and urged revision of the legislation to permit a memorial hall, "which would be more in keeping with the dignity and greatness of this county." The instruction reflected the rise of a City Beautiful district on East End farmland previously owned by Mary Schenley. She had donated 400 acres for a public park in 1889, and soon afterward Carnegie had chosen a lot near its entrance for the Carnegie Institute library, museum, and concert hall that opened in stages in 1895–96. His business associate Henry Phipps founded a conservatory and botanical garden in the park. Plans for the Civil War memorial intertwined with the neighborhood development that followed Schenley's death in 1903, leaving her land to a group of trustees that included Carnegie. The city had already purchased nearby property for the promised endowment of Carnegie Tech, envisioned as a trade school for working-class children, and a design competition for the campus took place in 1904. In the same year the Western University of Pennsylvania began preparations to relocate. When the legislature passed an act in 1905 that provided specifically for an Allegheny County memorial hall at a cost of $1,250,000, local leaders saw the building as a visual and thematic centerpiece for the spine of Oakland that extended from Schenley Park and the Phipps Conservatory through the Carnegie Institute and Carnegie Tech to the Schenley Hotel (1898), with the memorial hall anchoring Fifth Avenue and linking to the projected site of the renamed University of Pittsburgh in the hills beyond. The tribute would

FIGURE 2.4. J. C. Bragdon, *Pittsburgh's Fifty Million Dollar Beauty Center*, postcard, 1916. Author's collection.

insert patriotism at the heart of a district that celebrated cultural riches and individual opportunity presented through industrial capitalism.[21]

The program for the design competition announced in late 1906 blended martial remembrance with building uses attractive to local business leaders on the county's memorial hall committee. The commemorative core of the building would be tablets inscribed with the names of soldiers in thirty Union regiments and several batteries associated with Allegheny County, which ultimately added up to 23,885 names, one of the longest lists ever displayed on a memorial to that point.[22] GAR posts and other veterans' organizations would control two meeting rooms, headquarters offices, and a library. The largest space was an auditorium with a seating capacity of 2,550. The final major component was a banquet hall with kitchen facilities for functions too large to fit in the Schenley Hotel, which had hosted the "Meal of Millionaires" to celebrate the formation of U.S. Steel in 1901. Some critics questioned the combination of memorial and recreational purposes, but the program reflected the determination to justify a large structure and an aspiration to bring together all levels of society, from former rank-and-file soldiers to the fashionable crowd at gala concerts and balls.[23]

Henry Horbostel's winning design epitomized what "The Pittsburgher's Creed" of the era called faith in "Pittsburgh the powerful—the progressive."[24] By stacking the ballroom atop the auditorium, the adaptation of the Mausoleum at Halicarnassos achieved compact solidity and impressive height. Essentially identical facades on all four sides radiated central authority and helped to unify the Oakland district. Some features situated the work in the industrial economy. The final cost of $1,650,000 testified to Pittsburgh's wealth. Crowning the roof was a large urn that functioned as a smokestack for the boiler plant of the building, a conceptual link to the most remarkable feature of Horbostel's acclaimed design for Carnegie Tech, the elaborately encased smokestack that closed the main quadrangle at Machinery Hall.[25] The analogy between the two quasi-temples identified the dutiful servicemen honored at the memorial hall as particular models for the future laborers training at the vocational campus.

The main speaker at the October 1910 dedication embodied the overlap between public recognition of the GAR and the availability of state force to maintain labor discipline. Thomas J. Stewart served only a few months in the Union army as a teenager at the end of the war, but he became active soon afterward in the Pennsylvania militia, rebranded in the 1870s as the National Guard. He received his first commission as adjutant of the Sixth Regiment in the year of the great railroad strike. He served as assistant adjutant of the First Brigade during the Homestead strike in July 1892. Three years later he was appointed adjutant general of the Pennsylvania National Guard, a position he held until his death. For several years he was also adjutant general of the GAR, and in 1902 he became commander in chief of the society. Shortly before Stewart led the dedication of the Soldiers and Sailors Memorial Hall, the state and the county underscored his symbolic significance as project spokesman by selecting the adjacent lot as the site of a new armory for the Eighteenth Regiment of the Pennsylvania National Guard, the unit that had led the strikebreaking troops into Homestead.[26]

Despite the decisive exercise of state power against workers, memorial hall promoters preferred to imagine a voluntary social harmony grounded in patriotism. Horbostel commissioned sculptor Charles Keck to ornament the front facade with a colossal bronze statue of America in addition to making a vestibule tablet that honored Carnegie's role in the formation of the wartime telegraph corps.[27] The allegorical female figure sat upright in a heavy but sleek throne, her shield resting at her side. Looking forward vigilantly beneath a battle helmet wreathed with peaceful olive branches, she displayed a muscular arm as her left hand reached around to grasp her right in holding the hilt of a massive archaic sword. The association of the weapon with justice suggested America's blessing on the social relations she oversaw in

Models of Citizenship

FIGURE 2.5. Charles Keck, model of *America*, 1910. Courtesy of Soldiers and Sailors Memorial Hall and Museum, Pittsburgh, Pennsylvania.

the Oakland district. The swerve of her torso within her rounded chair and the crossing of her ankles created a lively spiral. The vigorous summons to loyalty incorporated many of the features that characterized soldier monuments dedicated at the same time as the proliferation of memorial halls from the 1880s to the 1910s, even though those statues largely eschewed allegory. Keck draped alongside his paragon of nationhood the starting point for that iconographic development, the American flag.

The rise of the flag-bearer was the most important design trend in soldier monuments during the last fifteen years of the nineteenth century. Communities installed only two statues of color-bearers from the 1860s through 1884 but more than fifty such figures from 1885 through 1899, followed by dozens more in the next fifteen years. Connected in origin to the memorial embellishment of battlefield parks, the new motif indicated both the enhanced influence of Union veterans and the expansion of business interests in Civil War remembrance. Although initially a static pose, the alternative to the sentinel contributed to the emergence of more active martial images. The conjunction of monuments and flags also contributed to changes in both of the symbolic forms energized by the wartime culture of death. Rather than sites for reflection on individual sacrifices, the icons increasingly became devices for enforcement of patriotic norms, often arbitrated by old soldiers. Inspirational emblems ripened into instruments of ideological, economic, and ethnic discipline.

Standard-bearers did not displace the dominant model for the soldier statue. Communities unveiled far more figures during 1885–99 that followed the sentinel templates popularized in the first years after the war. That default design for a modestly priced monument often revealed little, however, about sponsors' efforts to salute veterans. Daniel Butterfield, who had parlayed family wealth into a commission as major-general of Union volunteers, offered an ambitious history of war memorials at the 1888 unveiling of a monument in Ballston Spa, New York, to local citizens who served in the Civil War, the Mexican War, the War of 1812, and the Revolutionary War. But his oration did not address the remarkably typical decision to purchase what the *Ballston Journal* described as "a soldier standing in dress parade position" at a cost of $2,500. Instead the member and later commander of Lafayette Post #140, a unit known for its enrollment of New York City social elites, devoted much of his speech to a history and defense of the GAR. Even more than the granite statue, the veterans' organization was for Butterfield the late-nineteenth-century successor to the Western tradition of military monuments.[28]

Before the rebirth of the GAR, monuments that featured flags recalled the wartime identification of national and unit colors with the bodies of dead soldiers. Cemetery monuments in Tipton, Michigan (1866), and Cynthiana, Kentucky (1869), were among the flag-wrapped obelisks dedicated in the immediate aftermath of the war. A stoneworker in Swanton, Vermont, carved an allegorical monument to the town dead (1868) that depicted a somber female figure standing with a flag that echoed the folds of her gown. Chicago sculptor Leonard Volk particularly favored the motif. He made a flag-draped shaft, topped by an eagle, for the monument in Girard, Pennsylvania (1865), and a resplendently flag-draped cannon for the Rosehill Cemetery lot owned by survivors of a battery of the First Illinois Light Artillery Volunteers (1874).[29] He also created the first statue of a Civil War soldier with a flag for Rosehill Cemetery (1869). The marble effigy was not exactly a standard-bearer; he held the drooping banner in his raised right hand without a staff. The flag betokened battlefield death. In his other hand the soldier held a bugle that promised a summons to the afterlife.

Launt Thompson's color sergeant for Pittsfield, Massachusetts (1872), illustrated the individualistic and funereal connotations of one of the most emblematic figures of the war. Flag-bearers shared many of the features that prompted the early memorial focus on picket guards. The duties of both soldiers separated them from the impersonal mass of the army. Both soldiers were exceptionally nonaggressive. The flag-bearer did not have the picket guard's opportunity to meditate on home, but especially in the early stages of the war, his banner was often the precious gift of the community that had sent forth his unit. Finally, both soldiers were extremely vulnerable. Civil War reminiscences abounded in tales of color-bearers picked off by hostile fire and replacements who carried the banner forward. Thompson's work won praise for evoking the particularity of the honored dead. "It is not difficult to fancy a resemblance between the bronze form and face and that of some well known boy in blue," reported the *Springfield Union*. "There are thousands throughout these United States who would lead themselves to believe that the statue was intended for son, brother or lover," agreed the *Philadelphia Bulletin*. The flag-bearer's contrapposto stance, searching gaze, and smartly tilted cap suggested a personal distinctiveness in each Pittsfield soldier sealed by the precise circumstances of their deaths, for which the town recorded the time, place, and manner in the published proceedings of the dedication.[30]

The color-bearer statue dedicated in Magnolia Cemetery in Charleston, South Carolina, ten years later underscored the intersectional overlap of wartime flag culture. The Ladies' Memorial Association laid the cornerstone for a monument in 1870 but continued to debate its design. Although some supporters called for an effigy of a Confederate soldier, the women proposed in 1878 to raise an obelisk because a statue would exceed the association's resources and "instead of being a memorial of the dead, would be only the ob-

FIGURE 2.6. Launt Thompson, Soldiers Monument, Pittsfield, Massachusetts, 1871–72. Photograph by Stephanie Zollshan. Courtesy of *Berkshire Eagle*.

ject of cold, art criticism." After the grand dedication of the state monument in Columbia in May 1879, however, the association immediately tabled the obelisk plan and voted at the next annual meeting to commission a statue of a soldier holding the southern cross battle flag.[31] The capital ceremony had featured a substantial display of battle flags for the first time since the war; the published dedication proceedings included histories of more than a dozen. The survivors of Gregg's First South Carolina Volunteers reported that "twenty men, at least, were killed or wounded while bearing this flag." Orr's Regiment of Rifles recalled seventeen men shot down while carrying the unit banner. The monument unveiled at Magnolia in 1882 encapsulated these relic narratives. The *Charleston News and Courier* described the work, designed by a friend of the Ladies' Memorial Association president and executed in Munich, as "the bronze statue of a Confederate soldier accoutred for war, and wearing the famous tattered grey coat. He clutches his musket in one hand, and with the other seizes the standard which has just dropped from the hands of his fallen comrade. He looks defiantly at the enemy as he presses it to his heart! No doubt he will die ere he relinquishes it." If more melodramatic than Thompson's cool sergeant for Pittsfield, "apparently apprehending but defying danger," the Magnolia monument similarly illustrated the solitary fatalism of the color-bearer.[32]

Four monuments unveiled in 1885 turned flag-bearer statues in a different direction. The memorials were products of the Smith Granite Company, a leading enterprise in the flourishing Westerly, Rhode Island, stone industry; the firm worked a quarry site adjacent to the Westerly outpost of the Hartford-based New England Granite Works headed by James Batterson. The event that precipitated Smith Granite's promotion of a flag-bearer statue was apparently the expansion of memorialization on the Gettysburg battlefield, a result of the GAR revitalization in the wake of the Arrears Act. The Pennsylvania Department of the GAR conducted a well-planned takeover of the Gettysburg Memorial Association in 1880, electing enough members to the board of directors to gain control and purge nonveterans. The new administration launched an aggressive program of land acquisition, funded in large part by northern state legislatures, and warmly endorsed initiatives by several regimental associations to mark positions held by those troops during the battle. Massachusetts became the first state legislature to appropriate funds for such markers in 1883, and Smith Granite eagerly courted this patronage. The company produced ten Massachusetts monuments unveiled at Gettysburg in 1885. One of these works was a flag-bearer statue designed by Smith Granite sculptor Edward Pausch to express the Thirteenth Massachu-

FIGURE 2.7. Smith Granite Company (Edward Pausch), Monument to the Thirteenth Massachusetts Volunteers, 1884–85, Gettysburg. Courtesy of Gettysburg National Military Park.

setts veterans' decision to mark the spot where color sergeant Roland Morris was killed by Confederate fire on the first day of the battle.[33]

Even before the regimental association had finalized its order, Smith Granite sold the same statue in bronze to the town of Gardner, Massachusetts, and in granite to Tiffin, Ohio, and Branford, Connecticut, all of which also dedicated their monuments during 1885.[34] The replication of the work detached it from Morris's story and clarified that Pausch's composition did not necessarily imply imminent death. The soldier reaching across his body to draw his sword dramatized instead his readiness to defend the national flag. His relationship to the color-bearers in Pittsfield and Charleston was comparable to the contrast between Ward's vigilant sentinel and Milmore's contemplative picket guard. Like the Seventh Regiment Memorial, the monuments in Gardner, Tiffin, and Branford honored all men who had served in the military, not exclusively those who had died. As the survivors of the Thirteenth Massachusetts saluted their own efforts at Gettysburg, the veterans of Mason Rogers Post #7, formed in 1881, led the agitation for the Branford monument. The front of the pedestal featured the letters "GAR" surrounded by wreaths and crossed rifles. The inscription "ONE COUNTRY — ONE FLAG," endorsed a slogan that the GAR had begun to popularize as a prescribed incantation at the close of each post meeting. The update to Daniel Webster's antebellum call for "one country, one constitution, one destiny," measured the extent to which the banner of loyalty would displace the more complex charter as the principal symbol of the nation.[35]

Flag-bearer statues soon spread across the North. Monumental Bronze Company of Bridgeport, Connecticut, formed in 1879, developed a cheaper zinc imitation of Smith Granite's design that the corporation sold to sponsors in Salem, Massachusetts (1886), Biddeford, Maine (1887), Stratford, Connecticut (1889), and elsewhere. Color sergeants topped stone ensembles in other small communities like Kokomo (1886) and Logansport, Indiana (1887), and Elyria, Ohio (1888). The device also made inroads in monument campaigns with larger budgets. A memorial association in Winchester, Connecticut, commissioned George Bissell to make a more naturalistic bronze variation on Pausch's stiff pose to cap a picturesque fifty-five-foot-tall Gothic Revival tower dedicated in 1890 at a total cost of $16,500. Bissell's young friend Lorado Taft designed a flag-bearer for the ensemble installed in Joliet, Illinois, by the Muldoon Monument Company for $10,000 in 1889. Taft also provided the color-bearers that presided over infantry-cavalry-artillery-navy quartets in Yonkers, New York (1891), and Winchester, Indiana (1892). The latter monument, which the fresh graduate of the École des Beaux-Arts had hoped to crown with an allegorical statue of Mars at rest, cost $25,000. By the turn of the century, the flag-bearer had become an epitome of memorial convention. *Monumental News* editorials decried the "change from one monotony to another—from the soldier at 'parade rest' to the 'standard-bearer.'"[36]

Orthodoxy was the point of the new statuary mold to a much greater extent than it had ever been for the figures variously read as soldiers on guard or at rest. The turn to color-bearers was scarcely more organized than the grassroots emergence of the picket in the early postwar years, but the independent decisions of GAR posts and northern communities reflected veterans' coherent promotion of specific ideas about monuments and flags. The GAR codified its memorial doctrine in a ritual published in 1881 for use in the dedication of soldier monuments. In the central passage, recited at many towns and villages in the late nineteenth and early twentieth centuries, the GAR representative declared that the monument's "very silence is impressive. Without articulate speech, it is eloquent. It needs no words. It is itself an oration." These assertions repudiated any understanding of the memorial as a stimulus to interpretive imagination, including reflections on the ideological principles embodied by the monument and ruminations on the individual circumstances of commemorated soldiers and their families and friends. The GAR ritual directly challenged the authority who had often dominated dedication ceremonies, the orator of the day. The unveiling of the Pittsfield flag-bearer statue, for example, had featured a thoughtful address by George W. Curtis. Even though the GAR litany insisted that a monument spoke for itself, the prescribed text explained that the revered object was "significant of brave and loyal obedience to the command of the nation always and everywhere."[37] Regardless of the design selected for a memorial, its function was to enforce discipline.

Standard-bearer statues especially expressed this position because the GAR identified the American flag as a primary instrument for imposing coherence on an increasingly diverse and factious country. The innovation in Union monuments during the mid-1880s was a first step toward self-conscious promotion of a flag cult. Lafayette Post #140 initiated a widely publicized program of presenting the national banner to schools in 1888, soon emulated by another socially prominent post in New York City and within a few years by posts across the North, many of which sought to present flags purchased with government funds. The ensuing campaign to place the Stars and Stripes in every school by Columbus Day 1892 served as backdrop to the development of the Pledge of Allegiance. The salute drafted by

Union naval veteran George T. Balch, an active member of the Loyal Legion, concluded with the chant "One Country! One Language! One Flag!" The addition to the GAR shibboleth made clear the apprehensions of Balch and many veterans about the tide of immigration into the United States from southern and eastern Europe. Francis Bellamy published the eventually prevalent doxology in September 1891, a few weeks after the annual GAR national encampment introduced the practice of compulsory standing and uncovering for playing of "The Star-Spangled Banner." Like the GAR ritual for monument dedications, the consolidating flag culture positioned veterans as arbiters of patriotic practices that modeled ostensibly voluntary social unity.[38]

Two monuments dedicated in Maine in the early twentieth century completed the convergence of monuments and flags begun by the Smith Granite standard-bearer statues. In 1911 the town of Brownfield unveiled a soldier statue modeled from a photograph of Daniel A. Bean, who had enlisted at the age of fifteen in November 1861 in a company of the Eleventh Maine Volunteers and died in June 1864 of wounds suffered in the Bermuda Hundred campaign. Brownfield veterans named the GAR post formed in 1890 in his honor. Twenty years later, a former comrade funded a statue by John A. Wilson that depicted Bean with his cap in his left hand and his right arm raised as he took the oath of enlistment. Although the prescribed oath enjoined inductees to vow support of the Constitution, the monument inscription honored Brownfield's "SONS / WHO UPHELD / THE FLAG / 1861–1865" and listed the names of all 146 men who served in the war. The effigy served as a proxy for the thousands of youths who recited the Pledge of Allegiance in schoolrooms daily by 1911 with outstretched arms. The recognition of a specific individual was a tribute to conformity, unlike the generic statues of picket reveries that celebrated individuality. The next year, the town of Rockland merged Civil War monument and national banner by installing a memorial flagpole designed by architect R. Clifton Sturgis in front of the local GAR hall in conjunction with the observance of Flag Day. Correctly foreseeing that the hall might not long outlast the post, the GAR orator at the dedication expressed hope that "our children's children will in years to come point to the place where this memorial rests and tell of the patriotic organization of Civil War veterans which for years met here in weekly conclave." The flagpole aptly recorded the postwar influence of ex-soldiers as well as their wartime contributions.[39]

Confederate monuments participated more slowly in the late-nineteenth-century transformation of the color-bearer motif. Southern commemorations did share in the intensified emphasis on patriotic obedience, however, as demonstrated by the region's most prominent flag-related work of the era, the state monument to Confederate soldiers and sailors dedicated in Montgomery, Alabama, in 1898. Alexander Doyle's thoroughly commonplace design featured a tall column surrounded at the base by infantry, cavalry, artillery, and naval figures. More distinctive was the bronze finial statue of Patriotism, a woman who held a sheathed sword in her right hand and the staff of an enormous flag in her left hand. The dedication oration by former Confederate officer and corporate lawyer Thomas Goode Jones, who had spent much of his recent gubernatorial administration wrestling with Populist insurgency and had dispatched militia to break mining and railroad strikes in Birmingham, accentuated the conservatism of the exemplary southern patriot. "He was taught respect for authority," Jones reminisced. Hierarchical social institutions instilled deference as well as command. Because "not every man esteemed himself a statesman," the Confederate "followed almost blindly, as his father did before him, some great leader who appeared to him the most fit exponent of his thoughts." Like many orators at southern monument dedications, Jones vehemently rejected characterization of the Confederate as a rebel.[40] Subordination was the heart of patriotism in the South as well as the North.

The glorification of discipline partly undercut long-standing emphasis on the autonomy of Civil War soldiers. The former GAR department commander who spoke at the dedication of the Alton, New Hampshire, monument in 1897 declared that it honored townsmen who "were by the country called to arms, and without stopping to inquire whether the war was proper or expedient, buckled on the armor and upheld the flag." To be sure, neither Union nor Confederate commemoration expressed doubt that the war was proper and expedient. Southern orators were particularly insistent that "we cannot praise and commend the martyr and at the same time condemn the cause for which he gave his life." Mere sincerity did not discharge a soldier's political duty. The dedication speaker in Cumberland County, North Carolina (1902), scoffed that local sponsors "never, of course, entertained the idea of saying 'They Died in Behalf of a Cause They Believed to Be Right'" on the monument inscription. An orator in Carroll County, Mississippi, agreed three years later that such a sentiment was "but an apology, which is half confession."[41]

Some monument promoters continued to maintain that men in uniform preserved their independence. An artist from Louisa County, Virginia, which dedicated William L. Sheppard and Frederick W. Sievers's high-relief sentinel figure in 1905, congratulated the chair of the monument association on the original design because "no stereotype bronze could ever portray our hero in gray. For above all things, the Confederate soldier was an individual ... who could not become the indefinite portion of a mass." But industrialist Julian S. Carr, soon to become commander-in-chief of the United Confederate Veterans, struck a different note when he observed at the 1917 dedication of the Nash County, North Carolina, monument that "the glory of the private soldier of the South was that, an intelligent unit, he permitted himself, for duty and love, to be made into the cog of a wheel."[42] The granite standard-bearer statue atop the tall column that overlooked the textile mills of Rocky Mount punctuated Carr's parable for factory laborers. No longer redolent of death, the flag cult so vigorously championed by veterans had become an injunction against social disorder.

THE NEW TYPE OF FIGHTING MAN

Although the color sergeant with furled banner introduced by Smith Granite in 1885 was a compact emblem of poised readiness, the popularity of the standard-bearer contributed to the emergence of more aggressive poses. Unlike earlier representative soldiers whom narrative imagination might place in camp or at rest, the flag-bearer drew notice primarily on the battlefield. The adoption of the same statue by municipalities and the Thirteenth Massachusetts at Gettysburg also illustrated a link between community memory and the emerging institution of the battlefield park. These historical theaters aimed to excite as well as instruct visitors, and the veterans who dominated battlefield remembrance commissioned works that illustrated dramatic action. The common-soldier statues that followed Smith Granite's standard-bearer included a sharpshooter perched behind a boulder, a Zouave loading his rifle, and a skirmisher.[43] Large-scale reliefs dedicated to the First Massachusetts Infantry, 149th Pennsylvania Infantry, Thirteenth New Jersey Infantry, and Sixth Ohio Cavalry during 1886–87 all depicted battle scenes. In 1891 the association of the Seventy-Second Pennsylvania Infantry unveiled a statue of a soldier swinging his rifle by the muzzle as a club. A visitor in 1894 reported that "everywhere upon that great, great battlefield one sees the soldier in action."[44] Community monuments began to follow a similar pattern, intensified by city memorials of unprecedented scale that promoted the arrangement of figures in groups. Soldier monuments helped to inform a new ideal of manhood, in which the experience of war served as the preeminent school of citizenship.

Lorado Taft's work typified the role of flag-bearer statues in the emergence of active figures. Upon his return from Paris to Chicago the young sculptor found a substantial market in commissions for Civil War monuments. His first effort was a conventional sentinel unveiled in Morris, Illinois, in 1887. A year later he contracted to provide the American Bronze Company in Chicago with large reliefs of a color guardian, a sharpshooter, and a cavalry charge for three regimental memorials at Gettysburg. The standard-bearers he made for Joliet, Illinois (1889), and Warren, Ohio (1890), followed the Smith Granite template, but by the time he graduated to the more expensive monument in Winchester, Indiana (1892), he was fashioning a much larger and freer-falling banner than Pausch's furled ensign. Like Bissell's statue for Winchester, Connecticut, the modeling demonstrated the superiority of bronze to stone in sculptural animation. Taft amplified this approach when commissioned to make a monument for the Alpha Kappa Phi literary society at Hillsdale College, which supplied a substantial number of volunteers for the Fourth Michigan Infantry. Taft had commemorated this unit at Gettysburg in an 1889 stone relief that recalled Col. Harrison Jeffords raising the regimental colors immediately before his death in the Wheatfield. Although Jeffords did not attend Hillsdale, the college monument dedicated in 1895 was a three-dimensional bronze version of the battlefield image. The more youthful Hillsdale soldier lofted the flagstaff in the same determined stance with his right arm parallel to the ground at shoulder height and his left arm stretched upward. The gigantic unfurled banner spiraled gracefully behind the recent student, a reminder of his elevated principles and moral verve.[45]

Other sculptors further energized the flag-bearer's memorial profile over the next two decades. F. Wellington Ruckstuhl described the Confederate battle flag in his Little Rock monument (1905) as "very supple in movement and instinct with life."[46] The colors wrapped around the soldier's body to guide him forward. Theo Alice Ruggles Kitson's monument to the 124th New York Infantry in Goshen (1907) depicted an advancing standard-bearer as an extension of the sharp diagonal line of the eagle-topped staff he held. The flag waved in the wind at nearly full extension. Henry Kirke Bush-Brown enveloped the head of his mountaineer soldier for the grounds of the West Virginia capitol (1912) in a swirling banner. Girard College in Philadelphia replaced Joseph Bailly's canopied marble picket guard (1869) with John Massey Rhind's bronze soldier and sailor standing together beneath a large, billowing flag (1914).

During the 1890s the soldier with rifle in combat position began to join the flag-bearer as an iconographic staple. Apart from the work of Randolph

FIGURE 2.8. F. Wellington Ruckstuhl and Charles R. Lamb,
Monument to Confederate Soldiers of Arkansas, Little Rock, 1903–5.
Courtesy of the Arkansas Historic Preservation Program.

Rogers, almost all armed common-soldier figures installed in northern and southern communities during the first quarter century after the war depicted men holding the rifle with its stock, or occasionally its muzzle, on the ground. As in the case of the flag-bearer, battlefield commemoration was an impetus to change. Frederick Kohlhagen's statue for the Tenth Pennsylvania Reserves (Thirty-Ninth Pennsylvania Infantry) of a Union skirmisher striding forward, his rifle in his right hand, attracted attention even before its dedication at Gettysburg in 1890 because the project brought the Gorham Manufacturing Company into the business of casting bronze statuary. The Providence Association of Mechanics and Manufacturers donated a replica to Gorham's Rhode Island home in 1898, and at least three other northern communities later installed copies.[47] Taft included infantrymen wielding rifles menacingly at the base of the Yonkers and Winchester monuments. Caspar Buberl, who also did a considerable amount of sculpture at Gettysburg, made a skirmisher with his finger on the trigger that contractor Frederick and Field installed on monuments at Kingston, New York, in honor of soldiers from Ulster County (1890) and at Gettysburg in honor of the 111th New York Infantry (1891). Soldiers with raised weapons soon became commonplace. Joseph Klir's monument for the Bohemian National Cemetery in Chicago (1892) anticipated Bush-Brown's mountaineer in equipping the hero with both a rifle and a flag.

Confederate monuments shared in this development. Sculptor Herbert Barbee of Luray, Virginia, personally raised funds to execute a marble statue of a stalking picket (1898) that *Confederate Veteran* deemed "a vigorous embodiment of soldier and patriot." John Williams Bronze Foundry featured George Julian Zolnay's skirmisher for Owensboro, Kentucky (1900), in a full-page advertisement in *Monumental News*. Virginia sculptor Frederick W. Sievers placed soldiers cocking their weapons in Pulaski (1906), Abingdon (1907), and Leesburg (1908). *Monumental News* hailed Chicago-based expatriate Léon Hermant's similar Confederate for Parkersburg, West Virginia (1908), as "a strong, vigorous portrayal of the new type of fighting man, full of life and action." Gutzon Borglum made an energetic advancing figure of Henry Lawson Wyatt, the first North Carolinian to die in the war, for the statehouse at Raleigh (1912). More than fifty active single-figure soldier monuments and subordinate infantrymen in columnar ensembles guarded northern and southern communities by 1914, a striking departure from the previous quarter century.[48]

The development of active figures expanded when projects in Cleveland and Indianapolis led a radical increase in the scale of metropolitan monu-

FIGURE 2.9. Advertisement from *Monumental News* 13 (November 1901): 633.
Courtesy of Doe Memorial Library, University of California, Berkeley.

ments that encouraged depiction of groups in battle. The two ventures paralleled each other in several ways. Both resulted from veterans' lobbying that resulted in unprecedented state funding. The Ohio legislature introduced a tax levy in 1880 that with repeated supplementation eventually yielded $280,000 for a tribute to soldiers and sailors of Cuyahoga County, more than three times the previous record cost of the 1877 monument on Boston Common. The Indiana legislature appropriated $200,000 for a state monument in 1887, a mere down payment on a final expenditure of almost $600,000. Promoters secured central civic spaces for the undertakings, Public Square in Cleveland and the Circle in Indianapolis. Partly as the result of similar debates over the merits of memorial halls and monuments, the works both took the form of a memorial chamber from which projected a large shaft topped by a bronze figure. The committee in Cleveland listed on the interior walls of the chamber the names of almost 9,000 soldiers confirmed as honorably discharged. The committee in Indianapolis placed in the cornerstone eight volumes with the names of more than 210,000 state troops, tabulated by service branch on a large panel on one exterior wall of the chamber. In both cases, exterior walls of the chamber provided a backdrop for elaborate sculptural ornamentation, thematically focused on the infantry, cavalry, artillery, and navy in Cleveland and war and peace in Indianapolis.[49]

These prominent embellishments shared a resolution expressed by Franklin Simmons in 1888 as he took over a Portland, Maine, project with a budget of about $36,000. The sculptor lamented that "a general similarity seems to prevail in the style of soldiers and sailors monuments" by which "where a small sum of money is expended, there is one statue, and where a large sum is expended, there are only additional figures of about the same size." He proposed a much larger crowning figure supported "by a *group* of soldiers on one side and sailors on the other."[50] Simmons designed sets of three army and navy figures standing before large arrays of flags. The ensembles in Cleveland and Indianapolis were vivid battle scenes. The Cleveland monument commissioners called for bronze statuary "not in the stiff and inartistic attitudes of dress parade, but in fierce conflict." The resulting infantry group depicted an incident that architect and sculptor Levi Scofield reported he had witnessed at Resaca: a defense of the flag of the 103rd Ohio by its color sergeant and eight corporals, all of whom were killed or wounded in the clash. Scofield's cavalry group, also modeled in 1890, presented a close-range struggle over the guidon of an advance Union detachment.[51] Unlike these freestanding statues, the War and Peace groups proposed by German architect Bruno Schmitz in the design that won the Indianapolis compe-

FIGURE 2.10. Levi Scofield, Cuyahoga County Soldiers and Sailors Monument, Cleveland, 1887–94. Courtesy of the Library of Congress.

FIGURE 2.11. Bruno Schmitz, Herman Matzen, and Rudolf Schwarz, Indiana Soldiers and Sailors Monument, Indianapolis, 1888–1902. Courtesy of the Library of Congress.

tition in 1888 combined low relief, high relief, and sculpture in the round. Schmitz's plans for central female allegorical figures ensured comparison with François Rude's famous *Departure of the Volunteers of 1792* on the Arc de Triomphe in Paris (1833–36). Danish-born sculptor Herman Matzen, who taught at the Cleveland School of Art, won an 1895 competition to realize Schmitz's vision, and the architect brought Rudolf Schwarz from Ger-

Models of Citizenship

FIGURE 2.12. Levi Scofield, model of Infantry Group (*The Color Guard*) for Cuyahoga County Soldiers and Sailors Monument, Cleveland, 1890. Courtesy of Duke University Libraries.

many for the carving of the figures. The War montage incorporated a sniper, a prowler, a rider trying to control a frightened horse, and several dead soldiers. In front of the enormous relief, thirty-seven feet high and twenty-two feet wide, a smaller group that depicted the death of a drummer boy served as a transition to a fountain gushing into a lower pool.[52] Such glamorized depictions of battlefield deaths, unthinkable in early postwar monuments, typified the new ensembles of fighting men.

The Cuyahoga County monument dedicated in 1894 and the Indiana monument dedicated in 1902 both publicized the ideal of the combat group, and the Indianapolis project also furthered the aggressive model of soldiering in less direct ways. After completing Schmitz's commission, Schwarz became a prolific designer of Civil War monuments elsewhere in Indiana, including South Bend (1903), Franklin (1905), Crawfordsville (1906), Mount Vernon (1908), Terre Haute (1910), Princeton (1912), and Vincennes (1914), as well as Le Roy, New York (1906), and Little Rock, Arkansas (1911). Many of these works were conventional ensembles with a flag-bearer atop a shaft surrounded by four representative military figures. Like his colossal stone infantry and cavalry figures guarding the door to the memorial chamber in Indianapolis, the soldier statues Schwarz provided to smaller communities were highly animated.

Even more influential were two compositions superseded in Indianapolis by the Matzen-Schwarz groups. Before the monument commission acceded to Schmitz's plan for stone reliefs, it contracted with Frederick W. MacMonnies for bronze groups. The committee and the sculptor soon dropped each other, but MacMonnies was able to recycle his Indianapolis sketches when invited to provide large reliefs for another grand metropolitan monument, the Brooklyn arch completed in 1892 for $250,000 without sculptural decoration. Taft had a similar tale. Shortly after the initial Indiana legislation, a contractor set up an Indianapolis studio where the sculptor made a sketch of a large military group. Although pursuit of the state commission failed, Taft continued to develop this model over the next few years. The dynamic composition titled *Defense of the Flag* (1889) was much more like recent French memorials of the Franco-Prussian War, such as Étienne Pagny's ensemble in Lyon (1887), than the detached figures Taft was executing for midwestern communities. The group consisted of three figures: a grizzled, hawk-eyed veteran kneeling with his finger on the trigger of his rifle, a young color-bearer like the Hillsdale volunteer with a billowing flag, and a slumped soldier clutching the fatal chest wound he had just received. Taft eventually sold the work to a contractor who installed it as the Second Minnesota memorial for the opening of Chickamauga and Chattanooga National Military Park in September 1895. Copies later went to Battle Creek (1903) and Jackson, Michigan (1904); Gloversville, New York (1917); and the national cemetery in Marion, Indiana (1915).[53]

Other cities commissioned similar ensembles. *Monumental News* reported in April 1895 on the progress of two monuments like Taft's *Defense of the Flag*. The composition by John S. Conway unveiled in Milwaukee in 1898, titled *The Victorious Charge*, depicted an agitated color-bearer stepping over a fallen comrade; on the sides, soldiers brandishing a rifle and a revolver surged forward. Frederick Triebel's two bronze groups for Peoria, Illinois, collectively titled *Defense of the Flag*, were commissioned in 1893 and dedicated in 1899 with President William McKinley in attendance. The frenzied clusters consisted of flag-bearers surrounded by fallen men and soldiers raising their weapons.[54] Sigvald Asbjornsen followed with derivative groups in Decatur, Illinois (1905), and Madison, Indiana (1908), and Mil-

FIGURE 2.13. Lorado Taft, model of the first version of *Defense of the Flag*, 1889. Courtesy of the University of Illinois Archives.

waukee sculptor Gaetano Trentanove provided a battle scene to Oshkosh, Wisconsin (1907). Syracuse spent more than $100,000 for a seventy-five-foot-tall white-granite pylon ornamented with two large bronze reliefs by Cyrus Dallin (1910). The west-side group depicted a battlefield incident at Gettysburg in which the color sergeant of the 149th New York mended a flagstaff broken by attacking fire that also put eighty holes in the regimental banner. In the same week as the Syracuse dedication, Malden, Massachusetts, unveiled Bela Lyon Pratt's version of a "defense of the flag" ensemble.

The ideal of martial discipline embodied in standard-bearer statues and the ideal of martial vigor embodied in combat scenes both promoted reconceptualization of the army as a school for citizenship. Earlier commemoration had usually treated the Civil War as a testing of virtues developed in antebellum society. Connecticut politician Joseph Hawley, a former brevet major general of volunteers and frequent orator at monument dedications, anticipated the newer pattern when he maintained at Bridgeport in 1876 that "a few young men were demoralized, it may be, but hundreds of thousands now scattered through the land, learned lessons of duty, obedience, and respect for law which they carry with them." Such sentiments became more widespread as vindication of the prewar order lost relevance in an industrial economy. Washington, DC, lawyer Leigh Robinson, who had left the University of Virginia shortly before graduation to enlist in the Confederate army, recalled the Richmond Howitzers at an 1892 monument unveiling as "the best of all academies, the noblest university" because he had learned "the lesson of courage in daily jeopardy; of patience under privation and strain; the pursuit of high aims in disdain of earthly menace or disaster." Union veteran and Syracuse attorney Edwin S. Jenney argued the following year at Gilbertsville, New York, that peace and prosperity fostered "the dulling of the sensibilities, and lowering of the moral tone, a confusion as to the distinction of right and wrong, which do not obtain in war." GAR member Benjamin Harrison endorsed an 1893 call by Lafayette Post #140 for military training in public and private schools. The former president praised the proposal in a *Century* article as "good for the boys, good for the schools, and good for the country" because "the sluggish need to be quickened, the quick taught to stand, and the willful to have no will. The disputatious need to learn that there are conditions where debate is inadmissible."[55]

The Spanish-American War soon prompted more strident claims for martial progress. The speaker at the unveiling of a flag-bearer statue in New Bloomfield, Pennsylvania, in October 1898 declared that "wars have always been the source of commercial and educational development. The evidence is strong also that wars generally have advanced the civilization of the world." Tributes to Civil War soldiers, he noted, had inspired volunteers to enlist in the current conflict. Amid the revelations of American atrocities in the Philippines four years later, a dedication orator in Fayetteville, North Carolina, deplored the common intersection of economic stratification and militarism when he sighed that "the modern American of a certain class gloats in the savagery of war." At the unveiling of a standard-bearer statue in Bridgton, Maine (1910), former Union officer and New York railroad lawyer Thomas Hubbard, future national commander-in-chief of the Military Order of the Loyal Legion, illustrated the identification of soldiers as exemplary citizens when he urged civilian application of the army principle that "if each man does the things assigned to him co-operation and harmony become the rule." Even a Universalist minister who joined Hubbard on the platform agreed that "the advancement of civilization has always been accompanied by war." Consistent with the logic of the GAR dedication ritual, the minister extended the ennobling force of war into an observation that historical texts were "written, but, too often, by pens that have been prejudiced," while the histories "that endure, and that speak without prejudice, are written in granite and marble and bronze."[56] The monument, rather than the book, was the reliable guide for a nation shaped by war.

CIVIC COURAGE

Originally a counterpart to monuments that recalled soldiers' deaths, Memorial Day became an occasion for veterans' paeans to the martial virtue embodied by the newer statues. At the 1895 observance of Memorial Day at Harvard Memorial Hall, which Charles Eliot Norton had once hoped to consecrate to "the sacrifice of life for a cause wholly disconnected with ordinary warfare, and above it," Oliver Wendell Holmes Jr. exalted the long record of warfare in an address titled "The Soldier's Faith." The former Union officer and associate justice of the Massachusetts Supreme Judicial Court fretted that "war is out of fashion" and that "commerce is the great power." He denounced the fin-de-siècle temperament as a "time of individualist negations, with its literature of French and American humor, revolting at discipline, loving flesh-pots, and denying that anything is worthy of reverence." Holmes argued that warfare offered a classic education in moral values. It was "the business of youth and early middle age." The jurist approved the martial demand for subordination, and he took his title from his assertion that "the faith is true and adorable which leads a soldier to throw away his life in obedience to a blindly accepted duty, in a cause which he little understands, in a plan of campaign of which he has no notion, under tactics of which he does not see the use." He was even more rhapsodic about the martial demand for exertion. War taught that danger was essential to "the breeding of a race fit for headship and command."[57] The speech endorsed the civic religion of patriotism illustrated by standard-bearer statues and the cult of aggressive masculinity illustrated by sculptural groups of soldiers in battle.

Exactly two years later, Holmes sat among honored veterans on a Boston stage at the Memorial Day dedication ceremonies for a monument that presented a contrary viewpoint. Augustus Saint-Gaudens's basic design for the memorial to Robert Gould Shaw and the Fifty-Fourth Massachusetts Infantry preceded the commemorative initiatives that had bolstered the martial ideal synthesized by Holmes, including the emergence of battlefield parks, the rise of standard-bearer and skirmisher statues, the expansion in scale of metropolitan monuments, and the vivid representation of combat. The artist formed his working plan for the Shaw Memorial when lingering remembrance of the Civil War dead had not yet fully given way to celebration of Civil War veterans. The extraordinary composition managed to combine the nominally complementary but often conflicting themes of sacrifice and service. While the monument reclaimed a republican vision in danger of eclipse by the 1897 unveiling, William James's dedication address replied more directly to the challenge of "A Soldier's Faith."

The slow gestation of the Shaw Memorial reflected the mismatch between the artist's ambition and the project funding. Henry Hobson Richardson brought Saint-Gaudens onto the Shaw Memorial team three months before the 1881 unveiling of the Farragut monument in New York made the sculptor's reputation. Adapting sponsors' early postwar hopes for an equestrian statue that subverted the imperial form and recalled Shaw's departure from his hometown in May 1863, the committee announced plans in April 1882 for a horseback portrait of the unit commander set before an arched panel intended for insertion into the fence of the Massachusetts statehouse. Subordinate relief panels would depict the famous assault on Fort Wagner as well as the departure and return of the regiment. When Shaw's family vetoed the equestrian proposal because "only men of the highest rank should be so honored," Saint-Gaudens sought fuller incorporation of the black troops of the Fifty-Fourth Massachusetts into the composition. Rather than a mounted portrait set above narrative reliefs, his revised design merged the two elements. A sketch model of the new arched panel featured a high relief of Shaw riding alongside low reliefs of his marching troops at the depar-

FIGURE 2.14. Augustus Saint-Gaudens and Charles McKim,
Shaw Memorial, Boston, 1881–97. Courtesy of the Library of Congress.

ture from the capital; an angel floated overhead in low relief. Saint-Gaudens
contracted in February 1884 to produce this work within two years for only
$15,000. The conjunction of form and theme promised a classicizing realist's
rejoinder to the epic romanticism of Rude's *Departure of the Volunteers*. As
his sense of this potential expanded, particularly through fuller development
of the black soldiers and the angel, Saint-Gaudens took the gap between
his goals and his modest compensation as reason to work gradually on the
Shaw Memorial while fulfilling the more lucrative commissions that made
him one of the most acclaimed artists in the country.[58]

Immediate communion with death pervaded the Shaw Memorial
much more than most Civil War monuments begun in the 1880s. Even as
Saint-Gaudens completed his final touches he wrote to his niece about "the
feeling of death and mystery and love" involved in making the angel. The
commission brought Saint-Gaudens into contact with devoted keepers of
memory such as Shaw's mother and sisters and the vast cousinage that in-

cluded banker Henry Lee and railroad magnate John Murray Forbes, the dominant members of the monument committee. The artist's meditations on Shaw's acceptance of death doubtless deepened in the course of work during 1886–91 on the Rock Creek Cemetery memorial for another cousin, Clover Adams. Moreover, wartime tributes had long ago canonized Shaw as a model of Christian martyrdom. Anna Cabot Lowell Quincy Waterston, whose name encapsulated much of the Boston elite, had imagined the resurrected casualties of Fort Wagner at their last judgment in a poem that would be excerpted on the terrace of the Shaw Memorial. The final verse described Christ's greeting to the regiment commander: "And thou, young generous spirit, / What will thy welcome be? / 'Thou hast aided the down-trodden, / Thou hast done it unto Me.'" At the last minute Saint-Gaudens worried that his own interpretation was too "Christian martyr–like," and he substituted an olive branch of peace for the palm branch that the angel had previously carried with poppies, the floral emblem of eternal sleep.[59]

Saint-Gaudens depicted heroic immortality not merely by situating Shaw between the angel and his fellow soldiers but also by exempting him from the sense of movement that defined the composition. Auguste Rodin's maxim that "procession is the soul of the bas relief" found unsurpassed confirmation in the tread of the soldiers marching to the beat of the drummer in the lead. The strong diagonal formed by their back legs and the strong diagonal formed by their rifles and flagpoles and Shaw's sword intersected in a forward-pointing arrow pattern. The colonel pulled tightly on his horse's rein and sat bolt upright with his right arm hanging straight downward, the sole vertical line in the composition. The pose echoed Hippolyte Flandrin's mounted Christ in *Entry into Jerusalem* (1842–44), and the stillness within the flow achieved a transcendence that prefigured the afterlife. William James recognized Shaw as a typification of sacrifice when the orator told his audience that "you think of many as I speak of one. For, North and South, how many lives as sweet, unmonumented for the most part, commemorated solely in the hearts of mourning brothers, widowed brides, or friends, did the inexorable war mow down!" The dead subsumed within the representation most directly included those who fell alongside their leader at Fort Wagner, although Forbes and Lee declined the request of Shaw's sister Josephine Shaw Lowell to list the names of his rank-and-file comrades on the monument.[60]

Those martyrs were not the only black soldiers that the monument honored. Forbes wrote that "the change from a statue to a bas-relief" enabled the memorial "to serve as a record of the Era which the outgoing of the regiment from Boston, and its only memorable battle, some sixty days later, marks." That epoch was the enlistment of African Americans into the Union army; the principal inscription of the Shaw Memorial recorded that 180,000 African Americans served in uniform by the end of the war. Standard-bearer statues and other recent Civil War monuments might present military service as a citizen's duty, but the defeat of racial exclusion by the volunteers of the Fifty-Fourth Massachusetts was a democratic assertion of individual choice. Federal acceptance of long-offered black service was closely connected to the Lincoln administration's efforts to limit conscription at a point when the harrowing death toll of the war had stalled recruitment. Saint-Gaudens linked that voluntarism to the classical tale of the retired Cincinnatus leaving his plow to serve the Roman republic. The winged figure flying above the departing regiment made the composition of the relief panel an amplification of the reverse side of the medal of the Society of the Cincinnati, an order of descendants of Revolutionary War officers. The sculptor underscored the allusion by inscribing on the panel the motto of the society, "Omnia relinquit servare republica" (He gave all to serve the republic). Shaw's ancestry entitled him to membership in the hereditary organization, but its motto applied no less to the regimental rank and file.[61]

Like the story of Cincinnatus, this depiction of the black Union volunteer revolved around the qualities he brought to the war rather than the education he drew from it. The record of the Fifty-Fourth Massachusetts refuted skeptics who had attributed to African Americans a racial inferiority that would preclude exemplary military service. Saint-Gaudens's representations of the departing recruits stressed their full humanity. These reliefs were not portraits sculpted from wartime photographs like the rendering of Shaw. They were studies of black models whom the artist found striking. The care with which he explored the head of each anonymous man expressed the potential of African Americans as a subject for artistic representation, and by extension for other high callings of civilization. He showed a variety of facial features and beards and other particularities that testified to the individuality of the enlisted men. The rigidly forward-looking gaze they shared with Shaw and the presiding angel similarly marked their impending experience as psychologically isolating. Those about to die at Fort Wagner and those who would survive participated in a vision that they could not or would not extend fully to others, in contrast with monuments or speeches that purported to present veterans' patriotic viewpoint.[62]

James's address was unusual in the extent to which the orator proposed to parallel the design of the monument he was helping to dedicate. "Look at that monument and read the story," he said at an early point. He called attention to the "dark outcasts, so true to nature that one can almost hear them breathing as they march." As Saint-Gaudens had depicted a deliberate purposefulness among the volunteers that contrasted with the Gallic tribalism of Rude's fervent band, James repeatedly compared his epigrammatic account to an epic poem. He flouted memorial convention in his insistence on "how soon, indeed, are human things forgotten!" Dubious of other orators' expectations of imperishable oral traditions, he warned that someday "books of history and monuments like this alone will tell the tale" of the Fifty-Fourth Massachusetts. The essence of that saga was that "Americans of all complexions and conditions can go forth like brothers, and meet death cheerfully if need be, in order that this religion of our native land shall not become a failure on the earth," a phrase that echoed Lincoln's pledge at Gettysburg.[63]

The address was even more unusual in its strictures against war and its reservations about the Civil War. In a jibe directed particularly at Holmes though equally applicable to many orators, James observed that "war has been much praised and celebrated among us of late as a school of manly virtue, but it is easy to exaggerate upon this point." The professor of psychology and philosophy argued that "man is once for all a fighting animal; centuries of peaceful history could not breed the battle-instinct out of us." Men gave up life or treasure to go to war more readily than they sacrificed for any other cause. Given that inclination, "military virtue is the kind of virtue least in need of reinforcement by reflection, least in need of orator's or poet's help." James did not praise "the common and gregarious courage" Shaw showed at the outset of the war by enlisting in the Seventh Regiment. Instead the speaker honored "that lonely kind of valor" or "civic courage as we call it in peace times" that Shaw demonstrated by joining oppressed African Americans in the Fifty-Fourth Massachusetts. According to James, the Civil War reflected a failure of civic courage in the antebellum United States. Abolitionists, "the voice of the world's conscience," were a small faction, although "weak as they were, they drove the South to madness." Slavery had consequently ended through war, "destroying good and bad together," and inevitably leaving "miserable legacies" as well as overdue emancipation. "Democracy is still on trial," James concluded, and he looked to the monument to inspire dedication to a civic courage antithetical to the soldier's faith lauded by Holmes.[64]

The two Memorial Day observances indicated that sites of Civil War commemoration could still frame ideological debate within a local community, not merely across the divide between North and South. The GAR dedication ritual imagined the soldier monument as an icon that needed no interpretation and expressed a straightforward call to duty. In contrast, Saint-Gaudens's elegant complexity quickly prompted a variety of readings. With the dedication ceremony as a model, the Shaw Memorial exercised influence by stimulating creative reflection. Only three years after the unveiling, William Vaughn Moody's "Ode in Time of Hesitation" situated its speaker before the monument to condemn the forcible annexation of Puerto Rico, Guam, and the Philippines.[65] The protest testified to the frustration of James's hope that renewed civic courage might enable the United States to avoid war. Imperialism ignited the military enthusiasm that had built throughout the 1890s and presented new contexts for invigoration of white supremacism. Saint-Gaudens's invocation of the Revolution may have incorporated African Americans in an Enlightenment legacy of voluntary republican citizenship, but the exchange between Holmes and James over the promise or futility of "breeding" Americans measured the extent to which social appropriations of Darwinism had strengthened an organic view of the nation. That vision increasingly shaped Civil War monuments in the early twentieth century.

DRAWN FROM MOTHERHOOD

"The ideals of the past for men have been drawn from war, as those for women have been drawn from motherhood," declared Holmes. Insistence on the first claim implied elaboration of the second. Carl Rohl-Smith drew the parallel vividly in the Iowa soldiers and sailors memorial completed in Des Moines in 1896, another in the new line of more expansive monuments. The sculptor complemented his soldier statues with an allegorical figure of Iowa as a nude young woman seated with a blanket across her lap. Her hair was undone, her back arched, and her fingers cupped beneath her swollen breasts in what a contemporary guidebook called an image of "longing, waiting motherhood, with bounteous gifts for all her offspring."[66] As wartime cemetery monuments to female munitions workers killed by arsenal explosions in Pittsburgh and Washington indicated, however, women had participated in the Civil War in ways that ranged widely from a maternal model.[67] When remembrance of Union and Confederate women followed the pattern for men by turning from death to service, monuments aimed more often to contain than to advance innovative redefinitions of citizenship. Commemorative emphasis on wartime motherhood reinforced the exaltation of masculine aggression by promoting the gender differentiation characteristic of racialized adaptations of evolutionary theory.

Two projects of the 1890s illustrated the sectionally distinct possibilities and constraints in memorial reconsideration of women's relationship to the polity. Shortly after the death of wartime U.S. treasurer Francis E. Spinner, a group of women formed to honor him for promoting federal employment of female clerks, which opened a promising career to middle-class northern women with few antebellum prospects for wage labor beyond the underpaid field of schoolteaching. The organization commissioned Henry Ellicott to make a portrait statue for $10,000 and petitioned Congress to place it outside the Treasury Department. The proposal won considerable legislative support, but successive treasury secretaries resisted it. The statue languished in storage for years before the association turned it over to the Daughters of the American Revolution (DAR) chapter in Spinner's hometown of Herkimer, New York, which installed it in a park in 1909.[68] The female clerks' attempt to commemorate a citizenship fostered by the wartime nation-state had ended in a tribute to a local notable.

The monument to Confederate women installed in Fort Mill, South Carolina, in 1895 in contrast typified southern gender politics. As one veteran reported, the pendant to an 1891 soldier statue depicted a woman who "while kneeling in supplication for the success of a lost cause, dropped her country's flag around her knees and extended her clasped hands and turned her eyes to heaven." That veteran judged the work "the best-conceived memorial in all our bonnie Southland" because it so aptly distilled Confederates' claim that their cause was a sacred defense of home. While northern volunteers subordinated family to the nation-state and northern women left their supposedly separate antebellum sphere of moral influence to participate in Civil War political development, white southern ideology denied such tensions between social institutions. The purpose of the country was to protect the household. This merger invited desertion when continuation of military operations threatened starvation on the home front, but the ideal infused Confederate women with a symbolic power that Union women did not match. The sponsor of the Fort Mill monument, industrialist Samuel Elliott White, clarified its enthusiasm for domestic institutions by donating an adjacent monument to "THE FAITHFUL SLAVES" who during the war "TOILED FOR THE SUPPORT OF THE ARMY" and "GUARDED OUR DEFENCELESS / HOMES, WOMEN AND CHILDREN." Patriarchy and mastery converged in the proslavery republic. Although secession had failed and

White's textile mills portended economic transformation, the monuments implied continuity in the social order. The women listed on an inscription as exemplars of Confederate patriotism bore the names of wealthy families in the community, in sharp contrast with the middle-class women whose wartime precedent the Spinner Memorial Association sought to recall.[69]

Women's leadership in Confederate commemoration was crucial to representation of their wartime role. Soon after the war, women across the South formed local groups known as Ladies' Memorial Associations (LMAS), many of which were extensions of soldiers' aid societies. The LMAS' most conspicuous project was to tend to the remains of fallen Confederates, a responsibility assumed for the Union dead by the federal government. In addition to reinterring bodies and marking graves, the LMAS orchestrated ritual observance of Memorial Day, over which the GAR asserted early supervision in the North. This cemetery activism prompted LMAS and similar southern organizations to sponsor a much higher proportion of collective monuments than northern women. Northern women played a significant part in fund-raising for early Union monuments, but the dominant sponsorship narrative centered on municipal recognition of the local dead. The sectional divergence intensified as Civil War commemoration shifted in the 1880s. The revitalized GAR gained an affiliate, the Woman's Relief Corps (WRC), which took over the administration of Memorial Day in many communities and later joined the GAR in promoting the cult of the American flag. With eligibility for membership defined by women's personal loyalty to the Union rather than their kinship with Civil War soldiers, the WRC contributed to the surge of monuments dedicated to veterans but did not make those projects a primary emphasis. Sponsorship of monuments was in contrast the chief activity of the UDC after its chapters began to spread across the South in the 1890s. The UDC not only supplemented the narrower LMA focus on Memorial Day but also brought to Confederate memory the familial principle shared by many ancestry societies of the late nineteenth century, of which the recently founded DAR was the most direct parallel.[70]

Confederate monuments multiplied dramatically after the establishment of the UDC. The number of monuments dedicated in former slaveholding states during the twenty years after 1895 was well over twice the number dedicated during the previous thirty years. The total doubled even in Virginia, where the concentration of casualties had led to substantial early development of the memorial landscape. The number of monuments tripled in North Carolina and Mississippi. The effect was particularly extreme in Texas, where installation of Confederate monuments only began in the 1890s. The

UDC did not sponsor all of these monuments, but it was so closely associated with memorial fund-raising campaigns and solicitation of government support that even monuments built without direct financial aid sometimes acknowledged the UDC aegis in an inscription. The soldier statue unveiled in Shreveport in 1906 stood atop a cylindrical base surrounded below by busts of Confederate generals. In the front stood an allegorical female figure of History writing in an open book, "ERECTED BY THE UNITED DAUGHTERS OF THE CONFEDERACY," although Caddo Parish provided half of the $10,000 cost.

The courthouse location of the Shreveport monument also typified turn-of-the-century installation of Confederate memorials at sites more regularly visible to the community than the cemeteries where earlier white southern remembrance had centered. The proliferation of county courthouses in the urbanizing New South provided new public space for commemoration. The shift connected Confederate memory more directly to local government and the assertion of social order, especially the white supremacist racial order. Public-private partnerships like the Caddo Parish monument arrogated an authority intertwined with but broader than the electoral politics or legal administration of justice headquartered inside the courthouse. The prominence of white women underscored the range of this mandate, exercised most horrifically by lynching, of which Caddo Parish was an infamous center during the late nineteenth and early twentieth centuries. Six months after municipal authorities chose the site for the Shreveport monument, a large mob hanged three black men from a tree on the courthouse lawn.[71]

White southern women saw that their commemorative citizenship presented opportunities and pitfalls. Confederate memory was an important forum for women's associational enterprise in the postwar South, and the UDC was among the strongest organizations in the turn-of-the-century club movement. Women often combined passion for the Lost Cause with interests in education or social welfare; suffragists Rebecca Latimer Felton, Belle Kearney, and Nellie Nugent Somerville were all members of the UDC. Such women recognized tensions between exaltation of veterans and other objectives. UDC founder Caroline Meriwether Goodlett demanded that the 1908 annual convention decide whether it would "go on in the stone and mortar monument business, gratifying our own vanity by erecting monuments to our pet idols? Or shall we spend our money in a nobler cause — in raising the standard of Southern women?" Urging the completion of national initiatives at Arlington National Cemetery and Shiloh National Military Park

Models of Citizenship

four years later, the UDC president general added the increasingly common disclaimer that women should not be "mere monument builders."[72]

This ambivalence partly resolved in UDC opposition to proposals for monuments to Confederate women. To be sure, UDC members deeply admired Confederate women and originated some proposals for monuments to them. But most such initiatives came from men. Regional discussion centered on a campaign within the UCV that ripened in 1906 into a plan to replicate a monument to Confederate women at each southern capital, supposedly to demonstrate the universality of affection for the heroines. Women resented this challenge to their hard-earned leadership in the civic realm of the Confederate monument. They also saw that placement of Confederate women on a pedestal would not advance turn-of-the-century women's efforts to participate more fully in the polity. Rather than monuments, some UDC members proposed to honor their putative mothers through residential institutions for elderly southern women. Other suggestions revolved around education, including endowment of scholarships and construction of college dormitories. Men showed little interest in these options. They sought monuments to Confederate women that would counterbalance the feminist potential in the commemorative activism of Lost Cause women.

Veterans articulated this position in 1909 when a UCV committee put forward a design by Louis Amateis for the regional monument. The proposed embodiment of Confederate womanhood stood with a flagstaff and a sword in her outstretched arms. The banner was not controversial, but the unsheathed blade prompted veterans to denounce the figure as "a composite of the classic Amazon, the Wagnerian Brunehilda, and Carrie Nation." The inscription beneath the figure's feet looked to one critic like "the text of a stump speech," and another agreed that she was "declaiming like a candidate for the legislature an oration upon State rights!"[73] Closer to Amateis's energetic statue of a bugler for Corsicana, Texas (1908), than to White's patriarchal monument in Fort Mill, the design threatened to endorse the female political engagement that veterans aimed to inhibit. The UCV committee regrouped, but its plan for a uniform monument failed dismally. Only Mississippi (1917) and Tennessee (1926) would eventually install the substitute proposal; five states chose unique monuments. A few smaller towns also commissioned monuments to women or monuments that honored Confederate men and women together. UCV camps and UDC chapters in Thomson, Georgia (1913), and Camden, Arkansas (1915), found the readiest common ground in sponsorship of a stock statue of a woman in period dress clutching the folds of a Confederate flag. The joint monument in Yazoo City, Mississippi (1909), featured a Confederate woman presenting a flag to a soldier carrying a rifle.

Nursing was a dramatic aspect of women's wartime experience that endured in northern and southern memory in several forms. Like the clerical workers in the Treasury Department, Civil War nurses had helped to open an important career field to women. Nurses' memoirs, the passage of the Army Nurses Pension Act of 1892, and the postwar celebrity of some former nurses burnished remembrance of the wound dressers.[74] The soldier monuments in Boston and Cleveland included relief panels devoted to the Sanitary Commission and nurses. Above such commemorations loomed the legend of Florence Nightingale, whose adventures in the Crimean War had inspired many Union and Confederate women. A monument installed in Waterloo Square in London in 1915 reprised iconography already famous at the outbreak of the Civil War. Arthur G. Walker's portrait statue depicted "the lady with the lamp" patrolling the wards at Scutari. Relief panels showed the superintendent of nurses welcoming patients at a hospital door, advising a doctor on treatment strategy, meeting with high-ranking military officers, and surrounded in later life by nurses she had trained. The monument recalled Nightingale as an efficient and forceful executive who transformed the conjoined institutions of the hospital and the medical profession.[75]

Civil War monuments rejected this precedent and instead adapted the Christian motif of the pietà as a model of womanhood. The monument to Mary Ann Bickerdyke initiated by WRC leaders in Galesburg, Illinois, and dedicated there in 1906 depicted the hospital dynamo kneeling above a wounded soldier on the battlefield, cradling his head and giving him water. The muscular forearm displayed by a rolled-up sleeve in Theo Alice Ruggles Kitson's portrait statue suggested Bickerdyke's modest class origins and the hard physical labor of nursing. But the principal inscription highlighted Sherman's hollow quip, "SHE OUTRANKS ME," which obscured the extent to which Bickerdyke managed to assist Sherman's army at his personal sufferance because she remained outside of the federal Office of Women Nurses that male officers widely disdained. The memorial indicated that the middle-aged Bickerdyke personified her wartime nickname, "Mother." The monument to army nurses commissioned by the Daughters of Union Veterans in Boston and placed in the Massachusetts statehouse in 1910 shared much the same composition, although Bela Pratt's younger and prettier female figure corresponded to an inscription that described nurses as "ANGELS OF MERCY AND LIFE / AMID SCENES OF CONFLICT AND DEATH." Joseph

FIGURE 2.15. Theo Alice Ruggles Kitson, Bickerdyke Monument, Galesburg, Illinois, 1903–6. Courtesy of Special Collections and Archives, Knox College Library.

Maxwell Miller made a similar sculptural group for the Maryland monument to Confederate women (1917). Generic statues in Rome (1910) and Macon (1911), Georgia, underscored the maternal theme by placing two groups at the base of an obelisk, a cowled nurse succoring a wounded soldier and a woman on the home front with a child.

The UCV committee turned to a variation on the pietà motif in an attempt to recover from the Amateis debacle. The committee proposed a design by Nashville native Belle Kinney that featured a maternal representation of Fame seated behind and enveloping two figures, a young woman whom Fame crowned with laurel and a dying soldier on whom the young woman placed a palm frond. The composition did not satisfy members of the UDC, who objected that the maternal figure was inappropriately allegorical and lacked the sublime refinement they associated with Confederate womanhood. The younger woman in Kinney's group also drew sharp UDC criticism; New Orleans matron Margaret Drane Tichenor exclaimed that "the lank, limp, shrinking, nondescript figure" could never have inspired soldiers. When Mississippi installed a cornerstone for its monument at the state capitol in 1912, UDC division president Laura Martin Rose delivered an address that put a maternal gloss on the project. After a standard comparison of Confederate women to Spartan mothers, the future UDC historian-general reported that "the great Napoleon on being asked what was the greatest need of his country replied, 'Mothers.' The South had mothers, and these same mothers furnished to the world the Confederate soldier." Born in 1862, this daughter of the Confederacy looked beyond her own mother's experience in the war generation to emphasize reproduction of soldiers as women's most profound national mission.[76]

The other state monuments to Confederate women more clearly celebrated motherhood. F. Wellington Ruckstuhl complemented his colleagues' quotations of the pietà by offering a variation on the Annunciation in the South Carolina memorial (1912). J. Otto Schweizer's group for Arkansas (1913) depicted a Confederate volunteer taking leave of his mother; a much younger brother with a toy drum ensured the postwar continuity of martial virtue. Augustus Lukeman's monument for North Carolina (1914) presented a similar theme in a vignette closer to the twentieth century. A seated grandmother holding an open book told the story of the war to a rapt grandson kneeling alongside her with a sheathed sword; subordinate relief panels illustrated the departure of the boy's father for the war and the return of his dead body. Florida placed Allen G. Newman's bronze scene of a woman reading about the war to her young son and daughter beneath a granite canopy

FIGURE 2.16. Augustus Lukeman and Henry Bacon, Monument
to North Carolina Women of the Confederacy, Raleigh, 1912–14.
Photograph by Carol M. Highsmith. Courtesy of the Library of Congress.

topped by a statue of an allegorical figure holding a flag (1915). The last two
works most directly identified women as custodians of Confederate memory, although the domestic settings obscured the public implications of that
work. The strategy reflected the male sponsorship of the projects. The North
Carolina monument was the gift of a veteran, and the other three were the

products of state appropriations that matched veterans' fund-raising efforts. In a commemorative process marked by sectional differences and gendered divisions, motherhood provided a unifying memory of the war at the same time that Mother's Day assumed a place on the national calendar.[77]

As the institution of Mother's Day partly reflected anxieties about the pace of white Protestant family formation amid the surge of southern and eastern European immigration into American cities, the emphasis on motherhood in Civil War monuments supported ethnic purity. The monument in Decatur, Indiana (1913), to Union soldiers and women featured an allegorical female figure in a short-sleeved classical gown that showed off the well-toned arm she stretched along a horizontal array of flags. Charles Mulligan's well-publicized model for the robust figure was Margaret McMasters van Slyke, whom *Physical Culture* editor Bernarr McFadden had named Chicago's "most perfectly formed woman" as measured by the strength and athleticism that the eugenicist considered essential to sexual reproduction of the fittest national race.[78] The memorial drinking fountain dedicated the following year in Fayetteville, Tennessee, by a local UDC chapter honored women "WHO GAVE TO THEIR SOLDIERS, / THEIR CHILDREN, AND THEIR LAND THE WATER OF LIFE, HOPE AND COURAGE." The fluid symbol connected motherhood to the technological refinement of racial discrimination in the Lincoln County courthouse square. An allegorical statue of a woman stood atop a base ornamented with two sanitary drinking faucets of the sort that had spread across the country in recent years and become a new fixture of segregation in the South. The hygienic reform testified to the modernity claimed by Jim Crow.[79]

The most ambitious attempt to create a monument to women perhaps most fully transformed the Civil War legacy of political mobilization into an idealization of feminine sympathy with racial undercurrents. Telegraph cable magnate James A. Scrymser became interested in promoting a monument to Union women through his friendship with northeastern liberal culture hero Francis Channing Barlow, whose first wife had worked as a U.S. Sanitary Commission volunteer and nursed her wounded husband in field hospitals at Antietam and Gettysburg before she died of typhus near the end of the war. Shortly afterward Barlow married Robert Gould Shaw's sister Ellen, whose involvement in the Civil Service Reform Association, the Consumers' League, the National Committee on Prisons, and the promotion of black education typified the postwar women's civic engagement fostered by the Sanitary Commission. Scrymser persuaded the New York commandery of the Loyal Legion to lead a campaign for a grand monument to

Union women in 1911, but other units did not support the initiative. He then proposed that the Loyal Legion raise funds, matched by a congressional appropriation, for a Washington headquarters for the American Red Cross. The plan recalled that the Sanitary Commission, largely organized and sustained by women, had provided an important precedent for the founding of the International Red Cross in the Geneva convention of 1864 and that Clara Barton, the woman most famously brought to the public forefront by Civil War nursing, had played an instrumental role in congressional ratification of the Geneva treaty in 1881 and headed the American Red Cross for its first twenty-three years. President William Howard Taft's endorsement of Scrymser's project duly noted that "upon the American Red Cross has fallen the mantle of the Sanitary Commission."[80]

The memorial venture foundered in Congress on the trope of sectional reconciliation. Mississippi senator John Sharp Williams led southern objections that exclusive recognition of northern women was not appropriate for the international humanitarian representative of the restored United States. The Loyal Legion dropped from the project, and Congress approved the joint memorial to Union and Confederate women in 1913. Matching the $400,000 federal appropriation were large gifts from Scrymser, widowed philanthropists Olivia Slocum Sage and Mary Harriman, and the Rockefeller Foundation, for which the building donation was the beginning of a wide influence in global health and population management. A dedicatory tablet in the building honored "the Women of the North and the Women of the South, Held in Loving Memory by a now United Country, that Their Labors to Mitigate the Sufferings of the Sick and Wounded in War may be Forever Perpetuated." The WRC and UDC commissioned memorial stained-glass windows from Tiffany Studios.[81]

The mutations of Scrymser's initiative introduced ominous implications. Williams's address at the 1917 building dedication emphasized that Confederate women embodied "the cause of the white race, its physical and social and racial integrity, and its enlightened and enlightening domination."[82] The design, site, and ornamentation of the headquarters subtly amplified this theme. With an interest in Colonial Revival styles that matched the architects' bloodlines, Samuel Breck Parkman Trowbridge and Goodhue Livingston provided a Neo-Georgian blueprint to complement the neighboring headquarters of the DAR. The relationship with the snobbish lineage society inflected the Red Cross tribute to women, as the third major feature of the new Washington district, the Pan-American Union Building, linked the humanitarian enterprise to diplomatic ambitions for world leadership.

Inside the Red Cross headquarters, the UDC and WRC windows depicted a medieval scene in which robed maidens moved toward a wounded knight and his mounted comrades. Like Holmes's attempt to renew martial chivalry in "A Soldier's Faith," the stained-glass allegory imagined essential male and female identities contrary to the organizational narrative from the Sanitary Commission to the Red Cross. Even before the group took charge of the national blood supply, its memorial headquarters promised to protect the transmission of American purity.

ANGLO-SAXON ATHLETES

The sensational success of the soldier statue unveiled in Newburyport, Massachusetts, on July 4, 1902, reframed several patterns in recent Civil War monuments. Like Edward Pausch's standard-bearer, Frederick Kohlhagen's skirmisher, and Lorado Taft's battle scene, Theo Alice Ruggles Kitson's marching soldier illustrated the overlap between community commemorations and battlefield parks. Massachusetts ordered a slightly altered version for three times the $8,500 paid by the Newburyport sponsors and dedicated it in 1903 as the first state monument at Vicksburg National Military Park. Six more towns installed Kitson's work within a decade, and other sculptors turned to marching figures.[83] The motif echoed but also challenged the most acclaimed common-soldier monument, the Shaw Memorial. The Newburyport statue signaled a deepening concentration on race as the fundamental bond between the community and its armed champions. While many kinds of monuments shared that emphasis, the marching soldier placed the relationship between civilization and savagery in the specific kinesthetic context of military progress. As the federal government reconsidered its longstanding reliance on state volunteers, the fresh memorial model suggested the step in national ideals from an army comprised of citizens to a citizenry trained like soldiers.

The striding figure that Kitson titled *The Volunteer* presented a three-dimensional counterpart to long-standing representations of Civil War soldiers heading off to war. Beginning with the monument installed in Green-Wood Cemetery in 1869, many metropolitan monuments featured relief depictions of volunteers taking leave of family members. A subordinate panel of Milmore's monument on Boston Common portrayed prominent local officers and civilians in an imaginary departure review. The columns designed by architect George Keller for Manchester, New Hampshire (1879), and Buffalo (1884) and Utica (1891), New York, included wraparound

FIGURE 2.17. Theo Alice Ruggles Kitson, *The Volunteer*, Newburyport, Massachusetts, 1900–1902. Courtesy of the Museum of Old Newbury.

friezes with farewell scenes; Casper Buberl served as the sculptor for the first two projects and Karl Gerhardt for the third. William R. O'Donovan and Jonathan Scott Hartley's work for Michigan City, Indiana (1893), followed the same pattern. The genre climaxed in the Confederate Monument dedicated at Arlington National Cemetery in 1914. Moses Ezekiel's eight-foot-tall wraparound bronze frieze comprised much of the shaft. The former Confederate introduced about three dozen figures, many in high relief. In the front of the circle, uniformed soldiers and a black body servant rushed to the aid of a stricken allegorical female South. Vignettes stretching around the shaft depicted an officer kissing the infant child presented to him by a faithful black mammy, an officer embracing his wife, a muscular blacksmith buckling on his sword while his wife watched anxiously, and a clergyman and his wife bidding farewell to their boy soldier. Ezekiel's depiction of slavery as a cardinal domestic institution was specifically Confederate, but the ritual enactment of ties between troops and home was familiar in both sections.

As the ambitious Arlington frieze demonstrated, departure scenes flourished after the impetus given to large-scale relief by the unveiling of the Shaw Memorial, the Brooklyn arch ornamentation, and the Indiana monument within a five-year period at the turn of the century. Dallin's group for Syracuse titled *The Call to Arms* (1910) tried to combine the allegorical verve of *The Departure of the Volunteers in 1792* with the republican gravity of the Shaw Memorial, but other sculptors joined Ezekiel in adhering to domestic conventions. The Confederate monument dedicated in St. Louis in 1914 was a large granite pylon embellished with George Julian Zolnay's bronze relief of a southerner preparing to embark for the war, his wife and mother standing at his sides. In front of the volunteer, his young son waved a flag. Two years later Frederick Hibbard completed a similar monument for Evergreen Cemetery in Jackson, Michigan, that featured a volunteer in high relief flanked by his parents in low relief. These conflations of family, community, and army embraced the sentimentality that Saint-Gaudens had eschewed. In the monument for his hometown of Bellefonte, Pennsylvania (1906), George Grey Barnard submitted an allegorical representation of the social Darwinist axiom that the family was the biological basis for the moral sense which led to the development of nations. His version of *The Call to Arms* depicted a mother nursing an infant while sitting atop a cannon, an adaptation of the snow sculpture *Resistance* made by Jean-Alexandre-Joseph Falguière while serving in the Franco-Prussian War (1870). Barnard's juxtaposed relief *War* focused on two heroic male nudes, one of whom held an ancient sword in his right hand and supported a dying comrade with his left hand. The grief-stricken angel in the background confirmed that home life had nurtured the capacity for solidarity and sacrifice.[84]

The forward stride of Kitson's *Volunteer* linked it to the departure reliefs and Daniel Chester French's *The Minute Man*. The decisive step invoked enlistment, as the stable stance of early sentinels had illustrated perseverance. Kitson's soldier, however, was not leaving home for the first time. Commentators recognized the effigy as "a soldier who has seen service." A Newburyport newspaper listed the evidence of experience: "his uniform is tattered, his knapsack lost, bottoms of his trousers tucked in his stockings and his whole appearance indicative of a long, hard campaign."[85] The solitary veteran nonetheless remained closely connected to his family without depiction of parents or wife, without the farm implement in which French located the domesticity of husbandry, and without imputation of midnight longing for home. The bond between Kitson's soldier and his community was racial identity.

Ethnocentrism inflected soldier statues from the outset. An early critic of Randolph Rogers's *Soldier of the Line* "could not but regret that the model of the statue had been a brave Celt." A Brahmin newspaper echoed that the infantryman and sailor sculpted for Boston Common by Martin Milmore of County Sligo "*both* are apparently Irishmen — a manifestly unequal distribution of honor." Friends of the exclusive Seventh Regiment reported that J. Q. A. Ward's sentinel was "studied with care, evidently from the best models, and is a national head, a true American face, not to be mistaken for one of any other nation." Insistence on ethnic purity intensified with the influx of immigrants at the end of the century. The sponsors of the Indiana monument were emphatic that "the American idea is the unit of the monument. From this, no departure will be permitted." Legend reports that when a commissioner complained that the flowing beards of Schwarz's soldiers made them look too Germanic, the sculptor immediately seized a chisel and shaved away the offending whiskers. The Italian immigrant who sculpted the Union soldier for the Allentown, Pennsylvania, monument dedicated in 1899 initially chose a handsome compatriot as his model, but he switched under pressure to a model described as "a typical American boy of the kind that made the fiercest fighters during the Civil War."[86]

Ethnic anxiety shaped not only individual statues but also the institutional framework of public art. Several years after Bostonians of Irish ancestry gained a majority on the common council, they ordered the installation in the Public Garden of a portrait statue that the Society of the Ninth Massachusetts Regiment had commissioned to honor Thomas Cass, founding commander of the Irish American unit. The granite memorial, carved by a local stonecutter from a sketch supplied by sculptor Stephen J. O'Kelley, stirred fierce controversy upon its unveiling in 1889. Brahmin critics called it too small for the Public Garden and more suitable for a cemetery. Defenders of the tribute to the Malvern Hill martyr bristled that "there is no spot or place within the limits of the city that is too sacred for his features to be put there in granite." Former councilmember William R. Richards, who traced his Boston lineage to 1632, led a lobbying campaign that persuaded the Massachusetts legislature to establish the Boston Art Commission in 1890. The state agency entrusted the chief officers of the Museum of Fine Arts, the Boston Public Library, the Boston Society of Architects, and the Massachusetts Institute of Technology with veto power over the placement of art-works on municipal property. The legislation became a national model for urban elites eager to circumvent the political power of recent immigrants.[87] Boston mayor Josiah Quincy resolved the dispute over the Public Garden statue by arranging for a replacement by National Sculpture Society member Richard E. Brooks. An American journalist long resident in Paris, where the new portrait won a medal at the 1900 exposition, marked the extent to which Brooks reconciled his immigrant subject with Yankee morality when she reported that "the principal feature of the statue is its great simplicity and sobriety."[88]

Kitson's *Volunteer* participated in the assertion of an old-stock national type. Admirers saw a native in the lanky figure, long countenance, and square jaw. "His face is typical," observed the *Newburyport Herald*. "The face is really the best part of the statue. It is essentially American in its expression of alertness, high character and firm purpose." The newspaper concluded that "the whole figure is what we New Englanders call a 'speaking likeness' of a Yankee soldier." When Kitson used much the same features in a statue of a skirmisher for North Andover, Massachusetts (1913), a viewer thought "the face reveals an indication of breeding that is unmistakable." Bela Pratt's combat scene for Malden, Massachusetts, attracted similar plaudits. "The sculptor has seized for a motive upon the tense restless energy of our native population," stressed an approving description. Like Kitson's marching volunteer, Pratt's embattled color guard won the critical epithet "virile." A monument firm advertised its stock imitation of Kitson's *Volunteer*, installed in front of a sixty-three-foot-high shaft in Ebensburg, Pennsylvania (1913), as "one of the new race of soldier memorials."[89]

Confederate monuments were of course also avatars of whiteness. At the dedication of the state monument in Montgomery, Alabama, a speaker underscored the ethnic purity of southern soldiers by listing eighteen different ethnic groups in the polyglot northern army. Frequent dedication orator and future UCV commander-in-chief Bennett Young declared in Parkersburg, West Virginia, in 1908 that the Confederate army "constituted the most homogeneous organization that ever bore the Anglo-Saxon name." Southerners expected their monuments to realize this vision. Citizens of Elberton, Georgia, pulled down a locally carved marble they had nicknamed "Dutchy" for its supposed Germanic appearance. After the protesters buried the effigy face-down in dishonor, local sponsors substituted an acceptable stock work. The unveiling of a bronze sentinel in Raymond, Mississippi, prompted complaints against representation of the Confederate soldier with a brown figure.

In contrast, a 1911 compendium of Confederate monuments praised Caspar Buberl's soldier statue for the cemetery that had served the wartime hospital at the University of Virginia as a "handsome face, of pure Southern type."[90]

Northern and southern soldier statues increasingly suggested a ruggedness that added bodily training to the inner discipline for which Holmes had celebrated military life. Not merely enduring the war, Kitson's *Volunteer* stepped forward like a veteran "who has just come out of the 'Bloody Angle,' or Gettysburg, and is ready for anything more in that line that fate may have in store for him." Pompeo Coppini's *The Last Stand* for Victoria, Texas (1912), combined sympathy for Confederate privation with admiration for the muscular arms and chest revealed by the tattered, wide-open blouse of a soldier wearing a bandana. Louis Amateis's colossal *Dignified Resignation*, unveiled the same summer in Galveston, was equally brawny. *Monumental News* praised Zolnay's seated Confederate reaching for an ammunition pouch in Nashville (1909) as "a virile portrayal of the younger type of volunteer that has been seen in the better of our recent soldiers' memorials. . . . The close-fitting uniform shows the lines of the figure to good advantage." On the same day as the Nashville dedication, an orator in Trenton, New Jersey, aptly summarized the coalescing ideal when he described the Civil War as "a titanic combat between two Anglo-Saxon athletes."[91]

The extraordinary fitness of twentieth-century bronze warriors partly reflected a dramatic shift in military policy. The United States fought the Spanish-American War by temporarily expanding the regular army and accepting a few federal volunteer units like the Rough Riders. State volunteer units, which had comprised the overwhelming bulk of the Union army, mostly suffered through the imperial adventure in fatally unsanitary camps far from the theaters of action, including Camp George H. Thomas at the Chickamauga and Chattanooga National Military Park. In the aftermath of victory, Secretary of War Elihu Root pushed through Congress a quadrupling of the permanently authorized army force from 27,500 soldiers to 100,000 to subdue resistance in the Philippines and garrison the overseas possessions. Despite these deployments, the army became a larger presence in peacetime America than it had ever been, particularly because the end of Indian wars had prompted the urban consolidation of isolated frontier posts. National Guard units that had developed since the Civil War recognized this expansion as a threat to the heritage of a decentralized militia. A tenfold increase in annual congressional appropriations for the National Guard between 1900 and 1908 cemented the subordination of state forces outlined by the Dick Act of 1903.[92] Federal supplies and regulations sharpened the distinction between soldier and civilian traditionally bridged by the militia, and in mid-nineteenth-century mobilizations by the U.S. Volunteers.

Sally James Farnham's monument for the GAR lot at Mount Hope Cemetery in Rochester (1908) softened this transition. A vigorous young color sergeant, his manhood accentuated by the adolescent bugler next to him, bowed his head and doffed his cap for a Civil War veteran's funeral. His tightly fitted jacket was mostly unbuttoned, and he sported the thatched hair and clean shave fashionable among early-twentieth-century collegians. The figures stood atop a rough-hewn boulder, a trend popularized by Kitson's *Volunteer*. The inscriptions on a bronze plaque juxtaposed the title quatrain of "The Bivouac of the Dead" and the musical score for "Taps." Veterans' beloved poem led into the army's prescribed melody.[93] The Civil War origins of the dirge implied a martial continuity that transcended institutional restructuring.

Kitson's *Volunteer* cast military training as civic example in a more ideologically volatile site of Civil War memory, the march. It is certainly possible that statues of this thoroughly characteristic martial activity did not spread earlier because Americans so closely associated the marching soldiers of the war with the homeless population that traversed the country afterward, many of whom were veterans. The verb "tramp" came into common usage through volunteers' slang for their slogs, as in George Root's song "Tramp, Tramp, Tramp" (1864). The pejorative noun emerged in the depression of the 1870s.[94] The reception of Kitson's motif illustrates the relaxation of middle-class anxieties in the early twentieth century and a willingness to envision soldiering in one of its least individualized forms, on the march.

The soldier who strode atop Civil War monuments was not an unemployed vagrant or a Thoreauvian saunterer but a synthesis of primitivism and military discipline. The principal theorist of marching at the turn of the century was Edward H. Bradford, professor of orthopedics and later dean at Harvard Medical School. Bradford summarized his research in a paper presented to a national conference of military surgeons in 1899. The urban pedestrian, he reported, tended to draw the body forward from the back foot with a straight-leg heel-to-toe gait that more active walkers merely lengthened and quickened. "Moccasined and semicivilized nations" more efficiently leveraged gravity to advance over long distances by leaning forward and planting the entire front foot on the ground with the front knee still bent. Good soldiers adopted the same style in the field even if they exaggerated the urban manner when on parade. Citing a wartime observation that Ulysses S. Grant "does not march, nor quite walk—he pitches for-

Models of Citizenship

FIGURE 2.18. Sally James Farnham, *Defenders of the Flag*, Mount Hope Cemetery, Rochester, New York, 1905–8. Courtesy of the Albert R. Stone Negative Collection, Rochester Museum and Science Center.

ward," Bradford encouraged emulation of "the great exemplar of modern war, which disregards convention, but utilizes all forces in accomplishing the desired end." He told the military surgeons that "the subject is well understood in the War Department, and is in practical use in the regular service," but needed attention from the less expert state militias.[95]

Many sculptors doubtless already knew of Bradford for his 1897 study of "The Human Foot in Art," but Kitson was also in touch with sociological physiology through Dudley A. Sargent, director of Hemenway Gymnasium at Harvard and founder of the university program in physical culture that Bradford supported. Sargent had commissioned Kitson and her husband to model statues of "typical" men and women for the Columbian Exposition on the basis of extensive anthropometrical data. Kitson's *Volunteer*, noted for its "swinging gait portrayed in the strong lines of the body," paralleled Bradford's findings that "veterans have invariably acquired a rhythmic bent-knee swing," although "nobody cares to go shuffling along Tremont or Boylston streets after the manner of a hardy savage." The strenuous exercise modeled by the army promised to compensate for overcivilized weakness and lead to "a diminution, if not a disappearance, of a large number of the so-called nervous disorders which vex and hamper life."[96]

Bradford's research on the martial gait attracted national publicity when he delivered a set of public lectures in January 1908 that criticized the representation of marching in the Shaw Memorial as "physiologically incorrect, although possibly artistically serviceable as indicating the zeal and haste of those troops to get to the front." Boston artist and critic Darius Cobb argued that Saint-Gaudens's "mistake came from studying the models and not taking in the real life of the soldiers. The aspiring colored soldier should have been the real thing, not the coal-heaver who posed as a model to the sculptor." Saint-Gaudens's son shot back that the recently deceased master "was perfectly aware that the regulars of the latter years of the nineteenth century were of wholly different type of men from the volunteers of the '60s. The regulars were trig, trim, spick and span, clipperish and cleared for action, as it were, whereas the volunteers were of a wholly different physique — loose jointed, many of them, not set up, not finished in any sense." All sides saw a fundamental distinction between full-time soldiers and civilians. Cobb, who had served in a militia unit mobilized for nine months during the Civil War, typified the recent tendency to place the volunteers of his era on the martial side of that divide. When critics reviewed Frederick Hibbard's marching Confederate for Forsyth, Georgia (1908), they were delighted to see "a faithful portrayal of a real soldier on a real march," regardless of the extent to which the figure incorporated orthopedic theory in "the forward movement of his long, swinging stride."[97]

The vision of soldiering as a form of moral regeneration through physical culture was especially strong at elite colleges, which Harvard Medical School graduate and former Rough Riders commander Leonard Wood made the centerpiece of the public campaign to promote universal military training that he launched as U.S. Army chief of staff in 1912. Few leading administrators subscribed to the pacifism of Stanford president David Starr Jordan or the reasoning of Harvard president A. Lawrence Lowell that "military discipline, which means obedience to orders, is a very different thing from the self-discipline needed in civil life."[98] The soldier statue dedicated by the University of North Carolina in 1913 most directly recognized Confederate service as a form of education. The monument emerged from commencement plans for the fiftieth anniversary of the outbreak of the war, when the university would award degrees to students who had entered the Confederate army and had not followed the procedures established for postwar graduation. University trustee Julian S. Carr, who had reenrolled for the 1865–66 term but left school again to make his fortune as an industrialist, was the most prominent of these veterans and delivered the dedicatory address.

Although it fell too far behind schedule to be part of the semicentennial commencement, the Chapel Hill monument dramatized what the former students had learned by leaving school. John A. Wilson's composition, like his recent statue of Daniel Bean for Brownfield, Maine, depicted Civil War service as an initiation into adulthood. The active figure—holding his rifle up and ready with his finger on the trigger as he cautiously stepped into danger, eyes wide open—embodied the exhilaration of the strenuous life. The inscription reported that soldiers' experiences "TAUGHT THE LESSON OF THEIR GREAT COMMANDER THAT DUTY IS THE SUBLIMEST WORD IN THE ENGLISH LANGUAGE."[99] The most striking feature of the monument, a large front panel, emphasized that this essential military education was different from what the university provided. The relief depicted a callow young dandy with a half-read book on the floor and another book open on his lap. To become a man, to get what was necessary to strengthen the race, he had to accept the sword offered by a thinly robed allegorical female Carolina. Carr's oration, which fondly recalled that shortly after Appomattox he had "horse-whipped a negro wench until her skirts hung in shreds" because she had "maligned a Southern lady," emphasized that the experience of war prepared ex-soldiers for violent enforcement of white supremacy in the wake of emancipation. Carr exulted that Confederate veterans' "steadfastness and

Confederate Monument,
University of North Carolina,
Durham.—27

FIGURE 2.19. John Wilson, Confederate Monument, University of North Carolina, Chapel Hill, 1909–13. Courtesy of Durwood Barbour Collection of North Carolina Postcards, Wilson Library, UNC–Chapel Hill.

courage saved the very life of the Anglo Saxon race in the South" during Reconstruction and that "as a consequence, the purest strain of the Anglo Saxon is to be found in the 13 Southern States — Praise God."[100]

The memorial dedicated by Yale University at its commencement two years later similarly conjoined military service and college education. Launched in 1909, the project aimed from the outset to be the first civic monument of national significance to honor Union and Confederate soldiers on equal terms, a goal that extended the premise of federal military parks and the recently commissioned Confederate monument for Arlington National Cemetery.[101] Unlike many municipal and institutional monuments across the North and South, the Yale initiative embraced the idea that martial valor was a prime social virtue regardless of the cause for which men fought. Dedication of the memorial "TO THE MEN OF YALE / WHO GAVE THEIR LIVES IN THE CIVIL WAR" did not imply grief over long-ago deaths. When Daniel Chester French offered a mournful statue, the alumni sponsors rejected it with the comment that there was "not enough victory and action" in the composition.[102] The honored dead listed on marble walls in a rotunda that connected buildings erected for the Yale bicentennial were proxies for all who fought in the war; the restriction simplified the sponsors' name-gathering task and narrowed the sectional disparity in the participation record of the overwhelmingly Unionist school. The tribute to military service for divergent ends facilitated the later adaptation of Memorial Hall into a remembrance of Yale soldiers of other wars. The commemorative strategy also dovetailed with university president Arthur T. Hadley's view that the summer military training program established by Wood in 1913, in which Yale claimed a larger representation than any other school, provided students "great educational value for their individual development" and "in certain important respects supplements the deficiencies of our regular course of study."[103]

Henry Hering's sculptures for architect Henry Bacon's vaulted memorial passageway imagined a timeless martial virtue embodied by the collegians who started to fill the Yale Bowl in 1914. The classicized figures of Devotion and Courage announced the arrival of the male nude in Civil War common-soldier monuments.[104] Robed female figures of Memory and Peace, the latter holding an infant, offset the two students. The younger Devotion, who held a suggestively placed flag, sported a hairstyle popular at Frank Merriwell's school. An inscription promised that "DEVOTION GIVES A / SANCTITY TO STRIFE." The more muscular Courage wore an ancient helmet and held a

FIGURE 2.20. Henry Hering and Henry Bacon, Yale University
Civil War Memorial, 1912–15, detail. *Art and Progress* 6 (September 1915).
Courtesy of Thomas Cooper Library, University of South Carolina.

sword and a shield emblazoned with the Yale seal. A commentator noted that
"Devotion is a youth rather soft and undeveloped—the freshman, whereas
Courage is more representative of the senior, athletic and ready to take his
place in life." The ensemble looked to physical culture and military training
to refresh the ancient Olympian ideal.[105]

The contrast between the memorial halls of Harvard and Yale revealed
transformations within the entire genre of common-soldier monuments between the immediate aftermath of the Civil War and the eve of American
entry into World War I. The earlier memorial was at the same time more
fully consecrated to the loss of particular individuals and to an ideology of
military service inseparable from Union aims in the Civil War. The memorial
transept proposed a model of citizenship grounded in the liberal culture that
the commemorative fund-raising project sought to advance. The bicentennial complex at Yale testified to the rise of universities over the last several
decades. The white marble memorial illustrated the coalescence of a mascu-

Models of Citizenship

linity furthered by the development of military institutions during the same period, including veterans' groups, battlefield parks, and the National Guard as well as the army. The relationship between civilian and military realms would be an even more direct consideration in monuments to leaders of the Union and the Confederacy.

MODELS *of*
LEADERSHIP

Unlike the common-soldier memorials that emerged from the Civil War, monuments to military and civilian leaders extended a long artistic tradition. Equestrian statuary was the clearest example, dating back to sculptural precedents in ancient Rome and philosophical underpinnings introduced by Plato. Tributes to orators were another genre firmly established since antiquity. Americans in the decades before the Civil War had devoted considerable attention to the relationship between this heritage and democratic forms of leadership. The sectional conflict posed challenges to practices of military command and oratory that invited reconsideration of antebellum patterns of commemoration.

The opportunity to respond to a prestigious and dynamic canon was only one reason that artists especially prized commissions to honor eminent leaders. These projects usually involved large budgets. Equestrian statues routinely required expenditures exceeded only by the most ambitious common-soldier monuments. Remembrance of popular figures sometimes inspired impressive fund-raising campaigns. The costly monuments often prompted substantial spending by federal, state, or local governments and, in a few instances, extraordinary gifts by individual donors. Disproportionately installed in major cities, tributes to Civil War leaders attracted tremendous crowds to dedication ceremonies. More than 100,000 people attended the unveiling of the Robert E. Lee memorial in Richmond in 1890. An estimated 250,000 watched the unveiling of the memorial to Ulysses S. Grant in Chicago the next year. Such events drew extensive national publicity. The installation of monuments in the nation's capital added to the distinction. The *New York Times* called the ceremonies for the 1879 inauguration of the George Thomas equestrian statue "the most imposing witnessed in Washington since the Grand Review of the victorious Union armies in 1865."[1]

The relationship between military and political leadership gave multilayered significance to commander monuments. Many high-ranking officers later served in government, and those who did not nevertheless offered metaphorical models of individual authority. The Civil War was a crisis for the ideals of natural command personified in different eras by George Washington and Andrew Jackson. The Union and Confederate armies relied heavily on West Point graduates, though debate raged in both sections over the value of specialized training.[2] Commissions in the U.S. Volunteers provided postwar presidential springboards for "political generals" Rutherford B. Hayes, James Garfield, and Benjamin Harrison, but the professionalization that reshaped the officer corps eventually undermined this tradition. A military bureaucracy increasingly insulated from electoral politics found its representative image in a grand Washington monument to the victorious general of the Civil War.

Like military command, public art was an active site for discussion of professionalism. Commentators in both fields imagined polarities of innate genius and technical expertise. Artists aimed to combine popular and critical acclaim. The procedures for awarding government commissions stirred endless controversies. *American Architect and Building News* moaned on behalf of elite practitioners that "it would be hard to find a chapter in the history of human meanness presenting a greater variety of mendacity, brutal dishonesty, corruption, treachery and ignorance than would be afforded by a true account of American artistic competitions."[3] The sculptor who presided over a busy studio of assistants and laborers tended to develop a self-image as an executive and to stress that the defining act of artistic mastery was the clay model of a figure rather than its mechanical casting in bronze by foundry workers. The most innovative monuments to Civil War commanders identified not merely the admiral or general but also the artist as a model of leadership.

Monuments to Civil War commanders developed rapidly from markers of death to meditations on democracy. Soldiers began to memorialize fallen officers six weeks after the first battle of Manassas, when Confederates placed a shaft at the spot where Francis Bartow had died. Families, local communities, and military units commissioned a variety of quasi-public funereal monuments during and shortly after the war; perhaps the most ambitious was Franklin Simmons's marble portrait of Hiram G. Berry at Achorn Cemetery in Rockland, Maine (1865). Several higher-ranking casualties prompted efforts to address more broadly the relationship between an officer and his troops. These initiatives emphasized that an effective commander distilled the experiences and viewpoints of the men he led. Shortly after delivering the main address at the dedication of an equestrian statue, Stanley Matthews summarized the precepts he shared with many monument promoters. "Great men are so not by origination, but derivation," he asserted. Heroism rested on reciprocal interactions because "the purposes of individual life can be realized only by men in the relation of mutual help embodied in the institutions of the social organization."[4] Leadership incorporated these human relationships and personified the natural environment of the war. The general's task was to generalize.

The statue with which the First Corps of the Army of the Potomac honored John F. Reynolds, the highest-ranking casualty at Gettysburg, charted the emergence of public aims in commander memorials. While in winter quarters in January 1864 the corps formed a monument association that collected subscriptions limited to five dollars per officer and fifty cents per enlisted man. The group initially obtained permission from Reynolds's sister to place its tribute over his grave in his native Lancaster, Pennsylvania. But the undertaking soon came to mark both Reynolds's death and the demise of his unit, which the Union reorganized and attached to the Fifth Corps as a result of the heavy losses that the First had sustained at Gettysburg. The association abandoned the gravesite plan, and the proposed statue became a counter in the competition between the Gettysburg Battlefield Memorial Association and the Soldiers' National Cemetery. Battlefield promoters urged placement in the setting dramatized by Timothy O'Sullivan and Alexander Gardner's photograph *The Field Where General Reynolds Fell*

(1863). As Gardner's caption for the picture emphasized, Reynolds's death on the first day of battle and the Union triumph on the third day made him a potent symbol of pastoral regeneration. The site of his martyrdom was an immediate favorite of tourists, but the monument sponsors accepted a prominent position in the cemetery that Lincoln had consecrated in a similar cycle of mortality and immortality. J. Q. A. Ward's portrait statue, unveiled in August 1872, received praise for its "simplicity, strength and naturalness." Reynolds's "vigorous, earnest, courageous, self-possessed face" stamped him as "the beau-ideal of the modern American soldier," a leader by example.[5]

Placement of the Sixth Corps memorial to John Sedgwick at West Point made that project an especially important emblem of military leadership. A group of officers in the regular army had raised funds during the war for a campus monument to fallen colleagues; when George McClellan spoke at the dedication of the site in June 1864, the first name he invoked was Sedgwick, killed the previous month at Spotsylvania. That initiative stalled, and the statue unveiled by the Sixth Corps in October 1868 became the Academy touchstone for Civil War ideals of command. Dedication orator George William Curtis seized the opportunity to discuss military responsibility in democratic society. He frankly observed that West Point was often "accused of aristocratic tendencies" for promoting detachment from political decision-making. "If the charge be true, it is fatal to West Point," he warned. Curtis stressed that "a republic is possible only among thinking men" and that "no man has a right permanently to seclude himself from knowledge and interest in public affairs." He was pleased to report that only 197 of the 820 West Point graduates alive in June 1861 had betrayed the United States in the Civil War, but he stressed that patriotism was not a simple guide to duty. "I deny that in a noble breast, whether in or out of uniform, the sense of loyalty to the flag will be deeper and stronger than that of loyalty to conscience," he declared. He blamed Robert E. Lee not for resigning from the U.S. Army, where Sedgwick succeeded him as commander of the Fourth Cavalry, but for taking up arms to "raise the flag of injustice and inhumanity." The orator implored his audience, comprised partly of current cadets, to remain vigilant during Reconstruction, for "the magician who was a tiger yesterday will be a fox to-day."[6]

Sedgwick personified for Curtis a fulfillment of this political responsibility. Descendant of a general in Cromwell's army and a major who served at Valley Forge, the Civil War commander "was but one of the soldiers of the Union" in a struggle "as old as history . . . the contest for the largest individual freedom." The New Englander offered an example of the Puritan tradition that Curtis regarded as the trunk line of liberty. Sedgwick was an apt vehicle for the orator's emphasis that transplantation to America "modified and enlarged" the "gloomy and severe" Puritanism of England. Curtis reported that the general combined "all the cardinal soldierly qualities" with a "depthless tenderness" and that "simple in his habits, and of a rustic modesty of manner, Sedgwick's humor played pleasantly over every event." The commander was characteristically jesting at the moment of his death, encouraging his men to ignore Confederate sharpshooters because "they couldn't hit an elephant at this distance." Congeniality softened ideological rectitude. Sedgwick typically did not wear any insignia of rank, and the principal adornment on Launt Thompson's portrait statue was the badge of the Sixth Corps, consistent with Curtis's peroration to the former volunteers in his audience that "it is a monument of your valor as well as of his devotion. His modesty would have refused it for himself, but his affection would have accepted it from you."[7]

Similar wariness of military insularity shaped the dedication of the equestrian statue of James McPherson in Washington in October 1876 even though he was the golden boy of his West Point generation. McPherson graduated at the top of his class in 1853. After a year as an Academy instructor, he moved into a prestigious position in the engineering corps, where he remained until October 1862. The Society of the Army of the Tennessee launched a substantial postwar fund-raising campaign for an equestrian statue of the fallen commander, which contrasted with complete dependence on congressional funding for the monuments to Winfield Scott and John Rawlins unveiled in the capital in 1874. The dedication orator was John Logan, who had led the Army of the Tennessee to victory in the Battle of Atlanta after taking charge upon McPherson's death. Now a U.S. senator from Illinois, the powerful critic of military professionalism ascribed McPherson's success much more to character than training. Logan stressed that the engineering officer was an inexperienced field commander when he became major general of volunteers, after which "new and untried powers of mind and undeveloped talents" became manifest. He was "cast in a mold too grand and expansive to confine his fellowship and sympathy within the narrow limits of the trained military circle," and "his ear was ever open to the complaints and requests of the poor soldier." Logan's regionalism differed sharply from Curtis's portrait of Sedgwick and the Puritan tradition, but both orations described leadership as an emanation from community membership. McPherson understood his soldiers, and they understood him. "What was still dearer to the Western volunteers," Logan underscored, "they felt that, although a commander, he looked upon himself more as a comrade than a superior."[8]

Southerners also honored an ideal of accessibility. At the dedication of the Stonewall Jackson statue in Richmond in October 1875, minister Moses Hoge asserted that "the masses who compose the commonality, consciously weak and irresolute, instinctively gather around the men of loftier stature in whom them they find the great forces wanting in themselves." Jackson helped his soldiers find inner resources they had not recognized. According to Hoge, "he hedged himself about with no banner of exclusiveness," and more expansively, "no man was ever more susceptible to the impressions of the physical world," including the hum of bees, the streaks of dawn, or the fragrance of clover fields. Jackson was "the impersonation of our Confederate cause" because he shared virtues prized by white southerners, especially piety. Virginia governor and former brigadier James Kemper echoed that the Jackson statue, funded by British admirers, demonstrated intersectional and international respect for "the people of whom this christian warrior was a representative type and champion."[9]

Acceptance of risk was the heart of exemplary identification with the rank and file. The successful leader could not value his own life more highly than the lives of his soldiers. Civil War officers often directed assaults from the head of formations, as in the fatal charge at Shiloh commemorated by the equestrian statue of Albert Sidney Johnston installed atop the massive burial mound of the Army of Tennessee at Metairie Cemetery in New Orleans in 1887. Even the highest-ranking officers also exposed themselves in other operations near the front lines, which accounted for the deaths of Reynolds, Sedgwick, McPherson, and Jackson. The proportion of generals killed in the war was 50 percent higher than the proportion of privates.[10] Orators routinely observed that authority to ask for sacrifice depended on readiness to make the same sacrifice. Hoge testified that "it was his sublime indifference to personal danger . . . that gave [Jackson] such power over the armies he commanded."[11]

Antebellum artists translated these principles into specific poses. Thomas Crawford's monument to George Washington in Richmond (1850–58), the third equestrian statue in the United States, was the first to depict a leader in battle. During the final stage of the selection process, the sculptor's publicist Charles Sumner explained that Crawford had abjured classical gestures of imperial control and shown Washington's arm extended "not in an act of command but as though he were calmly and energetically pleading before his soldiers the importance of doing their duty to their country." Like

FIGURE 3.1. Thomas Crawford, Virginia Washington Monument, Richmond, 1850–58.
Courtesy of the Library of Congress.

Emanuel Leutze's contemporary painting of *Washington Crossing the Delaware* (1851), the monument imagined the Revolutionary leader sharing the hazards of war. Clark Mills's statue in Washington (1853–60) depicted the commander at the Battle of Princeton, controlling his balking horse as he advanced toward the British lines in front of his troops.[12]

Designers of early postwar monuments struggled to combine this democratic conception of leadership with the dignity of official authority. Henry Kirke Brown's equestrian memorial of Winfield Scott in Washington (1867–74) emphasized the weight of responsibility. The statue depicted "Old Fuss and Feathers," a hero of the War of 1812 and the Mexican-American War before he closed his career as the initial chief strategist for the Union army, as an aged, portly figure with his right hand testily arched on his hip. Pundits deemed the bronze general unfit for duty and his spindly horse "not daring to travel faster than a walk."[13] More sculptors tended in the opposite direction. Louis Rebisso, exiled from Italy because of his sympathies with Mazzini's republican movement, portrayed the youthful McPherson

Models of Leadership

in a rumpled uniform, setting aside his binoculars to fix his gaze on nearby action and poised to accelerate his spirited horse. John Rogers's equestrian monument to Reynolds in Philadelphia (1884) drew as much derision as Brown's effigy of Scott but for contrary reasons. The popular designer of tabletop statuettes wrote that he represented Reynolds shortly before the commander's death at Gettysburg. The horse was "startled and shying from the noise and danger" that the general decisively pointed out to the men at his side. Critics found the composition "so utterly wanting in dignity as to be utterly ridiculous."[14]

The equestrian monument to George H. Thomas unveiled in Washington in November 1879 synthesized ideas about leadership that prevailed for two decades after the war. The so-called Rock of Chickamauga was famously resolute and self-possessed. Dedication orator Stanley Matthews noted that "the internal, as well as the external, man was statuesque, massive, monumental." But Matthews stressed that Thomas was also "quick in his sensibilities," so attentive to public opinion that he died of a stroke in 1870 while writing a reply to a criticism from a rival Union general. This candid attachment to the community channeled an absorbed energy back into the army as the latent heat of Thomas's passion gradually intensified and "spread through all the particles that adhered and gathered to it, until the fused and molten mass, red hot with its combustion, consumed every thing that approached it." Matthews's description of the command relationship as a social exchange framed his observation that "Thomas was something more and better than merely a soldier" and prepared the conclusion that the monument was "also sacred to the memory of that invisible host without whom he was nothing."[15]

Admirers of J. Q. A. Ward's equestrian monument similarly found that "in this statue the spectator is reminded more of the man than of the warrior." Ward refreshed a Baroque conceit by depicting the commander riding to a summit. Viewers saw the general "reconnoitering the position of the enemy," a hazardous activity in the new age of the sharpshooter. The realistic portraits of man and horse also struck an egalitarian note. The corpulent Thomas was "not a particularly good horseman." Ward showed him "on a fine, not too handsome horse, and sitting with a gravity quite unpretending in gesture or look." The composition contrasted with "stagey and theatrical-looking" equestrians. Its vitality came from the sweeping diagonal and vertical lines and from the elimination of detail. "There is no flummery, no needless trapping," enthused one critic. "The General is free in his saddle and in trim for active work." This simplicity focused attention and prompted the reflection that "had one seen Thomas on the battle-field, it is highly improbable that

FIGURE 3.2. John Quincy Adams Ward and J. L. Smithmeyer, Thomas Monument, Washington, DC, 1874–79. Photograph by William Henry Jackson. Courtesy of the Library of Congress.

one would have recognized him as the Commander-in-Chief of the Army of the Cumberland." The general concentrated commonplace virtues.[16]

The monument to David Farragut unveiled in New York on Memorial Day in 1881 most fully elaborated the early postwar metaphor of military command. The admiral had some advantages over a general for this purpose. Sailing across the open sea was a better analogy for democratic leadership than the equestrian monument, which nature as well as history locked into an ideology of control. In a rhetorical image that invited comparison with Jacques-Louis David's famous painting of Napoléon heading into the Great St. Bernard Pass astride a rearing horse, Wendell Phillips commented that "if the Alps, piled in cold and still sublimity, be the emblem of Despotism,

Models of Leadership

the ever-restless ocean is ours . . . pure only because it is never still."[17] The commander of a ship also shared directly in the fate of his crew. Farragut had vividly symbolized his identification with the *Hartford* when he was lashed to its rigging as his flotilla entered Mobile Bay in August 1864. Although a precaution to secure the admiral, the incident lent itself to imaginative development. Randolph Rogers proposed to recreate the scene for the Farragut monument in Washington, a design that one critic called reminiscent of "martyrdom at the stake." The metal propellers of the *Hartford* supplied the bronze for the statue by Vinnie Ream that the federal government chose instead, at the foot of which was a portentous coil of rope. Joseph Choate remarked in his New York dedication address that Adm. Horatio Nelson had hoisted a signal at Trafalgar that "England expects every man to do his duty" but that it was reserved to his American counterpart "to hoist nothing less than himself into the rigging of his flagship, as the living signal of duty done."[18]

Augustus Saint-Gaudens's monument subsumed that narrative in a broader characterization of the commander. The portrait highlighted what one critic called the contrast between "a realism of particulars and a realism of generals; a realism cheap and false, and a realism penetrative and true." The memorial is a landmark in the history of American art for its beaux arts integration of the statue and the elaborate base. Saint-Gaudens suggested that Farragut similarly achieved greatness by unifying distinct elements. He presented the veteran sailor facing into a brisk wind, his frock coat buttoned to the top and its skirt flaring on his right and swirling on his left. Equally animated was the element of light, heightened by the sculptor's energetic and varied textural finish of the bronze surfaces and by the gilding of all that would have been gold in the uniform. Observers praised the modeling for its "rich living painter-like quality which is to be found only in modern works of the very highest rank." The most insistent element in the memorial was the water that defined the register of the bluestone base. If the wind and the sun enlivened the monument, the sea provided depth of character.[19]

The base that Saint-Gaudens designed with architect Stanford White placed viewers in a complex environment. Ripples and waves flowed across the surface, establishing horizontal lines to balance the vertical center section and reaching up to break near the foot of the statue. Carved dolphins sported at the ends of the semicircular exedra. The pebbled pavement in front of the monument, like a beach strewn with shells, featured a crab that carried the names of Saint-Gaudens and White. New Yorkers might sit on

FIGURE 3.3. Augustus Saint-Gaudens and
Stanford White, Farragut Monument, New York, 1877–80.
Courtesy of Photography Collection, New York Public Library.

the exedra bench to watch "as the rushing river of life goes by," one critic pointed out. This richly varied program included "freaks and sallies of the imagination" that troubled some commentators, but the monument made clear what Farragut had taken from a career at sea that began at the age of ten. Strong ideal figures of Loyalty and Courage dominated the two wings of the exedra. The naval hero rose from his characteristic medium.[20]

Saint-Gaudens situated Farragut in culture as well as nature. The *Times* thought the figures of Loyalty and Courage reminiscent of ancient Greek art. Another important decorative feature of the base, the lengthy inscriptions in stylized lettering and Roman numerals, evoked the Renaissance. A sword rising from the water on the pedestal linked Farragut to Arthurian legend. The eclectic allusions identified the warrior as the product no less than the subject of art and literature. "Sailor he is, every inch of him," observed the *Evening Post*, but at the same time, "this hero is an intellectual creature, a moral creature and spiritual creature, who plans with brains, who loves his country and who trusts himself."[21] The importation of pre-Raphaelite symbolism and beaux arts compositional principles complemented the unpretentious realism of the portrait statue. The thoroughly modern ensemble implied that the Union champion was not only loyal and courageous but also profoundly resourceful.

The placement of the Farragut monument suggested that those resources were not solely moral or intellectual. Stanford White summarized the decision for the north end of Madison Square Park as the "sweller part of the Park, just where the aristocratic part of the [Fifth] Avenue begins" and directly opposite Delmonico's restaurant, the dining capital of the Gilded Age. The site reflected the membership of the Farragut Monument Association, formed by a circle of powerful financiers and merchants in New York. Similar trends were evident in Washington. The monuments to Thomas and Farragut supplied new names and adornments to fashionable residential districts, as did the portrait statue of Rear Adm. Samuel F. Du Pont, installed in the former Pacific Circle in 1884.[22] The narrow funding base of the New York monument was also increasingly typical. The Society of the Army of the Cumberland contributed to the Thomas statue less than half of what the Society of the Army of the Tennessee raised for the McPherson statue. Even as the vision of Civil War leaders as representative of democracy reached a peak of artistic achievement, the economic underpinnings of that model were eroding. Groups that increasingly dominated American society would find new forms for the commander monument.

Classical tradition treated civic monuments and commemorative oratory as mutually reinforcing cultural institutions. Aristotle classified ceremonial speech as one of the three basic categories of oratory, alongside parliamentary and forensic rhetoric. Orators in turn became the subjects of important ancient statues. Daniel Webster exemplified the persistence of this reciprocal relationship in the mid-nineteenth-century United States. Delivering the main address at the unveiling of the Webster memorial outside the Massachusetts statehouse in 1859, his oratorical heir Edward Everett linked the occasion to Webster's famous performances at Plymouth and the Bunker Hill monument. Everett recalled that Demosthenes's "stony lips remained to rebuke and exhort his degenerate countrymen" long after the Athenian died, and he promised that in the event of a national crisis Webster's "bronze lips" would similarly "repeat the cry of the living voice."[23] A wealthy industrialist's donation of a Webster monument for Central Park reasserted the conjunction of statuary and oratory after the war. Thomas Ball's colossal portrait, the enlargement of a statuette he produced in large numbers at Webster's death, adapted a pose prescribed by classical convention. Celebrated speakers Robert Winthrop and William M. Evarts shared the dedicatory duties in November 1876.[24] But shifting styles of popular oratory doomed such simplistic claims of continuity. One brilliant monument captured a permanent glimpse of the lyceum ideal that prevailed during the peak of the sectional conflict, but that interactive format faded after the war. Most monuments to prominent orators of the Civil War era obscured the model of leadership that these figures had given the nation.

The ceremonial role of the orator remained an independent position of public responsibility in the dedications of early monuments to Civil War commanders, much as Webster's laurels from Plymouth and Bunker Hill were distinct from his triumphs in the Senate and the Supreme Court. John Logan's part in the McPherson unveiling reflected their service together in the Army of the Tennessee and the tendency of Washington ceremonies to feature federal officeholders, but the journalist George W. Curtis and the attorney Joseph Choate did not fight in the war and had never held office when they spoke at the Sedgwick and Farragut dedications. A lieutenant to Rutherford B. Hayes during and after the war, Stanley Matthews was a literary-minded lawyer like Choate or Choate's law partner Evarts or older cousin Rufus Choate. The selection of Curtis to deliver the address at West Point particularly showcased the commissioning of orators, like the choice

of monument subjects, as a forum in which private citizens elected representatives. For years one of the most popular lyceum lecturers in the country,
the *Harper's* editor had become friendly with Sedgwick's abolitionist cousin
Charles B. Sedgwick on repeated trips to Syracuse, but Curtis did not appear as a spokesman for the family. The Society of the Sixth Corps turned to
him as it had turned to sculptor Launt Thompson, as an outstanding figure
in his creative field.

The first major postwar effort to memorialize the orator as a model of
leadership resulted in disaster. Everett's wartime record invited idealization.
The conservative began to deliver speeches in support of the Union cause
within a few weeks of the firing on Fort Sumter. After a high-profile address
in New York on July 4, he presented his "Causes and Conduct of the War"
about fifty times between October 1861 and April 1862 to audiences in Boston, Brooklyn, Buffalo, Pittsburgh, St. Paul, and other cities, while Lincoln
clung closely to Washington and did not make any speeches. Logically invited to deliver the principal oration at the dedication of the Soldiers' National Cemetery, Everett filled out the ceremonial framework that created a
niche for the Gettysburg Address. He went on to speak in support of Lincoln's reelection in 1864, breaking with old allies like Robert Winthrop. His
death in January 1865, as Union victory became imminent, offered an opportunity to mark the redemption of a cultural and political faction under siege
since Webster's Seventh of March Address. Fund-raising for a monument in
Boston succeeded extraordinarily quickly. Commissioned sculptor William
Wetmore Story recognized that Everett's oratory was more deeply characteristic than his services in state and national office. The bronze portrait depicted the speaker with one arm uplifted in a gesture that classical convention reserved for epic rhetorical flourishes. A friend of the artist reported
that Story sought to show Everett at the high point of the speech about
Washington that he delivered 136 times during the late 1850s to raise funds
for the preservation of Mount Vernon and promote intersectional unity. Installed in the Public Garden without ceremony in November 1867 after the
sudden death of scheduled orator John A. Andrew, the monument honored
a champion of commemoration.[25]

Story expressed particular pride in the work when he sent it from Italy,
but local responses were withering. The statue was "a parasite on the firm
old trunk of classicism, yielding no new fruit." Wags ridiculed the histrionic
pose. The broadest critique found the defect in the type rather than the portrait, suggesting that Everett "is known to the present generation chiefly as
an orator, yet this is not his greatest claim to remembrance."[26] The fiasco was

FIGURE 3.4. William Wetmore Story, Everett Memorial, Boston, 1865–67.
Courtesy of the Library of Congress.

not unique. Partly on Story's recommendation, fellow expatriate Albert E. Harnisch received the commission for a monument to John C. Calhoun for which white women of Charleston, South Carolina, had raised funds before the war. Harnisch produced a statue of Calhoun standing before his Senate chair, his right index finger enumerating his arguments. Joel Tanner Hart had made similar portraits of Henry Clay dedicated in Richmond and New Orleans in 1860, much as Thomas Crawford's antebellum statue of Patrick Henry for the Washington equestrian monument in Richmond anticipated the theatricality of Story's memorial to Everett. Charlestonians protested the Calhoun monument long before its 1887 unveiling. They expressed several objections, but the rhetorical pose was among the most prominent. The indicative gesture was "peculiar to him during his speeches," admitted a local summary, but "amounted to a deformity" in the statue.[27] Within a decade the sponsors replaced Harnisch's work with a statue that depicted Calhoun holding a scroll, presumably a lawgiver rather than an orator.

These controversies reflected not only the depleted influence of the Italianate sculpture exemplified by Story and Harnisch but also the faded prestige of the oratorical style represented by Everett and Calhoun. Everett's autumnal vigor notwithstanding, a generational shift in public rhetoric had begun shortly after Webster's Second Reply to Hayne and shaped debate during the crisis of the 1850s. The transition was gradual and uneven. Charles Sumner's learned diatribes remained similar to Everett's speeches despite the ideological and temperamental contrasts between the two men. But most of the prominent speakers who came of age during the Jacksonian era rejected precedents informed by the earlier republic. The prevailing conception of the orator as public leader during the peak of sectional conflict was illustrated less by the selection of Everett to speak at Gettysburg than by the choice of Henry Ward Beecher for the next ceremony of comparable symbolic weight, the restoration of the American flag at Fort Sumter in April 1865.

The orators in their prime shortly before and during the war varied in some ways but shared essential characteristics. Although mostly educated at elite colleges that stressed the classics, these speakers sought less to dazzle audiences or lift them to an exalted plane than to engage them in everyday terms. Elevated rhetoric gave way to colloquial language and plain diction. Pithiness became a cardinal virtue. Ralph Waldo Emerson argued that Webster's rolling clauses constituted a failure of moral responsibility. The deplorable "want of generalization in his speeches" failed to articulate the principles beneath particular policies and generated "not a single valuable aphorism that can pass into literature."[28] As this criticism suggested, the newer pattern imported an intellectual radicalism, mostly antislavery though occasionally secessionist, even if some practitioners were political moderates. Observers described abolitionists Wendell Phillips and Theodore Parker and fire-eater William Lowndes Yancey as informal in manner, conversational in tone, and direct in language, their calm and often extemporaneous presentations enlivened by slashing sarcasm and acid dispatch of hecklers. Wit and wisdom increasingly flourished together, especially on the vibrant lyceum circuit that marketed public speaking as both entertainment and education. Beecher's self-deprecatory geniality and folksy metaphors aimed to establish rapport with his audiences rather than command over them. Curtis similarly spiced genteel self-improvement with clever charm. The two transplanted New Englanders helped to forge a Republican middle class that linked New York with the smallest audiences. Choate, forty-nine years old at the Farragut dedication in 1881, illustrated the trajectory of an oratorical culture in which he was too young to have participated prominently during the antebellum crisis. Mark Twain cited the attorney as one of his chief mentors in the art of delivering after-dinner speeches.[29]

The monument that best comprehended this oratorical culture focused on a literary-minded lawyer who shared ground with Emerson and Twain. Lincoln delivered his first enduring speech at the Young Men's Lyceum of Springfield in 1838. He presumably attended at least some of the lectures by visitors to the Illinois capital, who included Emerson and Beecher. After his defeat in the 1858 Senate campaign, he tried to join the circuit with a talk on discoveries and inventions that suggested a familiarity with Phillips's immensely popular "The Lost Arts," an account of ancient precedents to nineteenth-century technology. His outstanding sense of humor served him well on the platform, though it may also have caused him some diffidence toward ceremonial speaking. At a Springfield gathering after the death of Henry Clay, he self-deprecatingly reported that the Whig hero "never spoke merely to be heard. He never delivered a Fourth of July Oration, or an eulogy on an occasion like this." Lincoln did not seek to make such speeches as president. Obliged to do so at times, he delivered some of the greatest orations in American history. His inaugural addresses and Gettysburg Address illustrated the vernacular adaptation of classical structure and the talent for moral aphorism that characterized the most admired rhetoric of the period.[30]

The memorial that Saint-Gaudens designed with White for Lincoln Park in Chicago (1884–87) reworked formal and thematic elements of their re-

FIGURE 3.5. Augustus Saint-Gaudens and Stanford White, Lincoln Monument, Chicago, 1884–87. Courtesy of the Library of Congress.

cent Farragut collaboration to present the wartime orator, like the admiral, as a model of democratic leadership. The monument again featured a portrait statue in a setting shaped by an exedra, this time an ellipse that measured sixty feet across and thirty feet deep. The enveloped space invited quiet. The bearded president stood before an ornamental chair of state, but the long watch chain snaking across his creased vest indicated that his office was a position of toil rather than majesty. He rose to report to the national sovereign, the American people. The chair was the traditional emblem not only of the executive but also the philosopher; shortly before Saint-Gaudens received the Chicago commission, Rodin made his first plaster version of the seated statue that came to be known as *The Thinker*.[31] Like that muscular ideal figure, the statesman on the verge of speech represented what Emerson had described as "Man Thinking," a union of reflection and action. Saint-Gaudens depicted Lincoln's arms in symmetrical balance. His left hand touched the lapel of his coat, an updated reversal of an ancient pose.

His right arm, to which classical convention assigned the burden of gesture, reached behind his back, his fist tightly clenched in repudiation of stylized histrionics. Like many lyceum orators, he carried no notes and apparently preferred to speak extemporaneously rather than launch into a memorized text. Saint-Gaudens used the elevation of the statue to offer two views of Lincoln's bowed head. The orator looked inward to gather his thoughts, but he also looked directly at the viewer who served as the putative audience. The democrat found his ideas in the people.

Textual inscriptions were vital to this composition in a different way from the decorative lettering on the Farragut monument. Two golden balls inscribed with quotations marked the edges of the wide steps in front of the statue. Inscriptions on the exedra drew aphorisms from two of Lincoln's famous addresses. The earlier quotation was the conclusion of his 1859 lecture at the Cooper Union, an institution closely connected to the lyceum movement. Lincoln had called on his listeners to "let us have faith that right makes might, and in that faith let us to the end dare to do our duty as we understand it." The other inscription, from Lincoln's second inaugural address, similarly urged that "with malice toward none, with charity for all, with firmness in the right as God gives us to know the right, let us strive on." The breadth of these exhortations connected the Civil War monument to almost any moral struggle. Progressive journalist David Graham Phillips later described the work as an encapsulation of "the history of the human race, the long, bloody, the agonized struggle of the masses of mankind for freedom and light," and especially the history of the United States, "founded by common men for the common people, founded upon freedom and equality and justice."[32] The spotlight on Lincoln's talent for pithy generalization suggested a connection between the art of oratory and the art of public sculpture, comprehensible in an instant but sufficient to sustain detailed scrutiny.

By the unveiling of Saint-Gaudens's work in October 1887 the oratorical culture that nurtured Lincoln was disappearing. Six months earlier Curtis had written an affectionate essay for *Harper's* in which he recounted the role of Emerson and Beecher and Parker and Phillips in shaping northern opinion during the sectional conflict and noted that "the lyceum of the last generation is gone."[33] The principal speaker at the Chicago ceremony was Leonard Swett, a trusted ally of Lincoln since their days together at the Illinois bar but a figure with no higher intellectual ambition than adulatory reminiscences of his distinguished friend. During the same month the orator at the unveiling of the George Meade statue in Philadelphia was former corps commander John Gibbon. The dedication of the George B. McClellan statue in Philadelphia in 1894 similarly featured an address by loyal sub-ordinate William B. Franklin. The transition was gradual, and some lawyers continued to follow in the oratorical line of Evarts and Choate. George R. Peck delivered a thoughtful address at the unveiling of the Logan memorial in Chicago in 1897. The versatile Hampton L. Carson spoke at the inaugu-ration of the Grant monument in Philadelphia two years later. More typi-cal was the 1897 dedication of Grant's Tomb, an extraordinarily expensive and ambitious project. The orator of the day was the spearhead of the enter-prise, Grant's former staff officer and presidential secretary, Horace Porter, whose address complemented the publication of his memoir *Campaigning with Grant* (1897). The oratorical dominance of veterans, well established in dedications of soldier monuments since the waning of funereal connota-tions in those exercises, continued to deepen in the early twentieth century. When McClellan's widow asked that Supreme Court chief justice Melville Fuller or associate justice John Harlan speak at the unveiling of McClellan's equestrian monument in Washington in 1907, former Union general Daniel Sickles complained that "I fail to see any peculiar fitness in either of these gentlemen as orators on an occasion purely military." Sickles nonetheless proposed to cede his place on the program, but the secretary of the Society of the Army of the Potomac answered that this "suggestion to retire in favor of a Civilian is absurd."[34]

J. Q. A. Ward's acclaimed memorial to Henry Ward Beecher, unveiled in Brooklyn in 1891, testified to the fading memory of lyceum oratory. Within a year of the minister's death in March 1887 an impressively broad-based fund-raising campaign generated almost all of the $35,000 necessary to match the budget for Ward's recent statue of George Washington for Federal Hall on Wall Street. The sponsors chose to place the monument at City Hall Park in recognition of Beecher's services as a public citizen. Plymouth Church parishioners polled by a newspaper reporter "were unanimous in the opinion that the great preacher should be represented as standing by a small table, his left arm resting upon it and his right hand extended. This was the position in which Mr. Beecher was so frequently seen by his congregation. He assumed it when he argued, when he prayed, and when he brought laughter or tears by a slight inflection of his voice."[35] Ward chose a more sculpturesque but less historically accurate composition. Portrayed in a long coat and an In-verness cape, his Beecher was a massive figure. Sculptor and critic Lorado Taft rejoiced that the pose entailed "no weak gestures, no self-depreciatory remarks, no attempt to win us." Beecher's leonine head was "uplifted as if in command rather than exhortation." The result may have been, as Ward's

FIGURE 3.6. John Quincy Adams Ward and Richard Morris Hunt, Henry Ward
Beecher Monument, Brooklyn, 1887–91. Courtesy of the Library of Congress.

biographer echoed decades later, "the epitome of nineteenth-century public sculpture at its best," but the portrait differed sharply from Beecher's oratorical style. Corpulent though he became, he was essentially supple rather than imposing, beloved for his wit and charm and warmth. He aimed to win an emotional affinity with his audience. The implied setting at an outdoor speech, necessitated by Ward's desire for the volumetric cape, and the set of notes uncharacteristically held by the bronze Beecher further suppressed the conversational spontaneity for which the orator was famous.[36]

The lower register of the monument, which addressed the moral issues at the root of the Civil War, underscored Ward's indifference toward creative rhetoric. His portrait of Beecher stood atop a pedestal that featured on one side statues of a white boy and girl and on the opposite side a statue of a young black woman. If perhaps designed in part to highlight the domestic virtue of a celebrity whose career shipwrecked in sexual scandal, the white boy and girl also pointed toward Beecher's influence in the development of northern middle-class culture. The African American recalled the minister's role in cultivating the antislavery sentiment of that culture, particularly the sensational "auctions" at which Plymouth Church parishioners purchased the freedom of young women whom Beecher reported to be otherwise destined for concubinage in the lower South. Ward did not, however, relate that domestic ideology to Beecher's speaking style. Eloquence merely reflected the underlying political cause. Daniel Chester French adopted a similar approach in the memorial to Wendell Phillips dedicated in Boston in 1915. The statue held a slave's broken chain as a theatrical prop and leaned forward with animation, ready to pound a podium with his fist. When a visitor to French's studio complained that the statue looked nothing like Phillips's speaking manner, the sculptor replied that "whether it is a faithful portrait of the man himself or not, I should like to represent what he stood for in the zenith of his power and usefulness. . . . I am going to make my anti-slavery hero as inspiring as I know how." The strategy refused to acknowledge the educational and commercial frames of mid-nineteenth-century oratory as a context for antislavery politics.[37]

Many of the leading orators of the Civil War era did not figure with proportionate prominence in the memorial landscape. White southerners keener to discuss the war than the road to secession showed no interest in a monument to Yancey. Black northerners and their allies raised only enough money to commission a Smith Granite Company statue of Frederick Douglass for Rochester. The in-house sculptor portrayed a relaxed and agile Douglass presenting himself from the lecture platform as an American citizen after the adoption of the Fourteenth Amendment; bronze plaques on the base recorded memorable phrases from his speeches. The modestly budgeted work drew little lasting attention. Lorado Taft did not mention it in his magisterial *History of American Sculpture* (1903), which featured Saint-Gaudens's standing portrait of Lincoln as the frontispiece. Several monuments recalled key orators as statesmen or intellectuals but not as public speakers. Thomas Ball's monument to Charles Sumner in Boston (1878) depicted the senator holding a scroll generally understood to represent the Civil Rights Act of 1875. Jurors in the anonymous design competition had initially chosen a seated composition by Anne Whitney, whom they disqualified as a woman. Cambridge later installed that work in Harvard Square. Meanwhile the Boston Memorial Association sponsored a sitting statue of Theodore Parker.

The most conspicuous absence from this field was Emerson. He was vital to the rise of the lecture circuit, both as a widely traveled speaker and through the essays he based on his addresses, and he personified the political mobilization of the lyceum. An attentive observer noted in 1917 that Emerson was the highest vote-getter in the inaugural class of the Hall of Fame for Great Americans who lacked a statue in the national capital. He might have added that Emerson was also the only person in that top eight (after Washington, Lincoln, Webster, Franklin, Grant, Marshall, and Jefferson) without an outdoor public monument anywhere in the United States.[38] French, who met his fellow townsman when the sculptor was nineteen years old and Emerson was sixty-seven, made a seated marble statue for the foyer of the Concord Free Public Library (1914) that portrayed the sage in a dressing gown he wore in his study on cold mornings. Frank Duveneck's bronze statue for the interior of the Harvard philosophy building (1905) similarly depicted Emerson seated, his finger holding his place in the book on his lap.[39] These works placed him among literary men of reflection rather than men of action. Books and schools remembered that Emerson's achievement originated largely on the lecture platform, but he was not part of the commemorative realm constituted by civic monuments.

The limited tributes to Emerson and Parker and Douglass and Yancey, along with the distorted recollections of the lyceum style they had shared with Beecher and Phillips, effectively narrowed the remembrance of Civil War oratory to Lincoln. The celebrated Chicago installation and several twentieth-century works came to epitomize the triumph of vernacular rhetoric over the grand manner bequeathed by Webster and Everett and Clay and Calhoun. This pattern exaggerated the extent to which Lincoln's brilliant speeches resulted from his unique genius and obscured the institutional foundations of oratory during the sectional conflict, especially the lecture circuit that illustrated decisive values of northern society. The isolated commemoration of the president paralleled the growing domination of dedication programs by politicians and military personnel. Even more than the overlapping set of journalists, honored by seated statues of William Lloyd Garrison in Boston (1886) and Horace Greeley in New York (1890), the influential orators of the Civil War era had stood for the possibility of a spontaneous, unofficial democratic leadership. They had earned public recognition of intellectual creativity as a claim to authority. Incomplete remembrance of these orators ominously complemented an increasingly effusive celebration of military commanders.

SALUTES AND REVIEWS

Early memorial representations of military careerists like Thomas and Farragut updated the democratic challenge to imperial classicism initiated in antebellum tributes to Washington and Jackson, presidents as well as generals. The relationship between military and civilian authority continued to attract fresh attention in a series of works that explored Civil War soldiers' devotion to their commanders as a parallel to elected authority. This line of development soon reversed its premises and identified military rank as a model for political leadership. A nation once wary of the equestrian monument became the new home of the genre.

As Crawford's statue of Washington in Richmond imagined egalitarian leadership on the battlefield, Henry Kirke Brown's statue of Washington in New York (1852–56) envisioned republican subordination of military glory. Brown based his composition on the most famous ancient equestrian, the Marcus Aurelius moved to the Capitoline in the sixteenth century. That work showed the sovereign wearing civilian dress but signaling his martial power in a supervisory gesture of imperial advent that greeted his putative legions and subjects, as well as the later Romans who passed beneath the columns on which the statue stood.[40] Brown, an ardent member of the Young American movement, inverted this motif. He collaborated in planning the project with Horatio Greenough, and like that sculptor's depiction of a classicized Washington giving up his sword to his country, Brown's equestrian identified the Revolutionary commander's unwillingness to assume civilian authority as the definitive transcendence of Old World kingship. Situated in Union Square, the monument recalled the November 1783 celebration of British evacuation at which citizens of New York cheered Washington as he

FIGURE 3.7. George Hayward, *Equestrian Statue of Washington, Union Square, N.Y., 1856*, lithograph published in *Manual of the Corporation of the City of New York for 1857*, edited by D. T. Valentine. Courtesy of Wallach Division Picture Collection, New York Public Library.

bade farewell to his soldiers and returned to private life. The bronze counterpart to Aurelius raised his arm in a profoundly less condescending gesture of benediction and, as one critic observed, "uncovers his head in a token of deference to his country."[41] His subsequent presidency was not a continuation but a disruption of martial heroism.

Alexander Milne Calder's memorial to George Meade tried to apply similar ideas to a Civil War general. Stationed near his Philadelphia home for much of the postwar period, Meade served on the Fairmount Park Commission from its establishment in 1866 until his death in 1872. The new Fairmount Park Art Association decided to make its first project an equestrian statue of the general, who had largely directed the arrangement of bridle paths, drives, and walks in the park where he loved to ride. A contemporary critic called Calder's design for the ensuing monument, unveiled in 1887 after a slow fund-raising process, "almost a copy" of Henri Regnault's acclaimed 1869 painting of Spanish liberal strongman Juan Prim mounted in front of a column of adoring soldiers. Calder portrayed Meade doffing his cap to acknowledge a salute from his troops, but awkward execution compromised the conception. Most problematic was the highly agitated and sharply restrained horse, more appropriate to a combat crisis than a collective declaration of confidence in a leader who would go on after the war to promote recreational equitation in the public realm. If uneasily caught between Brown's statue of Washington and battlefield dramas like Rogers's statue of Reynolds, the monument built on democratic reinterpretations of the equestrian tradition.[42]

Robert E. Lee presented a much grander study in the relationship between martial and civic virtue. George Washington Cable wrote shortly after the 1884 unveiling of a bronze portrait of Lee standing atop a high column in the center of New Orleans that "this monument, lifted far above our daily strife of narrow interests and often narrower passions and misunderstandings, becomes a monument to more than its one great and rightly loved original. It symbolizes our whole South's better self."[43] Competing efforts to commission an equestrian statue in Richmond illustrated the tensions between Lee's military career and the role that Cable envisioned. Lee's wartime lieutenant Jubal Early aimed to raise the funds exclusively from veterans to "proclaim to all the ages, that the soldiers who fought under him remained true to him in death." Rival initiatives suggested other constituencies. The Ladies' Lee Monument Association sent a fund-raising circular to white churches throughout the South. Virginia governor James L. Kemper urged mayors of southern cities to appeal to regional business interests. An eventual compromise arrangement stressed juxtaposition of the Lee equestrian and Crawford's statue of Washington. The siting of the Lost Cause monument on the outskirts of town as a fulcrum for real estate development established an alignment along the new Monument Avenue with the antebellum monument at the statehouse. The two figures on tall pedestals both soared about sixty feet above the ground. When the Lee bronze arrived in Richmond in May 1890, thousands of residents joined in an elaborate reenactment of the improvised dragging of the Washington statue to the capitol in the 1850s after a mule team failed to climb the hill from the James River.[44]

Eager to project Lee's leadership beyond the battlefield, the monument sponsors selected a composition that highlighted rank-and-file admiration for the general. They rejected a variation on Crawford's democratic combat commander offered by sculptor Moses Ezekiel, who had fought at the Battle of New Market with his fellow Virginia Military Institute cadets. In Ezekiel's design the forceful restraint of a charging horse recalled the famous "Lee to the rear" incidents in which Confederate soldiers overruled the general's eagerness to lead assaults. The pose eventually chosen incorporated a hint of shared risk but focused on the devotion Lee inspired. French sculptor Antonin Mercié proposed a Napoleonic approach to the latter theme in an 1886 design competition, depicting Lee "as he passed along his dying troops on the field of Gettysburg—the horse rearing, the dying stretching for a last affectionate glance of their leader." Although Mercié considered the image "sublime," the monument sponsors helped him develop a less melodramatic substitute that "represents General Lee as having just ridden to some eminence where he may better view the movements of the enemy, and here his soldiers recognizing his presence, greet him with one of those outbursts of cheers which never failed to welcome his presence among them, and as the General for a moment reins in his horse and acknowledges the greeting by taking off his hat." At the unveiling in May 1890 orator Archer Anderson nodded toward Mercié's original conception by suggesting that the monument recorded the impressions of "the ragged, half-starved men in gray who stood with Lee" after the bloody setback at Sharpsburg.[45]

Anderson's speech articulated the New South underpinnings to this view of Lee. A staff officer during the war, Anderson joined afterward in the family management of the Tredegar Iron Works, the most advanced manufacturing enterprise in the Confederacy. His dedication address praised Lee for recognizing the centrality of industry to modern war and accordingly making the defense of Richmond his highest priority. Anderson's interests in intersectional economic development framed his response to the central

FIGURE 3.8. Antonin Mercié and Paul Pujol, Lee Monument, Richmond, 1886–90.
Courtesy of the Library of Congress.

question debated in the extensive press coverage of the unveiling, whether to regard Lee as a regional or a national hero. Many northern newspapers continued to condemn him as "the natural demigod of the slave-holding oligarchy that sought to destroy the Union" while some white southerners maintained that "no other people in the world, and certainly not the people with whom we so recently contended in war," could fully appreciate the Confederate general.[46] Anderson argued instead that "all who bear the American name may proudly consent that posterity shall judge them" by the embrace of Lee as a hero because "the character of the ideal commander is the grandest manifestation in which man can show himself to man." Military leaders achieved more than "poets, artists, historians, orators, thinkers who have sounded all the depths of speculation, princes of science who have advanced the frontiers of ordered knowledge." Lee's mastery of logistical challenges and human nature, along with his "moral perfection," had earned him the admiration that the statue depicted and ratified. His postwar demonstration of "the best qualities of citizen, sage, and patriot" as president of Washington College followed naturally from his military accomplishments since West Point, even if Confederate defeat "denied him that eminence of civil station, in which his great qualities in their happy mixture might well have afforded a parallel to the strength and moderation of Washington."[47] Anderson's call for national celebration of the eminent general capped the twinning strategy of the Lee equestrian at the same time that the industrialist abandoned the traditional wariness of Washington's military glory.

This conciliatory militarism overlapped with a growing attachment to commanders' perspectives on the war. The best-selling memoirs published by Sherman in 1875 and Grant in 1885 were peaks in a flood tide of reminiscences. *Century* organized its immensely popular 1884–87 series of articles titled *Battles and Leaders of the Civil War* around contributions by high-ranking officers, including Grant, Sherman, Joseph E. Johnston, P. G. T. Beauregard, and James Longstreet. Equestrian statues were one measure of the trend, as *American Architect and Building News* signaled by running a fifty-part series on the form from July 1888 to May 1892. The monuments in Washington to Scott, McPherson, and Thomas were the only Civil War equestrians unveiled in the United States during the 1870s. Four followed in the 1880s and eight in the 1890s in addition to the four statues of mounted state heroes on the Iowa Soldiers and Sailors Monument completed in Des Moines in 1896. Reporting on a parallel pattern in battlefield parks, *Monumental News* noted in 1898 that Civil War remembrance "bids fair to make equestrian statuary in this country a characteristic feature of our national art." The rapid rate of increase continued with the unveiling of twenty more Civil War equestrian monuments in American cities during the first twelve years of the twentieth century. The deaths of Grant in 1885, Sheridan in 1888, and Sherman in 1891 prompted immediate responses, but the overall pattern did not merely reflect the lifespans of Civil War generals. The Massachusetts legislature appropriated funds in 1896 for an equestrian monument to Joseph Hooker, who died in 1879. The Kentucky division of the United Daughters of

Models of Leadership

the Confederacy began in 1906 to campaign for an equestrian monument to John Hunt Morgan, who died in the war.[48]

The equestrian effusion expanded on the motif of commanders' acknowledgments of soldiers' admiration. The Sherman monument authorized by Congress in 1892 was an especially influential extension of the transformation begun by the Lee memorial in Richmond. The driving force behind the project was Grenville M. Dodge, successor to Sherman as president of the Society of the Army of the Tennessee and a key figure in the transcontinental railroad industry, one of the American institutions most directly dependent on the army and most deeply invested in civilian analogies to wartime organizational ideals.[49] Joining Dodge on the three-member federal Sherman Statue Commission were the secretary of war and the commanding general of the army, an apt arrangement because Sherman's postwar career centered on the tension between those positions. During his long tenure as commanding general from 1869 to 1883 he was often frustrated by the subordination of military to civilian authority. He supported his protégé Emory Upton's call for the autonomy enjoyed by the Prussian military, and he achieved some success in institutional aggrandizement of the army by founding an advanced school at Fort Leavenworth and articulating a peacetime mission of preparing for unexpected foreign wars as the close of Indian conflicts ended the standard rationale for army budgets. After Sherman's retirement, his wartime lieutenant John Schofield initiated a more bureaucratically sophisticated approach to the position of commanding general by working with the secretary of war as something akin to a chief of staff. Dodge and Schofield participated in a parallel entrenchment of army influence through the Sherman Statue Commission.

Dodge initially hoped to infuse military principles into government by placing statues of Grant and Sherman on the east and west Capitol plazas, but congressional refusal led to a more narrative exposition of his goals. The commission voted to accept a lot on Pennsylvania Avenue adjacent to the Treasury Department in January 1896, three weeks after the deadline for artists' submission of models. Carl Rohl-Smith's proposal for a statue of Sherman "acknowledging the plaudits of a grateful people" sounded the theme through which Dodge aimed to make the most of the location, and the commission awarded the Danish immigrant the assignment against the recommendation of the distinguished advisory jury.[50] When Dodge presided over the dedication seven years later, he opened the proceedings by explaining that the monument depicted the Grand Review of May 1865. Riding at the

FIGURE 3.9. Carl Rohl-Smith, Sherman Monument, Washington, DC, 1895–1903.
Courtesy of the Library of Congress.

head of the daylong procession of western troops, Sherman looked back down Pennsylvania Avenue as he reached the rise near the Treasury Department and "saw his old army coming, with their old spirit, energy, and swing, and was satisfied they would do their best. . . . The crowd seemed to appreciate his thoughts, and welcomed him with a great ovation." The composition recalled soldiers' devotion to Sherman and public appreciation for him. It also situated citizens walking along the principal boulevard of the republic in the position of the rank-and-file troops that the general had overseen. Dodge echoed Archer Anderson's insistence on the primacy of military leadership when he suggested that an appropriate inscription would be Sherman's remark that "I cannot subscribe to the naked sentiment that 'the pen is mightier than the sword,' because it is not true."[51]

The controversial Sherman competition prompted direct rebuke of Dodge's vision of the commemorative landscape. Frank Sewall lamented in an 1896 article in *American Architect and Building News* that "the eques-

Models of Leadership

trian military statue is already becoming so frequent as to leave no place for monuments of a different purpose." He looked for more monuments that would honor "great American scholars, poets, inventors, philanthropists, and statesmen." Five years later *Washington Evening Star* proprietor and Corcoran Gallery of Art president Samuel Hay Kauffman urged the Columbia Historical Society to ensure that "the National Capital shall in the future be adorned not so much by statues and memorials of those who have won fame by the shedding of blood as of those whose lives have been devoted to the nobler work of promoting the welfare and securing the happiness of mankind."[52]

Conversely, the Sherman dedication ceremony also produced emphatic affirmations of Dodge's goals. Theodore Roosevelt's zest for the "dominant quality of forceful character" he found in great military commanders harmonized with the claim of the souvenir program that Sherman would have been pleased by the "order, discipline, and array" of the military pageant because he was "one of the greatest of disciplinarians." Orator of the day David B. Henderson agreed that "subordination was the rule of his military life," a startling reinterpretation of a general distinguished in the Civil War for adroit encouragement and coordination of rank-and-file initiative. Daniel Sickles dismissed the complaints of Sewall and Kauffman with an exultation that "no visitor to Washington need be told that we are a martial people."[53]

The conflation of soldiers' salutes and commanders' reviews spread readily to volunteer generals elected to public office after the war. *Monumental News* praised sculptor F. Wellington Ruckstuhl in 1898 for his "perhaps unique" design for a monument to John F. Hartranft, who had parlayed his commission as a brigadier general of the U.S. Volunteers into two terms as governor of Pennsylvania. The statue depicted Hartranft "on his return from the war, saluting the people who applaud him." The horse assumed a complementary role. "As he proudly walks over the palm and laurel branches strewn at his feet," observed a description of Hartranft's mount, "he seems to show that he feels the occasion is as much a triumph for him as for his master."[54] A few years later Ruckstuhl sold a similar composition to the state of South Carolina for its tribute to Wade Hampton, the planter whose career in the Confederate cavalry positioned him to lead the 1876 campaign to overthrow Reconstruction. The sculptor explained that he "decided to represent Hampton as cantering down in front of the lines of his troops at review and saluting them as they cheered him." Once again Ruckstuhl tried "to show the horse as he hears these cheers as if he knew and said to himself 'this is the chief's

day but I am in it.'" In both northern and southern versions, the parallel enthusiasm of the imagined admirers and the horse underscored the mastery
of the reviewing commander. Similar disciplinary authority animated the
equestrian monument to Confederate general and postwar Georgia politician John B. Gordon unveiled in Atlanta in 1907. Like the Sherman equestrian on Pennsylvania Avenue, the Lost Cause hero depicted "majestically
in reviewing attitude on the northwest corner of the state capitol grounds"
established a mixed military and civilian tableau "where every year the long
Memorial day parade will pass it as if in review, on the way to the Confederate monument at the cemetery."[55]

The monument to Charles Devens dedicated in Worcester, Massachusetts, in July 1906 most fully elaborated the shift involved in widespread
adoption of the review pose. Shortly after Devens's death in 1891 his former
law partner, longtime U.S. senator George Frisbie Hoar, proposed a statue to
honor "our late eminent and beloved fellow citizen," but the idea languished
until taken up a decade later by the veterans' association of the Fifteenth
Massachusetts Regiment, of which Devens was the founding colonel. The
new campaign secured municipal funding for a monument to soldiers from
Worcester County, to be surmounted by an equestrian statue of Devens.[56]
The foregrounding of the commander in the courthouse memorial offered
a sharp contrast to the 1874 town monument on Worcester Common, less
than a mile away, which featured statues of three rank-and-file soldiers and a
sailor and listed the names of the 397 local men who lost their lives in the war.

The decision to honor Devens as a military leader typified the recent reconfiguration of American priorities. Although he advanced from his regimental commission to command a brigade and then a division in the Army
of the Potomac, he glaringly failed to achieve much battlefield success. Proponents of the monument acknowledged that his military record was less
distinguished than his postwar career as attorney general of the United States
and justice of the Supreme Judicial Court of Massachusetts. But even Hoar,
an outspoken critic of American jingoism, cagily maintained that Devens
should be remembered first as a soldier because "whatever may be said by
the philosopher, the moralist, or the preacher, the instincts of the greater
portion of mankind will lead them to award the highest meed of admiration
to the military character."[57]

William F. Draper, who chaired the Devens committee after Hoar's
death, confirmed by example his predecessor's argument. Like Devens a volunteer in the war, Draper rose to the rank of lieutenant colonel; his largest
command was a depleted regiment. After he accepted discharge in October

1864, he was awarded brevet rank as colonel and brigadier general. He returned to his family's large-scale textile manufacturing interests in Hopedale, Massachusetts, which led him to Congress and a plum appointment as U.S. ambassador to Italy. Upon his death in 1910, his widow commissioned Daniel Chester French to make an equestrian statue for Milford, Massachusetts, that depicted Draper in a resplendent dress uniform, evidently reviewing troops. Congressional representative and future secretary of war John W. Weeks amplified the image in observing that "'captain of industry' is a modern coined phrase, intended to describe the strong, masterful man who accomplishes results. General Draper was such a man." In French's statues of Devens and Draper, the lawyer and the industrialist blended into the army general, celebrating the extraction of obedience through compulsion.[58]

Devens's personification of the relationship between military command and civilian authority was especially dramatic because he had played an important role in the controversies over the Fugitive Slave Act of 1850. As federal marshal in Boston he had cooperated in the fiercely contested rendition of Thomas Sims, a runaway returned to Georgia with the assistance of U.S. Marines. Massachusetts governor Curtis Guild began his dedicatory remarks with Devens's enforcement of the "odious" law. Guild's excuse that Devens "executed the law as he found it" suggested how much the United States had changed since George William Curtis observed at the unveiling of the Sedgwick statue at West Point in 1868 that "discipline and obedience, indeed, are indispensable to military service; but when the position of any honorable man anywhere requires him to do what seems to him unjust, mean, wicked, he will resign his position, and retain his manly honor."[59] Curtis emphasized that military virtue was an incomplete and sometimes inaccurate guide to civic duty, even for men in uniform. The statue of Devens at the Worcester courthouse showed that groups powerful enough to sponsor monuments had come to favor a more regimented conception of public order.

Although the emergence of the review redefined leadership as an act of supervision rather than an act of representation, the motif did little to identify the attributes of an exemplary leader. The new imagery offered no replacement for the egalitarian interactions, sublimation of nature, and shared risks that constituted authority in the democratic memorials that culminated in Saint-Gaudens and White's monument to Farragut. As the basis for compliance shifted from consent to command, it became urgent to explain whether individuality mattered in an age of institutional power. That question shaped a separate set of Civil War monuments.

When Congress discussed the Sherman Statue Commission's disregard for its advisory jury in 1896, former Union general and longtime Connecticut senator Joseph R. Hawley declared that he favored "a popular statue of Gen. Sherman—such a one as his old soldiers would recognize at half a mile distance; not a mere work of art, which might be entitled 'The American General.'" The portrait of Sherman at the Grand Review was such a distinct pose, but the multiplication of the motif tended toward homogenization. The convention demonstrated the power of a metropolitan establishment that extended from the New England courts and mills administered by Devens and Draper to the New South interests represented by Hampton and Gordon. Firmly ensconced at the apex of that establishment, Saint-Gaudens took the occasion to address its stress points in the Logan monument commissioned in September 1888 but not begun until three years before its Chicago unveiling in July 1897. The sculptor's celebration of the inspiring hero envisioned a class unity achieved through patriotic restraint on elites' exercise of power. Several years after the Logan dedication, the vexing relationship between institutionalized authority and individual leadership prompted bitter controversy over an equestrian monument to Sheridan.

Embracing the narrative specificity he had eschewed in his Farragut and Lincoln statues, Saint-Gaudens imagined Logan at the peak of his war, metaphorically raising an American flag to rally the Army of the Tennessee upon McPherson's death in the Battle of Atlanta.[60] After that triumph, Sherman had passed over Logan for permanent command of the unit because the Illinois politician had not trained at West Point or served in the regular army. He had fought as a lieutenant of volunteer forces in the Mexican War and participated in the Illinois militia before his election to a seat in Congress, which he resigned to found the volunteer Union regiment that he headed as colonel, from which he advanced through the ranks to lead a brigade, a division, and a corps. Logan never forgave the slight, and during his long postwar career in the House and Senate he was a vigorous critic of the army and especially West Point. He was hardly antimilitary. He appreciated that the Prussian model of compulsory service in a large standing army was "too closely allied with the methods of monarchy to find any imitation in a republican government," but he sought widespread basic training "to make of every youth an inchoate and available soldier" in a time of crisis. Mostly he resented West Point for "arrogating to itself the sole military knowledge of a people military by natural impulse and by the general habits and sur-

FIGURE 3.10. Augustus Saint-Gaudens and Stanford White, Logan Monument, Chicago, 1894–97. Courtesy of Chicago History Museum.

roundings of their life." He ridiculed the Academy's record in identifying promising officers and emphasized the pool of talent that had not received special training, such as himself. His attack on the school had resonance beyond the military in a period when educational institutions increasingly defined American class structure. Logan's condemnation of "the spirit of aristocracy" at West Point encompassed not only the monopoly of rank but also the more general "class-feeling" exhibited by graduates who had benefited from a rare college education that afforded officers "ready entrée into every grade of society," while they disdained the men they commanded.[61] Saint-Gaudens, an immigrant shoemaker's son grateful for the opportunity to attend the École des Beaux-Arts, showed considerable sympathy for the challenges confronted by the capable outsider.

The monument particularly honored Logan's wartime response to the frustration of his ambition. Unlike Hooker, who gave up his corps command when passed over for the same assignment that Logan coveted, the volunteer served faithfully until the end of the war. He supposedly also resisted an opportunity for revenge when Grant sent him to take over the Army of the Cumberland in place of Thomas, who had advised Sherman against promotion of someone who was not a fellow West Pointer. By traveling to Nashville at less than his usual breakneck pace, Logan was said to have enabled Thomas to retain command upon unleashing the successful attack that Grant was impatiently awaiting. Dedication orator George R. Peck called this moment of temptation "one of the most picturesque situations of the war," especially because Logan "was not easily controlled." "But this is his glory," Peck concluded. "The self-willed, dominant temper always yielded submissively to the stronger spirit of patriotism."[62]

The politics of passion described by Peck had recently given rise to a new phrase, "the man on horseback." The term originated in the brief but spectacular career of French general Georges Ernest Boulanger, who built up huge popularity in the late 1880s through fierce *revanchisme*, shrewd gestures such as permitting soldiers to grow beards, and the fine figure he made astride his black horse. Sacked as war minister for his monarchical sympathies, he initiated a political movement that seemed likely in 1889 to ripen into a military coup that would topple the Third Republic. After he drew back at a key moment, he fell even more rapidly than he had risen and eventually committed suicide at his mistress's grave in 1891. Although the United States faced little prospect of a military coup, the idea of "the man on horseback" was highly pertinent to domestic anxieties. Labor strife, immigration, and economic distress deepened middle-class and elite fear of demagoguery in the Populist era. Apart from any radical prospects, the rapid expansion of metropolitan newspapers and mass-circulation magazines facilitated the building of individualized followings. Herbert Croly observed in *The Promise of American Life* (1909) that "each of our leading reformers is more or less a man on horseback."[63] Like *boulangisme*, political movements seemed increasingly tied to the strengths and weaknesses of personalities.

Saint-Gaudens, who adhered to the tradition that the equestrian monument was the highest form of sculpture, recognized the opportunity that the rise of "the man on horseback" presented for a genre that dramatized ideas about individual and social stability. Ever since the Renaissance, the Platonic image of the upright charioteer reining in his passions and appetites had pervaded the equestrian symbolism of the right to reign. Self-regulation, often through the etymologically equine chivalric code, was essential to governance of the body politic. The republican counterpart was Washington's

Models of Leadership

serene self-denial as portrayed by Brown and other artists. Equipoise generally defined the ideal of military command from Donatello's fifteenth-century *Gattamelata* through the end of the equestrian genre. Saint-Gaudens's statue of Logan, in contrast, depicted a battlefield commander and future statesman giving full vent to his passions, his long hair flowing and chest expanding as he dramatically clenched a flagstaff topped by an eagle spreading its wings. The painfully contorted front leg of the horse suggested the struggle that preceded Logan's next step after the victory at Atlanta. Like Peck's oration, Saint-Gaudens's statue indicated that the snubbed hero's passionate patriotism overpowered his proud temper. Lorado Taft, noting the contrast between this inner tension and the audience rapport that marked Saint-Gaudens's previous Chicago monument, observed that "psychologically, the Lincoln and the Logan statues present an analysis not less remarkable than is the technique which has given it visible expression."[64]

Although original, Saint-Gaudens's conception was not unique. It paralleled the Joan of Arc monument by Émanuel Frémiet installed at the Place des Pyramides in Paris in 1875, which featured a woman surmounting the carnality coded female in Neo-Platonic imagery. Frémiet's statue of a slight maiden controlling a hooded steed imbued the symbolically irrational arrangement with an aura of mystical faith. The patriotism of Joan, who raised the banner of France, provided a religious foundation for the patriotism of Logan. The monuments also served similar political purposes. Minister of public instruction Jules Simon commissioned Frémiet's work as a means of reconciliation between republicans and Catholics in the surge of patriotism that followed the Franco-Prussian War.[65] The Logan statue, which involved some of the Chicago businessmen who sponsored the 1895 dedication of a monument in Oak Woods cemetery to Confederates who died at the Camp Douglas prison, identified militant patriotism as a basis for postwar reconciliation of white northerners and southerners. Peck rejoiced that 200 members of a Chicago camp of the United Confederate Veterans joined in the dedication parade.

Saint-Gaudens's composition identified the flag as a bridge across not only the sections but also class and ethnic divisions in the home of the Haymarket bombing and epicenter of the Pullman strike. Governor John R. Tanner recalled Lincoln's observation that the war against secession was a fight against anarchy, and he emphasized that "national preservation and national supremacy are but equivalent words for law and order." The governor described the Logan monument as an answer to "the spirit of sedition" which whispered in the ears of the unfortunate "that their courts are an organized system of oppression, and that only the rich and the great can receive benefit from our laws and institutions."[66] The United States offered opportunity to self-made men like Logan, and his career showed that its leaders subordinated their desires to the good of the nation.

Frémiet's and Saint-Gaudens's hopeful images suffered similar fates. The French right wing gradually appropriated the public memory of Joan of Arc, who came to symbolize persistent divisions in the Third Republic. Led by the Grand Army of the Republic (GAR), which Logan had helped found in 1866 and with which he remained closely associated for the rest of his life, Union veterans were making the American flag an instrument of reactionary discipline. Saint-Gaudens designed the Logan monument shortly after the Columbian Exposition and could not have fully foreseen the long-term deepening of new rituals like the Pledge of Allegiance, but the veterans' flag regime was ominous for the sculptor's vision of patriotism as a force that restrained the exercise of power. A clearer measure of the self-subordination to be expected from Gilded Age elites was the 1896 decision by the U.S. Supreme Court under Chief Justice Melville Fuller, a founding member of the Logan monument commission, that ruled unconstitutional the taxation of personal income from corporate dividends and bond interest. Saint-Gaudens found little social harmony in his work on the Logan project. Reporting himself "completely disaffected with America" and worn out by urban friction despite the privileges he enjoyed, he moved to France shortly after the unveiling.[67]

If Saint-Gaudens's response to "the man on horseback" ultimately collapsed into ritualized enforcement of community order, the controversy over a Sheridan monument for Washington offered a clearer choice between a celebration of charismatic authority and the ceremonious hierarchy of the review motif. Officers of the Society of the Army of the Cumberland arranged for J. Q. A. Ward to meet Sheridan after the 1887 unveiling of the sculptor's monument to James Garfield in Washington, a work that satisfied Society members as fully as the Thomas equestrian they had previously commissioned Ward to create. In his interview with Sheridan, who had succeeded Sherman as commanding general of the U.S. Army, Ward found him especially proud of his career since the Civil War, "speaking lightly of the famous ride at Winchester and other incidents in his campaigns." Ward made a study of Sheridan's head, which the artist considered "a perfect type of the military commander" that "expressed the possibilities of his earlier fighting age, at the same time giving a larger view of his mature character as a great commander with indications of a capacity for statesmanship." When

FIGURE 3.11. John Quincy Adams Ward, model for
Monument to Philip Sheridan, 1891–1906.
Photograph © Peter A. Juley & Son Collection, Smithsonian American Art Museum.

approached by the veterans' committee upon enactment of federal legislation for a monument, Ward proposed to portray the middle-aged, heavy-set
Sheridan in full dress uniform, with his many decorations, as if leading a
parade past a presidential reviewing stand while a crowd cheered. The sketch
model approved by the veterans in 1892 anticipated the trend toward conflation of military and civilian authority in a review motif. But uneven health

and the pressures of a final major commission slowed the aging Ward, and when he finally exhibited a full-scale model after the unveiling of the Sherman, Hartranft, Hampton, Gordon, and Devens statues, a critic observed fairly that "the theme is the familiar one."[68]

From the outset Sheridan's widow wanted the monument to depict a lithe young Civil War cavalry hero, and Ward's delay eventually snapped her patience with his concept. She pressed for rejection of the full-scale model on the grounds that it was "not sufficiently characteristic of General Sheridan" and "did not suggest the brilliancy of his military achievements."[69] Ward tried to taper the girth of his rider, but compromise was impossible. The dispute left the War Department in a delicate position after it relieved the veterans of decision-making authority because the project relied almost entirely on federal funds. Ward was the acknowledged dean of his profession, the first and longest-serving president of the National Sculpture Society. Army officers sent by Secretary of War William Howard Taft to inspect the model reported that they admired it. In the end Taft decided to defer to the wishes of Sheridan's widow and his younger brother, a retired brigadier general. He dismissed Ward and in August 1907 turned to the replacement sculptor that Irene Sheridan favored, Gutzon Borglum.[70]

Less prominent at this point in his career than his brother Solon, whose cowboy statues had prompted one critic to call him "probably the most original sculptor that this country has produced," the forty-year-old Borglum saw that the Sheridan commission gave him a chance to match Solon's monument to Bucky O'Neill and other Arizonans who died in the Rough Rider unit during the Spanish-American War, dedicated in Prescott in July 1907.[71] Borglum chose to depict Sheridan on the October 1864 ride from Winchester to Cedar Creek in which the general turned around retreating soldiers and led them to a pivotal victory. Thomas Buchanan Read's poem "Sheridan's Ride," his painting with the same title, and numerous chromolithographs had made this incident the single most celebrated example of battlefield leadership in the Civil War. Borglum told Irene Sheridan that "no other point in his whole campaign gives me the opportunity to represent at once his action and the force of his character." His statue depicted Sheridan abruptly halting his horse Rienzi, whose head twisted sharply in response. Holding his hat in his fully outstretched arm, Sheridan waved back the soldiers he met on their retreat from Cedar Creek. Borglum unsuccessfully proposed the inscription "Turn back men — you're not beaten yet."[72] The transformation of defeat into victory demonstrated the leadership potential of a dramatic personality, and the incorporation of cowboy rhythms popularized

FIGURE 3.12. Gutzon Borglum, Sheridan Monument, Washington, DC, 1907–8.
Courtesy of the Library of Congress.

by Solon Borglum, Frederic Remington, Alexander Phimister Proctor, and other artists identified the military commander monument with the ideal of strenuous living so widely prescribed to the metropolitan establishment as a strategy for moral purification.

The orator at the November 1908 unveiling was President Theodore Roosevelt, "the man on horseback" in American public life since the defining moment imagined by Remington in *The Charge of the Rough Riders at San Juan Hill* (1898), in which the only mounted figure in the field led the regiment forward. Roosevelt liked to speak at Civil War monument dedications. He participated in ceremonies for statues of Sherman, Sheridan, Slocum, and McClellan, as well as several soldier monuments. He used the platform to promote his military buildup, arguing that "no man is warranted in feeling pride in the deeds of the Army and Navy of the past if he does not back up the Army and Navy of the Present." He warmly encouraged sectional reconciliation and hinted that the opposing sides shared a common purpose "in the great years when Grant, Farragut, Sherman, Thomas, and Sheridan, when Lee and Jackson and the Johnstons, the valiant men of the North and the valiant men of the South, fought to finish the great civil war." He maintained that the Civil War was an unsurpassed example of "the exalting of a lofty ideal over merely material well-being" and that its veterans had learned that "the life worth living is the life of endeavor, the life of effort, the life of worthy strife." Military service was the most broadly available social foundation for the masculinity that Roosevelt could also afford to pursue on his Badlands ranch and big-game hunts. His conclusion that "the qualities needed to make a good soldier, in their final analysis, are the qualities needed to make a good citizen" implied that the qualities needed to make a good battlefield commander were the qualities needed to make a good president.[73] Roosevelt rested his claim to this devotion from his constituents on his flamboyantly muscular personal character.

The extent to which the Sheridan monument paralleled Roosevelt's model of charismatic authority lent a current of self-reflection to the president's discussion of a general who "showed his greatness with that touch of originality which we call genius." Admiration mingled with frustration in Roosevelt's observation that "indeed this quality of brilliance has been in one sense a disadvantage to his reputation, for it has tended to overshadow his solid ability."[74] Exuberant though it was, the monument reflected a commitment to institutional regularity. The War Department rejected Ward's model not for lack of sympathy with his review motif but because Taft concluded that protocol required deference to Irene Sheridan. Although she had special leverage as the daughter of a brigadier general who was for many years the second-ranking officer in the Quartermaster's Department, federal monument commissions were similarly accommodating to Virginia Farragut, Almira Hancock, Ellen McClellan, and especially Mary Logan. Army officials did not ordinarily believe that the images of military commanders and cowboys should be similar.

In this judgement the military community was more in agreement with the National Sculpture Society than the dismissal of Ward indicated. A supporter of Ward's model argued that "distinctly 'Sheridan's Ride' is not a subject for an equestrian statue" because horse and rider were too volatile. The hero of Cedar Creek was "possibly a more picturesque but certainly a less statuesque subject than the Commanding General of the Army."[75] These aesthetic principles shaped equestrian monuments around the country. Beaux arts sculptors produced still portraits of such dynamic Civil War commanders as Nathan Bedford Forrest in Memphis (1905), George Armstrong Custer in Monroe, Michigan (1910), and John Hunt Morgan in Lexington, Kentucky (1911).[76] Solon Borglum's statue of John B. Gordon was more typical than his brother's interpretation of Sheridan. The culmination of the pattern was the campaign launched in 1914 by New York governor Martin H. Glynn to place a monument to Sheridan on the grounds of the state capitol.

Models of Leadership

Glynn sought a monument that would let "all the world know him as his soldiers knew him — mounted on the fieriest steed he could find, with his cap in his hand and an invitation on his lips to follow him to glory and to fame."[77] French recognized the opportunity to vindicate his former mentor and late friend, and he persuaded the Albany sponsors to adopt Ward's model.

The threat represented by the cowboy of individuality carried to the point of irresponsibility was only one reason that the image of the military commander turned in a different direction. The cowboy was also supposedly a vanishing figure produced by the era before the expansion of railroads and invention of barbed-wire fences. The icon epitomized nostalgia when the economic, military, and artistic communities most invested in monuments to Civil War commanders promoted a modernity identified with bureaucratic rather than charismatic leadership. They would find a fertile theme in the most successful general of the war.

THE BRAIN OF AN ARMY

Commemoration of Ulysses S. Grant offered the fullest test of the relationship between military and civil authority. The idealization of public endorsement that gave rise to the review motif entered only occasionally into the Grant projects that continued for many years after his death in 1885. The notion of charismatic power proved even less significant. Although disappointment in Grant's presidency may have caused some hesitation to celebrate his enormous popularity, more influential was the reconceptualization of the American state underscored by the eventual stakes of Grant remembrance. The most important monument was crucial to a reconfiguration of the national capital that paralleled a reorganization of the U.S. Army. At the same time that the equestrian group placed in front of the halls of Congress turned its back on the representatives, however, the transformation of American society so prominently traced to the Civil War opened space for artistic ambivalence toward the modern order. The centralization of authority ironically empowered some independent leadership.

The burial of Grant raised the question of whether the United States had a center and where it might be. After Julia Grant accepted an interment site overlooking the Hudson River, boosters exulted that this permanent adoption of the couple's last home ratified the status of New York as the first city of the nation. The predominance of finance in this claim, personified by monument committee treasurer J. P. Morgan, appalled Americans elsewhere. Veterans called on Congress to mandate burial of Grant in Washington or Arlington National Cemetery. The GAR soon commissioned a standing statue to be placed in the Capitol across from a statue of Washington. Chicago aimed for a national commemoration in Grant's native Midwest. The campaign for an equestrian monument, chaired by a former chief of staff of the Army of the Tennessee married to local potentate William B. Ogden's niece, concentrated on Chicago the commemorative interests of the Society of the Army of the Tennessee, which sponsored the McPherson and Sherman statues in Washington.[78]

Some of these initiatives enjoyed exceptional success in the standard attempt to present a monument as a voluntary outpouring of public admiration. With an eastward dig that the heartland campaign involved "no committee of a hundred millionaires," the *Chicago Tribune* reported that 100,000 people contributed a total of $65,000 to the equestrian statue unveiled in October 1891.[79] Fund-raising for Grant's Tomb had by this time reached $155,000, an extraordinary total diminished to the point of national ridicule by the widely publicized initial goal of $1 million. The committee set a budget of $500,000 in an 1890 design competition that resulted in the selection of a design by New York architect John H. Duncan based on French academic reconstructions of ancient mausoleum prototypes.[80] Horace Porter, vice president of the Pullman Palace Car Company since ending his long service on Grant's military and presidential staffs, led a reorganization of the monument committee in February 1892 and soon launched an ambitious effort to remedy the funding shortfall. The hallmark of the campaign was its recognition that economic relations rather than civic ties defined the community. More than 200 auxiliary committees, run by more than 2,000 volunteers, sought donations from workers in every conceivable trade in town, including locomotive engineers, wood dealers, stockbrokers, manufacturers of gas fixtures, plasterers, corset-makers, and restaurant entrepreneurs and employees (for which Charles C. Delmonico chaired the committee). Porter's plan for the businessmen "thoroughly to round up the people upon whom they are expected to call" may have fostered pressures along the lines that recent adoption of the secret ballot tried to dispel from politics, but the drive resulted in broad participation. The committee met its goal by raising $350,000 in little over two months and set the monument on the path to completion, although without most of the statuary that Duncan wanted to embellish the neoclassical building.[81]

Henry James, who was in 1904 one of the more than 500,000 visitors that Grant's Tomb attracted annually for several decades after it opened in 1897, reported that the monument restated long-standing questions about American inheritance of Old World forms. "Here, if ever," he observed, "was a great democratic demonstration caught in the fact, the nakedest possible effort to strike the note of the august." Taking up the invited comparison with Napoléon's tomb at Les Invalides, the novelist noted that the French military compound was "a holy of holies, a great temple jealously guarded and formally approached." In contrast, Grant's Tomb, "as open as an hotel or a railroad station," tried to "play its part without pomp and circumstance to 'back' it, without mystery or ceremony to protect it, without Church or State to intervene on its behalf, with only its immediacy, its familiarity of interest to circle it about." James concluded that the Riverside Park pavilion was no less successful than the Paris dome. The earnestness of Grant's Tomb and the moral legacy of Union victory showed that with "an original sincerity of intention, an original propriety of site, and above all an original high value of name and fame . . . publicity, familiarity, immediacy, as I have called them, carried far enough, may stalk in and out of the shrine with their hands in their pockets and their hats on their heads and yet not dispel the Presence." The provincialism he had lamented a quarter century earlier in a famous description of Nathaniel Hawthorne's barren cultural environment ("no aristocracy, no church, no army . . . no Oxford, nor Eton") did not preclude effective Civil War remembrance.[82]

The United States had changed more during James's long residence abroad than the author realized, as commemoration of Grant in Washington demonstrated. The commissioning of an equestrian monument intersected with two important developments in the elaboration of the American state, the design of a grand capital and the invigoration of the army. Both of those initiatives drew on European prototypes, and both gained momentum from the imperial powers asserted by the United States in the Spanish-American War. The architects who argued for formation of a national commission of fine arts and the army officers who called for the establishment of a general staff shared in a broader national pattern of professionalization that strengthened the influence of particular educational institutions. The advocates emphasized the rationalization of decision-making authority and the importance of city planning and military planning. Closely tied to the largest corporations of the era, the artists and army officers contributed to a consolidation of class structure by advancing alternatives to representative government. The Grant memorial in Washington epitomized the emerging administrative state.

Grenville Dodge launched the campaign for a Grant monument at the 1895 meeting of the Society of the Army of the Tennessee shortly after announcing that he had wrung an additional $30,000 from Congress to supplement the original $50,000 appropriation for the Sherman statue. Claiming to have "discovered" while in Washington that no arrangements were set for a Grant monument, he reported that he had begun to "prepare a way." Dodge had no intention of repeating Horace Porter's exhausting grassroots campaign for Grant's Tomb, for which Dodge served as vice president. Instead he proposed to establish the principle that "it is the duty of the Government to do this work."[83] A former member of Congress from Iowa, he found his task easier when political ally and Society of the Army of the Tennessee comrade David B. Henderson became speaker of the House of Representatives. Close friend William B. Allison of Iowa piloted Senate passage of the measure in February 1901. The authorized budget for the statue was $250,000, five times the original commitment to the Sherman and Sheridan memorials. Congress had previously paid for all of some Civil War commander monuments, and for most in the other cases, but Dodge's success bore the mark of a premier railroad lobbyist.

As Dodge knew, proposals had arisen shortly after Grant's death to link his remembrance in Washington to the construction of a Potomac River bridge to Arlington National Cemetery that would bring visitors to the graves of soldiers he had led and symbolize the Union he had restored. Prospects for bridge legislation were excellent when Dodge suggested to the veterans that a Grant statue might be part of the project, but opponents of the large expenditure parried it for several years. The Army Corps of Engineers continued to support the proposed bridge, though redesignating it after the Spanish-American War as a memorial to American patriotism, and in conjunction with the centennial anniversary of Washington in 1900 the Corps sponsored a design competition intended to lead to full funding. At the same time, superintendent of buildings and public grounds Col. Theodore A. Bingham released centennial plans to enlarge the White House and lay out Potomac Park, recently created by landfill west and south of the Washington Monument. James McMillan of Michigan, chair of the Senate committee on the District of Columbia, embraced a fervent appeal by the American Institute of Architects for the appointment of prominent artists to work with the Army Corps of Engineers on these plans. In addition to its influence at a crucial juncture in the development of the capital, the campaign looked toward establishment of a permanent national commission of fine arts like the boards created for Boston in 1890 and New York in 1896. The legislation to fund a Grant memorial proceeded alongside the parliamentary maneuvers by which McMillan fashioned the Senate Park Commission in March

1901, as Allison was a strong supporter of his colleague's initiative. Because Secretary of War Elihu Root, who supervised public buildings in Washington, also backed McMillan and was one of the three members of the Grant commission, the equestrian monument offered a tangible piece for the Senate Park Commission to incorporate into its semiauthorized planning.[84]

Root was currently orchestrating a series of measures to expand and restructure the army. Two weeks before it authorized the Grant statue, Congress quadrupled the permanent authorized strength of the force from 27,500 to 100,000 soldiers. This increase responded to Root's efforts to subdue the Philippines and garrison the new overseas possessions. The Wall Street corporate lawyer next aimed to channel public dissatisfaction with the army's performance in the Spanish-American War into a reorganization long sought by line officers eager to control the staff bureaus that reported directly to the secretary of war. Before Root took office, Dodge had given this program a boost as chair of a blue-ribbon panel investigating the war effort. The Dodge Commission report issued in February 1899 tried not to blame individuals for mismanagement but to identify structural flaws and recommend adoption of reforms that Emory Upton had formulated when Sherman was commanding general. Against the voluble protest of incumbent Nelson Miles, whose hope to exchange high military rank for the presidency was a last gasp of the nineteenth century, the plan would eliminate the position of commanding general when Miles reached mandatory retirement and create a chief of staff, who would report to the secretary of war but control all of the bureaus in the chain of command. The army would institute rotation between the staff and line for the new general staff and the bureau staff officers, traditionally accustomed to settling permanently in Washington or other major cities. The revamping connected closely to the expansion of officer education, especially the Army War College that Root established in November 1901.[85]

Military failures in the Spanish-American War had created the impetus for Congress to consider creation of a general staff, which would undercut legislators' influence over the bureaus. At the same time, Root also realized that intervention in the Pullman strike and other labor disputes of the 1890s had turned a national spotlight on the army and the National Guard. His call for reinforcement of military professionalism and executive responsibility aimed to establish a strong public image for the new army. The monument to Grant offered a useful means toward that end.

Coordination between the Grant Memorial Commission and the Senate Park Commission was a little-publicized negotiation. Two weeks after

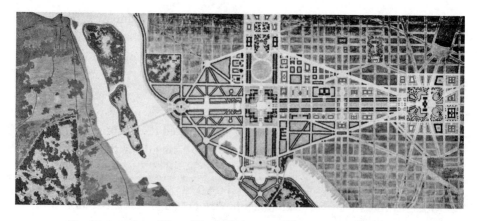

FIGURE 3.13. "Plan of the Mall Showing Development to 1914 in
Accordance with Recommendations of the Park Commission of 1901."
Courtesy of the Library of Congress.

passage of the authorizing legislation, Dodge, Root, and the chair of the joint
committee on the Library of Congress decided at their initial meeting to
place the Grant statue in the lot southwest of the White House that balanced
the southeast lot where the Sherman statue was under construction. The
two commissions met together a month later, by which point Root had with
characteristic foresight and tact secured Irene Sheridan's permission to place
the delayed monument to her husband in the southwest lot despite her preference to put it near her home on what was already called Sheridan Circle.
The Grant Memorial Commission issued a competition program in June
1901 that looked toward installation of its statue either in the southwest lot or
due south of the White House, flanked by Sherman and Sheridan and near a
large area designated as a military parade ground on the Potomac Park plans
prepared by Bingham, who was the executive and disbursing officer of the
commission.[86] Senate Park Commission members Daniel Burnham, Charles
McKim, Frederick Law Olmsted Jr., and commission secretary Charles
Moore took a summer study trip to Europe without the fourth commission
member, Augustus Saint-Gaudens, whose poor health had prompted him to
resume residence in the United States. While abroad the architects settled on
the basic plan to extend a realigned Mall past the Washington Monument to
a western anchor on the Potomac Park riverfront, at the site where Bingham
had envisioned a parade ground. The proposed structure would serve as the
Washington terminus for the memorial bridge to Arlington National Cemetery and the point of origin for a parkway along Rock Creek that would connect to the National Zoological Park opened in 1894.

Models of Leadership

In late August the Senate Park Commission reported to Root its plan to make the western anchor a Grant Memorial Arch, which would place the tribute to the Union commander in line with the monument to his Revolutionary predecessor Washington and the Arlington mansion of his Confederate counterpart Lee. Dodge endorsed the proposed site but would not switch from a statue, which the monument legislation specified, to an arch. Dodge thought a statue would better "represent the character and individuality of the subject," as the competition program hoped, and a return to Congress would jeopardize the Grant project. The Senate Park Commission had not mustered approval in the House of Representatives even for the artists' preparation of plans, let alone for execution of the controversial work that McMillan's team urged. McKim reassigned the western anchor to a Lincoln memorial and asked Dodge to consider placement of the Grant statue in the large plaza that would serve as a transition space between the Capitol and the Mall. This site would position the Grant statue as an entering wedge for the Senate Park Commission's plan to eliminate the Botanic Garden and clear the urban forest on the Mall. Dodge agreed, and the Senate Park Commission drawings and models displayed at the Corcoran Gallery in early 1901 featured a Grant memorial as the centerpiece of a new Union Square. Soon after that exhibit closed, the Corcoran presented the twenty-seven plaster models received in the Grant Memorial Commission's design competition. For assistance in reviewing these proposals Root empaneled a jury comprised of Burnham, McKim, Saint-Gaudens, French, and top-ranking retired generals John Schofield and Wesley Merritt. The group combined three members of the Senate Park Commission and Root's star witnesses in the ongoing congressional hearings on the bill to establish a general staff. McKim laughed that the meeting run by Schofield "seemed nothing less than a military tribunal," but Root's acknowledgment of artists' expertise tacitly refuted Dodge's disregard for jury advice in the competition for the Sherman statue.[87]

French's participation attested not only to his standing as one of the leading sculptors in the country but also and more specifically to the acclaim for his equestrian monument to Grant, unveiled at Fairmount Park in April 1899. French wrote that the work depicted "a moment when Grant was surveying a battle-field from an eminence and he is supposed to be intent upon the operations of the forces before him." The compliant horse, in French's words "merely obedient to the will of his rider," suggested a machine rather than a living force. Grant's sugarloaf hat and long military cape with upturned collar added an air of mystery, consistent with the sculptor's vision of the commander's "sphinxlike character" and French's effort "to give something of the latent force of the man, manifesting itself through perfect passivity."[88] This interpretation differed sharply from the "rude simplicity" attributed to Grant by Rebisso's equestrian monument in Chicago and from all monuments that emphasized the close relationship between a leader and his troops.[89] Despite Grant's wartime reputation for unpretentious directness, critics found the opacity compelling. The *New York Times* thought the rider's attitude "indicative of deep thought." *Monumental News* admired "the passiveness, the sphinx like character of the man, the soldier; the logical solver of strategic problems." French's portrait would exercise a strong influence on submissions in Washington.[90]

The entry favored by the artists and the generals served their goals in ways that the proposal did not entirely foresee. The official description from architect Edward Pearce Casey and sculptor Henry M. Shrady advised installation of the monument due south of the White House, between the commissioned statues of Sherman and Sheridan that both featured review motifs. Casey and Shrady suggested a long, low platform "facing the President's Parade, from which reviews of troops may be held as occasion dictates." Grant was to be "represented in repose, as if in the act of reviewing troops." The equestrian statue stood on a pedestal that had side panels with reliefs of infantry marching and hurrying into action. The flanks of the platform would feature animated ensembles of artillery and cavalry.[91] The Senate Park Commission's relocation of the monument to Union Square obviated its intended function as a presidential reviewing stand but made a large terrace ornamented by three separate groups highly desirable.

Casey and Shrady's proposal was much more firmly grounded in contemporary military thought than any of the rival submissions. Casey was the son of the army chief engineer who completed the Washington Monument and the grandson of another general. The architect and his collaborator Shrady had both joined the Seventh Regiment while studying at Columbia. Their emphasis on the distance between the contemplative leader and the harried artillery and cavalry units dramatized the role of the chief commander as, in a phrase given currency by an influential book about the German general staff, "the brain of an army."[92]

Consistent with the concept of the general staff, Shrady and Casey's design differed radically from all other entries in declining to focus on the resolution of the Civil War. The frenzied artillery and cavalry groups anticipated endless warfare, both in the sense of war without cease and war without specific purpose. This motif supported the fundamental premises of Root's re-

FIGURE 3.14. Daniel Chester French, Edward C. Potter, and Frank Miles Day, Grant Monument, Philadelphia, 1892–98. Photograph by Gregory Benson © 2008, courtesy of the Association for Public Art.

FIGURE 3.15. Henry M. Shrady and Edward Pearce Casey,
model of Grant Memorial, Washington, DC, 1902.
Courtesy of Thomas Cooper Library, University of South Carolina.

structuring: that the mission of the peacetime army was to expect and prepare for war, and that the most effective wartime organization of the army
should determine its peacetime organization. The ineptitude of the army
in the Spanish-American War provided an opportunity to implement this
policy far beyond any new geopolitical pressures. The vision of endless war as
a mandate for military reform dated back to the waning of Indian conflicts,
which eliminated the historic central purpose of the regular army.

Although propelled initially by institutional interests within the military,
the public traction exercised by the image of endless war reflected industrial
strife at least as much as international ambitions. If the statues of energetic
but disciplined soldiers that developed in the 1890s offered a model for the
dutiful worker, the Grant monument in Washington presented the attitude

of the twentieth-century corporate executive or government official. He was thoroughly detached from the messy labor of war, in which Shrady depicted one cavalryman pinned under a horse, about to be trampled. An artilleryman pitched back in the wagon, perhaps shot, as the bridle controlling a horse snapped; another soldier huddled in misery and desperation at the edge of the wagon. Shrady promised no harmony between the leaders and the led, or between classes in industrial society. The impassive commander focused on the broad battlefield rather than individual people.

This version of Grant resembled Root, the consummate insider whose daughter married the general's grandson in 1907, but the hero of the monument was also Shrady. Like Root's protégés Robert Bacon and Henry Stimson, the artist emerged from the heart of the social environment in which the ideal of the strenuous life took hold. The son of a prominent Manhattan physician who had attended to Grant's fatal throat cancer, Shrady dropped out of law school after a term and worked without enthusiasm in the firm of his brother-in-law, Jay Gould's son. At twenty-seven he began to seek a career in art, first trying painting but soon specializing in small bronze animals along the lines popularized by Remington. This trajectory invited anxieties about his usefulness, and throughout his life Shrady was, in French's words, "an intensely nervous man, working evidently all the time and at high tension." Apart from his conventional treatment of this condition through service in the Seventh Regiment, the sculptor pursued the disciplined aestheticism that critic and painter John C. Van Dyke prescribed in *Art for Art's Sake* (1893), which sought to purify the title phrase of its bohemian connotations. Van Dyke aimed to incorporate painters in the trend toward professionalization by spurning mere illustration of literary narrative and celebrating artists' visual acuity. Shrady's monument followed those strategies closely enough to prompt admiring critic William Walton to tell a friend, "Shrady is art for art's sake all right."[93]

Shrady's artillery and cavalry groups rejected storytelling as a memorial strategy. They could not exist in the same space and time as the sculptor's proposed depiction of Grant reviewing troops, unless such scenes wracked the mind of the commander as he inspected survivors. The composition advanced opposing ideas about hierarchy, for it was the subordinate figures who commanded viewers' attention and sympathy. At the same time, the monument stressed the limits of such imaginative engagement by foreclosing almost all access to the infantry, the overwhelming majority of the army, who were flattened into low reliefs on the pedestal for the statue of the mounted general. Shrady's reliance on indeterminacy and inner conflict,

FIGURE 3.16. Henry M. Shrady, model of Artillery Group, Grant Memorial, 1902. Courtesy of Thomas Cooper Library, University of South Carolina.

rightly compared with Stephen Crane's recent *Red Badge of Courage* (1895), made his work differ from such beaux arts precedents as Saint-Gaudens's memorials to Farragut and Lincoln, which used the monumental space to synthesize complex relationships between the individual and nature and between the hero and the public rather than dramatizing tensions between the chaos of life and the order of art.[94]

An artillery officer, Shrady understood the importance of technology in the ideology of military professionalism, and he put forward a parallel claim for the expert artist. He depicted the artillery unit attempting an urgent halt, apparently under fire. The variations in the three lead horses' responses to the bridle produced a serial treatment of forelegs that clearly evoked stop-motion photographs of horses' gaits. Walton praised Shrady both for his state-of-the-art research and his "positive conviction of the frequently un-artistic—and therefore unavailable quality of these facts, the uncouthness, the apparent destruction of the very action they represent." The secret to the sculptor's "very successful realization of the action sought" was his "careful selection of the natural facts combined with a skilful use of some of the traditional methods of affecting the eye of the spectator."[95] This version of the ancient equestrian form required a sculptor as modern as a general staff officer or a city planner. Through this self-reflexivity, Shrady adhered to Van Dyke's precept that an artist should propound ideas about art to avoid becoming a mere propagandist, even as he completed an immense monument to the deepening of military influence on American government.[96]

The Grant memorial in Washington turned out to be what architect and

Models of Leadership

critic Henry Van Brunt hoped for in an 1885 magazine forum on appropriate commemoration of the hero, "the product of a national evolution of monumental form."[97] The central figure surrounded by the branches of service updated a convention that traced from James G. Batterson's monument for Green-Wood Cemetery through the Sherman equestrian on Pennsylvania Avenue. The artillery and cavalry groups shared in an intensifying animation of soldier statues, though Shrady eschewed idealization of service and sacrifice. The spatial theater of the beaux arts monument recalled Saint-Gaudens's great memorials to representative military command and oratory. Conceived in the review motif through which artists often imagined popular submission to a general's supervision, Shrady's work came to provide an emblem for a bureaucratic model of the army and the polity. The artist had, however, bypassed one important strand of commemoration in presenting an image of endless war. As the other entries in the Grant design competition indicated, the close of the Civil War remained a theme of wide appeal. The idea of resolution stimulated many memorial projects.

VISIONS *of* VICTORY

Like memorial models of leadership, commemorations of victory comprised a genre with Old World precedents that traced back to antiquity. To be sure, almost all Union monuments were in a sense victory monuments, as were a remarkable number of Confederate monuments. Beyond statues of common soldiers and heroic leaders, however, postwar Americans turned to triumphal arches, columns, and allegorical figures to define the meaning of their war. These classical forms had stimulated extensive adaptation in nineteenth-century Europe, a process that would continue alongside the development of Civil War monuments. American sponsors of remembrance sought to enter into the venerable tradition. James C. Ayer, the wealthiest manufacturer of patent medicines in the country, scoured Europe during an 1866 tour for an appropriate work of public art to present to his home city of Lowell, Massachusetts. He settled on a bronze copy of one of the two statues of winged Victory that Christian Daniel Rauch made for the Royal Palace in Munich. Ayer remarked at the Lowell unveiling that he did not think the

German prototypes were "either as appropriate or as effective as this is here" as a Civil War monument.[1]

Much of this commemorative vocabulary was new to the United States. The post-Revolutionary republic had eschewed the triumphal arch for the same anti-imperial reasons that influenced equestrian statuary. The antebellum landscape did include a few works that might be characterized as victory columns, most notably Maximilian Godefroy's monument dedicated in Baltimore in 1825 to soldiers who died in the battle for the city during the War of 1812. The many Civil War variations on the column not only featured innovations in remembrance of the rank and file, such as the introduction of soldier statues surrounding the base, but also imbued crowning figures of Victory or Peace with the fervent sense of purpose that earlier Americans had devoted to representations of Columbia or the statue of Armed Freedom atop the U.S. Capitol. In arches and allegories, monument sponsors tried to identify the implications of success in the Civil War and situate the national epic in world history.

Victory monuments unfolded along a timeline comparable to the periodization of soldier monuments and leadership monuments. Union commemoration in the early postwar years demonstrated an appreciation for the limits of military achievement. Suppression of the rebellion implied a reinstatement of lawful order rather than a martial triumph. Confederate monuments of this period occasionally addressed the southern legacy of defeat. Countervailing interpretations also took root in the immediate aftermath of the war, however, and won ascendancy as the Gilded Age plutocracy strengthened its grip on the country in the 1890s. This memorial pattern avoided introspection in favor of martial self-congratulation, dramatically but not exclusively in the context of triumphalist Confederate monuments. Union celebrations of victory rejected constraints that iconographic convention had previously associated with the consummation of national desires. The Spanish-American War expressed and reinforced the new military culture. The controversial imperial venture also strengthened a professed interest in peace initiatives within elite commercial circles, which monument sponsors complemented by looking back to the conflict settled permanently in 1865. A half century of victory monuments in both the North and the South informed American thinking about the possible ends of war by 1914.

"The Triumphal Arch is the finest and grandest expression in the vocabulary of monumental art," declared art critic Truman H. Bartlett in 1883. The arch was "the form of Honor, of Victory, of Glory, of Renown" and the epitome of "every monumental idea and ambition of a national character." It was also a link between ancients and moderns. An invention of the Romans, who "left these crowning monuments as lasting and memorable records of their power and genius," the arch had enjoyed a nineteenth-century renaissance in Napóleon's imperial Paris and the Wellington Arch (1826–30) and Marble Arch (1827–33) in London. According to Bartlett, the form reached its fullest development at the Arc de Triomphe de l'Étoile (1806–36), distinguished alike for its proportions, its decorative sculpture, and its placement on the site of a former customs gate to symbolize entrance into the city and displacement of the old regime.[2] Northerners gradually embraced the arch as a form of commemoration after the Civil War. Variations on Old World precedent advanced different interpretations of the historic transition spanned by the war. The gateways inscribed the meanings of Union victory in several types of urban landscape that confronted postwar challenges.

The brief but sharp debate over an early proposal for a triumphal arch in Worcester, Massachusetts, tested the potential of the form within a changing New England town common. Worcester had in February 1866 appointed a committee headed by new mayor James Blake to raise funds for a memorial and in September 1867 authorized the group to select a design and location. After a competition, the committee reported in December 1868 in favor of an arch suggested by Henry Hobson Richardson for installation at the center of the Common. Worcester was no longer a village, the committee observed. The population had increased from 7,500 to 25,000 during the twenty years before the war and would pass 40,000 by 1870, which ranked behind only Boston, Providence, and New Haven among New England cities. The municipality now sought a nobler public square than the disintegrating colonial Common. Blake's committee looked ahead to the removal of Old South Church and elimination of railroad tracks that had crossed the Common since 1840. The proposal hoped that "the next generation will properly lay out the Common in conformity to the demands of the arch." This renovation of the wartime mustering ground corresponded to selection of "the strongest and most enduring form of architecture" to recall the sacrifices that "spanned the deep, broad space between the old and the new life of the nation." While eager to tap the prestige of European triumphal arches, the committee also expected the first American arch to bring luster to Worcester because Richardson's rusticated design offered an original complement to the New England setting rather than an imitation of works he had studied at the École des Beaux-Arts during the war.[3]

Although supported by local newspapers as well as the prominent citizens on the committee, the proposal fell before criticism that better anticipated the future of the Common. The imperial connotations of the arch drew objections. Some citizens preferred to join other Massachusetts towns in building a memorial library, and voters receptive to a monument saw vanity in the effort of "a third or fourth rate city of the nation, to assume the right or responsibility" to celebrate "the achievement of which she acted so small a part" through a form that invited comparison with great cities of Europe.[4] This argument intertwined with doubts about modernization of the Common. The city might, and before long did, arrange removal of Old South Church and the railroad tracks, but the original town burial ground had recently become more deeply entrenched after a descendant commissioned a Victorian monument for the grave of Timothy Bigelow, captain of the local minutemen. That project was completed in time for the anniversary of Lexington and Concord in April 1861, when the coincident crisis at Fort Sumter prompted a dedication ceremony that transformed the filiopietistic gesture into an important site of community memory.[5] The link between the Revolution and the Civil War, rather than any bridge to the postwar order, defined remembrance on Worcester Common. The city overwhelmingly rejected Blake's proposal and after the mayor's death in 1870 commissioned Randolph Rogers to provide the metropolitan version of a soldier monument, topped by an allegorical figure of Victory but fundamentally similar to the statues installed on the greens of many smaller New England towns.

Richardson brought his design to a different antebellum landscape in postwar transition, the waterfront city, and to a community readier to represent the national ambitions of an arch. Buffalo was the eleventh-largest city in the United States and growing rapidly when local leaders invited Frederick Law Olmsted in 1868 to propose a public park on the strength of his work with Calvert Vaux at Central Park in New York and Prospect Park in Brooklyn. Olmsted suggested a park system that included the Front, a scenic overlook near the Lake Erie shore that had given rise to the city; the Parade, an inland recreational space; and the Park, an expansive pastoral landscape at the northern edge of town. The major innovations were the parkways that connected the Parade to the Park and provided attractive transitions from the city center to the Park. Adapted from the boulevards that Baron Haussmann had recently cut through Paris, the parkways combined urban modernity with romantic nature. Civil War commemoration was an important part of this program. The western boulevard leading into the Park was Lincoln Parkway. The two avenues feeding it bore the names of fallen Buffalo officers. The point of convergence was Soldiers Place. Here Olmsted initially envisioned a monument that would function much like the Arc de Triomphe de l'Étoile, presiding over traffic circulation near the local Bois de Boulogne.[6]

By 1874, however, this plan gave way to a fresher approach to Civil War remembrance. Olmsted told the park commissioners that the memorial should be an arch installed not at Soldiers Place but in the long-standing heart of the port city, Niagara Square.[7] Formal ornamentation was inconsistent with the arcadian parkways. Moreover, the landscape architect had found a commemorative perspective that better extended his wartime efforts with the U.S. Sanitary Commission to promote Union idealism as the moral invigoration of a nation drawn toward enervating materialism. Olmsted proposed to place Richardson's slightly modified arch at the Niagara Square opening of Delaware Street, the only downtown road that extended through the Park. Because an arch implied a wall, the monument on the northern edge of the square would imaginatively enclose the busy crossroads to foster sociability and also suggest a permeable boundary between the downtown economy and the rejuvenating zones of domesticity and nature. The stretch of Delaware Street, soon renamed Delaware Avenue, near the proposed arch was the most prestigious address in town. As the road led into the Park three miles away, it supported the middle-class suburban housing crucial to Olmsted's economic and ideological vision of cities. Continuing northward, Delaware Street pointed toward Olmsted's hopes for a parkway that would connect Buffalo to Niagara Falls, for which he launched a preservation campaign. Worcester critics had dismissed Richardson's arch as "utterly meaningless" because it would embellish the Common without connecting anything, but the Buffalo version positioned Union triumph as the hinge between the dynamic Great Lakes economy and the splendors of nature's nation.[8]

Olmsted and Richardson's well-publicized plans failed when private fund-raising fell short and municipal spending focused on other facets of the parks project, but the Buffalo initiative influenced a variety of arches in Hartford, Brooklyn, and Manhattan. Connecticut's decision to follow New York, Kansas, Illinois, and Michigan in building a monumental new capitol after the Civil War framed planning in Hartford around the relationship between the statehouse finished in 1879 and the adjacent park named for its antebel-

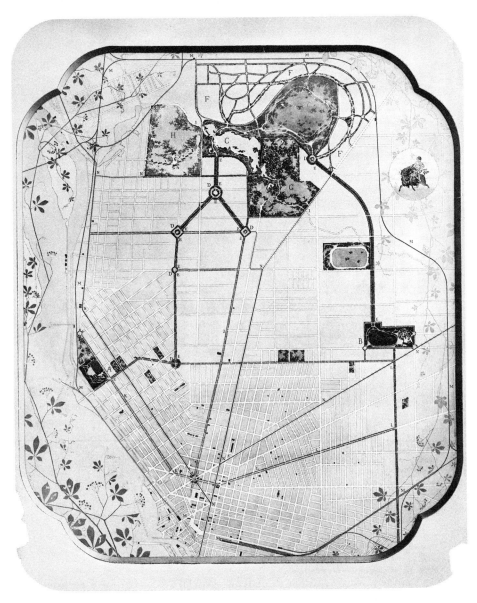

FIGURE 4.1. Frederick Law Olmsted, map of Buffalo parks and
parkways, 1876. Soldiers Place is the circular junction of the parkways
in the top third of the map. Niagara Square is the radial spot in the
lower left, connected directly to the parkways by Delaware Street.
Courtesy of the National Park Service, Frederick Law Olmsted National Historic Site.

FIGURE 4.2. Office of Henry Hobson Richardson (possibly drawn by Stanford White), Civil War Memorial Project, Buffalo, 1874–76. Courtesy of Houghton Library, Harvard University.

lum founder, Congregational minister and social theorist Horace Bushnell. Unlike the large Central Park that Bushnell's former parishioner Olmsted helped to create in the 1850s for the outskirts of Manhattan, the thirty-acre Hartford park sought to renew the industrial and tenement district that had emerged along the Little River (renamed the Park River) as the Hartford economy shifted inward from the Connecticut River. Consistent with Bushnell's anxieties about the challenge of individualism to the institutions of church and family, he envisioned parks—like public schools, or in the Civil War, the nation—as reinforcements for the social framework. Bushnell Park

Visions of Victory

promoted cross-class gentility rather than transcendental encounters with
nature. The minister called the space "an outdoor parlor, opened for the cultivation of good manners and a right social feeling."⁹ The neighboring capitol added the state to the celebration of powerful institutions. A local committee formed in 1881 to plan a Civil War monument focused from the outset
on the idea of an arch spanning the street that cut through the park to the
capitol.

    Hartford architect George Keller, who designed the arch dedicated in
1886, was keenly aware of developments in Buffalo as well as local understandings of Bushnell Park and the capitol. He had participated in an in-
conclusive Buffalo competition held after the abandonment of Olmsted and
Richardson's plan, from which Keller successfully recycled his entry for use
in Manchester, New Hampshire (1879), and he had won a subsequent Buffalo competition with a design executed in 1884. Like both of those columns
flanked by soldier statues, the Hartford arch featured bands of narrative relief sculpture. Visitors entering the park saw a battle frieze of War and statues
of a farmer and a blacksmith arming to fight; visitors leaving the park saw a

homecoming frieze of Peace and statues of a carpenter and a mason resuming civilian life. The eastern and western sides of the monument featured statues intended to embody transformation, a student and a slave breaking his chains and learning to read. The combination of a classical frieze, a pointed Gothic arch, and Norman castle towers echoed the eclecticism of R. M. Upjohn's statehouse, topped by its distinctive tower-dome, while the brownstone structure emulated the mass and organicism through which Richardson expressed the vigor of postwar America. If Keller's historical allusiveness suggested a nostalgia underlying Bushnell's social thought, the masculine war memorial complemented the implied femininity of the park as a public domestic space.[10]

The arch installed outside Prospect Park in Brooklyn more directly challenged Olmsted and Richardson's vision of the meanings of Union victory. The campaign for a grand Civil War monument, initiated by Seth Low shortly after Republicans wrested the mayoralty from Democrats, reflected the boom that accompanied the completion of the Brooklyn Bridge in 1883. Richard Morris Hunt and J. Q. A. Ward proposed a design with an estimated cost of $500,000 to a committee chaired by Low in 1886, but the ex-mayor concluded that half of that budget should yield a sufficient memorial. Ward proceeded to judge a competition won by another shaft ornamented with allegorical statues. Mayor Alfred C. Chapin vetoed the award of a contract, arguing that the conventional design was "essentially funereal. It does not recall to the mind the patriotic pride, the consciousness of sufficient strength which animated and sustained the Nation in that supreme hour." Chapin opened a new competition in 1888 specifically for an arch to be placed at the entrance to Prospect Park. All but two of the thirty-nine entrants proposed Gothic or Romanesque arches. The winner was one of those two, New York architect John H. Duncan, then best known for his recent Tower of Victory in Newburgh, a rusticated arch that canopied a statue of Washington. His Brooklyn submission marked a timely shift toward classicism that he would continue at Grant's Tomb and the Philip Lehman Mansion.[11] Installation of Duncan's arch on Prospect Park Plaza, which Olmsted and Vaux had marked with a wide, low circular fountain, reopened the conflict of the early 1870s over Hunt and Ward's proposal for an elaborate Warrior Gate in Central Park. Press coverage of the October 1889 cornerstone-laying ceremony promised "a structure, which, when competed, will rank second only to the famous Arc de Triomphe in Paris."[12]

Richardson's former assistant Stanford White, who had worked on the arch proposal for Buffalo, pushed the Brooklyn arch toward the flamboyant classical revival that would soon shape the Columbian exposition in Chicago. Appointed to head architectural embellishment of Prospect Park, he quickly supported the arch plan for the plaza with a set of Doric columns for the main entrance. Similar interventions in the park eventually included statuary, balustrades, a formal rose garden, and a peristyle presented as a shelter for croquet spectators. Olmsted lamented after the 1892 completion of the arch that the situation was "as if war had been formally declared" between proponents of the spiritual power of nature and a "strong and able, organized, systematic and methodic renaissance movement" that preferred to showcase human achievement.[13] The arch in Bushnell Park proposed restoration of a religious order that Olmsted thought outdated, but Grand Army Plaza (the name given to Prospect Park Plaza in 1926) pointed toward secular materialism.

White commissioned Frederick MacMonnies to ornament the arch with a crowning quadrigia, which Duncan had eschewed in his final design, and with Army and Navy groups for the piers. The elaborate compositions attracted wide notice that mostly divided along national lines. French critics dismissed the sculpture as derivative and confused. One Paris newspaper described the quadrigia as "desperate banality, copied from everything that ancient and modern art has produced in this genre, without the least movement and without the slightest personal note." Several journalists called MacMonnies's ensembles a pastiche of François Rude's work on the Arc de Triomphe. Some Americans agreed. The *Springfield Republican* thought the pier groups "theatrical, but vacant." But the majority saw a powerful expression of national spirit after the recent victory in the Spanish-American War. The *Brooklyn Daily Eagle* considered the arch sculpture "virile." The *New York Tribune* judged it "wonderfully vivid and effective." The *New York World* maintained that "the entire work is very beautiful and impressive and compares favorably with any work of its kind in the world."[14]

Ironically, White served as architect for the most radical construction of an arch to reshape an antebellum landscape in postwar transition, the Washington Parade Ground used for decades by New York City militia before the newly formed Department of Public Parks took charge of the renamed space in 1870 and militia units turned toward armories. Like the Victory Tower in Newburgh or the Alliance and Victory Monument that Hunt and Ward completed in Yorktown in 1884, the Washington Square Arch previewed in temporary form for the centennial anniversary of the first presidential inauguration and dedicated in marble in 1895 illustrated the extent to which Civil War commemoration had reshaped Revolutionary remem-

FIGURE 4.4. John H. Duncan and Frederick MacMonnies, Soldiers and Sailors Monument, Brooklyn, 1888–1901. Courtesy of the Library of Congress.

brance. Installation of the cornerstone for the arch took place on Memorial Day in 1890; orator George William Curtis argued that no occasion could be more appropriate than the red-letter day of the Civil War, for "its associations blend naturally with those of the Revolution."[15] The dedication orator was Horace Porter, representative of Washington's counterpart Grant. His speech typified the ways in which Revolutionary memory after the Civil War focused on the military conflict with Britain rather than the invention of American democracy.

Candid speakers acknowledged that the main theme of the arch was the gulf between wealth and poverty in the Gilded Age metropolis. Washington Square was the most fashionable address in the city from the early 1830s until the rich began to move uptown during the 1850s. After the Civil War the working class dominated the district, as indicated by the Garibaldi statue that Italian immigrants unveiled in the square in 1888. William Rhinelander Stewart, the driving force behind the arch, regarded his initiative as a permanent Knickerbocker imprint on his neighborhood. Pride and resentment intermingled in his treasurer's report that the private funding of the project reflected "the individual efforts of a few members of the committee, who sought large subscriptions by personal visits and letters." Slightly more than 400 donors accounted for almost four-fifths of the $128,000 spent for the arch. Some supporters, however, took a more optimistic view of class relations. Arch committee secretary Richard Watson Gilder, editor of the *Century*, headed the New York Tenement House Commission. Arch committee chair Henry G. Marquand, who lived in a Madison Avenue mansion designed by Richard Morris Hunt, noted at the cornerstone-laying ceremony that friends asked why he was involved in a project in a neighborhood that "in a few years will be all tenement houses." The financier and Metropolitan Museum benefactor called for an "arch of peace and good-will" that would bring together rich and poor not only by stimulating patriotic remembrance but also by providing an outlet for families too poor to afford the streetcar to Central Park.[16]

The extent to which White's arch achieved these cross-class goals resulted largely from following Olmsted and Richardson's precedent for placement of the memorial at the northern edge of the plaza. The implicit wall reinforced the spatial integrity that had been threatened when the Department of Public Parks began to route traffic through the square. Moreover, the arch dramatized the important boundary between the part of the city shaped by the 1811 grid plan and the less orderly downtown streets. Although Stewart hoped to showcase Washington Square as the source of Fifth Avenue, the partition also associated the plaza with the Bowery, the Lower East Side, and Five Points. The arch enclosed no mere outdoor parlor but a lively civic forum, available to labor parades as well as marching soldiers. Like the invitation at Niagara Square to uplifting encounters with nature, the facilitation of street politics in Washington Square encouraged a continuous renewal of the nation. Hope for the strengthening of the polity through these encounters drew on the confidence Curtis expressed at the cornerstone-laying ceremony that the legacy of the Revolution had already been "tried by fire" in the Civil War.[17]

The introduction of arches at Bushnell Park, Prospect Park, and Washington Square in the 1880s led to more ambitious projects that culminated in the Senate Park Commission proposal for a triumphal arch as the hinge between the extended Mall in Washington, DC, and a memorial bridge to Arlington National Cemetery. These efforts lacked the regenerative strategies proposed for Niagara Square and realized in Washington Square. The Smith Memorial in Fairmount Park originated in an 1891 testamentary bequest that became effective four years later. A colossal standing statue of entrepreneur Richard Smith, installed alongside a galaxy of Pennsylvania war heroes despite some local complaint, celebrated the captain of industry as a Union champion.[18] The appropriation of $250,000 for the Brooklyn arch soon prompted a parallel expenditure in Manhattan. Plans for a triumphal arch at the Central Park entrance at Fifth Avenue and Fifty-Ninth Street advanced with strong cooperation between veterans and artists until a joint committee of the National Sculpture Society and the Architectural League concluded that the fund was "quite inadequate" for "the most festal and decorative part of our mechanical and commonplace town." Estimates of $2 million for a gateway on the plaza (named Grand Army Plaza in 1923) caused the veterans and politicians on the monument commission to favor a column ornamented by statuary, which the National Sculpture Society vetoed under the Municipal Art Commission legislation of 1896.[19]

The eventual New York Soldiers and Sailors Monument illustrated the waning interest in triumph as a link between diverse civic spaces. The winners of the 1897 competition for a monument at Fifth Avenue and Fifty-Ninth Street, architect Arthur A. Stoughton and engineer Charles W. Stoughton, retained the commission upon transfer of the project to Riverside Park and developed a new design for a circular colonnade reminiscent of the Choragic Monument of Lysicrates in Athens. Olmsted had long ago expressed discontent with selection of Riverside Park as the site for Grant's Tomb, and one of his admirers sued to stop installation of the Soldiers and Sailors Monument. The protest succeeded in preventing obliteration of an eminence at Eighty-Second Street known as Mount Tom, but construction at Eighty-Ninth Street concluded in time for dedication ceremonies on Memorial Day in 1902. The work particularly pleased a vocal contingent of naval officers who had preferred the site to the Central Park plaza because it was visible from the Hudson River. The consideration underscored the aim of this memorial to provide an endpoint rather than a frame for a postwar vista. The colonnade, which in the words of one critic "suggests the Song of Victory," was like the ancient Choragic Monument essentially a trophy.[20]

Emphatically triumphal structures proliferated across the North in several forms during the late nineteenth and early twentieth century, but the arch retained particular prestige. Iowa completed one of the most extravagant victory columns in the country in 1896 only after a commission decided that Des Moines lacked a suitable setting for an arch.[21] Union veterans espe-

FIGURE 4.5. Lew F. Porter, Camp Randall Memorial Arch, University of Wisconsin, Madison, 1911–13. Courtesy of the University of Wisconsin–Madison Archives.

cially enjoyed the traditional symbol of victory. Temporary arches festooned annual encampments of the Grand Army of the Republic (GAR). Even a municipality as small as Gouverneur, New York, installed an arch in the center of the village park at the urging of the local GAR post in 1905. The most imposing monument in the national battlefield parks was the arched Pennsylvania Memorial dedicated at Gettysburg in 1910.[22]

The arch dedicated in 1912 at the former site of the Camp Randall training compound in Madison, Wisconsin, marked the resolution of the narrative arc opened at Worcester in 1868. No longer did anyone object that the arch was a form of commemoration reserved for great cities like Rome and Paris. Nor did arches necessarily inscribe historic social or political transitions in the community landscape. The span in the midst of the University of Wisconsin campus opened onto a small park that led to the football field laid out atop the former parade ground in the 1890s. The site reinforced an emerging athletic definition of masculinity but identified Union victory with the empty wins and losses of college sports. The statues in front of the piers, a soldier of 1861–65 and a veteran of 1912, revealed the focus of the gateway on the passage of time experienced by the GAR members who had lobbied for this recognition.[23] Such self-congratulatory nostalgia was the opposite of the creative tension behind the promise of the Niagara Square Arch and the achievement of the Washington Square Arch.

THE UNVANQUISHED

"It is a strange sight," observed Charles Colcock Jones Jr. at the 1878 unveiling of the Confederate monument in Augusta, Georgia, "this dedication of an august monument in the chief place of our city, by a people who were overcome in the contest, to the cause which they seemingly lost." The accomplished historian asked "whether history, in all her wide range of nations and ages, furnishes like example. To victors belong paeans, and triumphal arches and statues of bronze and marble and gold are usually accorded only to those who win the title of conqueror."[24] The clash between the conventions of the public monument and the experience of the Confederacy yielded innovations in memorial form and content. In contrast with the *revanchiste* monuments that spread across defeated France during the same period, white southerners reimagined the Civil War to generate bold narratives of Confederate victory. Monuments claimed not only that Confederate soldiers had won fame or honor but also that the South had achieved its political goals. Such assertions partly reflected the extent to which postwar white supremacism stifled federal initiatives to secure civil rights for African Americans. Retrospective rebranding of secessionists' attempt to establish an independent proslavery nation also typified and deepened an American failure to recognize failure.

The dedication of a truncated shaft near the graves of sixty-two soldiers in Cheraw, South Carolina, in July 1867 showed that former Confederates understood in the early years after Appomattox that they had suffered a crushing defeat. Joshua H. Hudson, who served in the army throughout the war and commanded a regiment at its end, praised his fallen comrades for their valor. "The Phalanxes of Miltiades, the Legions of Caesar, the battalions of Napoleon or the patriots of Washington deserve no higher encomiums for all soldierly virtues than the Confederate dead," he maintained. Hudson argued that the monument wisely honored private sacrifices on the public behalf, but he did not deny the futility of those deaths. Salutatorian of the class of 1852 at South Carolina College, the former state legislator was exceptionally candid in admitting that the dead "may have been misguided by the errors of others," whose advocacy of proslavery secession had led to emancipation throughout the restored United States at an enormous cost of human life. Although he hoped that "in the economy of an alwise God we may have become the chosen instruments of fulfilling His wonderful plans though in a manner different from what we supposed," he warned against roseate conjectures. "Alas the vain sacrifice of noble blood!" Hudson lamented. "All was lost — nothing achieved." The veteran observed a clear distinction between honor and success as he saluted the dead who had "saved our defeat from shame, and gave dignity to our disaster."[25]

Acceptance of defeat might have political uses, as Horatio Nash Ogden demonstrated in his address at the unveiling of a monument in Greenwood Cemetery in New Orleans in April 1874. Deeply involved in the resistance movement against Reconstruction, the attorney belonged to a mercantile faction in partial collaboration and partial competition with an older faction of elites that called on loyal ex-Confederates to support the fullest possible return to the antebellum social order. Ogden laid groundwork for policies of economic modernization and violent white supremacism by emphasizing that the monument "represents no successful, but a beaten cause." The road to prosperity and racial dominance did not lie in the recent past of a people gathered "in the face of defeat, disaster and suffering, with a country desolated and in ruins." Hoping to discredit his white opponents with the burden of failure, Ogden claimed for his faction the moral purity of remembrance unmixed with triumphant pride.[26]

Commemorations launched in other "reform" contexts culminated in distinctive recognitions of defeat. Women associated with the New Departure faction in Lexington, Kentucky, sponsored the 1874 cemetery installation of a marble cross carved to simulate two logs, which propped up a broken flagstaff. The fallen banner of the Confederacy draped across the rustic cross. Scattered across the base, which resembled a pile of rocks, were a broken sword and symbolic flora. *Frank Leslie's Illustrated Newspaper* called the monument "probably the most perfect thing of its kind in the South," in part because "it tells its own story — the tragic story of the Lost Cause — without the use of a single word."[27] Comparably acclaimed was the Alexandria, Virginia, monument adapted from John A. Elder's painting *Appomattox*. A map-maker at the Battle of the Crater, the artist aided the political career of William Mahone with an 1869 canvas that highlighted the counterattack led by the Confederate general. When the Readjuster movement flourished in the early 1880s, Elder painted a visual complement to Mahone's fusionist admonition to "live for the future, and not the dead past . . . while cherishing

FIGURE 4.6. George W. Ranck and Muldoon Monument Company, Confederate
Memorial, Lexington Cemetery, 1873–74. Photograph by J. Smith Soule.
Courtesy of the Special Collections Research Center, University of Kentucky.

memories of its honorable glories." The fund-raising campaign for the Alexandria monument featured a lecture by apostate Confederate commander
John S. Mosby, recently returned from Republican diplomatic service in
Hong Kong. The official description issued for the 1889 dedication characterized the statue as a soldier contemplating after surrender the hardships he
had endured "all for a principle which he deemed sacred and righteous, and
yet all apparently for naught." Postwar success depended on the flexibility
necessary to appreciate failure.[28]

Reform remembrance of southern defeat faced early opposition from
Bourbon insistence that the wartime successes of the Confederacy foreshadowed eventual vindication. Sponsors of a monument for a cemetery
in Warrenton, Virginia, invited South Carolina diehard Wade Hampton to
speak at the 1873 cornerstone ceremony, where he narrowly conceded that
white southerners must "accept our defeat with the consequences that legiti-
mately follow it" and more enthusiastically vowed to "stand manfully by the
great principles for which we fought" in anticipation of the inevitable "triumph of those principles." The monument featured a forty-foot-high shaft
topped by a draped figure of a woman sadly reading a book of remembrance
but carrying a laurel wreath in her right hand. An inscription identified the
dead as defenders of states' rights and expressed Byronesque confidence
that "THEY NEVER FAIL WHO DIE IN A GREAT CAUSE."[29] The monument dedicated at Augusta, Georgia, in 1878 provocatively featured the word

Visions of Victory

"WON" as the centerpiece of a nineteen-line hourglass-shaped inscription focused on the "FADELESS FAME" of the Confederate dead. Dedication orator Charles Colcock Jones Jr. described the monument as a tribute to "the labors and the triumphs of the private soldiers of the Confederacy." His assertion that "truth and justice are eternal, and remain unaffected by the accidents of war," typified Bourbon eagerness to dissociate the Confederacy from the irreversible failure of proslavery secession.[30]

The triumphalist strain in Confederate remembrance thrived at the turn of the century as the overthrow of Reconstruction solidified. The dedication of the Lee monument in Richmond in 1890 provided a vehicle for reconciliation of Bourbon, probusiness Democrat, and Readjuster factions in Virginia. *Confederate Veteran* published a poem in 1896 titled "Call It Not a 'Lost Cause,'" and two years later former Confederate general Clement Evans claimed at a monument dedication in Elberton, Georgia, that "ours is not a lost cause, for the world sits at our feet to learn lessons of valor." The staff of *Lost Cause*, a monthly published by the Kentucky circle responsible for the Lexington monument, felt obliged to defend the journal title by the outset of 1901. The editors noted that secession had in fact not produced an independent nation. They nevertheless described the southern cause as "lost but immortal, dead but triumphant." *Confederate Veteran* modified its masthead in 1905 to expand on long-standing objections to the term "Civil War" by denouncing the phrase "Lost Cause."[31] White southerners contended that the Confederacy begat what they considered the best features of modern America.

Commemoration of Jefferson Davis after his death in 1889 measured the strength and limits of Confederate triumphalism. Richmond civic leaders formed a monument association in a successful appeal to Davis's widow for the removal of the president's remains from New Orleans for permanent interment at Hollywood Cemetery. A year before the 1893 rail procession of the coffin to Richmond, the Jefferson Davis Monument Association (JDMA) forged an alliance with the United Confederate Veterans (UCV) and a Southern Press Association headed by future *Confederate Veteran* editor Sumner Cunningham and set plans for a public monument with a budget of $250,000. The group held a design competition that climaxed at the national UCV reunion in 1896 with cornerstone ceremonies at Richmond's Monroe Park, located about halfway between Capitol Square and the Lee equestrian statue installed on the western outskirts of the city six years earlier. The winning design by New York architect Percy Griffin, a large Palladian temple with a gold-leafed dome above a statue of Davis, suggested a determination to keep pace with Grant's Tomb. The promoters confessed to Griffin within a year that they had no prospect of raising enough money for such an edifice, and they still had only $20,465 on hand when they asked the United Daughters of the Confederacy (UDC) to take charge of the project in 1899. The UDC adopted the task as its first national monumental undertaking in collaboration with a reconstituted JDMA led by women officers.[32]

From the outset the new JDMA urged construction of an arch on Broad Street, the principal east-west thoroughfare, at an intersection two blocks south of the museum that Richmond women had recently established in the house where Davis lived during the war. A newspaper editorial acknowledged that arches traditionally symbolized victory and that the proposal was "an anomaly" by classical standards but maintained that "the idea strikes the southern mind as particularly appropriate" because Davis manifested a character and spirit "which failure and defeat cannot conquer." The UDC endorsed the plan at its 1901 national convention. As a design competition neared the exhibition stage in the following spring, however, Varina Davis raised strenuous objections. She observed that "a triumphal arch to the memory of a man whose cause failed . . . certainly will excite ridicule in many quarters," despite the president's efforts to achieve an impossible task. She mobilized the New York chapter of the UDC, which declared that the arch would be "a great mistake" because "an arch, the world over, has been the insignia of triumph." After some negotiation, including the dispatch of a UDC delegation to New York to persuade Davis to support remembrance of the Confederate "triumph in principle," she and the sponsors agreed to proceed with an arch characterized as "memorial" rather than "triumphal." The JDMA reluctantly deferred to the preference of the president's widow for installation of the monument in Monroe Park rather than on busy Broad Street.[33]

The debate was partly moot, for the artist awarded the commission soon discovered that he could not build the arch the sponsors wanted for the sum that they had raised, but the women salvaged much of their goal upon turning the project over to Richmond architect William C. Noland and Richmond sculptor Edward Valentine. Noland, who had placed third in the 1896 competition with a proposal for a linear colonnade, shifted the dream of an arch to a horizontal plane by designing a semicircular colonnade similar in proportions to the unbuilt span. From the center of the arc rose a sixty-foot-high fluted and banded column, atop which stood an allegorical female figure named Vindicatrix, who held her right arm upright and raised her eyes heavenward. The statue of Davis in front of the column depicted the president holding open the book of history, to which he appealed as vindication

FIGURE 4.7. Edward Valentine and William C. Noland, Jefferson Davis
Memorial, Richmond, 1903–7. Courtesy of the Library of Congress.

of the Confederacy. At the dedication ceremony in June 1907 orator Clement Evans invoked the putative shape of the monument when he described the project as the end to the rail procession that had carried Davis's remains through public observances in southern cities and towns on the route from New Orleans to Richmond. Evans suggested that on this train the Confederate president was "passing into immortality under an extended arch of triumph, erected with the living uplifted arms of his loving Southern people."[34]

The tribute to the oft-embattled chief executive showed that the short-lived nation had won the lasting affections of white southerners.

Evans's allusion to procession as the ritual expression of triumph aptly echoed the eventual decision about the site of the monument. After the city engineer vetoed the proposed return to Monroe Park, the Richmond women at last conceded to the logic of the speculative placement of the Lee equestrian on the western edge of town. Early-twentieth-century construction was finally creating the anticipated fashionable neighborhood in this area. Rather than building closer to the city center, the Davis sponsors agreed to place the colonnade a half mile west of the Lee statue on Monument Avenue. Substantial city funding quickened a weak campaign for an equestrian monument to J. E. B. Stuart and steered it to a site on Monument Avenue one block east of the Lee memorial. With the dedications of both the Stuart monument and the Davis monument during the 1907 annual UCV convention, Monument Avenue became a Haussmannesque boulevard of Confederate remembrance that culminated slightly off-axis in the long-awaited "Battle Abbey," or Confederate Memorial Institute, for which sponsors laid the cornerstone in 1912. By that time plans were under way for an equestrian monument to Stonewall Jackson, placed with city and state funding at the Monument Avenue intersection that led to the Abbey reliquary and archive. White southerners who traveled the mile between Stuart and Jackson saw three mounted generals and the Confederate president pass in glory.[35]

Confederate monuments relied on a mixture of combative inscriptions and designs to celebrate the postwar stabilization of white supremacism. A generic statue in Obion County, Tennessee (1909), honored the Confederate soldier "WHO HAS PRESERVED ANGLO-SAXON CIVILIZATION IN THE SOUTH." A monument in Milledgeville, Georgia (1912), claimed that the Confederate soldier's "UNCONQUERABLE PATRIOTISM AND SELF-SACRIFICE RENDERED ABORTIVE THE EFFORT OF HIS ENEMIES, AFTER HIS FLAG HAD FOLDED FOREVER, TO DESTROY HIS PROUD INHERITANCE." South Carolina, where memory of the overthrow of Reconstruction was especially strong, installed an equestrian monument to Wade Hampton at the statehouse (1906) that reproduced his appearance as redeemer governor rather than Confederate cavalry commander. The state monument to Confederate women, dedicated on the thirty-fifth anniversary of federal recognition of Hampton's election, recalled that "IN THE REBUILDING AFTER THE DESOLATION / THEIR VIRTUES STOOD / AS THE SUPREME CITADEL / WITH STRONG TOWERS OF FAITH AND HOPE / AROUND WHICH CIVILIZATION RALLIED / AND TRIUMPHED."

The monument at the county courthouse in Denton, Texas (1918), was an inexpensive but triumphal arch topped by a soldier statue and presenting on its piers twin drinking fountains that identified racial segregation as the measure of Confederate victory.[36]

Authors of southern monument inscriptions exhausted their repertories of superlatives in recounting the Confederate military achievement. Although the monument in Galveston, Texas (1911), featured a statue by Louis Amateis titled *Dignified Resignation* that depicted a sailor with a broken cutlass in one hand and a flag draped from a shattered staff in the other hand, the inscription maintained that "THERE HAS NEVER BEEN AN ARMED FORCE WHICH IN PURITY OF MOTIVES, INTENSITY OF COURAGE AND HEROISM HAS EQUALED THE ARMY AND NAVY OF THE CONFEDERATE STATES OF AMERICA." According to the monument in St. Louis (1914), Confederate soldiers "PERFORMED DEEDS OF PROWESS SUCH AS THRILLED THE HEART OF MANKIND WITH ADMIRATION" and "GAVE A NEW AND BRIGHTER LUSTER TO THE ANNALS OF VALOR." The monument in Ripley, Mississippi (1911), reported that "THEY WON IMPERISHABLY."

The thirty-foot-tall monument in Appomattox, Virginia, a place synonymous with Confederate defeat, illustrated the triumphalism that pervaded the Lost Cause in the early twentieth century. By the June 1906 unveiling the wartime courthouse had burned down, and the county installed the monument at the new courthouse five miles from the site where Lee had surrendered forty-one years earlier. A local newspaper remarkably called the dedication "by far the biggest day in the history of Appomattox." Governor Claude Swanson rehearsed the popular argument that the federal government had recently conceded the justice of the Confederate cause by recognizing the secession of Panama from Colombia. He exulted that "the Civil War was the greatest war of all time. History contained nothing like it." Lee was the most brilliant commander on record, and "the Confederate army stands preeminently as the greatest army ever organized or led by man." The ceremony included no hint of frustration. A newspaper reported that "everybody enjoyed themselves and the sun went down on a tired, but happy and enthusiastic crowd."[37]

The incongruous pattern did not escape notice. Pompeo Coppini, who incorporated a male nude allegory of the Lost Cause in his monument to Confederate postmaster general John H. Reagan for Palestine, Texas (1911), expressed dismay at F. Wellington Ruckstuhl's monuments for Little Rock (1905) and Columbia (1912), in both of which Coppini identified images of winged Victory. He considered such works better suited to "New England, Pennsylvania, New York, or any other Yankee state." The sculptor asked New Orleans matron Margaret Drane Tichenor, "Don't you think it is rather a puzzle to find out where the Lost Cause sentiment comes in?" Tichenor, however, was the leader of the UDC campaign to reject Belle Kinney's design for a multistate monument to Confederate women in part because the ensemble grouped around a dying soldier "has singled out one feature, Appomattox alone."[38] Citizens of Athens, Alabama, a town sacked by Union troops in 1862, demonstrated similar vigilance against defeatism when Limestone County replaced a courthouse statue of a soldier with downcast head in 1917 because in the words of one veteran, "He looks like we was whipped, but we know we wasn't!"[39]

Ruckstuhl's reworking of his former mentor Antonin Mercié's *Gloria Victis*, or "Glory to the Vanquished," illustrated differences between white southern and French responses to defeat. Mercié's bronze statue of a winged allegorical woman carrying away a fallen nude warrior who clutched a broken sword was a sensation at the Paris Salon of 1874. The composition touched an eagerness to rescue national honor after recent humiliation in the Franco-Prussian War. By the time Ruckstuhl prepared the adaptation unveiled in Baltimore in 1903 and reproduced in Salisbury, North Carolina, in 1909, French remembrance had long since turned toward threats of revenge. Mercié's *Quand même!* (Even So), dedicated at Belfort in 1884, was one of many monuments that linked a fallen soldier to a figure who resumed the fight.[40] Ruckstuhl's work, also labeled *Gloria Victis*, instead amplified the transcendence of defeat in Mercié's earlier work. The Confederate soldier was not nude. Although dead, he stood upright. The Nike-like figure held aloft a laurel wreath to crown the soldier. Far from assuaging or preparing to avenge defeat, the monument hailed Confederate victory. At the Baltimore dedication one veteran declared that southerners had managed to "win the rank, 'Invincible'; until, in the words of Robert Toombs, they were worn out at last by constantly defeating their opponents." Another speaker identified white southern satisfaction with the current social order as an example of the maxim "Peace has its victories as well as war."[41]

Confederate triumphalism rejoiced in the reconstruction of white supremacy through disfranchisement, segregation, convict labor, and lynching but exhibited an intensity that exceeded white confidence in racial control or regional liberation from federal oversight. Commemoration expressed a nationwide conception of history as a set of unforgettable moments elevated above the wearisome obscurity of human experience. White southerners

FIGURE 4.8. F. Wellington Ruckstuhl, *Gloria Victis*, Baltimore, 1902–3.
Courtesy of the Library of Congress.

considered the Confederate struggle such an epic. "AS AT THERMOPYLAE, THE GREATER GLORY WAS TO THE VANQUISHED," read the inscription on the monument in Yazoo City, Mississippi (1909). The gallant setbacks of Leonidas and Lee presaged ultimate success. The argument that secessionists had reshaped America facilitated convergent postwar loyalty to the Confederacy and the United States. Individual authors might build on the crushing failure recognized by Joshua H. Hudson in 1867 and propose that the South offered a corrective to dangerous illusions of national omnipotence because the region shared in "the common experience of mankind, all the great peoples of which have known the bitter taste of defeat."[42] The memorial landscape offered little support for this understanding of the past. Civic monuments instead contributed to a massive denial of unhappy historical truths. In deepening public reluctance to engage in critical retrospection, white southerners made good on their claim that the Confederacy anticipated the course of the United States.

As Grant's army continued to grind toward Vicksburg in April 1863, an archaeological excavation in the mountainous Aegean island of Samothrace uncovered fragments of a large Hellenistic statue of Nike, the winged goddess of victory. The French diplomat who had sponsored the dig shipped the marble to Paris, where Louvre curators installed the torso and legs in the Salle des Caryatides. Further investigations during the 1870s identified blocks at the site as pieces of a sculpted boat on which the statue originally stood, presumably to celebrate a naval victory. Using plaster to fill many gaps, French conservators reassembled the vessel and one feathered wing; they made a matching wing from plaster as well as sections to join the wings to the body. The Louvre unveiled the reconstruction in 1884 at the head of the staircase completed the previous year as the grand entrance to the museum.[43] Designed to complement the sanctuary of the mystery religion at Samothrace, the statue became one of the most familiar icons of Western civilization soon after its installation at the gateway to the temple of art. Although markedly different in their political perspectives, the Futurist Manifesto of 1909 and Marcel Proust's novel *Swann's Way* (1913) both identified the Nike as the emblem of bourgeois self-satisfaction.[44] Shortly before those publications, three prominent Civil War monuments presented alternatives to the Louvre image of victory. The influential works envisioned Union triumph as a more comprehensive consummation than the most celebrated successes of antiquity.

The headless statue at the top of the Louvre staircase accidentally updated Nike's chief classical attribute, her lack of individuality. She was, as Marina Warner has observed, "a goddess without a story." No myths recounted her adventures. She landed abruptly to deliver victory, and she flew away equally suddenly, like a rupture in the movement of time. Her corporeal identity was unstable. She could be an aspect of other deities, especially the martial Athena or Zeus. Some invocations conflated her with Fortuna, the goddess of luck, and others with the divine personification of a place. She might appear in several incarnations at the same time. Christian Daniel Rauch, who made more than thirty Nike statues during his career, illustrated the multiplicity of the figure in a suite of six ethereal marbles dedicated at the Walhalla memorial in Bavaria in 1842. Exemption from experience and physicality manifested itself in sexlessness. "Nike has no children, no lovers," Warner notes.[45] In this respect the goddess resembled one of her accessories, the laurel wreath, fashioned from the tree into which the nymph Daphne was transformed to protect her chastity from the pursuing Apollo. At the 1882 dedication of the soldier monument in Augusta, Maine, former Union officer John L. Swift argued that this "familiar mythological fable teaches the instructive lesson that personal disappointment and particular disaster often lead to unforeseen and general benefit."[46] Although Swift stretched to enlist Apollo and Daphne as forerunners of Union sacrifices, he pointed obliquely toward a paradigmatic tension between the particularity of sexual possession and the social ideal of victory. Private satisfaction was a poor metaphor for collective achievement.

Early postwar monuments adhered to this principle more cautiously than the dynamic figure at the Louvre. Randolph Rogers featured a scowling Athena Nike brandishing a sword atop the column dedicated by Worcester in 1874. The statue resembled Rogers's more fully armed representation of Michigan for the state monument in Detroit (1872), an example of the continued association of Nike with allegorical representations of a polity. Franklin Simmons's statue of Victory on the Naval Monument in Washington (1877) and the wingless laurel-bearing figures in other cities, often presented as America or Liberty or a civic embodiment, also wore substantial robes. Simmons's monument for Portland, Maine (1891), soon dubbed "Our Lady of Victories," was the most elaborate essay in the genre by the Italianate generation of sculptors. The muscular figure showed off chain-mail armor beneath her classical drapery and carried a shield as well as a weighty sword. George Brewster's figure of Victory for the Indiana state memorial, already known as "Miss Indiana" when unveiled in 1893, extended the convention to sculptors trained at the École des Beaux-Arts. Brewster emulated the Statue of Liberty not only in providing his figure with a torch intended to light, in both cases unsuccessfully, but also in relying on colossal size as the primary indication of supernatural power. The hefty Victory's full-length gown outlined her curves without any revealing folds or cutouts, and the bald eagle she wore as a tiara thoroughly suppressed any hint of sexuality.[47]

A different vision of Victory emerged at a potent site, the parade ground at West Point. The faculty formed a committee in 1890 to complete the wartime initiative of officers and enlisted men in the regular army who had contributed funds for a memorial to their fallen comrades. Stanford White won the design competition with a proposal for a victory column believed to be the largest polished shaft in the world. Ringing the monument was a set of sixteen cannons inscribed with the names of Civil War battles, all Union successes except for Bull Run and Chickamauga; the committee treasurer voted to exclude any defeats.[48] White commissioned a crowning sculpture of

Nike from twenty-seven-year-old Frederick MacMonnies, the American expatriate in Paris invited around the same time by his mentor Saint-Gaudens to create an immense fountain for the Columbian exposition. The Chicago centerpiece was a Barge of State helmed by an allegorical representation of the Republic and led at the prow by a winged Victory, much as the Nike of Samothrace bestrode a vessel. The projects advanced together to the point that Battle Monument Association secretary Charles W. Larned, longtime head of the drawing department, pressed White for assurance that the figure installed atop the Trophy Point column in June 1894 was not merely a reproduction of the statue unveiled at the White City in May 1893.

The architect identified differences between the Victory landing on a globe and the Victory perched at the front of a ship, but the sensation stirred by MacMonnies's exposition ensemble, in which the regally nude Republic inflected all parts, deepened the West Point committee's reservations about the Battle Monument bronze. Her legs splayed and skirt blown back as she balanced on one foot, she wore extraordinarily flimsy robes that exposed her thighs and stomach and vividly defined her breasts. Larned judged the work "far too sensual and revealing, particularly the drapery at the junction of the legs." He worried that "it would 'fire up' the young cadets too much." The committee also complained that MacMonnies's face of Victory had "the appearance of an individual likeness," a standard line of division between artistic nudity and wanton nakedness. White agreed that the statue was too large for the shaft and offered to supply a replacement at his expense. The architect promised to deliver not merely a smaller but a different work, for which the committee urged "greater maturity and dignity in the sentiment of the figure" and "more ideality in the face."[49]

MacMonnies's substitute, christened Fame, demonstrated the extent to which composition was only one strand in the web of associations through which a community found meaning in a memorial sculpture. Looking in the opposite direction from Victory and featuring new arrangements of wings, trumpet, and laurel wreath, the statue installed in May 1896 stood on two feet with her legs pressed closely together. Her diaphanous robes still displayed her body clearly, and her face may have remained faithful to a living model. The deposed Victory continued to circulate in bronze reductions sold to collectors who prized it as "suggestive in every way of dauntlessness."[50] Moreover, the West Point statue shared in the additional notoriety generated by MacMonnies's other work of the period, especially the outcry over the nude *Bacchante and Infant Faun*, which he gave to McKim in 1894 for the Boston Public Library, and the criticism of his allegorical statuary for

FIGURE 4.9. Stanford White and Frederick MacMonnies, Battle Monument, West Point, 1890–97. Photograph by Adolph Wittemann shows original statue of Victory. Courtesy of United States Military Academy.

the Prospect Park arch as "just a copy of a model, rather gross in proportions, and with that expression of unintelligent and not too modest complacency which seems to be the nearest to which Mr. MacMonnies can attain in the way of female dignity." The sculptor's defenders denounced this "prim finicality," but identification of the Battle Monument with its artists' libertinism proved more enduring after a jealous husband killed White in the rooftop theater of Madison Square Garden in 1906. Eventually cadets developed a legend that Evelyn Nesbit had posed for the statue at Trophy Point.[51] Although the future model, showgirl, and architect's mistress was about ten years old in Pittsburgh when MacMonnies made Fame in Paris, the West Point legend reinforced a design history that advanced a fantasy of sexual conquest in place of the traditional chastity of Victory.

Saint-Gaudens's monument to William T. Sherman for New York presented a more seasoned reflection on masculine fulfillment. The project began in 1888 when the forty-year-old sculptor persuaded the sixty-eight-year-old former general to sit for a portrait bust in preparation for a posthumous monument. Despite the busy schedules of both men, Saint-Gaudens modeled the bust over an astonishing eighteen sessions, each about two hours in length, during which Sherman "talked most delightfully of the war, men and things."[52] Women doubtless figured prominently in the conversations of the two inveterate gossips. Married to chronic invalids, both men were engaged in long-term extramarital affairs and relished briefer flings. Saint-Gaudens's mistress, a sometime model whom he had wishfully renamed Davida, would bear his child the next year. If not as aggressive as his close friend White, the sculptor was a central figure in the theatrical and artistic set that spurned bourgeois domestic morality. Sherman, who retired as commanding general of the army in 1883, had recently moved from St. Louis to New York partly to enjoy this metropolitan realm of gentlemen's clubs, theaters, and artists' studios.[53] Saint-Gaudens's energetically worked bronze depicted the Civil War hero as highly experienced but still ready to campaign. Too independent to straighten his cravat, he looked forward fearlessly with a hawklike gaze beneath a cerebral brow. His grizzled beard complemented the cropped thatch that remained thick atop his head. A leading critic wrote that "the hair writhes and twists with very virility."[54]

Shortly after Sherman's death in 1891, Saint-Gaudens signed a contract for an equestrian monument in New York that would feature a figure of Victory. He started work on the project six years later while awaiting the unveiling of the Shaw and Logan memorials. Animal specialist Alexander Phimister Proctor took initial responsibility for the horse, while Saint-Gaudens concentrated on the Victory that he envisioned as the defining element of the composition. He chose a model who personified Union triumph, an African American born in South Carolina shortly after emancipation, though the sculptor did not regard Hettie Anderson in that historical light. He told his niece that "I commence the nude of the Victory from a South Carolinian girl with a figure like a goddess." He later recalled Anderson as "certainly the handsomest model I have ever seen of either sex, and I have seen a great many." In addition to her long-legged beauty, he praised her "power of posing patiently, steadily and thoroughly in the spirit one wishes."[55]

FIGURE 4.10. Anders Zorn, *Augustus Saint-Gaudens*, 1897.
Courtesy of the Isabella Stewart Gardner Museum, Boston.

Swedish artist Anders Zorn visited Saint-Gaudens's studio during one
of these sessions, which he recorded in an etching that examined a popular
theme of Gilded Age art, the sexualized domain of the artist's studio. The
nude Anderson curled in the background of the picture, bright-eyed and
smiling. The densely etched lines that set her in shadow also dramatized the
energy she radiated. Saint-Gaudens sat in work clothes in the foreground
of the picture. He leaned forward and, eyebrow arched, looked frankly and
knowingly at the viewer. Although contrasted as dark and light, background
and foreground, horizontal and vertical, model and sculptor both propped
themselves on their elbows. They presumably rested on the model's stand
but would have looked the same on a bed. Saint-Gaudens sealed the fraternal remembrance of the encounter by promising to send Zorn "a reduction
of my nude of the Goddess-like Miss Anderson." He gave Anderson an inscribed portrait bust as a memento of their collaboration, but when he resumed work on the monument after settling in Paris he decided to base the
face of Victory on his longtime mistress Davida Johnson Clark, who came to
live nearby with their son during part of Saint-Gaudens's residence abroad.
The combination of two households, a backlog of commissions, and growing

FIGURE 4.11. Augustus Saint-Gaudens and Charles McKim, Sherman Monument, New York, 1892–1903. Courtesy of Print Collection, New York Public Library.

cancer wearied the sculptor. He complained to a friend that "in the streets the men and women he met seemed to him 'to be thinking about sex all the time.'"[56]

The Sherman monument dramatized Saint-Gaudens's conception of exaltation. His figure of Victory strode forward, though not toward the prow of a ship like the Nike of Samothrace. This goddess was firmly grounded, walking in rhythm with Sherman's horse. Her wings flared as she descended an incline that the stallion crested, accentuating the general's elevation and strengthening the "impulse of irresistible advance" that observers identified as the dominant motif of the group and its streamlined base.[57] A pine bough on the landscape evoked "Marching through Georgia," the theme song of Sherman's celebrity, and added musicality to the sense of movement that animated the statuary. The monument did not, however, imagine the commander on a contingent path from Atlanta to Savannah. The palm branch held by Victory signaled that the war was over. Her right arm elegantly raised, she served as the herald of Sherman's endless triumph. The goddess and the general both looked far ahead into the distance. The man of the world held the reins easily but decisively, while his right arm remained close to his side.

His dashing cape offered a visual rhyme for Victory's wings, emphasizing that the two figures inhabited the same realm. Saint-Gaudens boldly covered the entire bronze in gold leaf, which highlighted the characteristically virtuoso surface modeling known as "color," the sculptural antithesis of pure ideality.[58] The warm tone enlivened the figures even as the luster enriched the grandeur of the apotheosis.

The site of the monument affirmed its embodiment of Gilded Age materialism. Saint-Gaudens hoped to place his work on the Central Park mall, where it could command a long vista and benefit from a green background. That plan wound up losing its round in the ongoing battles between proponents of architectural embellishment and landscape effects in the parks developed by Olmsted.[59] The city and the monument sponsor, the New York Chamber of Commerce, instead placed the memorial on the plaza across from the Central Park entrance on Fifth Avenue at Fifty-Ninth Street. The recent debate over the city's soldiers and sailors monument had established that this intersection, surrounded by expensive hotels and shops, was the epicenter of commercial prestige. More than a half century after the 1903 unveiling, the conflation of Civil War victory and luxury retail still lent itself to Frank O'Hara's satirical observation that "that angel seems to be leading the horse into Bergdorf's."[60]

The equestrian group was a triumph for Saint-Gaudens. He exhibited it in 1899 at the Salon of the Société Nationale des Beaux-Arts, which elected him a corresponding member, and in 1900 at the Paris World's Fair, where the Sherman plaster occupied a position of honor beneath the glass dome of the Grand Palais and the sculptor received the Grand Prix. The following year he became a *chevalier* of the Légion d'Honneur. He showed the ensemble to further acclaim at the Pan-American Exposition in Buffalo in 1901, where he was awarded a special diploma and medal of honor. With the Nike of Samothrace clearly in mind, a French critic declared that Saint-Gaudens's statue of Victory "proves there are no subjects used up and done with, and that Art far from having said its last word, ceases not from renewing itself at the call of genius." Saint-Gaudens wrote that "for the first time in my life I had the swelled head." He exclaimed to his niece that "it's the grandest 'Victory' anybody ever made. Hoorah!"[61] He had challenged one of the most admired statues of Western civilization, and he had won.

Not everyone shared fully in this enthusiasm. The relationship between Saint-Gaudens and Henry Adams, tested by the making of the Rock Creek Cemetery memorial to Clover Adams after her suicide in 1885, was mutually rewarding but also mutually frustrating. Adams found Saint-Gaudens and his collaborator White unfamiliar with the Eastern religious principles that the widower intended to express, but he mostly left the anxious sculptor to devise his own solutions. The autobiography Adams circulated privately in 1907 returned to his differences with Saint-Gaudens in a climactic chapter set at the Paris Exposition of 1900. Drawing on the historian's study of Chartres and the Mont Saint-Michel, the chapter centered on parallels between medieval Catholicism and the new electric generator that powered the exposition hall of machines. Adams described the Virgin and the dynamo as "supersensual, occult; incapable of expression in horse-power." The materialist antithesis to this spiritual conjunction was the triumphal memorial in the Grand Palais. "For a symbol of power, St. Gaudens instinctively preferred the horse, as was evident in his horse and Victory of the Sherman monument," Adams quipped, relying on his intimate friendship with the general's niece Elizabeth Cameron to add that "doubtless Sherman also felt it so." Steeped in iconographical scholarship, Adams expected his readers to recall the Platonic understanding of equestrian statuary as a contest between intellect and carnal passion. As Saint-Gaudens's portrait of Logan revealed the ambition of the man on horseback, his Sherman monument rejected Old World convention by aligning his Victory with the horse rather than emulating the Catholic Virgin or the goddess Diana or any other sacrosanct personification of what Adams considered "the power of sex."[62]

The sources for the turn-of-the-century revision of Victory extended beyond the extramarital privileges enjoyed by White, MacMonnies, Saint-Gaudens, and Sherman. Daniel Chester French, whose domestic arrangements were more orthodox, developed a parallel conception for Andersonville National Cemetery, a somber site without the martial or commercial exhilaration of the West Point parade ground or Fifth Avenue. After working with Henry Bacon for several years on a Francis Parkman memorial that featured a Native American figure emerging from a marble slab, French adapted the method to propose an allegorical composition he later titled *Mourning Victory* to a committee established by the Connecticut legislature to dedicate a memorial to the state soldiers who had suffered in Confederate prisons. The committee of veterans rejected French's sketch in May 1906 and instead commissioned Bela Pratt's statue of a young soldier stripped of his rifle and gear, standing in stoic apprehension of the ordeal ahead.[63] French offered his design to James C. Melvin, a fellow townsman of Concord, Massachusetts, who had long ago broached the possibility of a memorial to three older brothers who had died in the Union army. Their former regiment organized the June 1909 dedicatory exercises for the Melvin Memorial at

FIGURE 4.12. Daniel Chester French and Henry Bacon, Melvin Memorial (*Mourning Victory*), Sleepy Hollow Cemetery, Concord, Massachusetts, 1906–8. Courtesy of the Library of Congress.

Sleepy Hollow Cemetery. The cenotaph in the final resting place of Ralph Waldo Emerson, Henry David Thoreau, Nathaniel Hawthorne, and Louisa May Alcott served as an autumnal flourish for the rural cemetery movement that had contributed so significantly to the early development of Civil War monuments.

French's image of Victory expanded on the ideal nudes by Horatio Greenough, Hiram Powers, Erastus Dow Palmer, and William Wetmore Story that had been central to the American sculptural canon of the mid-nineteenth century. The perfection and smoothness of marble testified to the moral purity of the women depicted in these works. Narrative furnished a logical explanation for display of the female body, as French's elegiac half-nude reflected her transition between the realm of death and the promise of afterlife. Pathos demanded a spiritualized view of flesh that ordinarily represented temptation. At the same time, French's allegorical figure was different from the captive maidens, the mythological or ancient heroines, and even the beautiful corpses that had proven most disquieting in this line of precedent. The latter works had treated death as an experience analogous to sexual knowledge, though with the certainty of no further ravishment.[64] French's goddess of resurrection moved easily from the forbidden underworld back into the light. Her long hair undone and undulating in harmony with the national flag that her bare arms lifted, she personified freedom from ordinary constraints. The creases on her drapery and the labial shape of the passage through which Victory emerged from the tomb-like slab provided a vivid reminder of the place of female sexuality in opening the prospect of life.

Eyelids half-open and full lips pressed softly, the marble face of the Melvin Memorial expressed a tenderness that critics also saw in other innovative depictions of Victory. The countenance of Ruckstuhl's winged figure for Jamaica, New York (1896), suggested "a message of reward for struggles gained, rather than the stern, solemn Victory of war that is so frequently shown." A review of Augustus Lukeman's monument for Somerville, Massachusetts (1909), reported that "a new meaning seems to be given it by the expression of this tall Nike—she is no bloodless, dispassionate goddess, serenely aloof, but there seems to be care and love and fear in her."[65] Sally James Farnham's crowning statue for the soldier monument in Ogdensburg, New York (1905), demonstrated that the sexualization of Victory was not limited to male sculptors.

After the Concord dedication Melvin supplied funding for a new carving of *Mourning Victory* that in 1915 became the first work by French to enter the Metropolitan Museum, which the sculptor served as a trustee. Two years later the museum purchased a gilded bronze reduction of Saint-Gaudens's allegorical figure from the Sherman memorial. The collection of these triumphs reflected the coalescence of an ideal that drew upon but departed from Old World imagery. Although informed by the Louvre precedent, the prevailing American remembrance was not a learned reconstitution and theatrical appropriation of classical tradition, ratifying the position of a settled social class. The most influential personifications of Victory instead expressed dreams of contentment commissioned by powerful but still avidly grasping elites. Civil War triumph augured further success, unbounded by ancient constrictions.

VICTORIOUS PEACE

Henry James anticipated his friend Henry Adams in criticizing the Sherman monument in New York. In a travel essay about his native city published in January 1906, the expatriate author praised the "dauntless refinement" of the group but objected that its underlying idea "strikes me as equivocal, or more exactly as double" because the allegorical figure implied that "the

destroyer is a messenger of peace." James expressed skepticism "of all attempts, however glittering and golden, to confound destroyers with bene-
factors." Like Adams's sarcasm, this argument addressed a primary element
of Saint-Gaudens's conception. The sculptor had even made a separate head
of the female figure and a relief version, both of which he labeled Nike-
Eirene, the goddesses of Victory and Peace. He complained to James that
"it is because I feel so strongly the damnation of the whole business of war,
that I made it, the very reason for which you want it otherwise!"[66] Saint-
Gaudens's sentiments reflected the prominence of peace initiatives within
elite metropolitan society since the Spanish-American War, culminating in
the founding of the New York Peace Society in February 1906. The main orator at the Sherman monument unveiling, Elihu Root, was a central figure in
the movement; he participated in lawyers' campaigns to promote international arbitration and would in 1910 be appointed by New York Peace Society
president Andrew Carnegie to head the new Carnegie Endowment for International Peace. James harkened back to a more radical tradition. His father
had maintained that "no existing government, nor indeed any now possible
government, is worth an honest human life," although like many pacifists he
gave his blessings to two sons who enlisted in the effort to end slavery.[67] A
variety of Civil War monuments amplified the brief debate between James
and Saint-Gaudens about the relationship between victory and peace, but
the Sherman equestrian illustrated an increasing tendency to merge the two
concepts by the early twentieth century.

The first northern monuments often articulated Union understanding
of the conflict as a criminal disturbance with an outcome that resembled
lawful order rather than a war with an outcome that resembled martial triumph, even if the federal enforcement personnel consisted of soldiers. This
rationale was fundamental to Lincoln's call for troops as well as the American Peace Society's endorsement of that measure. The monument installed
in Kensington, Connecticut, in July 1863 accordingly commemorated "THE
DEATH / OF THOSE WHO PERISHED IN SUPPRESSING / THE SOUTH-
ERN REBELLION." Constabulary formulations remained commonplace
in inscriptions for a decade, during which some monuments gave the idea
visual form. Batterson Monument Works furnished Greenfield, Massachusetts, with a granite column topped by a bronze eagle strangling serpents in
its nest, dedicated in 1870 to "HER PATRIOTIC SONS / WHO OFFERED
THEIR LIVES / IN SUPPRESSING THE GREAT REBELLION." Alfred B.
Mullett, supervising architect of the U.S. Treasury Department, designed a

similar composition for Delaware, installed in Wilmington in 1871 in honor of the state's "PATRIOTIC DEAD WHO SACRIFICED THEIR LIVES FOR THEIR COUNTRY / DURING THE REBELLION OF 1861–1865."[68]

Much as the Lincoln administration complicated the Union legal premise in such situations as the imposition of a naval blockade and the treatment of prisoners, a substantial portion of early inscriptions described the suppression of the rebellion as a war. The memorial in Stockbridge, Massachusetts (1866), recalled "HER SONS / BELOVED AND HONORED / WHO DIED FOR THEIR COUNTRY / IN THE GREAT WAR OF THE REBELLION." By the mid-1870s the term "war of the rebellion" and variants like "war for the suppression of the rebellion" routinely injected into Union memory the tension between police and military action. Lynn, Massachusetts, exemplified this ambiguity in an 1873 memorial that featured an allegorical representation of the city flanked by figures personifying Justice and War.

The Naval Monument conceptualized by David Dixon Porter and executed by Franklin Simmons most conspicuously dramatized the divergent views of the conflict's outcome. Originally planned to ornament the Naval Academy grounds when Porter raised funds as superintendent in the late 1860s, the design featured a statue of America weeping on the shoulder of History, beneath which a chastely draped Victory held up a laurel wreath while infants Mars and Neptune sat at her feet. Congress authorized placement of the monument in Washington after Porter left Annapolis, and the admiral's committee put it in 1877 on the foot of Capitol Hill. The statue of Victory looked westward down Pennsylvania Avenue, the route of the Grand Review celebration of Union triumph. Congress also provided funds for addition of a statue of Peace, installed on the opposite side from Victory so as to look east toward the Capitol, home of the representative democracy disrupted by secession. Simmons's seminude Peace, holding an olive branch, recapitulated long-standing views of commerce and learning as antitheses of war. Surrounding the allegorical figure were a horn of plenty, a shock of wheat topped by a dove, a gear, an angle tool, and a book. The fountain beneath the monument offered a placid foundation for the naval theme. Olmsted set up two bronze vases on the Peace side designed to create an arc of water lit by gas jets to produce a rainbow. Although the memorial partly saluted Union victory, the array of familiar peace iconography and the congressional funding for the Capitol-side statue at the close of Reconstruction soon caused the work to be known popularly as the Peace Monument rather than the Naval Monument.[69]

The Soldiers' National Monument presented a more transformative

FIGURE 4.13. Franklin Simmons and Edward Clark, Naval Monument (Peace Monument), west side, 1871–78. Courtesy of the Library of Congress.

vision of peace than the return to harmony imagined by Porter and Simmons. In the same tradition as the Capitol Hill group, the Gettysburg monument dedicated in 1869 situated Peace alongside Prosperity, which balanced the conversation between History and the Soldier that completed the set of four statues placed beneath an allegorical figure holding a laurel wreath. Prosperity was a classical female figure bearing fruits and a sheaf of wheat indicative of the regained national bounty, but Peace was a mid-nineteenth-century mechanic in a leather apron. He held a mallet in his right hand, and

FIGURE 4.14. Franklin Simmons and Edward Clark, Naval Monument (Peace Monument), east side, 1871–78. Courtesy of the Architect of the Capitol.

a cogwheel stood next to his chair, which was decorated with a picture of a steam locomotive. This personification of Peace reflected not only the restoration of commerce but also the free-labor ideology behind the Republican commitment to the extirpation of slavery. In a monument placed at the site where Lincoln had delivered the Gettysburg Address, the allusion linked the new birth of freedom to the future of representative democracy and suggested the necessity of social justice for lasting peace.

More often, the argument that the Union won rather than restored concord envisioned the clash of arms as a paradoxical prelude to peace. Civic monuments were less likely than literature to celebrate sectional reconciliation grounded in mutual respect for martial valor, as northern veterans' influence in the making of memorials deepened local disinclination to concede moral parity to Confederates. The censorious compound "war of the rebel-

Visions of Victory

FIGURE 4.15. Batterson Monumental Works, Soldiers'
National Monument, Gettysburg, detail, *Peace*, 1864–69.
Courtesy of the National Park Service, Gettysburg National Military Park.

lion" gradually became less commonplace but continued to appear in monument inscriptions into the early twentieth century. Some memorial projects
nonetheless embraced the northern romance of reunion. Fresh from their
collaboration on the Alliance and Victory Monument at Yorktown, Virginia (1884), Richard Morris Hunt and J. Q. A. Ward proposed to Brooklyn

a cylindrical drum crowned by an allegorical figure of Peace separating two combatants. The artists stipulated that "her sympathies seem more directed toward the weaker."[70] Allentown, Pennsylvania, demonstrated the surge of reconciliationist rhetoric that accompanied the Spanish-American War. The monument dedicated in October 1899 centered on statues of a Union and a Confederate soldier standing side-by-side beneath the American flag. A local newspaper claimed that the group was "the subject of more orators, even before the unveiling, than any ornament ever placed on any American monument." Dedicatory speaker George F. Baer, soon to become president of the Philadelphia and Reading Railroad and belligerent spokesman for mine owners in the 1902 anthracite coal strike, echoed the newspaper's observation that the statuary depicted both citizen-soldiers "in a most aggressive attitude." The industrialist emphasized that "in all ages and among all peoples, the warrior is honored above all other men."[71] The constabulary notion of a suppressed rebellion had foreshadowed no future resort to arms, but the martial triumph of national unity offered little prospect of tranquillity in international affairs or labor relations.

Northern monuments of sectional reconciliation appeared particularly in settings that patently addressed national audiences. Grant's Tomb, which featured his declaration "LET US HAVE PEACE" on the front pediment, flanked by allegorical figures of Victory and Peace, showed how fully the hero of Appomattox embodied the twin outcomes of the war. Although the federal Grant Memorial Commission chose Shrady and Casey's different motif for the equestrian monument in Washington, most proposals centered on the relationship between victory and peace. Several designs featured figures that specifically represented the North and the South.[72] The New York Peace Monument at Chickamauga and Chattanooga National Park, a federal site designed to celebrate blue-gray fraternity, attracted wide attention at its dedication in 1910. Roland Hinton Perry's sculpture atop the tall victory column on Lookout Mountain depicted a Union and a Confederate soldier joining hands beneath the American flag. In the memorial to the Yale dead of both sides, an inscription above one of Henry Hering's allegorical reliefs asserted that "PEACE CROWNS THEIR ACT OF SACRIFICE."[73]

Several southern monuments expanded on the theme of Confederate contributions to the triumph of peace. Moses Ezekiel's memorial for Arlington National Cemetery was the most dramatic example. Some white southerners feared that the initiative implied compromise and favored repatriation of the Confederate dead. Ezekiel made no concessions, however, in the circular relief sculpture that depicted southern soldiers leaving home to defend their slave society at the behest of helmeted Athena. Rising from this martial display was an allegorical figure crowned by an olive wreath and presenting a laurel wreath, images of peace and victory. The plowstock and pruning hook in her hand corresponded to a Biblical inscription placed between the lower and upper registers of the monument: "AND THEY SHALL BEAT THEIR SWORDS INTO PLOWSHARES AND THEIR SPEARS INTO PRUNING HOOKS." In this composition Peace rested on military gallantry, and the transformation of weapons into agricultural implements was an exercise of masterly dominion. UCV commander-in-chief Bennett Young's address at the 1913 dedication aligned the monument with white southern insistence on the ultimate triumph of the Lost Cause. "Right lives forever," he promised. "It survives battles, failures, conflict and death. There is no human power, however mighty, that can in the end annihilate truth." For Young, the monument marked "another step in the complete elimination of sectional passions, suspicions or prejudice" insofar as it demonstrated federal recognition of the just southern cause and Confederate battlefield heroism.[74]

The Gate City Guard monument dedicated in Atlanta in 1911 affirmed that southern military prowess undergirded sectional harmony. A bronze tablet inscription recalled that the socially elite militia unit had traveled north in 1879 to greet former foes on a "MISSION OF PEACE" and dedicated the memorial to these "PATRIOTIC CONTRIBUTIONS TO THE CAUSE OF NATIONAL FRATERNITY." Allen G. Newman's composition emphasized the southern mettle that made such pacific gestures meaningful. A young soldier wearing a slouch hat and knotted neckerchief knelt in firing position on a battlefield, his trousers tucked into his boots and his finger on the trigger of his rifle. An allegorical Peace bearing an olive branch prompted the Confederate to look up and turn his gun to the side. Sherman's juggernaut had not subdued this indomitable warrior. Peace arrived suddenly, wings flaring from her landing as in traditional representations of Victory. The soldier acceded to the female figure's restraining hand as a caption announced, "CEASE FIRING — PEACE IS PROCLAIMED." This account of the end and aftermath of the Confederacy provided fresh meaning for the prominently featured Latin motto that proclaimed the Gate City Guard first in war and first in peace.

The trope of soldiers' reconciliation and countless oratorical references to the arbitrament of the battlefield as a resolution of constitutional debates over secession established war as an indispensable element of peace. The Sherman equestrian in Washington, on which an inscription quoted the general's statement that "WAR'S LEGITIMATE OBJECT IS MORE PERFECT

FIGURE 4.16.
Moses Ezekiel,
Confederate Monument,
Arlington National
Cemetery, 1910–14.
Courtesy of the Library
of Congress.

PEACE," presented the relationship in ostensibly contrasting allegories. War was a hideous fury rending her garments as a vulture descended on a dead soldier; Peace was a seminude young woman who stood above playful children. As one critic observed, however, the lithe figure mirrored popular images of the quintessential female warrior, Joan of Arc.[75] Similarly, representations of peace as the homecoming of soldiers, such as the elaborate statuary group on the Soldiers and Sailors Monument in Indianapolis, merely shared perpetual reversibility with depictions of soldiers leaving home for war.

The column dedicated in Michigan City, Indiana, in 1893, which included a frieze of the call to arms, featured an elegant crowning figure identified in newspaper coverage as Victorious Peace. The double identity sealed the displacement of earlier commemorations that treated the suppression of the rebellion as fundamentally different from a war and not conducive to triumph. William R. O'Donovan and Jonathan Scott Hartley's allegory marked the path that Saint-Gaudens's ideal Nike-Eirene would follow. Other monuments expressed similar conceptions without such specific names. The so-called Peace Monument in Decatur, Indiana (1913), honored local soldiers who had fought in the War of 1812, the Mexican War, the Civil War, and the Spanish-American War, as well as battlefield nurses. On the rear of the pylon, the pacific connotations of a fountain paled alongside a tablet made of metal from the battleship *Maine*, a reminder of notorious warmongering. Fierce eagles embellished the upper corners of the rectangular pylon. The front side featured plaques listing the Adams County soldiers in the four wars, before which stood a heroic statue of Peace. She held a laurel twig, described by a local newspaper as "symbolical of perseverance, ambition and glory." A sheathed sword at her side, she rested her shield on the ground because "the conflict is over and she no longer has need of it on her arm."[76]

If Saint-Gaudens's image of Victory promised a fuller consummation than the success embodied by the Hellenistic marble at the Louvre, the conflation of Nike and Eirene also echoed the epic ambitions of Richard Wagner's protagonist Siegfried, whose name was a compound of Victory and Peace. The Albany Soldiers and Sailors Memorial, the result of an aggressive GAR campaign that yielded a $100,000 municipal appropriation in 1908, summarized much recent thinking about Civil War triumph. The commission initially favored "either a column somewhat similar to the one erected on Lookout mountain or a decorated arch" if the budget permitted, or otherwise a variation on the Jefferson Davis Memorial in Richmond.[77] Choosing to conduct a select invitational competition, the commission rejected an extraordinary proposal by Lorado Taft for an ensemble designed

FIGURE 4.17. Hermon A. MacNeil, Albany Soldiers and Sailors Memorial
(*The Nation of Peace Won through Victorious War*), 1909–12.
Courtesy of the Albany Institute of History and Art.

to recall the grief that swept through communities devastated by the loss of life during the war. The composition depicted a funeral cortège led by a soldier and sailor but dominated by a Rodinesque swarm of weeping mourners around a bier. Around the edges of the monument platform stood statues of soldiers with rifles grounded, hats removed, and heads bowed. In the era of active poses, the figures looked back to the immediacy of early postwar images of distressed soldiers. Flames in ornate cauldrons illuminated the scene. Newspaper coverage indicated that the Albany commission considered Taft's proposal "the most striking" but "too funereal for the purpose."[78]

Visions of Victory

The commission instead chose a design that Hermon A. MacNeil titled *The Nation of Peace Won through Victorious War*. A large rectangular marble slab served as the ground for relief scenes of the departure for war and a battle. The reliefs on the ends of the block represented Victory and Peace, now complementary figures rather than the opposing ideals represented on the Naval Monument in Washington. MacNeil's juxtaposition came together in a heroic-sized central statue of America risen from her chair of state, "bearing the sword as a symbol of war and palms as the symbol of peace, showing the esteem in which her armies are held." Unlike the sensuous allegories of MacMonnies, Saint-Gaudens, and French, this armed and helmeted bronze was a "figure of might and dignity, commanding in pose, almost grim in its classic severity." MacNeil sought extreme pathos as well as extreme grandeur, obtaining permission from the commission to depict a drummer boy dying at the front.[79]

Despite its pretensions to totality, the idyll of Victorious Peace lacked the social transformation that the Soldiers' National Monument at Gettysburg associated with the ends of the war. George Honig's bronze groups for the facade of the Soldiers and Sailors Memorial Coliseum in Evansville, Indiana, illustrated the tendency of the formula to collapse into the same self-satisfied complacency as the triumphal arch in Madison, Wisconsin. One side of the entryway presented a scene titled *The Spirit of 1861*, which featured "a striking figure of Victory with the flag swirling around the head and body" amid a "tense, dynamic" depiction of battle. The opposite side offered a peace group titled *The Spirit of 1916*, in which an allegorical figure stood above two aged GAR veterans "seated calmly and comfortably, as if telling each other briny yarns."[80] Dedicated in April 1917, two weeks after the United States declared war on Germany, the embellishments of the memorial convention facility illustrated the weakness in crisis of the business-centered peace organizations that had flourished since the Spanish-American War. Contrary to Woodrow Wilson's recent call for "peace without victory," the lesson of Union and Confederate commemoration was that war was the best means to end war. This moral was one of many ways in which Civil War monuments shaped American understanding of the Great War.

The GREAT WAR and CIVIL WAR MEMORY

"There has never been a period since the end of hostilities that monument-building was more active and incessant," the magazine *Confederate Veteran* observed in August 1914. Editor Sumner Cunningham rightly predicted that "when the historian comes to count the monuments builded to perpetuate the memories of heroes of the Confederate States, he will pause and question if his figures be really correct." The conspicuous phenomenon had recently prompted several attempts at measurement. Bettie A. C. Emerson reported a total of 634 Confederate monuments across the country in 1911. At the same time Mildred Lewis Rutherford identified 103 monuments in Georgia alone, or 16 more than Emerson had found, with 11 new monuments under way. In a claim that would often be repeated, Gen. Bennett Young declared at the June 1914 dedication of the Confederate monument in Arlington cemetery that "there are more monuments erected to commemorate Confederate valor and sacrifice than were ever built to any cause, civil, political, or religious."[1] But the boom in Civil War monuments was intersectional.

In the Midwest as well as the South the number of monuments increased more than twice as rapidly in the decade ending in 1915 as in the decade ending in 1905, and during the same period New England exceeded a regional pace that had previously been the highest in the country.

This acceleration could not continue indefinitely. Eventually the proliferation of monuments would satisfy the demand for commemoration of the Civil War in public spaces. The passage of time was rapidly thinning the ranks of the veterans whom recent monuments most often honored. The end of the semicentennial anniversary of the war would close an occasion for remembrance. The southern women for whom sponsorship of Confederate monuments had provided a political platform were considering new options for participation in the Lost Cause, or for moving beyond it. Expanding on their resistance to public memorials to Confederate women, UDC members began to urge that the resources invested in Civil War monuments should be redirected to academic scholarships.[2] This pressure for utilitarian alternatives was only one of several long-term challenges that confronted the civic monument as a cultural form. The maturation of the automobile portended fundamental changes in the spatial organization of American life. As early as 1914 the hazards posed by increasing traffic caused Coweta County, Georgia, to move its Confederate monument from a prominent intersection to the courthouse grounds.[3] Popular entertainments increasingly undercut or competed with the experience offered by civic monuments. On July 4, 1914, director D. W. Griffith started production on his cinematic monument to the sectional conflict, *The Birth of a Nation*.

At the time of Cunningham's assessment, the Civil War monument remained a vital institution despite these threats. Many towns and counties throughout the North and South still lacked monuments, and some communities had begun to replace or supplement older memorials now deemed inadequate. The W. H. Mullins Company of Salem, Ohio, expressed confidence in the market for lower-cost memorials by issuing a catalog in 1913 that promoted Civil War monuments made of sheet metal.[4] Similarly, the McNeel Marble Company reserved the back-cover advertisement of *Confederate Veteran* for almost half of all months from 1911 through summer 1914. At the other end of the budgetary spectrum, several major cities continued to debate grand municipal monuments. Tributes to women had recently expanded the thematic range of potential Civil War memorials. Abraham Lincoln, a relatively dormant figure in the late-nineteenth-century landscape of commemoration, was attracting a flurry of new monuments, especially in the years since the 1909 centennial of his birth.

The prospect that the making of Civil War monuments would continue to follow a foreseeable pattern over the next few decades, gradually entering a decline mitigated by important initiatives, lurched suddenly in a different direction in the same month Cunningham published his overview. The outbreak of the Great War immediately touched Civil War remembrance, and the interaction intensified after American intervention. Recollections of the 1860s became a framework for thinking about war-related topics ranging from battlefield strategy to financial policy to presidential-congressional relations.[5] In no field did the shadow of the Civil War loom more conspicuously than the postarmistice construction of public monuments. World War memorial promoters built logically on recent Civil War exemplars, for those works had helped to shape the vision of the military and society underlying structural innovations that characterized World War mobilization, including the elimination of the U.S. Volunteers, the coordination of the militia with the regular army, the introduction of the Selective Service System, the rise of reserve officer training programs, and the implementation of the general staff system. Some internationalists sought to align American remembrance with the Allied Powers, but Civil War precedents proved more influential. At the same time, the European cataclysm obliged Americans to reconsider their past as they unveiled Civil War monuments commissioned in peacetime and decided whether to initiate and how to design and dedicate new memorials. From the Lincoln Memorial in Washington to the granite steles placed in cemeteries across the country, Civil War monuments installed during the quarter century after 1914 were important sites of American reflection on the trauma of the World War and the challenge of modernity.

THE ORACLE

The Lincoln Memorial was the most important Civil War commemoration to span the years of the Great War. Originating in the Senate Park Commission proposals of 1901, the basic design phase of the project culminated twelve years later in congressional endorsement of the architectural plans developed by Henry Bacon for the Lincoln Memorial Commission established at the semicentennial of the Civil War's outbreak. Daniel Chester French agreed in late 1914 to provide the statue for his friend's building, and carving of the marble began in the same month as the European armistice. The dedication ceremony took place on Memorial Day 1922. A relatively minor theme in Civil War monuments since the unveiling of Thomas Ball's emancipation group in Washington and Boston and Augustus Saint-Gaudens's ac-

The Great War and Civil War Memory

claimed standing portrait in Chicago, the war president had begun to attract fresh attention in the early twentieth century, mostly from individual sponsors rather than public fund-raising. These precedents elaborated a martial interpretation of Lincoln that original plans for the Mall memorial proposed to amplify. Bacon and French instead developed a remarkable tribute to a philosophical leader, though the shadows of the Great War would counterbalance their avoidance of belligerence.

The civilian commander-in-chief of Union forces had the potential to embody a variety of political and military narratives. Inclusion of the president in a soldier monument could add ideological direction to a design that honored martial sacrifice. Leonard Volk's monument to the war dead of Rochester, New York, dedicated on Memorial Day 1892 in the presence of President Benjamin Harrison, former Rochester resident Frederick Douglass, and an estimated 250,000 other participants, was a leading example. Infantry, artillery, cavalry, and naval statues surrounded the central column, which featured panels depicting the assault on Fort Sumter, the battle between the *Monitor* and *Merrimac*, Pickett's charge, and Lee's surrender. The figure of Lincoln atop the central column, holding a scroll that presumably represented the Emancipation Proclamation, invoked the abolitionist legacy of the burned-over district. The inscription affirmed his Gettysburg pledge that "WE HERE HIGHLY RESOLVE THAT THE DEAD / SHALL NOT HAVE DIED IN VAIN."[6]

More often, however, turn-of-the-century tributes to Lincoln reduced the president to roles as orchestrator and supporter of the army and navy. Ornamentation of the Brooklyn victory arch included a large panel that depicted Lincoln on horseback, apparently reviewing the troops, much like the pendant relief of Grant on the opposite side of the archway. No less ambitious for the size of the community was the $73,000 ensemble in Muskegon, Michigan, funded by lumber magnate Charles Hackley. Surrounded by a public library and a high school that Hackley had donated to the town, the centerpiece of Hackley Park was a soldier monument that followed the same pattern as the Rochester monument except that its top was a figure of Victory. For the four corners of the park Hackley commissioned statues of Grant, Sherman, Farragut, and Lincoln, which the town unveiled on Memorial Day 1900. The president held a sheaf of oversized papers in his lap, perhaps the Emancipation Proclamation, but he clearly fit into the group as part of a military team. Businessmen in Kenosha, Wisconsin, partially emulated Hackley's model by commissioning Daniel H. Burnham to design a beaux arts public library with a column topped by Nike at the center of an adjacent park, dedicated in 1900, and later adding a copy of the Lincoln statue that Hackley had placed in Muskegon.[7] The other statues of Lincoln completed in the first years of the twentieth century also identified the president with the military. Union veteran John W. Kitchell commissioned a statue by Charles Mulligan for a cemetery near Rosamond, Illinois, dedicated in 1903 "IN MEMORY OF THE UNION SOLDIERS AND SAILORS AND THEIR BELOVED COMMANDER-IN-CHIEF." Two years later a GAR post installed a copy of the statue in Oak Woods cemetery in Chicago. Charles Clinton placed a Lincoln statue by W. Granville Hastings in a Cincinnati suburb in 1902 and a copy in Bunker Hill, Illinois, that honored Clinton's company in the First Missouri Regiment of Cavalry Volunteers, much of which he had recruited in the community.[8]

Senate Park Commission members Burnham, Charles McKim, Frederick Law Olmsted Jr., and Saint-Gaudens envisioned a similarly martial commemoration of Lincoln in the nation's capital. They first planned to honor Grant with a triumphal arch at the key point on the Mall that would extend the axis from the Capitol through the Washington Monument and also serve as the Washington terminus for the proposed memorial bridge to Arlington National Cemetery. When Grenville Dodge of the Grant Memorial Commission insisted on an equestrian statue rather than an arch, the Senate Park Commission reassigned the Mall junction to Lincoln, whose memorial had been planned for what eventually became the site of the Jefferson Memorial. Whether for Grant or his commander-in-chief, the artists wanted a monument that combined the theatrical traffic distribution of the Arc de Triomphe in Paris with the more extended horizontal profile of the Brandenburg Gate in Berlin. The commission report even recommended planting the surrounding landscape with linden trees, like the Unter den Linden, the boulevard running from the Brandenburg Gate to the Imperial Palace.[9] McKim's sketch of the Lincoln Memorial featured a large screen of Doric columns, embellished with tablets and sculpture and surmounted by a central crowning group. A statue of Lincoln would stand on the Capitol side of the portico, but the structure would also look across the river toward Arlington. McKim considered the two-sided design a crucial feature. Balancing the Lincoln Memorial in front of the Capitol was a monumental Union square, which would become the site of the Grant memorial and, the planners hoped, the commissioned equestrian monuments to Sherman and Sheridan that instead went to Pennsylvania Avenue and Massachusetts Avenue.[10] In this scheme, as at Muskegon, Lincoln was honored primarily as part of the Union military team.

FIGURE 5.1. View of proposed Lincoln Memorial, published in *Improvement of the Park System of the District of Columbia*, edited by Charles Moore (1902). Courtesy of the National Gallery of Art Library, David K. E. Bruce Fund.

The passage of almost a decade between the Senate Park Commission report in January 1902 and the Lincoln Memorial Commission's designation of Henry Bacon as consulting architect in August 1911 largely reinforced McKim's concept. Public discussion of the proposed Mall memorial contributed to enthusiasm for the 1909 centenary of Lincoln's birth. Observance of that anniversary naturally focused on Lincoln's origins and built on a mythology well established in print and oratory, though not in public monuments until Charles Mulligan's portrait statue of Lincoln as a railsplitter, installed in Chicago in 1911. Even as the centenary deepened public interest in the prepresidential Lincoln as an individual personality, however, martial themes dominated most of the monuments that the anniversary prompted. Louis Bell Post #3 of the GAR in Manchester, New Hampshire, led the fundraising campaign that culminated on Memorial Day 1910 in the unveiling of a life-sized version of John Rogers's portrait statue of Lincoln studying a battle map, adapted from the *Council of War* statuette group Rogers had sold widely in the 1860s. The town of East Orange, New Jersey, commissioned a statue by Francis Elwell, dedicated on Flag Day 1911, that depicted Lincoln reviewing troops while wearing a quasi-military cape over his suit. Gutzon Borglum's composition in Newark (1911) centered on one of the most popular martial Lincoln themes, the president's anguish over the casualty reports received in the White House telegraph office.[11] The monument claimed for the commander-in-chief, and personification of the nation-state, a lead role in the grief once reserved for soldiers' families and friends.

The primary alternatives to the Senate Park Commission plan for a Lincoln memorial on the Mall in Washington shared the militarism of McKim's design and the works by Rogers, Elwell, and Borglum. Most persistent was the agitation for a memorial parkway honoring Lincoln that would connect Gettysburg and Washington, or, in some advocates' proposals, continue beyond Washington to Richmond. The campaign benefited from the prestige of Gettysburg as a shrine and more broadly from the Civil War battlefield park movement. Promoters of the parkway proposed to rely for its embellishment on the same method that the battlefield parks had adopted: installation of works sponsored by state governments and voluntary organizations like veterans' groups. Some proponents believed that those tributes should focus not only on Lincoln but also on the Union soldiers he had led. The destination of the road similarly subordinated Lincoln to a military narrative. Gettysburg may have been the scene of Lincoln's greatest intellectual achievement, but the park there had never accepted Charles Sumner's observation that "the battle itself was less important than the speech. Ideas are more than battles." A memorial road to Richmond would even more bluntly celebrate the Civil War as a pageant of martial valor and sectional reunion. Other alternatives recommended making the bridge to Arlington National Cemetery, rather than a new monument or parkway, the commemoration of Lincoln. After McKim's death in 1909 opened the question of the memorial designer, McKim, Mead & White alumnus Harold Van Buren Magonigle put forward his bid for the commission by urging construction of a triumphal arch at the bridge entrance. The suggestion was ideologically if not formally similar to McKim's plan.[12]

That the Lincoln Memorial took a different form with different possibilities was due to the partnership of Henry Bacon and Daniel Chester French. The two men were close friends with similar family backgrounds and Emersonian inclinations. Bacon's biographer has rightly called them "the quintessence of New England Idealism in its autumnal phase." They had already collaborated on eighteen projects—including the home and studio near Stockbridge, Massachusetts, that Bacon had designed for French—when the Commission of Fine Arts (CFA), established by Congress to assist the Lincoln Memorial Commission, recommended Bacon as the architect for the Lincoln Memorial. A member of the seven-person CFA and soon to become its chairman on Burnham's death, French played an active role in the selection. One of the chief arguments in Bacon's favor was that he had worked directly with McKim in the 1890s before setting up his own practice. Christopher Thomas plausibly suggests that most members of the CFA as well as the Lincoln Memorial Commission that adopted its recommendation looked on the forty-four-year-old Bacon as the architect who could best realize the vision of his former mentor.[13]

This expectation failed to reckon with the independence Bacon had demonstrated while building a reputation as a consummate professional. He had left the University of Illinois after only one year to follow what was becoming the outmoded custom of working without college education as a draftsman in an architect's office. Upon achieving his goal of winning a prestigious traveling fellowship for rising architects in Boston, he ignored advice to enroll in the École des Beaux-Arts and irked the fellowship sponsors by pursuing a self-directed study program focused primarily on Greece that he developed with advice from his older brother, a protégé of Charles Eliot Norton and leader in the excavations at Assos supported by the founding of the American Institute of Archaeology. At the end of his fellowship Bacon joined McKim, Mead & White, where he was one of the first associates invited to enter the partnership. But he chose to remain a salaried employee and soon left the elite firm because he did not want to work at what he called a "plan factory," in which the principals increasingly devoted their time to the cultivation of clients while younger architects attended to most of the drawing.[14]

The solo practice that Bacon set up after several years in partnership with a fellow McKim, Mead & White alumnus satisfied his ideal of architecture as a craft. Although he designed a variety of buildings, his practice focused on settings for public monuments to a degree possible only during the peak period in the construction of memorials. These projects, well suited to the scale of the practice he sought to sustain, reflected both an academic temperament and an interest in collaboration with sculptors that expressed Bacon's collegial personality and his commitment to building as a profoundly social activity. Inevitably many of these monuments focused on the Civil War, and long before Bacon came under consideration to design the Lincoln Memorial he had enjoyed ample professional opportunity to reflect on the legacy of the sectional conflict.

Bacon and French had worked together on several Civil War projects, including the work that most foreshadowed the Lincoln Memorial, the monument unveiled on Labor Day 1912 in Lincoln, Nebraska. Unlike the statues by Rogers, Elwell, and Borglum that honored Lincoln as commander-in-chief, the French-Bacon composition developed Saint-Gaudens's emphasis on Lincoln as an orator. Modeled on Polyeuktos's statue of Demosthenes, French's portrait depicted Lincoln with head bowed, eyebrows furrowed, hands interlaced, and weight balanced on his back foot. Like the tightly

FIGURE 5.2. Daniel Chester French and Henry Bacon,
Lincoln Memorial, Lincoln, Nebraska, 1909–12.
Courtesy of the Chesterwood Archives, Chapin Library, Williams College.

wrapped himation worn by Polyeuktos's Demosthenes, the buttoned frock coat of French's Lincoln firmly enclosed the body of the orator, and the pressures within him, to direct attention to the inner life of the hero.[15] Bacon's setting for the statue was a large panel, only inches behind the figure, inscribed with the text of the Gettysburg Address in a square as tall as French's figure. More constrained and pensive than the Lincoln that Saint-Gaudens had depicted stepping forward from a chair, the Bacon-French memorial struck some observers as too reserved.[16] Few people would make the same criticism of the monument for the Mall on which Bacon began to work only seven months after completing the design for Nebraska, but the two works shared the same view of Lincoln's significance.

Bacon diverged from McKim's design for the Lincoln Memorial so successfully that the earlier proposal eventually became unimaginable, and rarely remembered. Bacon envisioned the monument not as a screen that would connect the Mall with Arlington National Cemetery but as a solid terminus. In place of the Brandenburg Gate or the Arc de Triomphe, he chose the Parthenon as his chief point of historical reference. Turning its back on Arlington National Cemetery, his Lincoln Memorial would evoke the democracy associated with Greece rather than the empire associated with Rome. Bacon's adaptation of a classical temple certainly did not lack a sense of state power. He argued that a closed building was better than a portico because the Parthenon statue of Athena showed that "the power of impression by an object of reverence and honor is greatest when it is secluded and isolated." But the Lincoln who deserved such reverence and honor was a distinctive individual more than a representative of state authority or a personification of the Civil War narrative. Long before French received the commission, Bacon called for the main room of the memorial interior to focus on a portrait statue "which through subtle interpretation of personality must dominate the hall."[17] Bacon's ideal of leadership had decided institutional implications, and his memorial linked with the Washington Monument to exalt the office of the presidency. Unlike McKim's proposal or most of the other Lincoln monuments commissioned at the same time, however, Bacon's design declined to celebrate the military as a model for American society.

Similar premises governed Bacon's plans for the subordinate elements of the Lincoln Memorial. He recognized immediately that the building could easily become a museum housing a wide range of relics associated with Lincoln or more broadly with the Civil War, and he adopted a firm policy of resistance to any such displays. More remarkably for a project that found inspiration in the Parthenon, the most famous example of narrative architectural sculpture in world history, Bacon eschewed any comparable decoration for the Lincoln Memorial. Relying for visual interest on the extraordinarily pure and white Colorado marble on which he spent much of his budget, he added little embellishment to the exterior of the building. The most notable ornamentation was the incision of the names of the states with the dates of their admission to the union, interspersed with small wreaths of pine and laurel that rather half-heartedly symbolized sectional reunion, as both kinds of trees grow in the North and the South. Inside the building, he devoted the side chambers to panels inscribed with the texts of the Gettysburg Address and Second Inaugural Address, above which he installed allegorical murals depicting *The Emancipation of a Race* and *Reunion*, respectively. The paucity of this decorative program drew strenuous protest from Borglum, who maintained that "the story must be wrought in great friezes and groups, including the great actors with Lincoln." Bacon defended his focus on the two speeches by insisting that the texts were more important than "guns or battle scenes." The separation of the side chambers from the central portrait statue reinforced Bacon's commitment to Lincoln's words as disembodied statements of principle, ensuring that his ideas would "not be confused with his personality, but pondered in seeming seclusion."[18]

For the statue in the main hall Bacon sought a work that expressed "the gentleness, power, and intelligence" of Lincoln.[19] The impression of power has often been central to discussions of French's figure, which is nineteen feet high from head to feet and would be twenty-eight feet tall if standing. The emphasis on the gentleness and especially the intelligence of Lincoln deserves further attention. If French's statue of Lincoln for the Nebraska capital updated Polyeuktos's portrait of Demosthenes, the statue for the national capital invoked a Hellenistic tradition of seated personality portraits of philosophers and philosopher-kings. The rippling panels of Lincoln's coat merged with the large shawl draped over his chair to encase him in classical folds. The president nestled into a chair of state with a deep seat and high sides, a piece of furniture more substantial and less purely ceremonial than the chairs of state that accompanied seated Lincoln statues by Saint-Gaudens in Chicago, Charles Niehaus in Muskegon, and Adolph Weinman in Hodgenville, Kentucky. This Lincoln planned to remain seated indefinitely. He embodied thought rather than action.

French's representational strategy differed sharply from the countless narrative monumental portraits set either at a specific or a generic moment in the sectional conflict. As the sculptor indicated in summarizing his motif

The Great War and Civil War Memory

FIGURE 5.3. Daniel Chester French, Lincoln statue,
Lincoln Memorial, Washington, DC, 1914–22. Photograph by Bernie Cliff.
Courtesy of the Chesterwood Archives, Chapin Library, Williams College.

as "work over, victory his," this Lincoln lived in the postwar world. Rather than reflecting on the sectional conflict, he was prepared to receive the visitors toward whom he tilted his massive head for discussion of their affairs. The forward-looking image drew upon a devotional style popularized by Theodore Roosevelt, who kept behind his presidential desk a Lincoln portrait and declared that "when confronted with a great problem, I look up to that picture, and I do as I believe Lincoln would have done." The question "What would Lincoln do?" became an increasingly common rhetorical expression in the 1912 presidential campaign and the years that followed, even providing the motif of a popular song published in 1918. William Howard Taft captured the sentiment behind the phrase when he observed that "we feel a closer touch with him than with living men."[20] French's statue installed a wise oracle in Bacon's adaptation of an Athenian temple.

Measured against any plausible alternatives to the Lincoln Memorial advanced in the years after the formation of the Senate Park Commission, the work of Bacon and French was remarkable for its commitment to what Bacon called Lincoln's "humane personality."[21] This emphasis was instrumental to the success of the monument in fostering political movements more progressive than Bacon and French, or Lincoln, ever anticipated. Civil rights strategists would have found less leverage in a Lincoln memorial modeled on the Brandenburg Gate or the Arc de Triomphe, or a building that firmly embedded remembrance of the Union commander-in-chief in the military narrative of the Civil War. Those alternative structures would have been inauspicious sites for the protests against the Vietnam War that took place at the Lincoln Memorial and contributed to the decision to place the Vietnam Veterans Memorial in its shadow. To the contrary, most proposals for Potomac Park and the Lincoln Memorial would have deepened the militarism of American culture. Bacon and French reversed what threatened to become a disastrous climax to the national enthusiasm for Civil War monuments.

Bacon's emphasis on Lincoln's speeches also brought the long line of Civil War memorials to one of its most thoughtful points of reflection on the institution of the civic monument. The architect took interest in the mid-nineteenth-century French *néo-grec* movement that had climaxed in Henri Labrouste's treatment of the relationship between architecture and literature in the design of the Bibliothèque Sainte-Geneviève in Paris (1838–50). The library explored Victor Hugo's argument that the ancient reign of architecture as the most profound record of human thought and social interaction had begun to end with the invention of the printing press and that literature had by the nineteenth century become the sovereign art.[22] Bacon aimed to adapt civic commemoration to the new order. The side chambers of the Lincoln Memorial, toward which the shallow central chamber directed visitors, implemented Bacon's conviction that the Gettysburg Address and Second Inaugural Address "will always have a far greater meaning to the

FIGURE 5.4. "Abraham Lincoln, What Would You Do?," 1918.
Courtesy of the Sam DeVincent Collection of Illustrated American Sheet Music,
Archives Center, National Museum of American History, Smithsonian Institution.

citizens of the United States and visitors from other countries, than a portrayal of periods or events."[23] Dimly lit and unfurnished with even a stone bench, the side chambers did not provide for careful study of the addresses so widely available in printed form. Instead the panels saluted the centrality of the texts for the exercise of citizenship that would later come to be known as cultural literacy. This vision of the republic resting on radically decentralized production and consumption of words, a highly elastic process inexhaustibly extended through society by the printing press, offered a modern counterbalance to the ritualistic associations of Bacon's temple. The architect's assertion of American inheritance of the Western tradition took shape precisely as that tradition spiraled into crisis on the Western Front.

LINCOLN AT WAR

The antimilitarism and the modernity of the Lincoln Memorial linked it with a contemporaneous monument often treated as its opposite, George Grey Barnard's portrait statue in Cincinnati. The project originated in the Lincoln centenary, when the widow of a GAR member decided to fund a work that would honor her husband as well as his former commander-in-chief. On its way to becoming a military tribute like so many Lincoln memorials of the period, with Borglum evidently on the inside track for the commission, the initiative veered in a different direction when local arts patron Charles Taft and other members of the monument committee expressed a preference for Barnard. The fin-de-siècle aesthete vividly illustrated the antimodern roots of modernism. Immersed in medieval art, he had begun to assemble the collection that would become the nucleus of the Cloisters Museum. His champions often compared him with Rodin, and he would exhibit in the Armory Show in 1913. When the widow's plans for Cincinnati collapsed in the ensuing discussions, Taft commissioned Barnard in 1910 to make a Lincoln monument for a city park near the sponsor's home.[24] The resulting work would become the most famous sculptural casualty of American intervention in the Great War.

Barnard portrayed Lincoln less as a personification of Union than as an embodiment of the inner division central to the modernist conception of personality. Only the second civic monument to depict Lincoln in the period before his presidency, the work rejected the straightforward upward mobility celebrated in Charles Mulligan's statue of the railsplitter. Barnard focused on a point later in his subject's life but showed a figure permanently at odds with the manners of the bourgeoisie. Lincoln's hands clutched awkwardly

FIGURE 5.5. George Grey Barnard, *Abraham Lincoln*, Cincinnati, 1910–17. Courtesy of the American Sculpture Photograph Study Collection, Smithsonian American Art Museum.

over his stomach; his collar and bow tie were askew. His bulging veins, protruding back muscles, and heavy shoes betrayed years of manual labor. This lack of physical elegance expressed the complexity that Barnard considered Lincoln's hallmark. The sculptor systematically pursued his theme of internal division in Lincoln's hair—neatly combed on the left side of the part, unruly on the right—and especially in the face. "The left side of Lincoln's face is the motherhood side," Barnard claimed. "The right side is the man's." The sculptor rhapsodized over Leonard Volk's life mask of Lincoln as not merely a tool for making an accurate likeness but also a metaphor for the means by which Lincoln combined without necessarily reconciling the contending forces within him. No simple Victorian exemplar of moral character, the national hero remained an enigma.[25]

This interpretation of Lincoln was obviously contrary to the Bacon-French conception in some ways. Barnard maintained that his Lincoln was "much more like a Gothic Cathedral than a Greek Temple."[26] But the contemporaneous projects shared modernizing impulses as well as an emphasis on Lincoln as an intellectual, a theme ably articulated by an admirer of both works, William Howard Taft. Assuming the chairmanship of the federal Lincoln Memorial Commission while president, Taft was a key figure from congressional authorization of the monument through the dedication ceremony. He was also a prominent supporter of the Cincinnati monument his half-brother had commissioned, and he delivered the oration at its dedication on March 31, 1917. Taking his lead from Barnard's depiction of Lincoln's social origins, Taft set the theme for his address with an opening parallel between the achievements of Lincoln and Shakespeare. Revisited twice more in the next ten pages of Taft's printed text, the pairing of president and dramatist amplified Barnard's observation that Lincoln could be understood only through his life mask. Taft described Lincoln's humor and modesty as public performances. His main purpose in invoking Shakespeare, however, was to identify Lincoln's mind as his chief attribute. Like most observers, Taft took Barnard's statue to represent Lincoln around the time of his 1858 debates with Stephen A. Douglas, and the ex-president devoted far more of his address to the antebellum career than he did to the war years. His version of the hero differed from ordinary men in the rigor with which Lincoln tested moral judgments. In the Lincoln-Douglas debates the future president vindicated the hopes of principled reasoning against an expert politician "entirely willing to deny or ignore perfectly logical distinctions" and ready to rely on prejudice, name-calling, and outbursts of temper.[27] Barnard's tribute to the debater, like the temple on the Mall, expressed admiration for intellectual achievement.

By the time of its dedication during the week before the United States declared war on Germany, however, Barnard's statue was becoming the center of one of the most heated controversies in American art history. With the financial backing of Charles Taft, cofounder John A. Stewart of the American

Centenary of Peace Committee (ACPC) proposed in February 1917 to install a copy of Barnard's Lincoln in the southwest corner of Parliament Square in London to commemorate the friendship between the United States and Great Britain that had lasted since the signing of the Treaty of Ghent in 1815. The initiative followed an unsuccessful effort by Stewart in 1913–14 to obtain funding for a copy of Saint-Gaudens's standing Lincoln for the prestigious site and paralleled attempts by the entrepreneurial Barnard to commission copies of his work for the other leading Allied capitals. The plans for Paris and St. Petersburg fizzled, especially after the Bolshevik Revolution of October 1917, but the British government agreed to accept Barnard's Lincoln in place of the Saint-Gaudens work previously intended. The substitution outraged Lincoln's only surviving child, Robert Lincoln, a notorious snob appalled by the depiction of his father as an ungainly former manual laborer. The well-connected Lincoln launched a campaign to revive the proposed reproduction of Saint-Gaudens's portrait, and the two statues soon became competing self-images of the United States as it entered the Great War.

The outcome of this competition was predictable. A former minister to Great Britain and secretary of war, Robert Lincoln enjoyed even more leverage in a contest over the representation of his father than most family members of Civil War heroes did. As he foresaw, many powerful people were delighted by the opportunity to embarrass William Howard Taft, including Henry Cabot Lodge, Elihu Root, and Andrew Carnegie. Stewart's unilateral shift in the plan previously announced by the ACPC irked officials of the Carnegie Endowment for International Peace, who had good reason to believe that the Carnegie Endowment had absorbed the ACPC upon paying its debts in 1915. Though Barnard's work attracted some distinguished admirers, including Roger Fry, Jacob Epstein, and George Bernard Shaw in Britain, its appeal hardly compared with national pride in Saint-Gaudens's statue, so widely considered the definitive portrait of Lincoln that American Institute of Architects executive secretary Glenn Brown had encouraged Henry Bacon to use a copy of the work for the focal statue of the Lincoln Memorial. The National Academy of Design, the American Federation of Arts, and other arts organizations expressed strong preferences for the Saint-Gaudens, as did the overwhelming majority of voters in newspaper and magazine polls. The Carnegie Endowment commissioned a cast of Saint-Gaudens's portrait that the British government accepted for Parliament Square in November 1918. Charles Taft presented the copy of Barnard's statue to the city of Manchester in recognition of British working-class support for the Union during the Civil War.

If the attempt to substitute Taft's gift for the canonical statue would have encountered some of the same obstacles a few years earlier, the reasons articulated for thwarting Stewart's proposal reflected the military mobilization underway. F. Wellington Ruckstuhl, the most voluble participant in the controversy, illustrated the anxieties pervading the debate by changing his Alsatian surname to Ruckstull, which he deemed less Germanic, during the war. His inflammatory editorials in the *Art World* are important if tricky evidence of the relationship between artistic and political attitudes. Albert Boime has ably situated Ruckstull's denunciation of "degenerate" and "insane" sculpture within a critique of modernism that culminated in the Nazi ideology of art, but Boime overstates the significance of those commentaries by asserting that the designers of the Lincoln Memorial "were closely allied to Ruckstull's way of thinking." In fact, French protested that Ruckstull's attacks overshot the proper scope of criticism.[28] French did raise objections to Barnard's interpretation of Lincoln, as did Bacon's friends Royal Cortissoz and Leila Mechlin, but the polemics of 1917–18 are an imperfect guide to the Mall design.

Discussion of Barnard's work returned regularly to military values as the United States prepared to enter into the European cataclysm. Barnard had candidly represented Lincoln as divided between male and female personalities, and many observers considered the figure lacking in virility. Ruckstull called it "a whining, weeping *idea* of Lincoln — an idea charged with the silly pest of patheticism — the fundamental source of the dangerous pacificism-at-any-price which has been manifested by the pathetics of the country." He and other critics who branded the work "queer" may have been thinking in part of Barnard's early association with the gay artistic circle centered on Alfred Corning Clark. Ruckstull urged readers to remember that "Lincoln was primarily a six-foot-four fighting reformer, a noble conqueror." The *New York Times* similarly described Lincoln in terms that would apply to a soldier, as a "heroic, self-sacrificing American leader who bore so bravely the great burden of his nation's troubles." The class divisions widely regarded as the central theme of Barnard's portrait found an antithesis in the social order projected by the army, "the militant democracy of our times." One university president remarked that "if that weird and deformed figure really represents the results of democracy, we can hardly expect Europe to fight that democracy may be made safe."[29]

The critique that imagined Lincoln as a doughboy also reconsidered the duty of an artist at work on a public monument. Commentators grouped Barnard's work with Rodin's controversial statues of Hugo and Balzac as per-

The Great War and Civil War Memory

sonal interpretations that could not be monuments because they deviated from "the unchanging traditions of a special form of art." The narrowing latitude for originality, paralleling the constriction of American civil liberties during the war, prompted Frederick MacMonnies to protest that "of all stagnations, standardization is the most sodden."[30] Ruckstull rejoined that the purpose of the Great War was to cleanse the immorality produced by anarchistic freedom of expression. Comparing designers of civic monuments with the conscripts sent to serve in the trenches, he argued that the nation rightly restricted individual liberty in both cases on the principle "that every man must contribute his share to the life of the state — or get out of it!"[31] The mobilization of culture left little distinction between public art and propaganda.

Conceived in the classical tradition by an architect secure within the elite of his profession, the Lincoln Memorial did not suffer the patriotic inquisition visited on Barnard's statue. The popular press paid little attention to Bacon's departure from McKim's plan, his indifference to the Arlington vista, his disdain for Civil War narrative, his tribute to Lincoln's intellectual achievement, or his debt to the *néo-grecs* in fashioning a civic monument consistent with print-based social organization. Leaving behind the prewar debate over the appropriateness of a classical monument, commentators agreed that the design was fitting for Lincoln because it was "simple."[32] On its day of dedication the memorial would be closer to McKim's vision than at any moment in its history since the appointment of Bacon. The selection of Memorial Day 1922 for the occasion ensured an overwhelmingly military resonance and an emphasis on the link with Arlington National Cemetery that Bacon had downplayed. A crowd of 100,000 attended ceremonies in honor of fallen soldiers at Arlington, far more than the 35,000 who attended the Lincoln Memorial dedication later on the same day. At an American Legion ceremony for the World War dead, Rear Adm. Charles Plunkett predicted that the United States would soon fight an even greater war and promised that "the next time, America will say when the war shall cease, and not a foreign power or group of politicians." Similar events took place at other cemeteries throughout Washington. Senator Wesley Jones declared at the Congressional Cemetery that the United States should exclude immigrants who failed to embrace the doctrine of "America first."[33] The grand parade of the day joined veterans from the Civil War, the Spanish-American War, and the World War, suggesting no difference among the causes for which soldiers had fought in those conflicts.

The addresses at the Lincoln Memorial dedication further obscured its antimilitaristic design. Warren G. Harding, interested mainly in the paral-

FIGURE 5.6. Dedication of the Lincoln Memorial, Washington, DC, May 30, 1922.
Courtesy of the Library of Congress.

lel between the embattled Lincoln and his underappreciated presidential
successors, called attention to Lincoln's first inaugural address rather than
either of the texts featured in the monument. With clear implications for the
ongoing suppression of radicalism, he approvingly quoted Lincoln's argument that secession was "the essence of anarchy." More surprising was the
contrast between Chief Justice Taft's brief remarks and his oration at the
dedication of the Barnard statue five years earlier. So eloquent in Cincinnati
on Lincoln as an antislavery thinker, Taft centered his Washington speech on
the progress in art that enabled the country to commemorate Lincoln and
the Civil War more effectively than it had in earlier monuments. The watershed in that narrative was the Columbian Exposition, from which it followed
that Bacon deserved praise as the "student and disciple" of McKim. Situating the Lincoln Memorial firmly in the ideological plan of the Senate Park
Commission, Taft bowed both to the Ulysses S. Grant equestrian monument
dedicated a month earlier at the foot of Capitol Hill and to Arlington Na-

The Great War and Civil War Memory

tional Cemetery, toward which work would later begin on a bridge designed by McKim, Mead & White. Taft's peroration on the reconciliation of North and South, often cited as an example of the disregard for emancipation in the dedication ceremony, appealed fervently to martial values. In his final lines he christened the Lincoln Memorial with a famous phrase of the World War as "an altar upon which the supreme sacrifice was made."[34]

In the aftermath of this ceremony, and doubtless thinking about Taft's early career as governor of the Philippines and secretary of war as well as the prominent passage in the ex-president's dedication speech that had quoted John Hay's identification of Lincoln and Washington as "the immortals" worthy of commemoration on the Mall, Lewis Mumford asked in 1924, "Who lives in that shrine, I wonder—Lincoln, or the men who conceived it: the leader who beheld the mournful victory of the Civil War, or the generation that took pleasure in the mean triumph of the Spanish-American exploit, and placed the imperial standard in the Philippines and the Caribbean?"[35] This disillusionment was a dark epitaph for the efforts of Bacon and French to redeem the built memory of the Civil War. Their vindication would await recognition that the Lincoln Memorial was more than a salute to the commander-in-chief of the restored Union.

THE SHADOW OF CIVIL WAR MONUMENTS

By the dedication of the Lincoln Memorial, its principal artists and almost everyone else interested in public monuments had shifted their focus to commemoration of the World War. Bacon took part in no fewer than a dozen projects by 1922. French was equally busy, and six weeks after the Lincoln Memorial dedication he returned to Exeter, New Hampshire, for the unveiling of the World War memorial he had designed for his birthplace with Bacon's assistance. Such events helped to measure American internationalism in the aftermath of intervention in Europe. Much as former presidents Roosevelt and Taft, Secretary of War Newton D. Baker, expeditionary force commander John J. Pershing, and other prominent leaders called on families to bury dead soldiers in overseas cemeteries as a permanent commitment to the Allied cause, some civic monuments adopted more self-consciously collective frameworks than the received canon of commemoration. And much as the large majority of polled families chose to repatriate remains for interment, most community monuments revealed the countervailing force of established memorial patterns.[36] Civil War precedent exercised a decisive influence on Great War remembrance in the United States.

French's work for Exeter offered a soldier monument closer to British and French counterparts than to Civil War templates. The doughboy stood straight, his cap in his dangling right arm and his left hand on his hip, without a rifle to serve as staff or rod. This pose was original, though its informally upright bearing recalled Ward's "parade rest" formula as a balance between individuality and discipline. The alert soldier's closely fitted, high-buttoned uniform suggested a physical fitness with more constraint and less aggressive muscularity than the active figures that had dominated critical acclaim for a generation. A maternal allegorical figure stood alongside the doughboy to signal his idealism, raising her arms in pride and holding an American flag. At her feet was a spray of oak leaves and poppies, which viewers readily associated with John McCrae's "In Flanders Field" (1915). French affirmed McCrae's oft-quoted injunction "To you from failing hands we throw / the torch; be yours to hold it high" in a monument for Milton, Massachusetts (1925), which depicted a nude classical warrior losing his grasp of the torch he held aloft as he died in a niche that resembled a trench. At least ten other American monuments featured similar uses of poppies or torches, and at least eight joined the Milton memorial in quoting "In Flanders Field" in an inscription. Like the militant pastoral elegy, these works envisioned the war as a crisis for a transatlantic cultural tradition.[37]

French's monument for Milton paralleled many French and British memorials that depicted dead or dying soldiers, most directly Richard R. Goulden's allusion to McCrae in Great Malvern (1923). French returned to the motif in a work for St. Paul's School in Concord, New Hampshire, titled *Death and Youth* (1929), in which the falling nude figure's broken sword vividly evoked the shattered manhood of the war. Anna Coleman Ladd presented a more gruesome view of the trenches in her bronze tablets for Manchester, Massachusetts (1923), one of which centered on a skeleton caught in barbed wire. These images differed sharply from heroic Civil War death scenes like Lorado Taft's *Defense of the Flag*.

Such assertions of shared international experience encountered conflicting patterns of representation developed in Civil War monuments. Veneration of veterans most decisively distinguished American commemoration from Allied patterns. The overwhelming majority of monuments in the United States continued to recognize all soldiers rather than reserving tributes to the dead. A monument in Salem, Massachusetts, revised Horace to proclaim that "It Is Sweet and Noble to Serve / One's Country in Her Hour of Need." Communities routinely listed the names of soldiers who survived the war. The only other country that so conspicuously honored veterans was

Australia, which relied throughout the war on volunteer enlistments. Great Britain, which did not implement a draft until 1916, recognized survivors in about half of the monuments dedicated. Exclusive focus on the dead characterized French *monuments aux morts*.[38]

As in Civil War monuments after the 1880s, recognition of veterans correlated with an idealization of belligerent masculinity antithetical to Allied monuments. The closest study estimates that more than 60 percent of American soldier statues in World War I monuments depicted combat scenes.[39] John Paulding and E. M. Viquesney together sold well over 100 copies of their similar statues of a doughboy going "over the top" to charge enemy lines. The inexpensive stock figures depicted a helmeted soldier stepping over barbed wire and carrying his rifle loosely in his left hand while raising his right arm to throw a grenade. In these works, warmly endorsed by the American Legion, the energetic American soldier rose above the degrading, muddy stalemate of the Western Front. Karl Illava's more elaborate

FIGURE 5.8. E. M. Viquesney, *Spirit of the American Doughboy*, Columbia, South Carolina, copyright 1920, installed 1930. Photograph by Carol E. Harrison.

memorial in Central Park to the 107th Infantry Regiment, a successor to the old Seventh New York Regiment, similarly presented a battlefield charge by seven soldiers, one of whom crumpled lifeless into the arms of his neighbor in a formula common in late Civil War monuments. Great Britain produced little that was remotely comparable. Less than one-fifth of British soldier statues depicted combat scenes; more than one-third portrayed soldiers in mourning position with rifle inverted. Memorials in France represented battlefield action more exuberantly than those in Britain but much less ubiquitously than those in the United States.[40] Civil War monuments in the quarter century before intervention had promoted a celebration of martial bravado that the Allies considered reckless by the latter stages of the Great War and tragic afterward.

The athleticism introduced in twentieth-century Civil War monuments developed further in World War monuments. Henry Hering expanded on his allegorical nudes for Yale (1915) in a set of figures for the Indiana World War Memorial (1928), part of the headquarters complex for the American Legion. Bodybuilding champion Charles Atlas posed for Pietro Montana's *Dawn of Glory* for Highland Park, Brooklyn (1924), in which a male figure raised his arms to lift a veil that covered him. Charles Niehaus's *Planting the Standard of Democracy* in Newark, New Jersey (1923), depicted four muscular classical warriors securing a flagpole in preparation for raising a banner.[41] These heroic nudes differed dramatically from the broken men depicted by French and other internationalists. Building on Civil War precedents like Pompeo Coppini's *Last Stand* in Victoria, Texas (1912), other figures were clothed but displayed extraordinary brawn behind open shirts, including Giuseppe Moretti's doughboy for Canonsburg, Pennsylvania (1924), and Pietro Montana's soldier for East Providence, Rhode Island (1927). R. Tait McKenzie, a physician who was friendly with the Kitsons and shared anthropometric research with Dudley Sargent, carried the kinesthetic and ethnological ideas behind T. A. R. Kitson's *The Volunteer* (1902) to culmination in *The Homecoming* in Cambridge, England (1922), and *The Victor* in Woodbury, New Jersey (1925).[42]

Much as new monuments relied on previous models, American memorials of the World War failed to follow Allied patterns that lacked a Civil War precedent. Images of desolate family members were among the most important images in French commemoration after 1918, but Civil War monuments had rarely explored the theme beyond early allegories like the weeping America on the Naval Monument in Washington (1877) or Moses Ezekiel's *Virginia Mourning Her Dead*, modeled in 1869 though not cast in bronze until the sculptor's alma mater installed it in 1903. Lorado Taft was unable to sell a female nude titled *America Mourning Her Dead* that he sketched in 1889–90 while working regularly on Civil War monuments.[43] American monuments of the World War included allegorical mourning civilians that varied in gender ideology and antiwar sentiment, but almost all avoided the

FIGURE 5.9. Charles H. Niehaus, *Planting the Standard of Democracy*,
Newark, New Jersey, 1921–23. Courtesy of the Newark Public Library.

realistic depiction of bereft parents, wives, and children common in French
monuments.[44] George Julian Zolnay's caped figure crouched over a dead
doughboy in Nashville (1923), known as the *Gold Star Monument*, was typically closer to the celebration of stoic Confederate motherhood.

In some cases World War monuments not only followed Civil War ex-

The Great War and Civil War Memory

amples but merged the two commemorations. Communities added plaques to expand the ambit of memorials installed years ago.[45] Other works made the connection visually. More than a dozen monuments paired soldiers from the Civil War and the World War, accompanied in several instances by representatives of other conflicts.[46] Red Bank, New Jersey, unveiled a granite monument in 1926 that featured a Civil War soldier passing an American flag down to the outstretched arms of soldiers from the World War and the Spanish-American War. Such links to the Civil War extended into the South, where communities had insisted on the uniqueness of the Confederate soldier in monuments dedicated after the Spanish-American War. The doughboy monument in Knoxville, Tennessee (1921), inserted key phrases of the World War, like "the supreme sacrifice," into William Henry Trescot's oft-copied text for the monument to the Confederate dead of South Carolina. Belzoni (1923) and Poplarville (1926), Mississippi, and Carrollton, Alabama (1927), all installed monuments that depicted a Confederate soldier, a doughboy, and a mother.

Civil War memory was in some ways a powerful negative influence on World War monuments. Continued critical condemnation of most Civil War soldier statues as "a travesty and a plague" contributed to the popularity of what some commentators called utilitarian memorials.[47] *American City* magazine reported during World War II that communities had completed or committed to 452 such buildings after World War I. These initiatives prompted considerable discussion. State and municipal contributions to commemoration, legitimated by Civil War remembrance, made the issue different from the situation in Britain, where reliance on voluntary donations as the essence of a memorial limited the stakes of disagreement about the form of that memorial. In the United States, in contrast, architect Ralph Adams Cram compared utilitarian memorials to "the disingenuousness of presenting a pair of rubbers to a child for Christmas."[48] This debate revealed little awareness of the antimonumental impulse in the immediate aftermath of the Civil War. World War utilitarian memorials instead expressed a judgment that soldier monuments, especially figurative statuary, had too often failed in Civil War commemoration and were unlikely to improve. Alternatives in the 1920s and 1930s accordingly took a wide variety of forms, including bridges, roads, hospitals, forests, parks, auditoriums, athletic stadiums, recreational facilities, and clocks.

Supporters praised all of these projects as enrichments of American life, but no proponent advanced an argument as directly grounded in the moral foundations of the recent conflict as the call for memorial libraries, town

FIGURE 5.10. Frank J. Manson, *Handing Down Old Glory*,
Red Bank, New Jersey, 1926. Photograph by Douglas McVarish.
Courtesy of the New Jersey Historic Preservation Office.

halls, and educational buildings after Appomattox. American aims were murkier in the World War, and compulsory military service did not stimulate broad institutional conceptualization of citizens' voluntarism. The most significant attempt to single out an appropriate form of utilitarian memorial, the promotion of community centers, drew not on the purposes of American intervention in Europe but on the legacy of national mobilization. Municipal reformers backed these neighborhood houses as the successor to wartime facilities established near army bases to foster harmony among the heterogeneous troops and strengthen relations between uniformed personnel and civilians. The memorial halls of the 1860s and 1870s underscored the political basis of military service; the postarmistice initiatives identified the army as a model for society.

The expanded influence of the army also shaped another important renunciation of Civil War memorial precedent. The American Battle Monuments Commission (ABMC), established by Congress in 1923 and headed for a quarter century by Pershing, banned state governments and militia units from contributing monuments to American military cemeteries in Europe, setting those sites on a different path from Civil War battlefield parks. Veterans of the U.S. Volunteers had dominated the battlefield parks during their formative stages, with funding supplied by state governments. The ABMC would be more thoroughly insulated from civilians. Although initially concerned with projects outside the United States, it created a long-term bureaucratic wedge for military management of high-profile domestic monuments after the War Department yielded control of public buildings and grounds in Washington.[49]

Conversely, the elevated prestige of the army led to the most prominent World War imitation of a Civil War monument, the First Division Memorial unveiled in Washington in 1924. Maj. Gen. Charles P. Summerall and his fellow officers on the monument committee, fondly recalling from their cadet days the Stanford White–Frederick MacMonnies monument at West Point, sought to install a similar victory column across from the State, War, and Navy Building. The CFA strongly preferred a fountain in this vista, but the former First Division commander and future army chief of staff prevailed. The importation of the West Point model signaled the triumph of the regular army over its former rivals in the U.S. Volunteers and the militia. The recapitulation included a controversy over the allegorical figure designed by Daniel Chester French for the top of Cass Gilbert's column. Like the Academy faculty who had ordered the removal of MacMonnies's original figure, Summerall was shocked by the sensuality of French's winged Victory. He complained that the figure was "too voluptuous and not sufficiently spiritual." She thrust her hips forward too suggestively; the bare arms and scantily clad legs "suggest material rather than spiritual emotions"; and "the breast plates emphasize the development in a way that is most beautiful but that in my judgment is not of the highly spiritual type desired." The depiction challenged Summerall's vision "of spiritual exaltation, of sacrifice glorified by renunciation, of pride, and of reward," but he eventually acquiesced.[50] The Second Division followed twelve years later with a gilded bronze flaming sword designed by James Earle Fraser, extending the army's memorial beachhead in the nation's capital.

The Tomb of the Unknown Soldier, the most important American memorial of the World War, epitomized the tensions between the legacy of the Civil War and efforts to coordinate with the Allied Powers. The initiative recalled the hundreds of thousands of unidentified dead bodies that had haunted the American imagination after the Civil War, acknowledged at gravesites and cenotaphs across the North and South and prominently at Arlington National Cemetery.[51] The later commemoration, however, was explicitly international in origin. France had started the momentum by placing an empty casket at the Arc de Triomphe to focus salutes to the dead at the Bastille Day ceremonies of 1919, two weeks after the signing of the Treaty of Versailles. For the corresponding London parade at the end of July, the cabinet commissioned Edwin Lutyens's wood-and-plaster cenotaph on Whitehall for the British dead buried abroad as a result of national nonrepatriation policy. The sensational popular success prompted its transfer to stone, completed one year later despite the belief of some ministers that Lutyens's austere design was "of too mournful a character as a permanent expression of the triumphant victory of our arms."[52] Pressure from the Church of England for a more religiously inflected memorial led to the decision to establish a Tomb of the Unknown Warrior in Westminster Abbey. France placed a similar shrine beneath the Arc de Triomphe. The interment of both unknowns on the second anniversary of the armistice inspired the American movement for a Tomb of the Unknown Soldier. The ceremonies in the United States on November 11, 1921, took place on the same day as parallels in Italy, Belgium, and Portugal; other countries soon followed.[53]

The logic of Civil War commemoration repeatedly conflicted with the impetus to align with the Allies. The sponsor of the federal legislation was first-term representative Hamilton Fish Jr., a personification of the strenuous life. Renamed in childhood for a cousin who died in the Rough Riders, Fish starred for the Harvard football team and trained at Plattsburg for an officer's commission in a New York militia unit mobilized for the war. He called in December 1920 for interment of an unknown soldier on the next Memorial Day as a gesture of North-South harmony in the aftermath of the World War. This timetable failed as a result of its compressed schedule as well as the significance of the armistice anniversary, but the placement of the tomb caused a deeper debate. Fish proposed the rotunda of the Capitol, a plan endorsed by the American Legion on the grounds that Arlington National Cemetery was too closely associated with the Civil War and insufficiently prestigious to match the London and Paris installations. Newton D. Baker's selection of Arlington partly accomplished what Fish had sought in a Memorial Day ceremony and also expressed confidence in architect Thomas Hastings's new cemetery amphitheater as a vehicle for expanding the significance of Arlington beyond its origins in the Civil War.

The presumptive favorite for the tomb commission, Hastings designed a sarcophagus modeled on the Cenotaph. The allusion shared in a wide acclaim for Lutyens's streamlined modernism. *Monumental News* had suggested that American communities might adapt the Cenotaph in smaller versions, as British municipalities often did.[54] Hastings's international cordiality also paralleled the coordination between the interment ceremony and the opening of the Washington Naval Disarmament Conference the following day. The office of the army chief of staff soon worried that "the Unknown Soldier will continue to personify a policy of disarmament" and sought to make the memorial "more an inspiration of patriotism rather than sadness." Secretary of War John Weeks rejected Hastings's design.[55] A subsequent competition resulted in selection of a submission from sculptor Thomas Hudson Jones and architect Lorimer Rich that featured a sarcophagus embellished with allegorical figures of Victory, Valor, and Peace. Made from the same Colorado marble as the Lincoln Memorial, the monument installed in 1931 featured an inscription that left conceptual room for the addition of bodies from future wars. This flexibility was unthinkable at the Cenotaph or the tombs of Great War unknowns in Britain and France but fit readily with American understandings of soldier monuments and paralleled the development of Arlington itself from a site of Civil War remembrance into a broader national shrine.[56]

The defining feature of the American tomb soon came to be the way it fulfilled the ambition for military ritual that had informed the initial design of the Grant memorial in Washington as a presidential reviewing stand. Civilians primarily shaped the everyday experience of the Cenotaph and the Tomb of the Unknown Warrior, on Whitehall by male pedestrians' customary removal of hats as they passed and in Westminster Abbey through the presence of family members and clergy. Former *poilus* dominated the grave of their comrade in Paris, and the eternal flame they arranged in 1923 became an emblem of antiwar vigilance. At Arlington, the guard instituted by the U.S. Army in 1926 after lobbying by the American Legion and expanded to a round-the-clock performance in 1937 became an astonishing military spectacle. Rendering hierarchy invisible, the new showcase idealized martial achievement of coveted prestige through relentless, unquestioning execution of a precise task, regardless of impediments.[57] Far removed from the sentimental popular culture of the 1860s, this display of overwhelming state discipline transformed as it realized the literary vision selected by Montgomery Meigs for inscription on the entrance arch at Arlington: "AND GLORY GUARDS WITH SOLEMN ROUND / THE BIVOUAC OF THE DEAD."

THE SHADOW OF THE WORLD WAR

The production of Civil War monuments declined sharply with the outbreak of the World War. The number of monuments unveiled in 1915–19 was less than half what it had been during either of the two previous five-year periods. The pace fell by another third during the 1920s and then again by more than half during the Great Depression. The number of monuments installed during the 1930s was about half of the lowest total for any previous decade. By the early 1920s, a UDC historian could describe "the era of local monuments" as a period now in the past.[58] Most new Civil War memorials were inexpensive works that sponsors often placed in cemeteries. Larger projects were scaled back or modified to incorporate recent history. The city of Philadelphia, where discussion had recently centered on a proposed $350,000 soldiers and sailors monument, appropriated $88,000 in 1918 for Hermon A. MacNeil's work installed without ceremony in 1921. Newark used Union veteran Amos Van Horn's bequest for a Civil War monument to commission Gutzon Borglum's *Wars of America* (1926), a bronze procession of forty-two figures representing conflicts from the Revolution through the World War. Pompeo Coppini persuaded University of Texas benefactor George W. Littlefield to jettison plans for a Confederate memorial arch at the entrance of the Austin campus and instead commission a $250,000 fountain honoring school casualties of the World War, supplemented by portrait statues in which Woodrow Wilson stood with Jefferson Davis and other Confederate heroes (1933).[59] As the Newark and Austin cases indicated, ambitious new

Civil War memorials tended to be gifts of individual donors, like the soldier monuments in Wilmington, North Carolina (1924), Stafford, Connecticut (1924), and Charleston, South Carolina (1932), or the equestrian statues of Jackson (1921) and Lee (1924) in Charlottesville, Virginia. The World War not only slowed the proliferation of Civil War monuments; the larger conflict also influenced fresh tributes to the Union and Confederacy.

Efforts to align past and present crises occasionally invigorated Civil War memorialization instead of framing World War remembrance. The prominence of Lincoln in mobilization publicity helped to make statues of him the sole form of Civil War monument installed in approximately equal numbers during the twenty years before and after the dedication of the Lincoln Memorial. Several works reinforced the martial representation of Lincoln typified by Borglum's initial plan for the *Wars of America*, which featured a crowd of confused citizens organized into a fighting force by Washington and Lincoln. Alliance, Ohio, which had in 1915 installed statues of a Union infantryman and cavalryman on opposite sides of a pylon topped by a bronze eagle, substituted a Lincoln portrait as the crowning figure at a 1924 rededication that also added flanking monuments to soldiers of the Spanish-American War and the World War. Minnesota units of the GAR dedicated a statue of Lincoln on Memorial Day 1930 at the head of a tree-lined Victory Memorial Drive in Minneapolis that honored fallen soldiers of the World War. Five months later, Spokane unveiled a monument on Armistice Day that presented Lincoln as commander-in-chief in a military cape, looking across a battlefield. Dixon, Illinois, followed two years later with a statue of Lincoln as a soldier in the Black Hawk War.[60]

The deployment of Lincoln prompted competition from the Jefferson Davis birthplace memorial in Fairview, Kentucky (1924), which received strong support from *Confederate Veteran* and was in its final stages one of the few monument projects of the national UDC. Billed as the tallest obelisk in the world except the Washington Monument, the unreinforced concrete structure described the slaveholding planter as a fitter pendant to the first American president than the hardscrabble railsplitter. The Fairview project originated in direct response to the consecration of Lincoln's supposed birthplace log cabin in nearby Hodgenville, one of the most elaborate and highly publicized undertakings of the 1909 bicentennial. But promoters only began serious fund-raising for the Davis obelisk in 1916, when they sought to spur a backlash to the Lincoln adulation that accompanied the World War. Complaining in 1920 that "a wave of Lincoln hysteria seems to have swept this country during the late war period about as thoroughly as the influenza,

and it lingers even more persistently," *Confederate Veteran* offered an anti-
dote in a poem titled "The Great Obelisk" that repeatedly referred to Union
soldiers as "huns."[61]

The World War posed a stern challenge to key premises of Civil War
memorialization. The tragedy in Europe made many Americans uneasy
about glorification of martial achievement. "I am not in the mood, nor is the
world in the mood, merely to praise war or to exalt force as an agent of human
discipline," observed University of Virginia president Edwin Alderman at the
dedication of the Jackson equestrian in Charlottesville.[62] The Bacon-French
replacement for Launt Thompson's monument to Samuel Francis Du Pont
in Washington, DC, offered a sensitive response to the problem of the war
memorial in the age of catastrophe. Initiated by the admiral's family on the
grounds that Thompson's 1884 portrait statue was undistinguished and listing badly, the new design infused a pacific sensibility into a small urban park.
In place of a depiction of military command, Bacon and French substituted
an elegant fountain adorned with wistful allegorical figures representing the
sea, the wind, and the stars. The fountain as a memorial form was not necessarily inconsistent with zeal for martial values, as Coppini's work at the University of Texas demonstrated, but the Du Pont Memorial Fountain dedicated in 1921 celebrated the reflective and renewing qualities of its waters
and the oceans on which the admiral had sailed during his long career.[63]

Few war memorials so neatly omitted the concept of war, and Civil War
monuments mostly continued to identify peace as the fruit of victory. The
Woman's Relief Corps Department of Ohio, which had raised funds since
1908 for a monument in honor of men's and women's contributions to Union
triumph, commissioned former Kitson protégé and Ohio State University
professor Bruce Wilder Saville in the early 1920s to make an allegorical figure
of peace at the statehouse. Although waving an olive branch, the winged and
robed female dedicated in 1923, armed with a shield, was clearly a sister of
Nike. The ceremony featured a release of doves when Governor A. Victor
Donahey intoned, "Let us have peace," which was also an inscription on the
monument, and the *Ohio State Journal* reported that the monument "speaks
the protest of motherhood against war."[64] But other inscriptions indicated
that "MEN WIN GLORY IN THE / FIERCE HEAT OF CONFLICT" and
honored the loyal women "WITHOUT / WHOSE HELP NO VICTORY / OR
LASTING PEACE / COULD EVER HAVE / BEEN WON." Saville went on to
provide the state a doughboy statue titled *Victorious Soldier* (1926) that resembled R. Tait McKenzie's homeward-striding soldiers.

The monument dedicated on Armistice Day 1927 on the field of the 1864

FIGURE 5.11. Daniel Chester French and Henry Bacon, Du Pont Memorial Fountain, Washington, DC, 1917–21. Decorated for dedication ceremony. Courtesy of the Library of Congress.

battle of Nashville was the most revealing attempt to fuse international and intersectional remembrance. The city board of trade launched a campaign in 1908 to promote preservation of the battlefield as a park for the growing city. The effort attracted strong support from Nashville banker James E. Caldwell and his wife, May Winston Caldwell, whose Longview mansion had served as John Bell Hood's headquarters before the engagement. The initiative reorganized in 1921 amid local debate over commemoration of the World War. Like most leaders of Nashville arts organizations, May Winston Caldwell argued that the city memorial should be a permanent version of the Parthenon replica built for the centennial exposition of 1897, which in twenty-five years had become an emblem of "the Athens of the South" and a valuable cultural and social resource. State legislative leaders instead adopted a sweeping plan to combine a memorial auditorium, suitable for large conventions, with the construction of the first state office building since the antebellum capitol and the condemnation of several blocks of property to create a grand plaza as the fulcrum for a revitalized downtown. The thoroughly utilitarian scheme won the support of the Caldwells' political ally Luke Lea, a prominent real-estate developer as well as founder of the *Nashville Tennessean*, former U.S. senator, and leading World War veteran in state organization of the American Legion. The Caldwells' son Rogers, building one of the most important southern fortunes of the 1920s in municipal bonds, directed purchase of the record-breaking state, city, and county issue for the War Memorial Building. While the state razed property and chose a team of beaux arts architects, May Winston Caldwell turned to a monument for the battlefield park as a nonutilitarian remembrance of the Civil War and the World War.[65]

Caldwell soon identified a compatible artist in Giuseppe Moretti, whose entrepreneurship in bronze casting and marble quarrying as well as his public sculpture made him an outstanding champion of corporate culture. Best known for the cast-iron sculpture of Vulcan commissioned by the Commercial Club of Birmingham to represent Alabama at the 1904 St. Louis World's Fair, he similarly experimented with an aluminum portrait of smelting pioneer Charles Martin Hall at the request of former Alcoa president Richard Beatty Mellon. He worked on the Nashville project at the same time as his equestrian Dayton monument to National Cash Register founder John H. Patterson (1928). His home in Pittsburgh led him to make triumphal World War memorials in Bellevue (1921) and Canonsburg, Pennsylvania (1924), but in 1925 he returned to his native Italy, where he was a vocal admirer of Benito Mussolini.[66] In consultation with May Winston Caldwell, the sculptor designed for Nashville a tall stone pylon topped with an angel of peace.

FIGURE 5.12. Giuseppe Moretti, Battle of Nashville Monument, 1926–27.
Courtesy of the Tennessee State Library and Archives.

The center of the composition was a bronze statue of a nude young man restraining with each hand a horse rearing on its hind legs. An inscription explained that "THE SPIRIT OF YOUTH HOLDS IN CHECK THE CONTEND-
ING / FORCES THAT STRUGGLED HERE." The athletic youth absorbed the
power of North and South. An arch connecting the horses bore the motto
"UNITY." Like Moretti's captains of industry or the Fascist dictator in Italy,
his memorial hero was a superman.

The monument inscriptions elaborated the national ambitions of the
Nashville undertaking. A quotation from Emerson's address at the dedication of the Civil War obelisk in Concord paid homage to the North and
claimed high ground in the recent local debate over war memorialization.
More suggestive was the complementary southern inscription, the closing
verse of John Trotwood Moore's poem "Reunited," written for the 1898 dedication of the Tennessee monuments to soldiers of both sides at the Chickamauga and Chattanooga National Military Park. Moore, the state librarian
and archivist, was a prime exemplar of New South local color and a partial

link to the poets who published the *Fugitive* magazine during 1922–25. His son was a contributing member of the Vanderbilt circle, and the elder Moore occasionally attended meetings of the Fugitives to share common interests in regional history and oral tradition.

Those ties notwithstanding, the poet quoted on the Nashville memorial differed profoundly from the southern modernists. They recoiled from the sing-song schmaltz typified by the monument inscription. They were also deeply alienated from the public authority personified by Moore and symbolized by the battlefield memorial. Allen Tate's "Ode to the Confederate Dead," first published in the same year as the monument dedication, focused precisely on this sense of isolation in the aftermath of a war that left psychological fragmentation rather than national unity. While the Nashville monument envisioned the armistice as a triumphal culmination, much as Moore's poem treated victory in Cuba, Tate saw a deeper disruption in arguing that "with the war of 1914–1918, the South reentered the world—but gave a backward glance as it stepped over the border," which produced "a literature conscious of the past in the present." Robert Penn Warren similarly stressed the corrupting force of celebratory World War remembrance in his novel based on the devastating collapse of Rogers Caldwell's financial empire.[67]

The fresh urgency of commemoration tested remembrance of the Civil War as a historical watershed. Orators at monument dedications disagreed about the implications of changes in combat across the half-century gulf. One viewpoint saw the Civil War as the cradle of modern warfare. A speaker at the 1916 dedication of the Sheridan statue in Albany boasted that "the Civil War revolutionized, through the inventive genius of Americans, this art [of war], just as today American genius is responsible for much that has occurred abroad and for that which has made the mailed fist more terrible." Albert Lyman Cox, an artillery commander in Europe whose father was a general in Lee's army, noted at the 1923 unveiling of a Confederate monument in Holly Springs, North Carolina, that "I like to think of the World War as modeled after the great engagements of the War Between the States." A different argument placed the Civil War on the opposite side of the line that defined modernity. Poughkeepsie school superintendent Sylvester R. Shear articulated this position in an address at the dedication of a flag-bearer ensemble in Hillsdale, New York, on July 4, 1916, three days after the opening hostilities at the Somme claimed the lives of 19,240 British soldiers— more than five times the combined Union and Confederate fatalities on the bloodiest day of the Civil War. "It is said that modern warfare is more brutal than ever before in the history of the world, but I doubt it," Shear declared.

The Great War and Civil War Memory

"Today, the personal equation in battle is strangely lacking. The soldier is a portion of a whole, hidden generally in a trench. . . . Th[e] boys in blue looked calmly into the enemy's eye or into the mouth of the enemy's cannon. Officers waved their swords and personally led their men to the combat." For Shear, the Western Front was a departure from the moral testing ground provided by all wars "from Israel to Appomattox."[68]

The different interpretations competed with each other but also complemented each other. From one standpoint, the Civil War revealed the forces that now dominated the world. Remembrance of the war offered valuable guidance for forward-looking Americans. From the opposite perspective, the Civil War was the best measure of what had been lost in the advance of time. Tate, Warren, and other authors fused the positions into a profound ambivalence toward the sectional conflict, but such reservations did not come readily to public monuments.

The memorial to George Meade dedicated in Washington, DC, in October 1927, the last of the sixteen monuments to Union generals and admirals to be installed in the capital, was the most dramatic statement that the Civil War anticipated contemporary life. Authorized by Congress in 1915, the project became one of the starkest clashes between Civil War veterans and proponents of beaux arts design principles. Funding for the monument came from the state of Pennsylvania, represented by a commission comprised of former soldiers whose chief goal was to promote recognition of the battle of Gettysburg as the pivotal moment of the war. The veterans proposed a variety of plans toward this end, including installation of a Lee statue alongside the Meade memorial; the adjacent area on the Mall, they suggested, would be the logical place for the national monument to the American Expeditionary Force.[69] The Commission of Fine Arts regarded the Meade project as useful primarily as an opportunity to develop further the Union Square laid out by the Senate Park Commission and headed by the Grant memorial but bypassed by the Sherman and Sheridan memorials. The state commission insisted that the Meade memorial should feature a faithful portrait of the commander and perhaps an animated depiction of a soldier at Gettysburg. The CFA responded that the purpose of the monument was to "express that combination of qualities which made General Meade a great military leader."[70]

The sculptor appointed by the state commission, Charles Grafly, embraced the CFA viewpoint. Trained in Paris by a beaux arts sculptor after several years as a student at the Pennsylvania Academy of Fine Arts, where he would spend most of his career on the faculty, Grafly was fond of the

FIGURE 5.13. Charles Grafly, Meade Memorial, Washington, DC, 1915–27. Courtesy of Special Collections and University Archives, Wichita State University Libraries.

allegorical symbolism that appalled the veterans. His design for a portrait statue of Meade in front of a circle of ideal figures prompted the complaint that "General Meade never had any naked women with him at the Battle of Gettysburg!"[71] As Grafly explained in a 1918 memorandum, however, his composition was thoroughly "martial in character." The "dominant force" in the sculptor's conception was the demonic allegorical statue of War situated diametrically opposite from Meade, holding tablets that recorded the commander's battles. Grafly called it "a figure militant, but with the attitude of a guardian spirit." Four of the six intermediate allegorical nudes were male. The wings of War arched above Meade in tribute and protection as Loyalty and Chivalry, supported by Fame and Progress, removed the general's cloak. Meade's confident forward step highlighted his "military and statesmanlike progressiveness."[72] As emphatically as any Civil War monument, and certainly more forcefully than Meade's quiet postwar career might have suggested, Grafly's work presented the army as a foundation for the peacetime United States. One critic summarized the memorial as an argument that "civilization came riding in on a gun carriage." Another critic reluctantly agreed that "we are forced to admit the rightness of the artistic conception that qualities that make for progress have their origin in war."[73]

Some of the most important Civil War monuments of the 1920s and 1930s departed from the celebration of modern martial virtue to treat the war as a misty past. Representation of the Civil War from the standpoint of youth matched the experience of monument promoters who had been children during the war and could no longer address their commemorative efforts to living parents. The most explicit expression of this generational self-consciousness was the Lee memorial unveiled in Dallas in June 1936. The small group of socially prominent sponsors instructed equestrian specialist Alexander Phimister Proctor to depict Lee riding Traveler alongside a mounted young Confederate who, according to a plaque placed on the monument, "represents the entire youth of the South to whom General Lee became an inspiration." The tablet and other authorized explanations emphasized that the young man was not Lee's orderly or a junior officer. He may have been born well after the Civil War but was inspired by Lee's example and metaphorically set out to ride through life with the general. The project endorsed "nobility of character, achieved in one generation, inspired and passed on to the next."[74] Franklin D. Roosevelt, angling for white southern votes in his reelection campaign, attended the dedication ceremony.

Such nostalgia idealized particular visions of the social order. The proposal of the Jefferson Davis Chapter of the UDC in Washington to erect a monument in the capital to "the faithful slave mammies of the South," which the U.S. Senate approved in February 1923 but which made little headway in the House of Representatives, also sought to present the Civil War era from the perspective of a white southern child.[75] Longing for youth merged with regret about the loosening of racial hierarchy through emancipation. Sometimes the war also offered a locus for northern misgivings about mid-twentieth-century modernity. A local newspaper reporter described Raymond Averill Porter's sentinel statue for St. Johnsville, New York (1937), as "a true conception of the soldier boy of the Civil War" because it was "not a military figure" and had "none of the stiffness, eyes front, of the professional soldier." The commentator rhapsodized that "there is no sophistication in the features; life is still worth living and there is no disillusionment expressed" and sighed that the monument "will typify a past that will never come again."[76]

Confederate monuments denied that irretrievability. The Lee-Jackson memorial dedicated in Baltimore in 1948 was already old-fashioned in its

FIGURE 5.14. A. Phimister Proctor, *Robert E. Lee and Young Soldier*, Dallas, 1931–36.
Courtesy of the Proctor Foundation and Museum.

use of the horse-and-rider motif as an urban form when donor J. Henry Ferguson established the fund for the project in 1928. Ferguson directed that this tribute to "my boyish heroes" should exactly follow Everett B. D. Julio's painting of *The Last Meeting of Lee and Jackson*, first exhibited in 1864 and reproduced countless times over the next forty years in the commercial prints central to the visual culture of Ferguson's early life.[77] Like Julio's image, Laura Fraser's double equestrian froze the Confederate saga at its high point before the death of Jackson much as William Faulkner would write, in the same year as the Baltimore unveiling, that "for every Southern boy fourteen years old, not once but whenever he wants it, there is that instant when it's still not yet two o'clock on that July afternoon in 1863. . . . It hasn't happened yet, it hasn't even begun yet, it not only hasn't begun yet but there is still time for it not to begin."[78] Ferguson's memorial wrapped the adolescent fantasy of a reversible past in a sculptural program that recalled ways of life long since replaced by automobiles and illustrated magazines.

The Great War and Civil War Memory

The interwar contrast between the complexity of much Civil War literature and the bombast of the Nashville memorial or the nostalgia of the Lee-Jackson equestrian highlighted the extent to which Civil War monuments faced a crisis of form. Lewis Mumford famously wrote in 1937 that "the very notion of a modern monument is a contradiction in terms" because civilization now centered on change and life rather than fixity and death. His claim did not prove entirely correct in the long term, but he accurately sensed a current impasse. Other modernists echoed Mumford. The "idiot" of the title allusion in William Faulkner's *The Sound and the Fury* (1929) relied on the Confederate monument in the town square of fictional Jefferson, Mississippi, as a compass point for his feeble mental orientation; driven around the wrong side of the statue at the end of the novel, he exploded in panic. Charlie Chaplin's *City Lights* (1931) opened with a send-up of monumentality. Paul Green and Kurt Weill's antiwar musical play *Johnny Johnson* (1936) parodied soldier memorials. Walker Evans mocked F. William Sievers's melodramatic statue of Confederate general Lloyd Tilghman at Vicksburg National Military Park (1926) as absurdly out of touch with the national life documented elsewhere in *American Photographs* (1938).[79] The most heavily publicized Civil War commemorative project initiated after the outbreak of the World War, the Confederate memorial at Stone Mountain, illustrated the mutually reinforcing depiction of the sectional conflict as both a model for the future and a refuge from modernity and also offered a glimpse of the medium that would absorb much of the authority of the civic monument as a site of American memory.

FROM STONE TO FILM

The commemorative possibilities of the sheer 800-foot-high monolith outside Atlanta became a topic of discussion in 1914 when a local attorney proposed the insertion of niches in the rock for statues and the dedication of a templelike Confederate museum on its crest, a popular picnic and tourist destination since the early nineteenth century. Lorado Taft's recent completion of a fifty-foot-tall statue of Black Hawk overlooking the Rock River in Oregon, Illinois, helped to prompt the suggestion that Georgians place a portrait of Lee on the Decatur promontory. Eighty-five-year-old Helen Plane, honorary life president of the Georgia Division of the UDC, took up the idea with the plea that "the time has arrived for us to cease the erection of small and perishable local monuments . . . and concentrate our efforts on one which shall be a shrine for the South and of which all Americans may be justly proud."[80] Among the artists Plane contacted was Gutzon Borglum, who had demonstrated an interest in large stone monuments in his colossal marble portrait head of Lincoln, installed in the U.S. Capitol in 1908. Borglum visited the site in August 1915 and not only embraced but dramatically expanded on the Georgians' conception. He called for a relief across the face of the mountain comparable in cost and importance to the Lincoln Memorial under construction in Washington that he had criticized so vigorously. Supporters predicted that as the Lincoln Memorial capped decades of Union commemoration, the proliferation of Confederate monuments would culminate at Stone Mountain in "the final as well as the finest expression of this memorial impulse."[81]

If projected as the end of an era in Civil War landmarking, the Stone Mountain undertaking was in its social and economic framework distinctive to the period after the World War. Confederate veterans never played a significant part in the project. Women's managerial authority declined sharply after Helen Plane's early role, partly by choice and partly by displacement. The UDC's national leadership steered the organization away from the potentially bottomless budgetary drain. Women comprised most of the founding leadership of the Stone Mountain Confederate Memorial Association (SMCMA), but Atlanta businessmen pushed them aside by the early 1920s. The organization adopted a commercial spirit nourished by long-standing use of the mountain as a granite quarry. The SMCMA employed fund-raising agents and publicists who supplemented Borglum's extraordinary attention-getting talents. Salaries, commissions, office space, and other overhead expenses consumed almost two-thirds of the $1.2 million generated by the SMCMA during 1916–28. Of those revenues, straightforward donations accounted for only a fifth of the total. Another fifth came in exchange for naming rights on the several honor rolls that the SMCMA promised to include in the memorial. Almost 60 percent of the funds raised by the SMCMA resulted from the sale of merchandise and especially from the Stone Mountain commemorative half-dollar coins minted by the U.S. Treasury Department in 1925 and sold by the SMCMA for prices ranging from a minimum of $1 to as much as $200 in auctions of serially numbered coins.[82]

Borglum, who scorned but personified this entrepreneurial ethos, was also divided in his thinking about the relationship between warfare and modern America. No artist was more stridently committed to the notion that the martial ideal provided a model for personal and social progress. The

FIGURE 5.15. Gutzon Borglum, general plan of the sculptures at Stone Mountain
Confederate Memorial, published in *World's Work* 34 (August 1917).
Courtesy of Thomas Cooper Library, University of South Carolina.

pugnacious sculptor titled his manuscript memoirs "One Man War," which
aptly summarized a life consistently centered on intense conflict. His professional career was a long series of feuds with fellow artists; his personal
life was marked by bitter clashes with family and friends. It was not surprising that he eventually broke with the Atlanta businessmen in control of the
SMCMA, who fired him in January 1925 after he charged them, not implau-
sibly, with corrupt intentions for the distribution of the memorial coins.
Before that point, Borglum had fashioned a project with an emphasis on
military organization that would have pleased his political hero, Theodore
Roosevelt. Invited to carve a portrait of Lee, the sculptor instead proposed to
carve "a Panorama representing the Confederate armies mobilizing around
their leaders," similar in basic conception to his *Wars of America* group in
Newark and also reminiscent of late-nineteenth-century panoramic paintings, including depictions of the Civil War, that foreshadowed cinema. Borglum envisioned a procession that would begin at the right of the precipice,
seeming to come from behind the summit and sweep down and across the
mountain face. The entire frieze of artillery, cavalry, infantry, and commanders would include between 700 and 1,000 individual figures and would in
total be as much as 2,000 feet long, 50 to 200 feet wide, and up to 200 feet
deep in key segments like the central group, on which carving began in June
1923. Though he shrewdly started with the figure of Lee, and never advanced

much beyond the gigantic head unveiled in January 1924, Borglum insisted that the memorial was not primarily a tribute to an individual. "The perpetuating of a battle, of a defeat, of a movement — that is what is needed," he told a newspaper reporter.[83]

Borglum's sensational medium at Stone Mountain fused the Civil War with a contest between humanity and nature. The sculptor attacked the mountain like an invading general, planning to imprint his dominion permanently across its face. The monolith was a worthy adversary, repeatedly though incorrectly described in promotional literature as the largest exposed body of solid granite in the world. The confrontation required tremendous physical bravery. Borglum and the workers under his direction routinely walked along narrow edges of the sheer cliff and spent long days on scaffolds suspended at dizzying altitudes. They wielded advanced weapons of destruction, including pneumatic drills and precision blasting with dynamite, that demonstrated technological progress. But if Borglum sought to subjugate nature, he also identified it as the source of meaning in the project. He proposed not only to shape his figures from the granite but also to burrow into the base of the mountain and make a cave-like memorial hall. Here the records and relics of the Confederacy, as well as the names of contributors to the SMCMA, would be embedded in the mountain foundations. Civilization would be firmly grounded in the earth.

This understanding of nature as the basis of human achievement matched Borglum's biological views of American society. He was a Bull Moose progressive whose political outlook increasingly contracted into narrow racialism after the World War. An outspoken anti-Semite, he became a rabid supporter of immigration restriction as he lost all hope in betterment of the "homeless, hapless, poor overflow that comes from old Europe" to "corrupt our cities, schools, and management of our Government." Lowest of all in his regard were people of African descent, though they performed much of the most dangerous and difficult labor at Stone Mountain.[84] His panoramic frieze of the Confederate army, preparing to do battle in defense of racial hierarchy, aimed to depict the basis of the social order by celebrating it through nature.

The relationship between the Stone Mountain project and the Ku Klux Klan reinforced this effort to look to the Civil War era for guidance in contemporary politics. Local discussion of plans for the Confederate memorial and the recent release of D.W. Griffith's *Birth of a Nation* converged in the refounding of the Klan at the summit of Stone Mountain on Thanksgiving night in November 1915. Adoption of the name and rites of the original Klan eagerly identified the anti-Catholicism, nativism, and white supremacism of the later organization with Reconstruction resistance to the promise of black citizenship. Stone Mountain became sacred ground for the Klan, and the owner of the property granted the organization an easement for its ceremonial uses. On Helen Plane's suggestion, Borglum incorporated a Klan altar in his plans for the memorial after the project received a portion of the proceeds from the opening run of *Birth of a Nation* in Atlanta in December 1915.[85] The gathering place for Klan assemblies offered a stage for vows to move toward the future along a path defined by the Confederate legacy.

Yet the Stone Mountain memorial also depicted the Lost Cause as a vanishing golden past. Borglum shared the doubts of Madison Grant's and Lothrop Stoddard's other readers that "the great white race" could maintain its supremacy. The recent transformation of warfare added to these concerns. Armed conflict had supposedly strengthened Anglo-Saxons internally in addition to imposing dominion on other peoples. As a process of vitalization warfare was similar to childbearing, and the Civil War was important because it had marked the birth of a nation. "Revolution under Washington was a misnomer," Borglum maintained. "We had nothing like revolution until 1860 when America bled freely." But the World War had destroyed that means of racial regeneration. Even Borglum now sighed that "I hate war, that is, war of submarines, gas, guns, airplanes, etc."[86] Augustus Lukeman, who took over the project in April 1925 after Borglum's clash with the SMCMA, brought the design of the monument into closer conformity with his predecessor's thinking even as he ordered Borglum's head of Lee blasted from the face of the mountain. Lukeman arranged the mounted figures of Lee, Jackson, and Davis in a more formal stylized frieze to emphasize that the Civil War was the last great moment in the Western tradition that ended on the Western Front.[87]

Such anxieties contributed to the ambivalence with which the supporters of the Stone Mountain memorial stressed its permanence. One of the defining tropes of the public monument as a cultural form, the expectation of longevity assumed an obsessive quality in this project. Smaller bronze and marble monuments were frail in comparison. Borglum noted dismissively that even the Pyramids were "built of cut stone and long since have fallen into decay." But unlike other monument promoters who had treated the Civil War as a sustaining national epic similar to classical myths, the sponsors of the Stone Mountain memorial invoked antiquity to emphasize that the carved monolith would outlast the United States and record American existence for societies that took on different forms. Lukeman called it "the

FIGURE 5.16. Augustus Lukeman (drawing by Gerald K. Geerlings),
plan for Confederate Memorial at Stone Mountain, 1925.
Courtesy of Rose Library, Emory University.

Rosetta Stone for future ages." This conception of an alien distant audience extended to apocalyptic visions that aligned the project with the southern religious fundamentalism of the 1920s. "God created Stone Mountain and none but God can destroy it. In the dawn of Creation it was born; until the end of Creation it will endure," declaimed the SMCMA fund-raising handbook. Someday judgment would come, and "when earth's final cataclysm rends asunder the continents and lifts the oceans from their depths, the last remaining fragment to pass into oblivion will be Stone Mountain, bearing upon its face and holding in its breast the deathless story of Confederate heroism."[88] If the Confederate memorial conflated the past and the future, it also dramatized the transience of the present.

Even as it failed to materialize, Borglum's well-publicized vision for Stone Mountain helped to bring into focus a transition in the dominant forms of American commemoration. The Stone Mountain project shared similarities with the burgeoning motion picture industry that extended far beyond the early momentum both received from the success of *Birth of a Nation*. The suburban Atlanta leisure resort chosen as the site of the memorial was a commercialized retreat from everyday life in some ways more like a theater than the public spaces associated with monuments. Borglum loved movies, and the spectacle he planned in Georgia showed a cinematic imagination. He insisted that the giant flat surface should be filled with action, and he considered depicting a battle scene before settling on the mobilization of the Confederate army. His informal name for the work was "a memorial to a movement," a title with a double sense. The topical importance he claimed for the project was that it represented "the first effort in America to build a monument to a nation, to a movement of a hundred thousand or ten hundred thousand people." Its formal significance was that he had invented a world of "colossi that are not static, as are those of Egypt, but that are full of life and movement." Lighting was crucial to this effect. "In a dusk or soft light at a proper distance," Borglum promised, "the general appearance will be that of the natural mountain, over which, silently, this great gray army moves." The technical innovation most enthusiastically recounted by Borglum's project historian was the development of a special lamp that "looked much like an ordinary moving-picture projector." It cast shadow pictures of the sculptor's design on the face of the mountain and enabled workers to paint an outline to guide the carving.[89] The story located the monument in an era shaped by film.

The long-term relationship between Stone Mountain and motion pictures added a final indignity to the outcome of the challenge that Borglum had issued to the Lincoln Memorial. No movie would more piously demonstrate the uses of a Civil War monument than *Mr. Smith Goes to Washington* (1939), in which western senator Jefferson Smith made a pilgrimage to the temple and found in his encounter with its oracle the wisdom and strength to resolve contemporary national problems far removed from the issues that Lincoln faced. Later the same year, the unfinished Confederate memorial at Stone Mountain became a satellite of the most monumental Civil War film of the mid-twentieth century, *Gone with the Wind*. The excitement that followed the Atlanta premiere in December 1939 prompted a pivotal reorganization of the Stone Mountain venture, in suspension since the property owner had in loyalty to Borglum refused to renew the SMCMA's lease on its expiration in 1928. Public acquisition of a purchase option on the property led to establishment of a state commission to develop a park that would include the monument. The deepening of American involvement in World War II interrupted progress on the project, which added plans for a memorial to Margaret Mitchell when work resumed around the time of her death in 1949. That idea evolved into a proposed *Gone with the Wind* museum and then into one of the chief features of the state park that opened in the early 1960s, a recreated antebellum plantation staffed by Butterfly McQueen, the actress who had played the part of Prissy in the movie. Sculptor Walker Hancock supervised the completion of Lukeman's figures of Lee, Jackson, and Davis, but within a dozen years of the 1970 dedication the chief attraction at the site was a laser show that transformed the mountain into a projection screen. Cinematic animation now bolstered Borglum's intended illusion that the Confederate horsemen rode across the cliff face. Iconic musical selections provided the pulse to the pyrotechnics and illumination. Of course the soundtrack included the theme music from *Gone with the Wind*.[90]

By the time the movie began to resuscitate the Stone Mountain memorial, Borglum was in the final stages of the Mount Rushmore project to which he had moved after leaving Georgia. Five thousand spectators attended the unveiling of the sixty-foot-high granite face of Lincoln on September 17, 1937, the seventy-fifth anniversary of the battle of Antietam. The link to the issuance of the Emancipation Proclamation was ironic: Borglum's celebration of manifest destiny in the Black Hills of South Dakota transposed the Confederate essay on the nature of racial hierarchy he had begun at Stone Mountain.[91] Mount Rushmore became what the sculptor had promised his Atlanta sponsors, a counterpoint to the Lincoln Memorial. The western monument also became what its southern sponsors had envisioned, the finale to an era of memorialization.

Epilogue

TOWARD A NEW
ICONOCLASM

Over the last seventy-five years the careers of the several thousand Civil
War monuments have combined subtle potency with occasional eruptions
of visibility. The broad decline in the prestige of public monuments evident
in the 1930s lasted for another four decades.[1] World War II yielded fewer and
mostly less ambitious memorials than World War I despite the expanded
scale of American mobilization and victory, perhaps in part because fascist
and communist regimes embraced monumentality so ardently. Long before
this point the influence of Civil War monuments had transcended the particular cultural form they established in the United States. The reverent style
of patriotism stimulated by war memorials flourished in veneration for the
American flag. Beyond the realm of civic symbolism, the militarization facilitated by monuments continued to accelerate in policies and spending priorities; Herbert Hoover noted in 1929 that the United States had the highest military budget in the world despite an absence of foreign threats.[2] Civil
War precedents almost inevitably shaped the most prominent monuments
dedicated after World War II and the Vietnam War. Some memorials to the
sectional conflict also remained significant presences in the mid-twentieth-
century racial landscape. That salience intensified after public monuments
returned to favor in the 1980s. More spectacularly, in the 2010s Confederate
monuments became a key site of protest against violent oppression of African Americans, prompting the most important season of American iconoclasm since the destruction of the equestrian statue of George III in 1776.

The upheaval posed a fresh challenge to the convergence of martial and racial order that had prevailed in the first seventy-five years of Civil War commemoration.

As Civil War monuments had guided the development of Revolutionary War and World War I monuments, the core of the national memorial tradition likewise informed the most notable monument commissioned after World War II. Felix de Weldon's Marine Corps Memorial, dedicated in Arlington, Virginia, for the first federal observance of Veterans Day in 1954, adapted in bronze a photograph that had circulated widely in many forms, including the Hollywood movie *Sands of Iwo Jima* (1949). Behind the identification of Joe Rosenthal's successful composition for a monumental picture of Marines raising the American flag at Mount Suribachi, however, was a memorial iconography that traced to Lorado Taft's *Defense of the Flag* (1889). Depictions of embattled Civil War squads with banners, originally promoted as an alternative to less vigorous solitary figures, had already influenced World War I monuments like Charles Niehaus's *Planting the Standard of Democracy* (1923). The visual lineage of flag-raising in conquest or discovery predated Columbus, but Gutzon Borglum's recent projects provided well-publicized models for transposition of warfare into a struggle with nature. Interpretive emphasis on the desolate volcanic soil of Iwo Jima erased the Japanese civilians who bore the brunt of the American war in the Pacific, much as the Confederate champions at Stone Mountain fought against granite rather than the United States or the presidents on Mount Rushmore stamped a face of adventure on the forcible dispossession of Indians.[3]

The origin of the Marine Corps Memorial in the branch's strategy of avid self-promotion connected the bronze to another legacy of Civil War monuments. Even in the nation's capital, early equestrian monuments to McPherson and Thomas expressed the ideology of the U.S. Volunteers rather than the regular army despite the careerism of those generals and the administration of the projects by the War Department. The subsequent institutional self-interest that marked the Grant memorial remained prominent in completion of the capital monuments to McClellan and Sheridan. This turn-of-the-century awakening distinguished the Naval Monument urged by David Dixon Porter to honor comrades who had died in the Civil War, installed in Washington in 1877, from the Navy Memorial dedicated seven blocks away on Pennsylvania Avenue in 1987. The dispute between the twentieth-century sponsors and sculptor Stanley Bleifeld over the sufficiency of his *Lone Sailor*, an update of Saint-Gaudens's tribute to Farragut, mirrored tensions between contemplative and strenuous phases of Civil War soldier statues. The reliefs of battle scenes added to the Navy Memorial, over Bleifeld's objections, brought it more fully in line with the pattern that had culminated in the Marine Corps Memorial.[4]

The entry of the American Battle Monuments Commission into domestic commemoration after World War II was the most far-reaching bureaucratic extension of the memorial mobilization of the War Department. Congress expanded the jurisdiction of the ABMC in 1946 to include sponsorship of monuments within the United States. This authority led to the dedication of memorials in San Francisco (1960), New York (1963), and Honolulu (1966). Congress also directed the ABMC in 1956 to plan a memorial to longtime agency chair John J. Pershing, who had died eight years earlier.[5] Dedication of that work in Washington in 1983, followed by ABMC sponsorship of the Korean War Veterans Memorial (1986–95) and the National World War II Memorial (1993–2004), reinforced military control of commemoration in the capital.

The Vietnam Veterans Memorial dedicated on the Mall in 1982, in many ways the polar opposite of the Marine Corps Memorial, revealed the imprint of both the earlier and the later phases of Civil War monuments. Maya Lin's acknowledged debt to Edwin Lutyens's haunting Thiepval Memorial to the Missing of the Somme showed precisely the creative empathy with European responses to the Great War that American internationalists encouraged in the 1920s but that turn-of-the-century Civil War precedent forestalled.[6] Behind the list of more than 72,000 names inscribed on Lutyens's stone piers, however, stood the importance of Civil War commemoration to the advent of what Thomas Laqueur has dubbed the age of necronominalism. The unprecedented efforts in the 1860s to identify soldiers' bodies and provide individual headstones constituted the vanguard of this era. Tablets installed in public buildings and other community memorials bearing lists of names complemented the vast reinterment project. Many such Civil War lists eventually expanded to include the dead of other wars, like the sets of names that Lin often saw in Memorial Hall at Yale before she designed the Vietnam Veterans Memorial as a college student, but her brilliant concept was more firmly grounded in a specific historical remembrance and less amenable to martial generalization. Completed only seven years after the last of the approximately 58,000 deaths listed on the black granite wall, the Vietnam Veterans Memorial resembled the emotional linkages of names and bodies in the immediate aftermath of the Civil War. As the first wave of soldier monuments focused on tensions between individual realms and mass mobilization, Lin's enumeration tolled the intimate costs of a traumatic war in which draftees comprised a large share of combat deaths. The architect's determination to provide a space for "personal reflection and private reckoning" returned to the intense particularity of mourning that early Civil War monuments sustained through a more sentimental vocabulary.[7]

At the same time, the Vietnam Veterans Memorial also shared key features with later Civil War soldier monuments. Although Lin wrote in her proposal that "this memorial is for those who have died, and for us to remember them," the name of the project made clear that it honored survivors as well as the dead.[8] This emphasis followed the pattern that had gained ascendancy across the North and South by the early twentieth century and continued in American monuments of other wars. The Vietnam Veterans Memorial differed from its predecessors insofar as it recognized ex-soldiers as especially in need of the healing that the therapeutic site offered visitors, but a commonplace interpretation came to be that insufficient appreciation from civilians was a central aspect of veterans' sufferings. In alleviating that condition, the memorial identified veterans as moral arbiters of the nation in succession to the Union and Confederate soldiers who had promoted tributes to themselves.[9]

Apart from the influence of Civil War precedents on midcentury war memorials, some works retained vitality as sites of racial politics despite the overall eclipse of the public monument. The Lincoln Memorial developed into the premier national forum of civil rights protest during the years between Marian Anderson's open-air concert on Easter 1939 and the March on Washington in August 1963. Sporadic rallies turned into a ritualized program in which the Lincoln Memorial furnished a privileged liminal place, outside of ordinary politics, in which to seek national transformation.[10] Literary and artistic reflections renewed the aura of the Shaw Memorial. A line of wartime and early postwar poems about the Fifty-Fourth Massachusetts refocused around Augustus Saint-Gaudens's relief. Charles Ives's orchestral composition *Three Places in New England* (first performed in 1931), Robert Lowell's poem "For the Union Dead" (1960), and Lincoln Kirstein's album *Lay This Laurel* (1973) recognized the sculptural tribute to black soldiers and white officers as a canonical synthesis of history and art. Kirstein played an early role in the making of the cinematic monument *Glory* (1989), which brought wide attention to the Shaw Memorial as interest returned to its civic form.[11]

Racism kept other Civil War monuments alive. NAACP leader Walter White dramatized the long shadow of Confederate memory in his novel *The Fire in the Flint* (1924), in which a Georgia lynch mob burned the body of an African American at the feet of the soldier statue in the local court-house square. After winning reelection to the U.S. Senate in a campaign that stressed his resistance to federal antilynching legislation, "Cotton Ed" Smith stood before the Wade Hampton equestrian statue at the South Caro-lina statehouse dressed in a red shirt emblematic of the overthrow of Re-construction and declared, "We conquered in '76, and we conquered in '38." Rioters determined to stop James Meredith from integrating the Univer-sity of Mississippi in 1962 chose the Confederate monument on campus as a rallying point. The intersection of the Civil War centennial with resistance to the civil rights movement prompted the commissioning of a cluster of mod-est Confederate monuments as well as the anticlimactic completion of the Stone Mountain memorial. By then, however, the Confederate battle flag had become a much more potent reactionary instrument than any south-ern monument.[12] Alice Walker depicted a Confederate soldier statue in need of reinforcement against the civil rights movement in her novel *Meridian* (1976), in which an army tank added by local authorities to the public square of a Georgia town crushed the leg of the effigy.

The period beginning in the 1980s ended the half century of commemo-rative desuetude that began in the Depression. Soldier monuments were again the center of the memorial flurry, as some sponsors imitated Lin's masterpiece and others joined in backlash commemorations more akin to the Marine Corps Memorial.[13] Initiatives focused on twentieth-century con-flicts extended the lineage of Civil War monuments. The legacy of emanci-pation ensured more direct Civil War participation in the profusion. Rep-resented on the civic landscape for the first 125 years after the war by the Shaw Memorial, the All Wars Memorial to Colored Soldiers and Sailors in Philadelphia (1934), and a few modest monuments at an African American church and segregated or national cemeteries, the black Union soldier be-came a prominent memorial figure after the box-office and critical success of *Glory*.[14] Sponsors unveiled more than fifteen monuments with this theme between 1990 and 2015. Some of these projects were quite substantial. The budget for the African American Civil War Memorial in the Shaw neighbor-hood of Washington, DC (1998), which listed the names of 209,145 black soldiers as well as 7,000 white officers on a concentric series of curved walls, was $2.5 million.[15] The centerpiece of the installation, Ed Hamilton's sculp-ture *The Spirit of Freedom*, invited comparison with the Shaw Memorial by depicting a black volunteer taking leave of his family in the interior of a semi-cylindrical setting. The vigorous soldiers holding their rifles at alert on the exterior of the composition staked a claim to the masculine ideal promoted a century earlier in monuments to white soldiers. Set in relief above them, an African apparition watched over the struggle for black self-realization.

Defiant whites responded with fresh Confederate monuments. Perhaps the most extreme example was the equestrian statue of Nathan Bedford Forrest installed on private land alongside an interstate highway in Nashville in 1998. Created by Jack Kershaw, the white supremacist best remembered for his legal defense of Martin Luther King Jr.'s assassin, the twenty-five-foot-tall fiberglass group depicted the leader of the Fort Pillow massacre and postwar Ku Klux Klan on a rearing horse in front of an array of Confederate battle flags. The berserk general turned backward to fire his revolver at pursuers. Startling clashes in proportion and color between the small silver rider and the gigantic golden mount added to the cartoonish effect of the composition. Kershaw and the sponsoring landowner expressed disdain for the aesthetic conventions of public art as well as the constitutional principle of racial equality.[16]

Racial politics not only sustained older Civil War monuments through the middle of the century and inspired new works afterward but also placed Confederate monuments at the center of a return to iconoclasm in American memorial culture. The civil rights movement logically impelled confrontation with public endorsements of slavery. Indignant residents of Natchitoches, Louisiana, forced the 1968 removal of a statue of an elderly black man, bowing his head and doffing his hat, dedicated in 1927 "In Grateful Recognition of The / Arduous and Faithful Service Of / The Good Darkies of Louisiana," but such monuments were few.[17] College students led an increase in protests against memorials to the proslavery republic. The campus newspaper at the University of North Carolina published a letter in 1965 calling for removal of the school's Confederate soldier statue. Two years later, activist and poet John Beecher read from his verse collection *To Live and Die in Dixie* (1966) in a "debate" with the bronze infantryman. A group of African American students at the University of Texas petitioned in 1969 for removal of what they called "racist statues," including a portrait of Jefferson Davis. Student protests at the University of Missouri prompted local officials in 1974 to remove a boulder monument installed at the center of campus in 1935 to honor Confederate soldiers of Boone County; supporters arranged its transfer to the county courthouse.[18]

Criticism of Confederate monuments expanded somewhat with heightened interest in memorialization but remained much less fervent than the campaign against governmental display of the Confederate battle flag that roiled southern states from the late 1980s into the beginning of the twenty-first century. A short-lived 1997 request to remove the courthouse monument in Walterboro, South Carolina, was the only proposal of its kind in a state where the flag controversy dominated politics at the end of the millennium. Apart from memorials on college campuses, the works most likely to stir resistance were those that most squarely insulted the mid-twentieth-century civil rights movement. In 1999 a black resident of Denton, Texas, began a long effort to dismantle or alter the triumphal arch equipped with dual drinking fountains to highlight racial segregation as a Confederate victory. An especially provocative monument to Nathan Bedford Forrest unveiled in 2000 in Selma, Alabama, a city better remembered by then for the civil rights march that started there in 1965 than for the battle that the Confederate cavalry commander lost there a century earlier, stirred an uproar that caused removal of the work to a cemetery and later its theft and replacement. More typical of American commemoration were attempts to dilute the Confederate presence with the 1996 placement of a monument to black tennis champion Arthur Ashe on Monument Avenue in Richmond or the 2011 installation of a Frederick Douglass statue across from the Confederate monument at the county courthouse in Easton, Maryland.[19]

New Orleans, which became the epicenter of iconoclasm after 2012, had demonstrated the limits of that movement only a few years earlier. Protest long centered on the Liberty Place Monument, an 1891 obelisk that was not a Confederate memorial but a celebration of violent resistance to Reconstruction. The mayoral administration of Moon Landrieu, who as a city council member during the 1960s had supported removal of the Confederate battle flag from the council chamber, installed an explanatory plaque in 1974 intended to neutralize the memorial. After the city placed the obelisk in storage during a construction project and announced plans to move it to a museum, Ku Klux Klan leader David Duke instigated a campaign to restore it. Officials moved it to an obscure location behind a parking garage in 1993. The continued controversy contributed to an extraordinary local memorial activism that included renaming of public schools that honored slaveholders. Agitation directed specifically toward Confederate monuments nonetheless remained slight. A rally held in 1998 to urge removal of the Robert E. Lee statue towering above Lee Circle attracted four participants.[20]

Civil War monuments began to attract more of a spotlight amid the nationwide protests that followed the killing of black teenager Trayvon Martin by a Miami vigilante in February 2012 and, within the next few weeks, local protests against the killing of two young black men by the New

Orleans Police Department. New Orleans sympathizers painted inscriptions with the names of the three victims on the Liberty Place monument, the Lee monument, and the Jefferson Davis monument. The incident was not the first time that racial remonstrance had led to the defacing of Confederate memorials, but it achieved exceptional public traction.[21] The pastor of a church located near the Davis statue remarked that he had not previously noticed that the uninspiring monument honored the Confederate president. Protesters reached a wider audience by emailing photographs of the defaced monuments to New Orleans newspapers and helping to circulate the images through a variety of digital media. Baton Rouge soon reassigned its Confederate soldier statue, temporarily removed during a construction project, to the Old State Capitol Museum. Another round of graffiti at the Davis monument in New Orleans followed shortly after the acquittal of Martin's killer in 2013 prompted the launch of the online campaign Black Lives Matter.[22]

These protests reanimated dormant Confederate monuments through a remarkable combination of old and new strategies. Mourning for black lives harnessed the primal impetus of monuments in recognition of death, a crucial purpose in the initial emergence of Civil War memorials. Graffiti also tapped the creative tension between monuments and writing. Like the pasquinades posted on the talking statues of Rome, the anonymously spray-painted lamentations and imprecations challenged the memorials' claims to represent the voice of the community. Circulation of photographs updated the outlets through which local monuments had once reached across the country in prints, illustrated magazines, and postcards. The conjunction of the "tagging" of Confederate memorials and the rise of hashtags like #blacklivesmatter yielded an ironic mix of ancient and contemporary media, the public monument and the digital photo feed.[23]

The dissident New Orleans graffiti led to the formation of a group called Take 'Em Down NOLA amid the national turmoil that followed the police shooting of black teenager Michael Brown in Ferguson, Missouri, in August 2014. The organization condemned Lost Cause monuments as foundations for persistent white supremacy and more specifically as models for a social organization of violence that extended from slavery through lynch mobs to current police, prison, and death-penalty policies. The attack on Confederate monuments exposed their original energy as metaphors for forcible regulation of the racial order. Identification of the Confederacy as a precursor to agencies that acted as occupying armies in black communities connected secessionist battalions to later institutions of state-sanctioned aggression. Although the armed services had made important contributions to civil rights, repudiation of the war memorials suggested that a society in which the military provided a template for the civilian polity tended to be hierarchical and rigid and violent.[24]

Racial violence and digital media propelled the iconoclastic campaign to fruition after a white supremacist murdered nine African Americans attending a Bible study session at Emanuel A.M.E. Church in Charleston in June 2015. The perpetrator's online archive featured a manifesto calling for race war and photographs of himself posing with the Confederate battle flag. Discovery of these pictures redoubled the long-term recoil against the southern cross. Many retailers stopped selling the battle flag or items emblazoned with its design. South Carolina and Alabama, which had been flying the flag on their capitol grounds since removing the banners from their statehouse domes, eliminated those displays. The uprising swept beyond the battle flag to more widespread tagging of Confederate monuments. Charlotte, North Carolina, took down a defaced stele for cleaning and later shifted it to a city-owned cemetery, which underscored the political attenuation of cemeteries since the installation of early Civil War monuments.[25] The University of Texas moved its Jefferson Davis statue in August 2015 from the South Mall of the Austin campus to a history research center. Fifteen months later Louisville and the University of Louisville jointly removed a municipal Confederate monument at the school and sent it to a park in Brandenburg, Kentucky. The New Orleans city council voted in December 2015 to remove the local statues of Lee, Davis, and Beauregard as well as the Liberty Place Monument, though resistance delayed implementation of that decision for more than a year. In spring 2017 the four designated works came down in dramatic spectacles that drew national attention.

The response to the Charleston murders galvanized defenders as well as critics of Confederate monuments. During the turn-of-the-millennium controversies over the Confederate battle flag, Republican legislatures in South Carolina, Georgia, and Mississippi adopted laws that required state approval for removal or alteration of Confederate memorials. North Carolina enacted such a statute two weeks after South Carolina struck its Confederate battle flag in response to the Emanuel shootings. Tennessee soon reinforced the restrictive regulatory scheme established in 2013. Alabama adopted its law in May 2017 to thwart a vote by Birmingham officials to remove the local Confederate memorial after the Charleston murders. Though billed as "protection" of Confederate monuments, these centralizing measures redefined the memorials in a manner that illustrated the militarized legacy of commemoration. White southern monuments installed from the last third of the nineteenth century through the first third of the twentieth century identified localities with the Lost Cause and sought to honor the community no less than the Confederacy. When grassroots iconoclasm divorced those two fundamental themes, Republican legislatures prioritized remembrance of the Civil War rather than everyday civic engagement.

A different mobilization of Confederate monument defenders took place in Charlottesville, Virginia, where discussions of possible removal of Lee and Jackson statues had begun after the killing of Trayvon Martin and accelerated after the Charleston massacre. After a Democratic governor vetoed Republican legislation that would have tightened state limitations on municipal control over monuments, the city council voted in February 2017 to remove the equestrian statues. A right-wing candidate for governor made the issue central to his campaign for the Republican nomination, and belligerent white supremacists held a torch-lit rally at the Lee monument in May 2017 that attracted extensive media coverage several days before the climactic removal of the Lee statue in New Orleans.[26]

Like the Charleston murders, the Charlottesville rally invigorated Confederate monuments by embracing the white supremacism denied by the Sons of Confederate Veterans and other apologists who maintained that slavery was incidental to a secession focused on state sovereignty. Communities responded to this renewed potency with further iconoclasm. St. Louis removed its Confederate monument in June 2017. A middle-aged African American who frequently visited Forest Park told the *New York Times* that he had not noticed that the monument was a tribute to the Confederacy until the defacement campaign.[27] Rockville, Maryland, and Orlando, Florida, removed Confederate monuments around the same time.

The pattern expanded sharply after aggressive white supremacists staged another Charlottesville rally in August 2017, at which a vehicular assault by a white supremacist killed an antiracist counterprotester. Fifteen southern communities removed outdoor Confederate monuments in the next two months. Baltimore took down its Lee-Jackson double equestrian and its monuments to Confederate soldiers and Confederate women. Dallas removed its equestrian statue of Lee. San Antonio exiled a common-soldier statue. State laws limited this activity, though a crowd in Durham, North Carolina, toppled a Confederate soldier statue in defiance of the legislative restriction of municipal autonomy. Authorities in Memphis capped the wave in December 2017 by transferring legal title for two city parks to circumvent Tennessee supervision and remove statues of Jefferson Davis and Nathan Bedford Forrest. Since the outcry over the death of Trayvon Martin, twenty-

FIGURE E.1. Removal of the statue of Robert E. Lee from Lee Circle, New Orleans, May 19, 2017. Photograph by Scott Threlkeld. Courtesy of Associated Press.

three communities where slavery was legal in 1860 had removed thirty-three freestanding outdoor Confederate monuments.[28]

This surge was the most important American revival of iconoclasm since July 1776, even if Durham was the only community that destroyed a statue. Towns across the country also took down some Confederate commemorations that were not monuments, such as highway markers. The reexamination of the civic landscape extended beyond the Civil War. Municipalities and institutions renamed buildings and other facilities that honored advocates or perpetrators of violent white supremacism. New York City moved a statue of nineteenth-century gynecologist J. Marion Sims from Central Park to Green-Wood Cemetery. Confederate monuments remained the nucleus of the turmoil, and several controversies continued to simmer after 2017. A long-running series of demonstrations against the Confederate soldier monument at the University of North Carolina culminated in the toppling of the statue by a resolute crowd in August 2018.[29]

Much as protesters' turn to Civil War monuments linked racism to militarization of law enforcement, the martial framework of the memorials clarified the achievement of the iconoclastic movement. Tributes to Jefferson Davis, which did not benefit from deference to uniformed service, were especially vulnerable because they were readily recognized as ideological.[30] More remarkable was the repudiation of Confederate officers, especially Robert E. Lee. The general had thrived in twentieth-century commemoration as an epitome of military professionalism. The removal of several grand Lee monuments as well as prominent indoor memorials at the Episcopal National Cathedral, the chapel of Duke University, and the Hall of Fame for Great Americans reasserted the political accountability of military commanders urged by George W. Curtis at the dedication of the Sedgwick statue at West Point. Even more extraordinary was the removal of fourteen common-soldier monuments and two monuments to Confederate women. This iconoclasm indicated that ordinary Americans who sacrificed their lives at the call of the state were nonetheless morally wrong. In contrast, the city council of Demopolis, Alabama, illustrated the continued power of the martial ideal to forge compromise by voting to replace a motorist-damaged Confederate soldier statue with an obelisk dedicated to the local dead of all wars.[31]

Artists responding to the cultural moment stressed that the sudden salience of Confederate monuments arose from the intersection of white supremacism and organized violence. Even a few years earlier, this theme had not been central to the Tony Kushner–Jeanine Tesori musical *Caroline, or Change* (2003), which revolved around the incompatibility of Confederate monuments with the civil rights movement of the 1960s. Fred Wilson's vanguard meditation on race and war memorials in the public art project *E Pluribus Unum* (2009–11) addressed a Union rather than a Confederate monument. Wilson reproduced the statue of a freedman that formed part of the

Indiana Soldiers and Sailors Monument, extricated the figure from the celebration of northern victory, and supplied the resituated representation with a slanted flagpole reminiscent of the Marine Corps Memorial. Not the soldier statue that many Indianapolis residents wanted to see, this embodiment of emancipation carried a banner of the African diaspora. Local opposition in the politically conservative home of the American Legion led to cancellation of the commission.[32]

Iconoclasm refocused attention on the Confederate example of militarized racism. Kara Walker, an artist with a long interest in the Civil War, turned to the Stone Mountain memorial after the Charleston murders. Her exhibition *Go to Hell or Atlanta, Whichever Comes First* (2015), featured pencil drawings of figures reminiscent of Trayvon Martin and Michael Brown — a youth wearing a hoodie and a naked black man peaceably holding up both hands — as well as a drawing of military-grade weaponry of the sort that municipal police forces had obtained from the army. The centerpiece of the exhibition was a sixty-foot-long silhouette panel, installed next to a wall-sized photograph of Stone Mountain, that reimagined the Confederate memorial as a vast tableau of racial violence, often sexual violence enacted with implements of martial order like a sword and a flag. The High Museum of Art purchased this monumental work for permanent display as an Atlanta countermemorial to the monolith. Walker had grown up in and around the town of Stone Mountain, and the black artist's triumph in her former home reclaimed the black-majority area. Sierra Pettengill's short documentary film *Graven Image* (2017) similarly leveraged the resilience of the granite frieze, unlikely to suffer removal even though the tribute to the Confederate high command and birthplace of the twentieth-century Klan paralleled monuments that other communities were dismantling.[33] An-My Lê's photography exhibition *The Silent General* (2017) highlighted a picture of the condemned P. G. T. Beauregard statue in New Orleans as seen through a scrim. The shadowed figure dramatized civic rejection of the former hero. Placement of the image in a set of Louisiana landscapes of violence continued the Vietnam War refugee's studies of militarized environments.[34]

Such works aim to perpetuate the iconoclastic moment, much as a long series of paintings, prints, performances, and other artistic representations deepened American remembrance of the Revolutionary overthrow of the George III equestrian statue. Like a flourishing monument, meaningful iconoclasm requires sustained engagement. How well that effort will succeed, and how often it will be refreshed by removal of additional memorials,

FIGURE E.2. An-My Lê, *Monument, General P. G. T. Beauregard,*
New Orleans, Louisiana, 2016, from the portfolio *The Silent General,* 2015–17.
Courtesy of the Whitney Museum of American Art and Marian Goodman Gallery.

remains to be seen. The critical reappraisal of Civil War monuments adds a vital dimension to the resurgence of war memorials since the late twentieth century. Controversy has established broad recognition that Civil War monuments constitute an influential cultural form with a particular history. Appreciation for the complexities and contingencies of that history promises to reacquaint Americans with the democratic visions and tragic decisions that have contributed to making a national identity.

Epilogue

Acknowledgments

I have worked on this book for far too long to list all of my debts. My research began at the age of seven when my family moved to the suburbs of Washington, D.C. Weekend family trips explored all the famous landmarks of the capital, though my fondest memories are of walking together on the streets and frequently running off course with my siblings to identify the figures portrayed in nearby statues. We became familiar with many monuments, and I felt sure that I had mastered the code by which the arrangement of a horse's legs in an equestrian statue indicates whether the hero died in battle. I have subsequently had to set aside some of my early learning, but I have never lost the sense that civic memorials can be extraordinary sites of encounter between past and present. I am deeply grateful to my mother and father and sisters and brother for encouraging my interest in history. I am especially glad that my parents resisted the temptation to leave their petulant child behind at Arlington National Cemetery when he was violating the solemnity with a bored tantrum.

Other people have been immensely helpful in later phases of the project. David Blight, Kirk Savage, and Nina Silber have been the best supporters any scholar could find. I am particularly thankful to Kirk for carefully reading the manuscript and making extensive suggestions informed by his superb studies of public monuments. Fitz Brundage, John Coski, Gaines Foster, and John Neff also shared their expertise and showed their generosity. Many colleagues made valuable contributions in discussions of presentations. Ed Ayers offered welcome advice after a conference talk I gave when I was still using a slide carousel. Mark Peterson asked a question at a brown-bag lunch that haunted me for years. For similar interventions and more casual conversations I am especially grateful to Martin Berger, Doug Egerton, Alice Fahs, Drew Gilpin Faust, June Hargrove, John Quist, Heather Richardson,

Daniel Sherman, Frank Towers, Michael Vorenberg, Joan Waugh, and Elizabeth Young.

Family and professionalism converge in my debts to my wife and colleague, Carol Harrison. Her love has made me a better person, and her counsel has made this effort a better book. Despite my thorough investigation of public tributes, I do not know how to acknowledge her role properly. She personifies the good luck I have been fortunate to experience in life.

The project has received gratifying support from many institutions and the people who administer them. Research advanced decisively at the National Gallery of Art's Center for Advanced Study in the Visual Arts, where Elizabeth Cropper, Peter Lukehart, and Therese O'Malley welcomed me to an ideal scholarly community. During this period the staff of the Smithsonian American Art Museum helped me scour the files of the Inventory of American Sculpture. Fellowships provided by the American Antiquarian Society, the Gilder Lehrman Institute of American History, and the Virginia Historical Society were similarly fruitful. The National Endowment for the Humanities funded the initial phase of writing, and the National Humanities Center was a perfect site for completion of a first draft with the aid of its wonderful staff. Fulbright Sweden and the Swedish Institute for North American Studies at Uppsala University sponsored a magical year. Dag Blanck was an exemplary academic host, and Danuta Fjellestad and Margaret Hunt were particularly gracious and stimulating colleagues. At the University of North Carolina Press, the book has benefited from the expert support of Mark Simpson-Vos, Jessica Newman, Mary Carley Caviness, Alex Martin, and the editors of the Civil War America series. The Watson-Brown Foundation kindly provided a grant for the illustrations. The University of South Carolina has generously facilitated every stage of the process, and I am thankful for the backing of a series of department chairs, deans, and provosts, as well as the goodwill of many faculty members and students.

I did my first archival research for this project around the time Veronica Brown was born. It is a great joy to be able to present the book to her as a young woman embarking on her own career, and it is a great sorrow not to be able to present the book to her brother. I will be pleased if the book makes a contribution both to the party of hope and to the party of memory.

Acknowledgments

Notes

ABBREVIATIONS

AA	*American Architect*
AABN	*American Architect and Building News*
AAI	*American Art Illustrated*
AMA	*American Magazine of Art*
ANJ	*Army and Navy Journal*
BET	*Boston Evening Transcript*
CT	*Chicago Tribune*
CV	*Confederate Veteran*
HW	*Harper's Weekly*
IAS	Inventory of American Sculpture Files, Smithsonian American Art Museum
MN	*Monumental News*
NAR	*North American Review*
NT	*Nashville Tennessean*
NYT	*New York Times*
RD	*Richmond Dispatch*
WES	*Washington Evening Star*
WP	*Washington Post*

INTRODUCTION

1. Bellion, "Performing Iconoclasm"; Marks, "Statue"; Savage, *Monument Wars*, 1–2. Robert Mills and Enrico Causici made the monument in Baltimore (1815–29), Horatio Greenough the monument in Washington (1832–41), and Henry Kirke Brown the monument in New York (1853–56). See also McInnis, "Revisiting Cincinnatus."

2. Upton, *What Can and Can't Be Said*, 11–13, 196.

3. Criblez, *Parading Patriotism*; Ryan, *Civic Wars*, 58–93; Travers, *Celebrating the Fourth*; Waldstreicher, *In the Midst of Perpetual Fetes*.

4. Newell and Shrader, *Duty*, 42.

5. Tocqueville, *Democracy in America*, 224; Coffman, *Old Army*, 49–55, 137–41; Cunliffe,

Soldiers and Civilians, 101–34, 142–44, 179–212; Foos, *Short, Offhand, Killing Affair*, 23–25; Mahon, *History of the Militia*, 83, 97; Pitcavage, "Equitable Burden." Illinois, the fourth most populous state in 1860 and home of the showiest late antebellum volunteer militia unit, the U. S. Zouave Cadets, reported fewer than 800 uniformed militia members at the outbreak of the Civil War, less than one-fifth of the state requisition under the "amiable legal fiction" that Lincoln called 75,000 militia troops into federal service in April 1861. Hicks, "Organization of the Volunteer Army," 329–30.

6. Foos, *Short, Offhand, Killing Affair*, 101; Winders, *Mr. Polk's Army*. Greenberg, *Manifest Manhood*, demonstrates that filibusters exercised a cultural influence that exceeded their numbers, but characterization of these armed adventurers as "martial" obscures the institutional and ideological distinctions between their version of aggressive masculinity and the militarized citizenship that emerged in the late nineteenth century.

7. Anbinder, "Which Poor Man's Fight?"

8. Higginson, "Regular and Volunteer Officers," 350. In the large scholarship on Civil War soldier culture, see especially Carmichael, *War*; Foote, *Gentlemen and Roughs*; Giesberg, *Sex*; Glatthaar, *General Lee's Army*; McPherson, *For Cause and Comrades*; Ramold, *Baring the Iron Hand*; Reardon, *With a Sword*; and Weitz, *More Damning than Slaughter*. Foote, "Soldiers," is a valuable historiographical overview. Casey, *New Men*, chap. 1; and Fahs, *Imagined Civil War* are penetrating analyses of civilians' views of the army.

9. "The Army and the Nation," *ANJ* 1 (August 29, 1863): 8; "Military Government for the South," *ANJ* 8 (March 18, 1871): 492.

10. Wingate, *Sculpting Doughboys*, chap. 4.

11. Savage, *Standing Soldiers*, analyzes these developments brilliantly.

12. Prost, "Monuments to the Dead," 2:310. King, *Memorials*; and Sherman, *Construction of Memory*, both apply Prost's advice by structuring chapters around the different phases in making common-soldier monuments in the 1920s. This book addresses a wider variety of memorials across a longer period of time.

13. Panhorst, "Lest We Forget," remains a valuable overview.

14. My quantitative reports draw from a database compiled from the sources specified in the bibliography. I realize that my list of memorials is not comprehensive, but I am confident that it is sufficient to identify major patterns. My definition of Civil War monuments does not include roadside signs and other simple markers of historical places.

15. For overviews of this literature, see Cook, "Quarrel Forgotten?"; and Silber, "Reunion and Reconciliation."

16. Faust, *Republic of Suffering*; McElya, *Politics of Mourning*; Neff, *Honoring the Civil War Dead*.

17. Foster, *Ghosts*; McConnell, *Glorious Contentment*.

18. See especially Jordan, *Marching Home*; Kelly, *Creating a National Home*; McClintock, "Binding Up"; and Rosenburg, *Living Monuments*.

19. Clark, *Preparing for War*; Hoganson, *Fighting for American Manhood*; Pettegrew, *Brutes in Suits*. Lears, *Rebirth of a Nation*, is an important account of turn-of-the-century militarization, though the interpretation is compromised by the dated argument that the shift resulted largely from reverberations of what Lears calls a "total war" (12–13). See Hsieh, "Total War"; and Neely, *Civil War*.

20. Finseth, *Civil War Dead*, cites much of this large body of scholarship.

21. Becker, "Monuments aux morts après la guerre"; Fussell, *Great War*; Inglis, *Sacred Places*; Mosse, *Fallen Soldiers*; Winter, *Sites of Memory*.

22. H. P. Caemmerer to J. J. Vetter, November 12, 1925, General Files, National Commission of Fine Arts, relays Lorado Taft's statement that he knew of no such pattern. The belief must have been fairly new if it had not previously come to the attention of Taft, author of the leading survey of American sculpture and a prominent practitioner and teacher of the art.

CHAPTER 1

1. Stow[e], *Address*, 9; J. H. Hudson, "Dedication Address for Confederate Monument, Cheraw, SC, July 26, 1867," 1, Confederate Memorial Records; Reichel, *Historical Sketch*, 96.

2. Cray, "Commemorating the Prison Ship Dead"; Purcell, *Sealed*, 103–7, 144–49; Savage, *Monument Wars*, chap. 1.

3. Chambers, *Memories of War*; Purcell, *Sealed*, 125–26.

4. Melville, *Israel Potter*, 1–2; Purcell, *Sealed*, 197, 201; Roeser, "Bunker Hill."

5. "About Monuments," *HW* 4 (February 11, 1860): 82.

6. The unveiling of Herman W. Bissen's *Landsoldaten* statue in Fredericia, Denmark (1858), and the Crimean War Memorial at Waterloo Place in London (1861) exercised no discernible influence in the United States. Sherman, *Construction of Memory*, 8–9, discusses the contested process of emergence that informs this chapter.

7. Aaslestad, "Remembering," 395–96; Clark, "Wars of Liberation"; Easton, *Hegel's First American Followers*, 159–203; Hagemann, *Revisiting Prussia's Wars*, 235–38.

8. Reinhart, *August Willich's Gallant Dutchmen*, 26–27, 47, 52–53, 56, 59, 61, 191–92; Trowbridge, *America's Oldest Civil War Monument*.

9. Hillard, *Last Men*; Ransom, "Connecticut's Monumental Epoch," 58: 83–86; Young, *Shoemaker*, 135.

10. Faust, *Republic of Suffering*; Grant, "Patriot Graves"; Kinsel, "From These Honored Dead," 126–29; Neff, *Honoring the Civil War Dead*, 108.

11. Linden-Ward, *Silent City*, chap. 9; Rogers, *Randolph Rogers*, 92; [Strauch], *Spring Grove*, 55.

12. Scee, *Mount Hope*, 87–90. The well-publicized arrangements at Mount Hope may have contributed to the installation of monuments at cemeteries in Kittery and Hampden later in 1864. On antebellum rural cemeteries and war memory, see Schantz, *Awaiting the Heavenly Country*, 82–85.

13. Smith, *History of Newton*, 589–601.

14. "Inauguration of the Bristol Soldiers' Monument," *Cleveland Morning Leader*, October 20, 1863; George, *Civil War Monuments of Ohio*; Wheeler, "Local Autonomy."

15. Roe, *Fifth Regiment*, 21–22, 120, 271; Samuels and Kimball, *Somerville*, 105–10, 409–10; "To the People of Massachusetts," *BET*, March 7, 1863. Service records from American Civil War Research Database, Historical Data Systems, Inc., 1997–2013.

16. McGraw, "Minutemen"; Samuels and Kimball, *Somerville*, 109. See generally Gallman, *Defining Duty*.

17. Hight, *History of the Fifty-Eighth Regiment*, 131–45, 248, 534–35 (quotation at 131); Ramold, *Baring the Iron Hand*, 249–50, 256.

18. "The Bull Run Monuments," *HW* 9 (July 1, 1865): 401–4. The dedication exercises provided the concluding image in Gardner, *Gardner's Photographic Sketch Book*. Another well-publicized example was the cornerstone-laying for the monument at West Point in June 1864.

19. Whitney, *Oration*, 28, 31.

20. Brown, *Dorothea Dix*, 323; Jacob, *Testament*, 153–57.

21. Janney, *Burying the Dead*, 8–9, 95–98.

22. Faust, *Republic of Suffering*, 236; Hacker, "Census-Based Count"; Neff, *Honoring the Civil War Dead*, 134.

23. Richard Edes, "Biographical Notices of the Deceased Soldiers of Bolton," in Loring, *Oration, Delivered at Bolton*, 30.

24. *Report of the Soldiers' Monument Committee, of the City of Fitchburg*, 30. Harris, "Sons and Soldiers," is an excellent case study.

25. Pittsfield, Massachusetts, where Parthenia Fenn led an early fundraising campaign, described municipal sponsorship as the antithesis of the Ladies Memorial Association campaigns in the former Confederacy: "While it was felt that it would give additional interest to the monument, that Mrs. Fenn and other ladies who had labored for the health and comfort of the soldiers while in the field should have a more conspicuous share in its erection, it was also generally deemed proper and fitting that the town in its corporate capacity should take the greater part in thus honoring the memory of its representatives in the armies of the Republic." Smith, *Proceedings at the Dedication of the Soldiers' Monument at Pittsfield*, 4.

26. *Ceremonies at the Dedication of the Soldiers' Monument in Concord*, 29, 52. Halttunen, *Confidence Men*, chap. 5, discusses mid-nineteenth-century anxiety over sincerity at funerals.

27. *Proceedings at the Dedication of the Soldiers' and Sailors' Monument in Providence*.

28. Savage, "Unknowable Dead"; Sherman, "Bodies and Names."

29. Broadside, June 10, 1865, and Minority Report of the Sub-committee of Six, September 23, 1865, both in Miscellaneous Records of Memorial Hall.

30. Brooks, *Address*, 3, 20.

31. *Oration Delivered by General Francis A. Walker*, 18–19, 24; Ellis, *Massachusetts Andrew Sharpshooters*, 73–75.

32. *Quincy (MA) Patriot*, June 27, 1868.

33. *Woonsocket (RI) Patriot and State Register*, June 3, 1870.

34. *Erection and Dedication*, 38–39.

35. *Lewiston (ME) Evening Journal*, February 28, 1868; *Dedication of the Confederate Monument at Greenwood Cemetery*, 22.

36. *Dauphin County Soldiers' Monument*, 5; *Services at the Dedication of the Memorial Library, Framingham*, 45.

37. *Soldiers' Monument in Cambridge*, 75; *Dedication of the Soldiers' Monument, at Peterboro*, 15, 18. On Webster's rhetorical use of the vision convention, see Seelye, *Memory's Nation*, 75–76.

38. *BET*, August 10, 1869; "Dead on the Field," 17.

39. *Ceremonies at the Dedication of the Soldiers' Monument in Concord*, 12; *Dedication of the Soldiers' Monument at Cherryfield*, 6.

40. Sedgwick, *Address*, 3–4.

41. Brown, *Civil War Canon*, 28; *Waltham (MA) Free Press*, June 5, 1868.

42. *Town of Wayland*, 7. See also Huntington, *Stamford Soldiers' Memorial*, 5.

43. *Reports of the Soldiers' Memorial Society*, 2–3.

44. "The City's Memorial," *BET*, September 18, 1877.

45. "News and Views," *Harvard Alumni Bulletin* 21 (October 10, 1918): 53; Mitchell, "Harvard's Heroes."

46. *Alumni Hall*, 19–22; Higginson and Ware, "Memorial Hall," 2:50–51, 72. Amherst debated construction of a memorial hall before accepting a donated set of memorial chimes for the college chapel. "Gov. Claflin at Commencement," *Springfield (MA) Republican*, July 15, 1870. Lafayette (1867), Williams (1868), Girard (1869), and Oberlin (1871) were leading examples of colleges that chose monuments rather than buildings. Brown (1866) dedicated a memorial tablet.

47. Roe, *Monuments*, 26; [Sturgis], "Something about Monuments," 155.

48. Dowling, *Charles Eliot Norton*, 65; [Norton], "Harvard and Yale," 35.

49. [Howells], "Question of Monuments," 647–48.

50. City of Boston, *Report*, 5; *Dedication of the Memorial Hall in Dedham*, 23.

51. *Soldiers of Oakham*, 13.

52. Breisch, *Henry Hobson Richardson*, 9, 14, 93–97; Brown, "Ohio's Veterans' Memorial Halls"; Walton, "Northampton Local Monuments." Northampton (1888) and Shelby County (1900) much later placed military statues outside their memorial halls.

53. Thayer, *Address Delivered at the Dedication of Memorial Hall, Lancaster*, 39; Brooks, *Address*, 5.

54. Chambers, *Memories of War*, 176–77; Loring, *Oration, Delivered at Lexington*, 25, 70–72.

55. "Harvard University," *NYT*, June 24, 1874. Cohen, *Reconstructing the Campus*, 52–73, describes the postwar movement for collegiate military training.

56. Brown, "Reconstructing Boston," 135.

57. *Springfield (MA) Republican*, December 23, 1872; *First Report of the Free Public Library Commission*, 118–20.

58. Minority Report of the Sub-committee of Six, Miscellaneous Records of Memorial Hall.

59. [Sturgis], "Something about Monuments," 155; *Ceremonies at the Dedication of the Soldiers' Monument in Concord*, 13; *Waltham (MA) Free Press*, June 5, 1868. See also Giguere, *Characteristically American*.

60. "Soldiers' Monument in Erie County, Pennsylvania," *HW* 9 (November 25, 1865): 737; "Soldiers' Monument at Stockbridge, Massachusetts," *HW* 10 (November 3, 1866): 700; "Soldiers' Monument," *HW* 12 (February 1, 1868): 77 (Lancaster, Grant County, Wisconsin); "Soldiers' Monument at Plymouth, Massachusetts," *HW* 13 (August 29, 1869): 532; "Soldiers' Monuments in Pennsylvania," *HW* 13 (October 23, 1869): 684 (Norristown); "Soldiers' Monument at Glenn's Falls, N.Y." *HW* 14 (January 29, 1870): 77.

61. Giguere, "Americanized Sphinx."

62. [Howells], "Question of Monuments," 647; Jacob, *Testament*, 51–54; *WES*, June 16, 1877; Gibbs, "Franklin County Military Chapter," 448; Wheeler, "Our Confederate Dead." Ossining, New York, similarly replaced a kneeling angel in the town monument unveiled in 1879 with a soldier statue in 1887.

63. Harrison, "Edouard Laboulaye." Viano, *Sentinel*, examines the many currents of French thought reflected in the Statue of Liberty.

64. Joseph C. Brand to J. Q. A. Ward, April 18, 1866, Ward Papers.

65. Rogers, *Randolph Rogers*, 92.

66. Kinsel, "From These Honored Dead," 126–30.

67. Heath, *Roxbury Soldiers Monument*, 4–5, 7; Tuckerman, *Book of the Artists*, 600.

68. *Ceremonies at the Dedication of the Soldiers' Monument in West Roxbury*, 9. Batterson monuments with downward-looking soldier statues include works at Deerfield (1867); Lafayette College, Pennsylvania (1867); East Bloomfield, New York (1868); Granby, Connecticut (1868); Williams College, Massachusetts (1868); Green-Wood Cemetery in New York City (1869); Evergreen Cemetery in New Haven, Connecticut (1870); Woonsocket, Rhode Island (1870); Meriden, Connecticut (1873); Lancaster, Pennsylvania (1874); and Norwich, Connecticut (1875).

69. *Soldiers' Monument in Cambridge*, 31–32.

70. *Middlesex County (NJ) Journal*, October 14, 1869; *South Carolina Monument Association*, 48.

71. *"Dead on the Field,"* 16.

72. *History of Antietam National Cemetery*, 21; Hughes and Ware, *Theodore O'Hara*, 62–71; McElya, *Politics of Mourning*, 129–30; Pfanz, *Where Valor Proudly Sleeps*, 92–93.

73. Wrenn, *Wilmington*.

74. *Columbia (SC) Register*, May 11, 1879.

75. Baker, *Richard Morris Hunt*, 152 (quotation); Kowsky, "Central Park Gateways"; Sharp, *John Quincy Adams Ward*, 52–54, 172–77.

76. Unidentified scrapbook clippings in Ward Papers.

77. "The Seventh's Memorial," *NYT*, June 23, 1874.

78. *Soldiers' Monument in Cambridge*, 31; "Dedication of the Soldiers' Monument in Salem," *NYT*, September 5, 1869; "The Statue of a Soldier of the Seventh Regiment for the Central Park," *NYT*, October 31, 1869.

79. Olmsted, Vaux & Co., undated memorandum (emphasis in original), Ward Papers; "The Seventh Regiment's Memorial," *NYT*, June 23, 1874.

80. "The Antietam Soldiers' Monument," *BET*, July 13, 1874; Strahan, *Masterpieces*, 63; Gold, "Imaging Memory," 59–79; Trail, "Remembering Antietam," 117–18.

81. Magazine publication of short stories about the war declined even more precipitously. Fahs, "Feminized Civil War," 1483.

82. Devens, *Oration*, 8, 15; *Address of Hon. Jno. T. Morgan*, 7; *Dedication of Tomb of Army of Northern Virginia*, 20.

83. Brown, *Civil War Canon*, 98.

84. Soldiers' Memorial Society Records; Brown, "Peaceable War Memorial," 263n27.

85. Breisch, *Henry Hobson Richardson*, 13–17.

86. Memorial Hall at the University of North Carolina (1885) originated as a tribute to school president David Lowry Swain and developed into a university hall of fame, including tablets that set forth the roll of the Confederate dead. Kirby, "UNC's Ambiguous Memorial."

87. [Howells], "Question of Monuments," 646; Savage, *Standing Soldiers*, 52–128 (quotation at 73); Bullard, *Lincoln*, 11–72.

88. Savage, "Ream's Lincoln," 173–75; Power, *Abraham Lincoln*. See also Hosking, "Lincoln's Tomb"; Hill, "Lincoln Landscape."

89. Davenport file (080), IAS.

90. Savage, *Monument Wars*, 112–13; Stone, *History of the Saratoga Monument Association*, 13–18; Gold, "Imaging Memory."

91. Khan, *Enlightening the World*, 167–68; Viano, *Sentinel*, 363–65. Kammen, *Season of Youth*, identifies a similar shift in paintings and literature about the Revolution.

92. *Proceedings at the Centennial Celebration of Concord Fight*, 11–13, 16, 89–91; Beetham, "Sculpting the Citizen Soldier," chap. 4.

93. "The Seventh's Memorial," *New York Herald*, June 22, 1874, scrapbook clipping, Ward Papers; *Proceedings at the Centennial Celebration of Concord Fight*, 17.

94. "The Seventh's Memorial," Ward Papers; Charles De Kay, "Ward and His Art," *New York Tribune*, March 11, 1894; Bruce, *Century*, 172–73; McDowell, "Martin Milmore's Soldiers' and Sailors' Monument," 65; *AABN* 2 (September 22, 1877): 301.

95. Unidentified clipping, Macon file, IAS (552); *Manchester (NH) Union*, October 31, 1884, Londonderry file, IAS (538); *Exercises Held at the Dedication of the Soldiers' Monument*, 11; *Cortland (NY) Evening Standard*, May 31, 1893, Gilbertsville, New York, file, IAS (1051).

CHAPTER 2

1. Beath, *History of the Grand Army of the Republic*, 651.

2. On the darkening image of the farmer, see Meixner, *French Realist Painting*.

3. Chickamauga Memorial Association, *Proceedings at Chattanooga*, 7.

4. "Shiloh Monuments," *MN* 13 (December 1901): 673.

5. "Art Troubles in New Jersey," unidentified clipping, Ward Scrapbook.

6. Henry James, *The Bostonians*, chap. 25, in *Century* 5 (September 1885): 693–96; Koehler, "Our Public Monuments," 9, 11.

7. Keller, *Affairs of State*, 311; McConnell, *Glorious Contentment*, 146–47.

8. Mehrota, *Making the Modern American Fiscal State*, 88. Dearing, *Veterans*, 445–46, attributes the membership decline to veterans' satisfaction with the Dependent Pension Act. Economic circumstances doubtless played an important role after 1893.

9. McDaniel, "Caspar Buberl."

10. Wilson, *Business of Civil War*.

11. Hobbs, *Lynn*, 126–27; Lewis and Newhall, *History of Lynn*, 2:335.

12. *Soldiers' Memorial Building, Toledo*; Howe, *Historical Collections*, 2:414; Fogelson, *America's Armories*. During 1889–94 six small Ohio cities took advantage of 1884 legislation that authorized them to build memorial armories or to issue bonds for a memorial hall. Brown, "Ohio's Veterans' Memorial Halls."

13. "Notes," *The Nation* 32 (June 2, 1881): 390; Blanchard, "Soldier and Aesthete."

14. Hawes, *Condensed History of Dearborn Park*, 14.

15. Roe, *Monuments*, 93, 98.

16. *Kingman v. City of Brockton*, 153 Mass. 255 (1891); Kingman, *History of Brockton*, 746–69.

17. Roe, *Monuments*, 70; Webster, *Story of the City Hall Commission*; Austin, "Grand Army of the Republic Building"; Soldiers and Sailors Memorial Hall, Rockford, Illinois, National Register of Historic Places Inventory–Nomination Form, 1975.

18. Brown, "Ohio's Veterans' Memorial Halls," 51; Bates, *Annotated Revised Statutes of the State of Ohio*, section 3107—44a–k (March 12, 1902), 1:1750-a–c. On the Hamilton County Memorial Hall, see Painter, *Architecture in Cincinnati*, 162.

19. *Roll of the 40th National Encampment*, 119, 130, 133.

20. Wall, *Andrew Carnegie*, 190.

21. Gangewere, *Palace of Culture*, 17–22; Rosenblum, "Architecture of Henry Horbostel," 163–81. Carnegie Tech became the degree-granting Carnegie Institute of Technology in 1912. Much of the growth of the University of Pittsburgh did not take place at the anticipated site.

22. *History of the Origin and a Description of Memorial Hall*; "Competition for the Selection of an Architect," i–iii; Evans, *Allegheny County*, 7. Installed during 1914–16, the list was shorter than the list of 34,530 soldiers on the Pennsylvania memorial at Gettysburg, dedicated in 1913 and completed in 1914. Both would soon be surpassed in length by British memorials to the dead of the Great War. Fleming, *Pittsburgh*, 99; Laqueur, *Work of the Dead*, 449–51.

23. Rosenblum, "Architecture of Henry Horbostel," 206.

24. Fleming, *Pittsburgh*, 5.

25. Rosenblum, "Architecture of Henry Horbostel," 202–5; Aurand, *Spectator*, 137–201.

26. Thomas B. Cochran, *Smull's Legislative Hand Book*, 140; Logan, "History of the Eighteenth Regiment," 94.

27. Evert and Gay, *Discovering Pittsburgh's Sculpture*, 202–4. Frederick Hibbard's soldier and sailor statues *Parade Rest* and *Lookout* were added to the entrance in 1923.

28. *Ballston Journal*, June 23, 1888, IAS files (Ballston, New York, #1358).

29. "Soldiers' Monument in Erie County, Pennsylvania," *HW* 9 (November 25, 1865): 737; Kimbell, *History of Battery "A."* The allegorical figure in Swanton prefigured Martin Milmore's crowning bronze for the ensemble on Boston Common (1877). Leonard Volk's brother Cornelius designed the flag-draped, eagle-topped obelisk in Woodland Cemetery in Quincy, Illinois (1867). On wartime flag culture, see Bonner, *Colors and Blood*.

30. Smith, *Proceedings at the Dedication of the Soldiers' Monument at Pittsfield*, 10, 12, 20, 52–59.

31. *Charleston (SC) News*, June 20, 1871; *Charleston (SC) News and Courier*, May 21, 1879; Porcher, "Brief History," 211; *Confederate Monument at Charleston*, 15.

32. *South Carolina Monument Association*, 54, 60; *Charleston (SC) News and Courier*, December 1, 1882; Smith, *Proceedings at the Dedication of the Soldiers' Monument at Pittsfield*, 10.

33. Kinsel, "From These Honored Dead," 173–89; Panhorst, "Lest We Forget," 20–21.

34. Westerly Granite Records illuminate the connections among these monuments. See also Ransom, "Connecticut's Monumental Epoch," 1:95–97; "News of the State," *Meriden (CT) Daily Republican*, September 11, 1885.

35. *Ritual of the Grand Army of the Republic*, 31. The phrase may derive from Oliver P. Morton's declaration to the Indiana legislature in November 1865 that "we are many states, but one people, having one undivided sovereignty, one flag, and one common destiny," quoted in full on the inscriptions to monuments in Elkhart, Indiana (1889), and Three Rivers, Michigan (1893). *Oliver P. Morton*, 72. Webster's version appears in *Speech Delivered by Daniel Webster at Niblo's Saloon*, 5.

36. Ransom, "Connecticut's Monumental Epoch," 2:210–14, 260–66; Weller, *Lorado Taft*, 39–50; *Winchester Herald*, July 27, 1892, clipping in IAS Files (Winchester, IN 74220011); "Battlefield Monuments," *MN* 16 (August 1904): 482. See also *MN* 9 (July 1897): 406; "Stock Statuary on Soldiers' Monuments," *MN* 13 (June 1901): 338; and "Responsibility in Monument Designing," *MN* 16 (December 1904): 722.

37. Levering, *Services*, 26.

38. Guenter, *American Flag*, 104–7; McConnell, *Glorious Contentment*, 224–30.

39. Unidentified clipping, June 18, 1912, Rockland file, IAS.

40. Ockenden, *Confederate Monument on Capitol Hill, Montgomery*, 4, 23, 36. See also Panhorst, "Devotion."

41. *Dedication of Monument to Confederate Dead of Florida*, 12; E. J. Hale, "Oration at the Unveiling of Cumberland's Monument, May 10, 1892," Confederate Memorial Records; *Unveiling Ceremonies of Carroll County's Confederate Monument*, 45.

42. Wright, "Confederate Monument," 8–9; "Confederate Monument Unveiling: General Julian S. Carr's Eloquent Address," 18, Confederate Memorial Records.

43. Second Co. Massachusetts Sharpshooters (1885), 114th Pennsylvania Infantry (1888), Twenty-Third Pennsylvania Infantry (1888).

44. Weeks, *Gettysburg*, 64.

45. Weller, *Lorado Taft*, 35–48.

46. Emerson, *Historic Southern Monuments*, 59.

47. Whitman, Massachusetts (1908), Randolph, Massachusetts (1915), and Stillwater, Minnesota (1916).

48. "Beautiful Monument at Luray, Va.," *CV* 7 (March 1899): 109; *MN* 12 (November 1901): 633; *MN* 20 (July 1908): 514.

49. Gleason, *History of the Cuyahoga County Soldiers' and Sailors' Monument*, 16, 19, 23, 43, 48–49, 331, 338, 341, 477, 769; Grimaldi, "Indiana Soldiers' and Sailors' Monument," 6–7, 23. See also Bodnar, *Remaking America*, 78–82, 93–95.

50. Hawkes, "Our Lady," 92 (emphasis in original).

51. Gleason, *History of the Cuyahoga County Soldiers' and Sailors' Monument*, 35, 55, 612, 614–16.

52. Grimaldi, "Indiana Soldiers' and Sailors' Monument," 9, 27, 40, 61.

53. The Battle Creek version did not include the dying soldier. On Franco-Prussian monuments, see Hargrove, *"Qui vive?"*

54. "Among the Sculptors," *MN* 7 (April 1895): 246; "The Milwaukee Soldiers Monument," *Brush and Pencil* 3 (November 1898): 78–81.

55. *Special Report of the Soldiers' Monument Association*, 24; *Souvenir of the Unveiling of the Richmond Howitzer Monument*, 39; undated clipping, *Ostego Journal*, Gilbertsville, New York, file (#1051), IAS; Harrison, "Military Instruction," 469. On the militarized masculinity of the 1890s, see especially Pettegrew, *Brutes in Suits.*

56. Unidentified clipping, New Bloomfield, Pennsylvania, file (#1373), IAS; E. J. Hale, "Oration at the Unveiling of Cumberland's Monument, May 10, 1902," 8–9, Confederate Memorial Records; McIntyre, *Account*, 22, 34.

57. Holmes, *Speeches*, 56, 59, 62–63.

58. Saint-Gaudens, *Reminiscences*, 1:332. On the making of the memorial, see the essays in Blatt, Brown, and Yacovone, *Hope and Glory.*

59. Saint-Gaudens, *Reminiscences*, 2:120; Mills, *Beyond Grief*; Schiller, "Artistic Collaboration."

60. "Oration by Professor William James," in *Monument to Robert Gould Shaw*, 86; McDaniel, "Caspar Buberl," 321; Kresser, "Power and Glory," 50–53; Savage, "Uncommon Soldiers."

61. Brown, "Reconstructing Boston."

62. Kresser, "Power and Glory," 46–49; Follini, "Speaking Monuments," 33. The wartime debate over the potential of African Americans had prompted a particular racialized insistence on the transformational power of military service. Emberton, "Only Murder

Makes Men," examines this vision of martial citizenship. Savage, *Standing Soldiers*, 169–70, points out that the talismanic power attributed to the Union uniform in the case of black recruits sometimes masked uneasy recognition that slavery might be logical preparation for soldiering. He stresses that Saint-Gaudens's sensitive depictions aimed "to defy military uniformity, on the one hand, and racial caricature, on the other" (201).

63. "Oration by Professor William James," in *Monument to Robert Gould Shaw*, 74–75, 77, 83–84.

64. "Oration by Professor William James," 75–76, 84–86.

65. Moody, "Ode."

66. Holmes, *Speeches*, 58; Noun, "Iowa Soldiers' and Sailors' Monument," 93.

67. "Arsenal Explosion Recalled by Completion of New Monument," *Pittsburgh Press*, May 13, 1928; Jacob, *Testament*, 21–23.

68. "Statue of Francis E. Spinner"; "Statue to the Late Gen. Spinner," *CT*, November 6, 1893; J. Harry Shannon, "The Statue without a Site," *Pittsburgh Post-Gazette*, September 13, 1908; "Counted Money 49 Years," *NYT*, June 9, 1913; Moyer, "Spinner Memorial"; Aron, "To Barter Their Souls"; Silber, *Daughters*, 78–82.

69. "Monuments at Fort Mill, S.C.," *CV* 5 (May 1899): 210; Savage, *Standing Soldiers*, 155–56; Seigler, *Guide to Confederate Monuments*, 331–41. Silber, *Gender*; and Manning, *What This Cruel War Was Over*, contrast northern and southern understandings of home and nation.

70. Cox, *Dixie's Daughters*; Janney, *Burying the Dead*; O'Leary, *To Die For*, chaps. 5–6.

71. Equal Justice Initiative, *Lynching in America*, supplement; Trenticosta and Collins, "Death and Dixie," 132.

72. *Minutes Fifteenth Annual Convention of the United Daughters of the Confederacy*, 23; Mrs. Alexander B. White, "United Daughters of the Confederacy," *CV* 20 (May 1912): viii.

73. Howard M. Hamill, "Confederate Woman's Monument," *CV* 17 (April 1909): 150; Smith, "Belle Kinney," 13.

74. Schultz, *Women at the Front*, chaps. 6–7.

75. Bostridge, *Florence Nightingale*, 523–25.

76. "A Protest Offered by Mrs. Geo. H. Tichenor, Little Rock, November 20, 1910," in Margaret Drane Tichenor, "Tributes and Memorials of the Women of the Southland, 1861–1865," Confederate Memorial Records; "New Members of Mississippi Division, U.D.C.," *CV* 20 (September 1912): 414.

77. Brown, *Civil War Canon*, 117–24.

78. Tyndall and Lesh, *Standard History*, 1:165; Todd, "Bernarr McFadden."

79. "Memorial to Women of the Confederacy," *CV* 22 (August 1914): 348–49; Tomes, *Gospel of Germs*, 180, 232.

80. Scrymser, *Personal Reminiscences*, 145; Davis, "Sanitary Commission."

81. *Congressional Record*, 62nd Cong., 2nd sess., August 12, 1912, 10743; *American Red Cross Magazine* 10 (May 1915): 169–74.

82. Records of Commission on Memorial to Women.

83. Other communities that installed *The Volunteer* include Walden, New York (1904); North Providence, Rhode Island (1904); Ashburnham, Massachusetts (1905); Pasadena, California (1906); Sharon, Massachusetts (1908); North Attleboro, Massachusetts (1911); Westbrook, Maine (1917); and Townsend, Massachusetts (1932). Panhorst, "Lest We Forget," 306n74. One of Rudolf Schwarz's subordinate figures on the Indiana monument unveiled six weeks before the Newburyport dedication was a marching figure. Schwarz

returned to the marching motif at Le Roy, New York (1906). Marching figures were also installed during 1901–14 in Wareham, Massachusetts (1905); Goshen, New York (1907); Gainesville, Texas (1908); Forsyth, Georgia (1908); Somerville, Massachusetts (1909); Baltimore, Maryland (1909); Marengo, Iowa (1910); El Dorado, Arkansas (1910); Waycross, Georgia (1910); Carnesville, Georgia (1910); Philadelphia, Pennsylvania (1911); Orlando, Florida (1911); Houghton, Michigan (1912); Bloomington, Indiana (1913); Ebensburg, Pennsylvania (1913); Lebanon, Virginia (1914); and the national cemetery in Winchester, Virginia (1907).

84. *MN* 14 (November 1902): 643 reported that Bellefonte had awarded the commission to Barnard and described the design. The monument is usually attributed to W. Clark Noble, who may only have contributed the statue of Andrew Curtin. On Barnard's evolutionary thinking and doubling of figures prior to the nude soldiers in the Bellefonte memorial, see Hack, "American Acropolis," 19–77.

85. "Sculpture," *MN* 13 (February 1901): 116.

86. Walker, "American Studios," 102; *BET*, September 22, 1877; "Ward's Statue for the Seventh Regiment Monument," unidentified scrapbook clipping, Ward Papers; Grimaldi, "Indiana Soldiers' and Sailors' Monument," 17, 27–28; "Monument Which We Unveiled Today," *Allentown Daily-Leader*, October 19, 1899, IAS file—Allentown, Pennsylvania. Savage, *Standing Soldiers*, chap. 6, is an important analysis of whiteness in common-soldier monuments. Kelman, *Misplaced Massacre*, treats the racial implications of the Colorado monument to Union soldiers in Denver (1909).

87. The mayor also sat on the Boston Art Commission as originally organized. It was reconstituted in 1898 to provide for the mayor to choose from persons nominated by these four organizations and the Boston Art Club. *AABN* 60 (May 21, 1898): 58, 62. *Report of Proceedings of the City Council of Boston for the Municipal Year 1889*, 721, 748, 950–51, 1011–12; *Report of Proceedings of the City Council of Boston for the Municipal Year 1891*, 72–73; *BET*, November 12, 1889; McNamara, *History of the Ninth Regiment*, 423–24. On O'Kelley, see "Irish-American Sculptors," *Donahoe's Magazine* 7 (May 1882): 432. Bogart, *Public Sculpture*, 61–70, traces the 1898 establishment of the New York Art Commission to a similar controversy over a memorial to Heinrich Heine.

88. Emma Bullet, "Richard Brooks' Statue of Col. Cass," *MN* 11 (April 1899): 222.

89. "Sculpture," *MN* 13 (February 1901): 116; "Massachusetts and Iowa Monuments at Vicksburg," *MN* 16 (July 1904): 419; "Pratt's Malden Monument," *MN* 20 (September 1908): 646; "A Fine Type of Soldiers' Monument," *MN* 22 (December 1910): 873; *MN* 25 (April 1913): 267; Jones Brothers Company advertisement, *MN* 27 (March 1915): 183.

90. Ockenden, *Confederate Monument on Capitol Hill, Montgomery*, 45; *Parkersburg (WV) Daily State Journal*, July 22, 1908; Beetham, "Sculpting the Citizen Soldier," 90–164; Raymond file (028), IAS; Emerson, *Historic Southern Monuments*, 388.

91. "Sculpture," *MN* 13 (February 1901): 116; *MN* 21 (December 1909): 888; Rusling, *Mercer*, 19.

92. Cooper, *Rise of the National Guard*, 109–10; Zais, "Struggle for a 20th Century Army," 160–61, 252.

93. Schneider, *Taps*, 14.

94. DePastino, *Citizen Hobo*, 17–29.

95. Bradford, "Flexion or Bent-Knee Marching."

96. "Massachusetts and Iowa Monuments at Vicksburg," *MN* 16 (July 1904): 419; Bradford, "Science of Walking," 225, 227; "Spoke on 'The Human Gait,'" *BET*, January 6,

1908. On Sargent, see Townsend, *Manhood at Harvard*. Kitson's monument to the 124th New York Volunteers in Goshen, New York (1907), also illustrates Bradford's argument.

97. "Human Gait as Illustrated in Shaw Monument"; "Personal and Pertinent," *HW* 52 (March 28, 1908): 8–9; "Some Stories of Saint-Gaudens," *MN* 20 (January 1908): 33–34; *MN* 20 (February 1908): 124; "Annual Exhibit of Chicago Sculptors," *MN* 21 (March 1909): 221.

98. Pearlman, *To Make Democracy Safe for America*, 84. Nichols, "Education," provides an introduction to debate over the relationship between education and military preparedness on the eve of American intervention in World War I.

99. On this spurious quotation, see Heuston, "Most Famous Thing Robert E. Lee Never Said."

100. "Unveiling of Confederate Monument at University," June 2, 1913, Carr Papers.

101. The zinc monument dedicated in Morgantown, Kentucky, in 1907 to Butler County combatants in all wars listed the names of Union and Confederate soldiers and featured relief portraits of Lincoln, Grant, and Confederate cavalry commander Joseph Wheeler. It did not receive wide notice beyond "Monument for Morgantown, Ky.," *CV* 15 (June 1907): 283. Princeton graduate W. A. Coursen of Marietta, Georgia, began campaigning around 1909 for a monument at his alma mater that would honor Union and Confederate soldiers together, which culminated in the 1922 unveiling of a memorial that listed the names of the college dead without identifying the sides on which they fought. "Soldier's Monument, Princeton University," *CV* 19 (May 1911): 226.

102. Frick, "Mingled Dust," 33.

103. Hadley, "Military Training," 10, 14.

104. George Grey Barnard's quasi-Biblical figures for Bellefonte and Louis Amateis's warrior angel for Houston (1908) were earlier examples. Pompeo Coppini's allegory of the Lost Cause in a monument to Confederate postmaster general John Reagan for Palestine, Texas (1911), was a much less heroic male nude.

105. "The Yale Memorial," *Art and Progress* 6 (September 1915): 420; Clark, *Nude*, 130–65.

CHAPTER 3

1. "A Pageant in Washington," *NYT*, November 20, 1879; "The Lee Statue Unveiled," *NYT*, May 30, 1890; Karamanski, "Memory's Landscape," 66.

2. Goss, *War within the Union High Command*; Reardon, *With a Sword*.

3. *AABN* 65 (July 8, 1899): 2.

4. Matthews, *Address*, 8, 26.

5. Gardner, *Gardner's Photographic Sketch Book*, 1: plate 37; Sharp, *John Quincy Adams Ward*, 183; unidentified scrapbook clipping, Ward Papers. Frassanito, *Gettysburg*, 222–29, explains that O'Sullivan did not make this glass negative at the site of Reynolds's death.

6. *Description of the Ceremony of Dedication of the Statue of Major-General John Sedgwick*, 15–20, 32. For more recent calculations of the number of West Point graduates who served in the Confederate army, see Hsieh, *West Pointers*, 91–92.

7. *Description of the Ceremony of Dedication of the Statue of Major-General John Sedgwick*, 12–14, 22, 25, 30, 34.

8. "A Soldier's Laurels," *National Republican*, October 19, 1876.

9. *Inauguration of the Jackson Statue*, 3–4, 9, 10, 12, 13.

10. Adams, *Living Hell*, 74.

11. *Inauguration of the Jackson Statue*, 15.

12. Dimmick, "Altar Erected to Virtue," 22; "Equestrian Monuments: No. 34," *AABN* 31 (January 24, 1891): 59; Kauffman, "Men on Horseback," 14–15.

13. Jacob, *Testament*, 100–101.

14. Fairmount Park Art Association, *Sculpture of a City*, 149; L. W. Miller, "The Reynolds Memorial in Philadelphia," *AABN* 16 (October 14, 1884): 162.

15. *Unveiling of Ward's Equestrian Statue*, 5–6, 11, 14, 27.

16. Sharp, *John Quincy Adams Ward*, 195; "Ward's Statue of Gen. Thomas," *NYT*, May 3, 1879; "The Statue of Thomas," *NYT*, November 18, 1879; "A Pageant in Washington," *NYT*, November 20, 1879.

17. Phillips, "Public Opinion," 54.

18. Jacob, *Testament*, 103; *Farragut*, 17.

19. Clipping from *Evening Post* ("realism of generals") and unidentified clipping ("painter-like"), scrapbook, Morgan Papers; Gilder, "Farragut Monument," 166.

20. Unidentified clipping ("rushing river") and clipping from *Times* ("freaks and sallies"), scrapbook, Morgan Papers.

21. Scrapbook clipping, Morgan Papers; "The Farragut Statue," *NYT*, May 25, 1881.

22. White to Saint-Gaudens, February 24, 1880, in White, *Stanford White: Letters*, 101–2; Bohan, "Farragut Monument," 236; Jacob, *Testament*, 189–90; Savage, *Monument Wars*, 89.

23. *Daniel Webster, an Oration, by the Hon. Edward Everett*, 179, 210.

24. Burnham, *Proceedings*; Crawford, "Classical Orator," 68.

25. Varg, *Edward Everett*, 178, 200–202, 215–16; *BET*, December 13, 1867.

26. Seidler, "Critical Reappraisal," 650–60; *BET*, December 5, 1867.

27. *Appendix to History of the Calhoun Monument*, 2; Brown, *Civil War Canon*, 80–84.

28. Emerson, "Fugitive Slave Law," 77.

29. Bode, *American Lyceum*; Grodzins, *Heretic*, 77–78, 343–44; Seelye, *Memory's Nation*, 488; Walther, *William Lowndes Yancey*, 14, 25.

30. Wills, *Lincoln at Gettysburg*.

31. Allison, "Seated Philosopher."

32. Flower, "Saint Gaudens' *Lincoln*," 428. White, *Republic for Which It Stands*, criticizes Jane Addams's similar turn to the Lincoln statue for inspiration during the Pullman strike as "anodyne" (862).

33. "Editor's Easy Chair," *Harper's New Monthly Magazine* 74 (April 1887): 824.

34. H. C. King to William Howard Taft, March 5, 1907, enclosing Daniel Sickles to King, March 4, 1907, Records of McClellan Commission.

35. "Carried to His Grave," *NYT*, March 13, 1887; "City and Suburban News," *NYT*, May 28, 1887; "The Beecher Monument Site," *NYT*, March 16, 1888.

36. Taft, *History of American Sculpture*, 221; Sharp, *John Quincy Adams Ward*, 239.

37. Daniel Chester French to Charles William Eliot, January 28, 1914, French Papers. French's monument to lyceum prodigy and Union spokesman Thomas Starr King in San Francisco (1892) similarly depicted oratory as patriotic didacticism rather than informal engagement.

38. Charles Moore, "Out-Door Art in Washington," *AMA* 8 (October 1917): 474.

39. "Where's Waldo?"

40. Brilliant, *Gesture and Rank*, 96, 141; Haskell and Penny, *Taste and the Antique*, 252–55.

41. "Brown's Colossal Equestrian Statue of Washington," *Crayon* 1 (January 3, 1855): 5–6; Lemmey, "Henry Kirke Brown," 135–82.

42. Victoria Donohoe, "General Meade," in Fairmount Park Art Association, *Sculpture of a City*, 118–22; "Monthly Record of Art," *AAI* 1 (August 1887): 319; Walter Percy Lockington, "Among the Sculptors," *MN* 7 (November 1895): 684.

43. Cable, "Silent South," 674.

44. Early, "Campaigns of General Lee," 73; Knox, "Général Lee"; Savage, *Standing Soldiers*, 129–55.

45. "Monument Complete," *RD*, May 25, 1890; Anderson, *Robert Edward Lee*, 28.

46. Brown, *Public Art of Civil War Commemoration*, 98–99.

47. Anderson, *Robert Edward Lee*, 1, 5–6, 42–43.

48. *MN* 10 (November 1898): 620; *Equestrian Statue of Major General Joseph Hooker*, 9; Ramage, *Rebel Raider*, 256. The Veteran Cavalry Association of the Army of Northern Virginia similarly launched efforts in 1891 to sponsor a monument to J. E. B. Stuart, who also died in the war. *Richmond Times*, October 2, 1891.

49. White, *Railroaded*, 247–49.

50. John R. Dunlop to John Sherman, January 14, 1896, Records of Sherman Commission. The jury consisted of sculptors Saint-Gaudens, French, and Olin Levi Warner, and architects George B. Post and Bruce Price. "The Sherman Statue," *WES*, January 24, 1896, reported that the commission overruled the jury's exclusion of Rohl-Smith from the set of finalists "at the instance of Gen. Dodge."

51. G. M. Dodge to W. S. Coursey, January 2, 1901, Records of Sherman Commission. Dodge slightly misquotes and takes out of context a passage from the oft-quoted letter of Sherman to Edward Bok dated February 6, 1883, and published in *ANJ* 20 (March 3, 1883): 700.

52. Frank Sewall, "The Man on Horseback!," *AABN* 51 (March 14, 1896): 115; Kauffman, "Men on Horseback," 29.

53. Keim, *Sherman*, 45, 65, 76, 82.

54. *MN* 10 (November 1898): 621.

55. "Ruckstuhl's Conception of the Hampton Monument," *State* (Columbia, SC), November 20, 1906; *Atlanta Constitution*, May 13, 1905, May 25, 1907.

56. *Dedication of the Equestrian Statue of Major-General Charles Devens*, n.p. [2–11].

57. J. Evarts Greene, "The Proposed Devens Statue," *Worcester Magazine*, 41, undated clipping, Devens Statue Papers. On Hoar, see Hoganson, *Fighting for American Manhood*, 165–72.

58. *Address Delivered May 30, 1910 by John W. Weeks*, 59. Weeks spoke at the unveiling of a statue on Draper's estate in Hopedale. Draper's widow commissioned the Milford equestrian later that year, and French and Potter completed it in 1912. *MN* 22 (November 1910): 805.

59. *Description of the Ceremony of Dedication of the Statue of Major-General John Sedgwick*, 17; *Dedication of the Equestrian Statue of Major-General Charles Devens*, n. p. [33].

60. Henry Strong, "Monumental Art," *AA* 7 (February 1898): 344, reported that "there is among the soldiers a feeling that Logan should never have been represented with a flag. Those who were with him in that supreme hour when he turned defeat into victory say it was not the flag, but his old war-battered hat that was waved in the air, as he cheered them on to greater effort."

61. Logan, *Volunteer Soldier*, 119–20, 399, 406, 421, 580, 603, 608.

62. James, *Logan Monument*, 84.

63. Croly, *Promise of American Life*, 144.

64. James, *Logan Monument*, 42.

65. Winock, "Joan of Arc," 3:455–61. "Few Display the Horse," *CT*, July 25, 1897, noted a similarity in the positions of the horses as well as the device of the banner.

66. James, *Logan Monument*, 72.

67. Saint-Gaudens, *Reminiscences*, 2:82.

68. Sharp, *John Quincy Adams Ward*, 268; Michael V. Sheridan to Henry C. Corbin, June 21, 1902, Records of Sheridan Statue Commission; "The National Academy Exhibit," *MN* 21 (January 1909): 28. Ward's equestrian statue of Winfield Scott Hancock for the Smith Memorial in Philadelphia, a project he began in 1898, adopted a similar premise.

69. Proceedings of Commissions on Statues of Logan, Hancock, and Sheridan, June 14, December 24, 1906.

70. George B. Davis to William Howard Taft, April 25, 1906; J. W. Barriger to James Wade, May 12, 1906; J. A. Wade to William Howard Taft, May 12, 1906; Theodore F. Rodenbough to James Wade, May 17, 1906; Irene Rucker Sheridan to William Howard Taft, June 15, 1907; William Howard Taft to Henry C. Corbin, August 19, 1907; all in Records of Sheridan Statue Commission.

71. Caffin, *American Masters*, 149.

72. Gutzon Borglum to Irene Sheridan, October 11, 1907; Gutzon Borglum to J. H. Poole, October 20, 1908; in Records of Sheridan Statue Commission.

73. Theodore Roosevelt, "At the Unveiling of the Sherman Statue, Washington, D.C., October 15, 1903"; "At the Unveiling of the Statue to Major-General George B. McClellan, May 2, 1907"; "At the Unveiling of the Monument to General Sheridan," Wednesday, November 25, 1908"; all in *Complete Speeches*.

74. Roosevelt, "At the Unveiling of the Monument to General Sheridan." Blum, *Republican Roosevelt*, emphasizes Roosevelt's organizational virtues.

75. "J. Q. A. Ward's New Figure of Sheridan," *NYT*, May 20, 1906.

76. Carney, "Contested Image of Nathan Bedford Forrest," 612–18.

77. *Unveiling of the Equestrian Statue of General Philip H. Sheridan*, 23–24.

78. Waugh, *U. S. Grant*, 270–82.

79. *CT*, October 8, 1891.

80. Kahn, "Grant Monument."

81. "Making the Final Effort," *NYT*, April 24, 1892; "Ready for the Ceremony," *NYT*, April 26, 1892; "Laid by the President," *NYT*, April 28, 1892; "Rounding Up the People," *NYT*, April 29, 1892; "Good Work for the Grant Fund," *NYT*, June 1, 1892.

82. James, *American Scene*, 141–42 (emphasis omitted); James, *Hawthorne*, 43.

83. *Report of the Proceedings of the Society of the Army of the Tennessee at the Twenty-Seventh Meeting*, 69.

84. My account of the development of the Mall relies on Longstreth, *Mall*; Montagna, "Henry Merwin Shrady's Ulysses S. Grant Memorial"; Reps, *Monumental Washington*; Savage, *Monument Wars*; and Zangrando, "Monumental Bridge Design."

85. Zais, "Struggle for a 20th Century Army," is the most detailed narrative. See also Clark, *Preparing for War*, chaps. 5–6; Gough, "Battle of Washington," chap. 1.

86. Reps, *Monumental Washington*, 76–79.

87. Montagna, "Henry Merwin Shrady's Ulysses S. Grant Memorial," 12–13, 82–84, 186; Savage, *Monument Wars*, 180–85; Zais, "Struggle for a 20th Century Army," 261–62.

88. Daniel Chester French to Charles Cohen, October 1, 1898, Fairmount Park Art Association Archives, Historical Society of Pennsylvania.

89. "Equestrian Monuments 43: The War of Secession," *AABN* 34 (October 31, 1891): 67.

90. "Grant Statue Unveiled," *NYT*, April 28, 1899; "Philadelphia's Tribute to General U. S. Grant," *MN* 11 (June 1899): 339–40; Montagna, "Henry Merwin Shrady's Ulysses S. Grant Memorial," 117–18. Paludan, *"People's Contest,"* 295, sketches Grant's wartime image as "a man that ordinary men could understand."

91. Henry Merwin Shrady, "Description of Design for Grant Monument," Records of Grant Memorial Commission.

92. Wilkinson, *Brain of an Army.*

93. Montagna, "Henry Merwin Shrady's Ulysses S. Grant Memorial," 15–16, 37, 51; Burns, *Inventing the Modern Artist*, 109–11, 125.

94. Savage, *Monument Wars*, 228–36.

95. Walton, "Field of Art," 382–83. "'Action' in Equestrian Groups," *NYT*, July 5, 1900, discusses the challenge of stop-motion photography for equestrian sculptors.

96. Van Dyke, *Art for Art's Sake*, 23–25.

97. "Grant's Memorial," 284.

CHAPTER 4

1. Typescript in Lowell file (137), IAS; Cowley, *Reminiscences of James C. Ayer*, 98–99.

2. Bartlett, *About Monuments*, 11; Marrinan, *Romantic Paris*, 98–105.

3. "The Soldiers' Memorial Committee Recommend an Arch," *Worcester (MA) Daily Spy*, December 1, 1868; editorial, *Worcester (MA) Evening Gazette*, December 1, 1868; O'Gorman, "H. H. Richardson."

4. B. H. K., "Letter," *Worcester (MA) Evening Gazette*, December 11, 1868.

5. *Ceremonies at the Dedication of the Bigelow Monument.*

6. Kowsky, *Best Planned City in the World*, 45–46.

7. Frederick Law Olmsted to Buffalo Park Commissioners, December 15, 1874, in Beveridge, *Papers of Frederick Law Olmsted*, 7:99–103.

8. "The Worcester Soldier's Memorial," *Worcester (MA) Daily Spy*, December 19, 1868.

9. Baldwin, *Domesticating the Street*, 25.

10. Ransom, *George Keller*, xxx, 120–35. The figure of the ex-slave replaced a statue of a merchant that was on the arch at the dedication.

11. Kahn, "Grant Monument," 224; Sharp, *John Quincy Adams Ward*, 67–68.

12. "In Memory of Her Heroes," *NYT*, October 31, 1889.

13. Olmsted to William A. Stiles, March 10, 1895, Beveridge, *Papers of Frederick Law Olmsted*, 9:905–8.

14. MacMonnies Scrapbooks, reel D245A.

15. *History of Washington Square Arch*, 42.

16. *History of Washington Square Arch*, 16, 41, 84–140.

17. *History of Washington Square Arch*, 43. The fountain installed in 1852 and replaced in 1871 eliminated the center of the square as a possible position for the arch. (Olmsted's plan for Niagara Square had similarly envisioned a central fountain.) The temporary arch of 1889 spanned Fifth Avenue a half-block north of the square, in front of the Rhinelander mansion occupied by Stewart's aunts. Folpe, *It Happened on Washington Square.*

18. "Smith Memorial in Jeopardy," *Philadelphia Press*, May 6, 1895; unidentified clippings, Smith Memorial Scrapbook A, Fairmount Park Art Association Archives,

Historical Society of Pennsylvania; Lewis Sharp, "The Smith Memorial," in Fairmount Park Art Association, *Sculpture of a City*, 168–79.

19. "Senator Murphy's Little Scheme," *NYT*, March 22, 1889; "Our Memorial Arch," *NYT*, November 19, 1893; Russell Sturgis, "The Question of a Site," *NYT*, March 24, 1895; "The Monument and the Park," *NYT*, November 25, 1897. Plans for a Dewey Arch or Naval Arch in Manhattan followed soon afterward. Bogart, *Public Sculpture*, 97–110.

20. Roper, *FLO*, 398–99; "The Soldiers' and Sailors' Monument," *NYT*, July 18, 1897; Samuel Parsons Jr., "Save Mount Tom," *NYT*, February 21, 1899; "The Soldiers' Monument," *NYT*, June 14, 1899; "Legal Notes," *NYT*, January 5, 1901; John Walker Harrington, "Artistic War Memorials Being Sought by Many Civic Societies," *New York Sun*, February 23, 1919. New Britain, Connecticut, unveiled Ernest Flagg's variation on the Choragic Monument of Lysicrates topped by a winged victory in 1900. Ransom, "Connecticut's Monumental Epoch," 59:47–51.

21. Noun, "Iowa Soldiers' and Sailors' Monument," 84–86.

22. O'Leary, *To Die For*, 43; Panhorst, "Lest We Forget," 57, 119–20, 182–83.

23. Williams, *Camp Randall*, 24–36.

24. *Oration Pronounced by Col. Charles C. Jones, Jr.*, 3.

25. J. H. Hudson, "Dedication Address for Confederate Monument, Cheraw, SC, July 26, 1867," 4–7, Confederate Memorial Records.

26. *Dedication of the Confederate Monument at Greenwood Cemetery*, 9, 11.

27. Marshall, *Creating a Confederate Kentucky*, 84–85.

28. Jacob, *Testament*, 176; *Unveiling of the Monument to the Confederate Dead of Alexandria, Va.*, 31; Levin, *Remembering the Battle of the Crater*, 40–42. "Confederate Monument, Alexandria, Virginia," *CV* 2 (December 1894): 367, more buoyantly described the soldier as "standing with his head a little drooped, as if he was preparing to make another vigorous battle."

29. "Memorial Address of Wade Hampton"; Sedore, *Illustrated Guide to Virginia's Confederate Monuments*, 167–68.

30. *Oration Pronounced by Col. Charles C. Jones, Jr.*, 3, 7.

31. Savage, *Standing Soldiers*, 138–39; Pegram Dargan, "Call It Not a 'Lost Cause,'" *CV* 4 (June 1896): 195; clipping, *Elberton (GA) Star*, July 22, 1898, IAS (Elberton 386); "The Name 'Lost Cause,'" *Lost Cause* 4 (January 1901): 88; *CV* 13 (January 1905): 5.

32. Jefferson Davis Monument Association Minutes, Museum of the Confederacy; "Adopt the Design," *RD*, June 30, 1896; "Tribute of South to Memory of President Davis," *Richmond Times-Dispatch*, May 30, 1907.

33. Jefferson Davis Monument Association Minutes, Museum of the Confederacy; "Our Confederate Column," *RD*, November 24, 1901; "The Davis Arch," *RD*, April 2, 1902; "Mrs. Roger A. Pryor Speaks for Mrs. Davis," *RD*, May 31, 1902. "Jefferson Davis Memorial, Richmond, Va.," *MN* 14 (July 1902): 404, provides an illustration.

34. "Fine Oration Delivered by Gen. Clement Evans," *Richmond Times-Dispatch*, June 4, 1907.

35. Ellyson Scrapbook, VHS; Christian, *Sketch*, 15; Driggs, Wilson, and Winthrop, *Richmond's Monument Avenue*. A monument to Matthew Fontaine Maury followed in the 1920s west of the Jackson equestrian.

36. Caroline Baldwin et al., "Confederate Soldiers Monument" (2007), Portal to Texas History, University of North Texas Libraries, texashistory.unt.edu/ark:/67531/metapth 34974/m1/1/.

37. Confederate Memorial Records. Janney, "War," documents later white southern resistance to proposals for a federal monument in Appomattox that would have highlighted Confederate defeat.

38. Pompeo Coppini to Margaret Drane Tichenor, January 24, 1912, in Margaret Drane Tichenor, comp., "Tributes to and Memorials of the Women of the Southland, 1861–1865," Confederate Memorial Records; Smith, "Belle Kinney," 19.

39. Unidentified clipping, IAS/Athens, Alabama (024).

40. Hargrove, *"Qui vive?,"* provides illustrations of more than a dozen French monuments that followed the more menacing pattern, which essentially did not exist in the postwar South.

41. *Gloria Victis*, 5, 36.

42. Woodward, "Irony of Southern History," 4.

43. Haskell and Penny, *Taste and the Antique*, 333–35; Kinnee, "Nike of Samothrace"; Perkins, "Victory of Samothrake."

44. The *salonnière* who epitomizes bourgeois smugness in Proust's *Swann's Way* (1913) adores the Nike of Samothrace, Beethoven's Ninth Symphony, and Rembrandt's *Night Watch* as "the three supreme masterpieces of the universe."

45. Warner, *Monuments and Maidens*, 130–31; Cheney, *Life of Christian Daniel Rauch*, 242–50.

46. *Kennebec (ME) Journal*, September 22, 1882, clipping in IAS Files (Augusta 378).

47. Grimaldi, "Indiana Soldiers' and Sailors' Monument," 22–23, 34, 51–52, 85–86.

48. Larned, *History of the Battle Monument at West Point*, 75; Circular, April 27, 1894, Battle Monument Proceedings.

49. Battle Monument Proceedings, September 9, December 10, 14, 1894; Smart, *Flight with Fame*, 100, 104.

50. *Collector* 7 (June 1, 1896): 227.

51. *New York Evening Post*, July 22, 1899, *Philadelphia Telegram*, July 24, 1899, clippings in MacMonnies Scrapbooks; Atkinson, *Long Gray Line*, 21.

52. Saint-Gaudens, *Reminiscences*, 1:378–81.

53. Schiller, "Artistic Collaboration," chap. 2; Fellman, *Citizen Sherman*, chap. 19. Savage, "Ream's *Lincoln*," helpfully balances Fellman's conjectures by pointing toward the "erotic fantasy" in Sherman's relationship with sculptor Vinnie Ream (164), regardless of the level of physical intimacy. See also Dabakis, *Sisterhood of Sculptors*, 181–99, 207–11.

54. Taft, *History of American Sculpture*, 304.

55. Dryfhout, *Work of Augustus Saint-Gaudens*, 197; Hagans, "Saint-Gaudens," 81.

56. Hagans, "Saint-Gaudens," 84–85; Wilkinson, *Uncommon Clay*, 297–98; Saint-Gaudens, *Reminiscences*, 2:137.

57. Taft, *Modern Tendencies*, 113; see also Cox, "Sherman Statue."

58. Hutt, "Thoughts and Things."

59. Schiller, "Winged Victory."

60. O'Hara, "Music."

61. Schiller, "Winged Victory," 48; Saint-Gaudens, *Reminiscences*, 2:135, 201.

62. Adams, *Education of Henry Adams*, 381, 385, 388.

63. *Dedication of the Monument at Andersonville*, 70–72; Richman, "Daniel Chester French and Henry Bacon."

64. Kasson, *Marble Queens*, chap. 5.

65. "In Streets and Papers," *Architecture and Building* 24 (February 29, 1896): 103; "The National Academy Exhibit," *MN* 21 (January 1909): 27–28.

66. Henry James, "New York: Social Notes–I," *NAR* 182 (January 1906): 19–31; Augustus Saint-Gaudens to Henry James, February 8, 1906, in Saint-Gaudens, *Reminiscences*, 2:296; Dryfhout, *Work of Augustus Saint-Gaudens*, 257, 288.

67. Croce, "Calming the Screaming Eagle," 8–10; Marchand, *American Peace Movement*.

68. Foster, "What's Not in a Name," 418–21, analyzes this terminology.

69. Jacob, *Testament*, 51–54; Peace Monument Files.

70. Sharp, *John Quincy Adams Ward*, 222.

71. "Monument Which We Unveiled Today," *Allentown (PA) Daily Leader*, October 19, 1899; "Baer's Splendid Monument Oration"; both in Allentown file (1326), IAS.

72. Records of Grant Commission.

73. Frick, "Mingled Dust," 55.

74. Jacob, *Testament*, 170.

75. "A Criticism on the Sherman Monument: The Work from an Artist's Point of View," in *Souvenir: Sherman Statue*.

76. *Decatur (IN) Daily Democrat*, July 11, 1972, clipping in Decatur file, IAS (quoting newspaper coverage of dedication).

77. *Albany (NY) Argus*, October 3, 1908, clipping, Records of Albany Memorial.

78. Unidentified clipping, May 6, 1909, "The City of Albany Memorial to the Soldiers and Sailors of the Civil War, 1861–1865," Records of Albany Memorial.

79. Unidentified clipping, May 6, 1909, "Albany Memorial"; "Albany's Civil War Memorial, Long Desired, Is a Masterpiece," *Knickerbocker Press* (Albany, NY), October 5, 1912, clipping, H. A. MacNeil to James H. Manning, October 2, 1911; both in Records of Albany Memorial.

80. "Sculptor at Work in Evansville on Groups of Statuary to Adorn the Front of the Coliseum," *Evansville (IN) Courier*, January 23, 1916, reprinted at www.georgehonig.org /sculptures/coliseum/coliseum.cfm.

CHAPTER 5

1. "Praise of the Veteran by Miss Rutherford," *CV* 19 (December 1911): 563; "Confederate Monuments by States," *CV* 20 (January 1912): 43; "The Monument at Arlington," *CV* (July 1914): 297–98; "The Monumental Spirit of the South," *CV* 22 (August 1914): 344.

2. Mabel C. R. Wrenn, "Scholarships or Monuments," *CV* 23 (March 1915): 131.

3. McKenney, *Standing Army*, 45.

4. *Blue and the Gray*.

5. Kennedy, *Over Here*, 100.

6. "Rochester's Great Day," *NYT*, May 31, 1892.

7. "Memorial Day at Muskegon, Mich.," *MN* 12 (July 1900): 388; "The Soldiers' Monument, Kenosha, Wis.," *MN* 12 (August 1900): 443; Bullard, *Lincoln*, 99–101, 107–13.

8. Bullard, *Lincoln*, 114–22.

9. Kohler and Scott, *Designing the Nation's Capital*, 348; Reps, *Monumental Washington*, 127–28.

10. Reps, *Monumental Washington*, 117; Thomas, "Lincoln Memorial and Its Architect," 359.

11. Schwartz, *Abraham Lincoln and the Forge of National Memory*, 182.

12. Thomas, "Lincoln Memorial and Its Architect," 385, 465n81; Sumner, "Promises of the Declaration of Independence," 12:272.

13. Thomas, "Lincoln Memorial and Its Architect," 207, 459–60, 670–73.

14. Thomas, *Lincoln Memorial and American Life*, 45.

15. Pollitt, *Art in the Hellenistic Age*, 59–78.

16. Thomas, "Lincoln Memorial and Its Architect," 219.

17. "A Memorial to Lincoln Worthy Alike of the Nation and the Man," *New-York Tribune*, January 7, 1912, II, 1:1, 59; Mechlin, "Proposed Lincoln Memorial," 374.

18. Thomas, *Lincoln Memorial and American Life*, 97–98; Mechlin, "Proposed Lincoln Memorial," 374.

19. Lincoln Memorial Commission Report, 13.

20. Peterson, *Lincoln*, 164; Concklin, *Lincoln Memorial*, 83.

21. Lincoln Memorial Commission Report, 26.

22. Levine, "Romantic Idea of Architectural Legibility."

23. Lincoln Memorial Commission Report, 13.

24. Moffatt, *Errant Bronzes*, 46–47. On antimodernism, see Lears, *No Place of Grace*.

25. *Barnard's Lincoln*, 24.

26. Moffatt, *Errant Bronzes*, 108.

27. *Barnard's Lincoln*, 40. Thomas, *Lincoln Memorial and American Life*, 104–7, discusses modernizing features of Bacon's work.

28. Boime, *Unveiling of the National Icons*, 282; Moffatt, *Errant Bronzes*, 152.

29. "A Calamity in Bronze!," *Art World* 3 (November 1917): 99; "How to Give Europe a Worthy Lincoln Monument," *Art World* 3 (January 1918): 267; *NYT*, August 26, 1917, II, 2:3, October 3, 1917, 12:4, January 1, 1918, 17:1, January 2, 1918, 10:3.

30. "On Monuments," *New York Tribune*, October 4, 1917, 8; "Barnard's Lincoln," *NAR* 206 (December 1917): 838.

31. "How to Give Europe a Worthy Lincoln Monument," 267.

32. "The Lincoln Memorial," *NYT*, May 30, 1922, 9. The obfuscation was not unanimous. Ralph Adams Cram applauded Bacon for choosing a predominantly Greek vocabulary because "the architecture of Roman Imperialism, superb, magnificent, tyrannical" was "out of the question." Cram, "Lincoln Memorial," 490.

33. "Greatest Throng in City's History Takes Part in Honoring Heroes," *WP*, May 31, 1922, 3; "Harding Leads Tribute to Heroes at Arlington," *WP*, May 31, 1922, 1–2; "Pleads for Social Peace in Address at Cemetery," *WP*, May 31, 1922, 2.

34. Concklin, *Lincoln Memorial*, 86, 88.

35. Mumford, *Sticks and Stones*, 141–42.

36. Budreau, *Bodies of War*, 47.

37. Monument inscriptions in Hartford City, Indiana (1921); Marlborough, Massachusetts (1923); Gloversville, New York (1923); Rockaway Beach, Queens, New York (1927); Germantown, Philadelphia, Pennsylvania (1928); Romney, West Virginia (1928); Clinton Park, New York City (1930); and Llano, Texas (1930), quote the poem. Monuments in Exeter, New Hampshire (1922); Des Moines, Iowa (1926); and Clinton Park, New York City (1930), feature poppies, and monuments in Greene City, Arkansas (1924); Milton (1925), Williamsport, (1925), and Woburn, Massachusetts (1926); Glens

Falls, New York (1927); and Winnetka (1928), Lockport (1930), Moline (1930), and Pana, Illinois (date unknown), depict torches that are not inverted. Wingate, *Sculpting Doughboys*, helpfully discusses many of the monuments treated in this section but aims to situate works on a spectrum of pacifism rather than relate them to Civil War precedents and European counterparts. French's invocation of McCrae's poem was not pacifist, but his internationalism pointed Americans toward a less militarist memorial vocabulary than the Civil War inheritance offered. Malvina Hoffman's *The Sacrifice* (1922) for Harvard University similarly participated in the international medievalism discussed in Goebel, *Great War and Medieval Memory*.

38. Inglis, "War Memorials" and "World War One Memorials." Of the World War I monuments in the Smithsonian database for which the record is clear, about four-fifths are dedicated to all soldiers who served.

39. Wingate, *Sculpting Doughboys*, 9.

40. Moriarty, "Narrative and the Absent Body," 237–40; King, *Memorials*, 208; Choubard, *L'histoire des 500 plus beaux monuments aux morts*; Hébel, *36,000 cicatrices*; Sherman, *Construction of Memory*, 170–213. Inglis, *Sacred Places*, 169, estimates that in Australia "for every figure showing warlike action, about ten depict repose."

41. Wingate, *Sculpting Doughboys*, 146–59.

42. Inglis, "Homecoming."

43. Weller, *Lorado Taft*, 52–53, 141.

44. Wingate, *Sculpting Doughboys*, chap. 4, discusses several such works.

45. See, e.g., Enfield, Connecticut (1885, plaque 1922); Paola, Kansas (1916, plaque 1925); New London, New Hampshire (1914, plaque 1919); Hudson Falls, New York (1887, plaque 1921); Rensselaer, New York (1910, plaque 1920).

46. Carrolton, Alabama (1927); Danbury (1931) and Darien, Connecticut (1936); Lebanon, Connecticut (1922); Resaca, Georgia (1927); Bedford (1924) and Bloomington, Indiana (1928); Belzoni (1923) and Poplarville (1926), Mississippi; Tekamah, Nebraska (date unknown); Red Bank, New Jersey (1926); Memphis, Texas (1924); University of Texas (1933).

47. Adams, "War Monuments," 351; "Combating Utilitarian Memorials," *MN* 33 (October 1921): 716.

48. Shanken, "Planned Memory," 136; "When the Boys and Girls Come Home," *American City* 58 (August 1943): 1. The tally included 218 community buildings, 79 auditoriums, 43 hospitals, 42 museums, galleries, or college buildings, 16 club houses, 14 city or town halls, 14 libraries, 12 churches and chapels, 8 schools, and 6 YMCA buildings.

49. Shanken, "Planned Memory," 137; Piehler, *Remembering War*, 98–100, 105–9.

50. Richman, *French*, 190; "First Division Monument, Washington, D.C.," *AA* 126 (December 3, 1924): 525–30.

51. McElya, *Politics of Mourning*, 111–16, 118, 129; Savage, "Unknowable Dead."

52. King, *Memorials*, 144.

53. Piehler, *Remembering War*, 116–25; Inglis, "Entombing Unknown Soldiers."

54. "The Cover Illustration," *MN* 33 (May 1921): 358.

55. Piehler, *Remembering War*, 123; Dickon, *Foreign Burial*, 70–71, 75.

56. McElya, *Politics of Mourning*, 170–90.

57. Trout, *On the Battlefield of Memory*, 124–56.

58. Mrs. A. A. Campbell, "The United Daughters of the Confederacy — Some of Their Aims and Accomplishments," *CV* 30 (March 1922): 86.

59. *MN* 24 (March 1912): 275. Bzdak and Petersen, *Public Sculpture,* 98–99; *Daily Texan,* June 17, 2003.

60. Bullard, *Lincoln,* 246–47, 276–79, 282–83; Lerner, "Capital City," 231.

61. "The Mythical Lincoln," *CV* 28 (March 1920): 85; Grace Murray Mastin, "The Great Obelisk," *CV* 28 (March 1920): 86; Giguere, "Young and Littlefield's Folly."

62. "The Jackson Monument at Charlottesville, Va.," *CV* 30 (February 1922): 44.

63. Jacob, *Testament,* 128–30.

64. "The Peace Monument," *Ohio State Journal,* June 28, 1923.

65. "Parthenon in Centennial Park War Memorial to Tennessee Soldiers," *NT,* March 16, 1919, 18; "The Soldiers' Memorial," *NT,* March 19, 1919, 6; "The Soldiers' Memorial," *NT,* March 26, 1919, 6; "State Sells Bonds for Memorial to Local Financiers," *NT,* February 15, 1921, 1. The state completed the War Memorial Building in 1925.

66. Fowler, "Giuseppe Moretti."

67. Underwood, *Allen Tate,* 123–24, 218; Warren, *At Heaven's Gate.*

68. "Cullin Monument Dedicated," *Hillsdale (NY) Harbinger,* July 4, 1916, clipping in Hillsdale file, IAS; *Unveiling of the Equestrian Statue of General Philip H. Sheridan,* 106; unidentified clipping, Holly Springs file, IAS.

69. John W. Frazier to William Mitchell Kendall, July 18, 1918, Meade Memorial Papers.

70. William W. Harts to M. G. Brumbaugh, July 24, 1916, Meade Memorial Papers.

71. Simpson and Knaub, *The Sculptor's Clay,* 62.

72. Charles Grafly, memorandum with model, July 27, 1918, Meade Memorial Papers.

73. Grace E. Emerson, "The Meade Memorial," *WP,* April 18, 1926, 3; Wilcox, "Tribute to Peace," 198. James Earle Fraser's monument to John Ericsson at the opposite end of the National Mall (1926) complemented the forward-looking Meade Memorial, as the *Monitor* designer was a patron saint of military technology and industrialized society.

74. *Washington Sunday Star,* May 12, 1935; *Dallas Times Herald,* May 24, 1936, clippings in Proctor Papers.

75. McElya, *Clinging to Mammy,* chaps. 4–5.

76. *St. Johnsville (NY) Enterprise and News,* July 17, 1937, clipping, St. Johnsville File (1625), IAS.

77. Neely, Holzer, and Boritt, *Confederate Image,* plate 11.

78. Faulkner, *Intruder in the Dust,* 194.

79. Mumford, "Death of the Monument," 264; Evans, *American Photographs,* pt. 1, no. 30. North, *Final Sculpture,* examines additional literary examples.

80. Freeman, *Carved in Stone,* 57.

81. *Cincinnati Times-Star,* quoted in "The South Expressed Artistically," *CV* 31 (October 1923): 396.

82. Freeman, *Carved in Stone,* 101, 120.

83. *Handbook of Information;* "Mountain a Monument," *NYT,* January 2, 1916, 4:1.

84. Shaff and Shaff, *Six Wars,* 126; Lerner, "Capital City," 183; Johnson, *Undefeated,* 49–50.

85. Shaff and Shaff, *Six Wars,* 150. On the refounding of the Klan, see MacLean, *Behind the Mask.*

86. Lerner, "Capital City," 149, 188.

87. Freeman, *Carved in Stone,* 101.

88. "Mountain a Monument," *NYT,* January 2, 1916, 4:1; August Lukeman, "An

American Monument to Surpass the Pyramids," *World's Work* 51 (March 1926): 492; *Handbook of Information.*

89. Johnson, *Undefeated*, 35, 79; "Mountain a Monument," *NYT*, January 2, 1916, 4:1.

90. Freeman, *Carved in Stone*, 132–88; Hale, "Granite Stopped Time."

91. Boime, *Unveiling of the National Icons*, 136–79.

EPILOGUE

1. Janson, *Rise and Fall of the Public Monument*, 1, documents the nadir.

2. Herbert Hoover, "Statement on Military Expenditures," July 23, 1929, www.presidency.ucsb.edu.

3. Boime, *Unveiling of the National Icons*, 180–252; Marling and Wetenhall, *Iwo Jima.*

4. Bleifeld, "Lone Sailor."

5. *U.S. Statutes at Large*, 79th Cong., 2nd sess., 60 Stat. 502 (June 26, 1946); *U.S. Statutes at Large*, 84th Cong., 2nd sess., S.J. Res. 95 (April 2, 1956).

6. Maya Lin, untitled essay, in Lin, *Grounds for Remembering*, 8–14, identifies the Thiepval Memorial as "the prime inspiration" for the Vietnam Veterans Memorial. Facknitz, "Getting It Right," discusses the relationship between the projects.

7. Lin, untitled essay, 12 (quoting her submission); Laqueur, *Work of the Dead*, 413–88.

8. Lin, untitled essay, 12. The inscription that precedes the names reads, "In honor of the men and women of the armed forces of the United States who served in the Vietnam War. The names of those who gave their lives and of those who remain missing are inscribed in the order they were taken from us."

9. Frederick Hart's ensemble *The Three Soldiers*, installed in 1984 to appease Lin's critics, more obviously updated the combat groups popularized in turn-of-the-century Civil War monuments. In the large literature on the Vietnam Veterans Memorial, see especially Hagopian, *Vietnam War*; and Savage, *Monument Wars*, 261–84.

10. Sandage, "Marble House Divided."

11. Blatt, Brown, and Yacovone, *Hope and Glory.*

12. Brown, *Civil War Canon*, 160, 201–35; Coski, *Confederate Battle Flag.*

13. Doss, *Memorial Mania*, provides a valuable guide to this outpouring, of which war memorials were "without doubt" the largest subset (221).

14. These monuments stood at an African American church in Hertford, North Carolina (1910); segregated cemeteries in Portsmouth (ca. 1916) and Norfolk, Virginia (1920), and Frankfort, Kentucky (1924); and a national cemetery in St. Louis. The latter monument, embellished on its 1939 relocation to Jefferson Barracks National Cemetery with the remains of 175 cholera victims in the Fifty-Sixth United States Colored Troops, had stood since the soldiers' burial in 1866 on Quarantine Island in the Mississippi River. Yockelson, "Their Memory Will Not Perish."

15. Blatt, "*Glory*," 229. Other notable monuments were in Cumberland, Maryland (1991); Fort Myers, Florida (1998); Chestertown, Maryland (1999); Donaldson, Louisiana (1999); New Bedford, Massachusetts (1999); Columbia, South Carolina (2001); Nashville National Cemetery, Tennessee (2003); Vicksburg National Military Park, Mississippi (2004); Ithaca, New York (2006); Danbury, Connecticut (2007); Lincoln University, Jefferson City, Missouri (2007); Decatur, Illinois (2008); New Haven, Connecticut (2008); Butler, Missouri (2008); Lexington Park, Maryland (2012); Helena, Arkansas (2013); and Columbia, Missouri (2016).

16. Peter Holley, "The 'Terrifying' Confederate Statue Some Tennesseans Want to Hide," *WP*, June 25, 2015. "Lee Rides Again on Statue in Antietam," *Washington Times*, June 19, 2003, and "Confederacy Marker Unveiled in Abbeville," *State* (Columbia, SC), November 25, 2018, describe other examples of Confederate monuments installed on private land. Lees and Gaske, *Recalling Deeds Immortal*, 264–89, identifies more than twenty Confederate monuments unveiled in Florida between 1982 and 2011.

17. The statue spent four years in storage, after which the artist's daughter donated it to the Rural Life Museum at Louisiana State University. See https://sites01.lsu.edu/wp/rurallife/2014/07/29/uncle-jack-bronze-statue/.

18. Al Ribak, "Silent Sam Should Leave," *Daily Tar Heel* (Chapel Hill, NC), March 17, 1965, 2; Rick Nichols, "Poet John Beecher Will Be in 'Debate' with Silent Sam This Afternoon at 4:30," *Daily Tar Heel*, May 18, 1967, 8; Task Force on Historical Representation of Statuary at UT Austin, "Report to President Gregory L. Fenves" (August 10, 2015), 15; Whites, "You Can't Change History by Moving a Rock."

19. Bernd, "Texas Town Retains Confederate Monument"; Edgemon, "Nathan Bedford Forrest Bust." Upton, *What Can and Can't Be Said*, 34–50, describes the Forrest controversy. The book ably analyzes what Upton calls the pattern of "dual heritage" illustrated by the monuments in Richmond and Easton.

20. Powell, "Reinventing Tradition"; Cook, "Unwanted Monument"; Kevin Sack, "Blacks Strip Slaveholders' Names Off Schools," *NYT*, November 12, 1997; Kevin Litten, "Efforts to Remove Confederate Monuments in New Orleans Go Back Decades," *New Orleans Times-Picayune*, March 13, 2017.

21. Brown, *Civil War Canon*, 84–89; and Kytle and Roberts, *Denmark Vesey's Garden*, 107–12; examine the best-known precedent, vandalism of the Calhoun Monument in Charleston. Doss, "Process Frame," 409, notes the defacing of several Confederate monuments during 2004–11.

22. Shay Sokol, "Sipp, Allen, Martin Protesters Vandalize City Monuments," *NOLA Defender*, March 27, 2012; Katy Reckdahl, "3 Defaced New Orleans Monuments Are Cleaned by Volunteers," *New Orleans Times-Picayune*, March 29, 2012; Levin, "Trayvon Martin"; "Local Businessman Cleans Up Defaced Monuments," *Civil War Talk* forum, civilwartalk.com, April 6, 2012; Good Witch of the South, Twitter post, October 29, 2013; "That Time Baton Rouge Moved a Confederate Monument," *Independent*, March 15, 2016.

23. Woodley, "Hashtags and Monuments."

24. See especially the statement that accompanied the March 2012 photographs of graffiti, printed in Sokol, "Sipp, Allen, Martin Protesters." Ransby, *Making All Black Lives Matter*, surveys the broader movement within which Take 'Em Down NOLA emerged.

25. That diminution was not total. The Confederate monument in Reidsville, North Carolina, damaged by an automobile in 2011 and shifted to a cemetery in 2014 over strenuous protest from the Sons of Confederate Veterans, drew extensive graffiti protest after the Charleston murders. Beetham, "From Spray Cans to Minivans," 20–26.

26. Abramowitz, Latterner, and Rosenblith, "Tools of Displacement"; Britton, "Monumental Questions."

27. Julie Bosman, "In Popular Park, a Point of Contention," *NYT*, May 27, 2017.

28. Florida: soldier monuments in Bradenton, Gainesville, Orlando, Tampa, and West Palm Beach. Kentucky: John C. Breckinridge and John Hunt Morgan statues in Lexington; soldier monument in Louisville. Louisiana: soldier monument in Baton Rouge; Davis, Lee, and Beauregard statues in New Orleans. Maryland: Lee-Jackson

statue, soldier monument, and monument to Confederate women in Baltimore; soldier monuments in Ellicott City and Rockville. Missouri: monument to Confederate women in Kansas City; soldier monument in St. Louis. North Carolina: soldier monuments in Charlotte, Durham, and Reidsville. Tennessee: Davis, Forrest, and J. Harvey Mathes statues in Memphis; Edmund Kirby Smith monument at the University of the South. Texas: Davis, Lee, Albert Sidney Johnston, and John Reagan statues at the University of Texas; Lee statue in Dallas; soldier monument in San Antonio. Virginia: George Morgan Jones statue at Randolph College. This list does not include the midnight vandalism of a cemetery soldier monument in Sylvania, Georgia. Some northern communities also removed freestanding outdoor monuments, such as the Confederate Memorial Fountain in Helena, Montana.

29. "Removal of Confederate Monuments and Memorials," en.wikipedia.org/wiki /Removal_of_Confederate_monuments_and_memorials, is a helpful list.

30. In addition to the removal of Davis statues in Austin, Memphis, and New Orleans, a blue-ribbon commission in Richmond recommended removal of the Davis statue on Monument Avenue but not the tributes to Lee, Stuart, Jackson, or Matthew Fontaine Maury. *Monument Avenue Commission Report*, 33. Statues of U.S. Supreme Court Chief Justice Roger B. Taney, author of the *Dred Scott* decision, were vulnerable for the same reason and taken down in Annapolis, Baltimore, and Frederick, Maryland.

31. David Montgomery, "After the Fall," *WP*, July 20, 2017.

32. Pollack, "Civil War in Art"; Rooney, "It's Not about One Statue."

33. Sierra Pettengill, *Graven Image*, video, *Field of Vision*, December 1, 2017, fieldofvision .org/graven-image; Walker, Hannaham, and Marcopoulos, *Go to Hell or Atlanta*; Walker and Marcopoulos, *Stone Mountain*. Stokes-Casey, "Richard Lou's *ReCovering Memphis*," discusses the "conceptual iconoclasm" of the Forrest equestrian in the years before its removal.

34. See also "5 Artists Respond to: Charlottesville," T Magazine, *NYT*, August 29, 2017; and "Monuments for a New Era," *NYT*, August 10, 2018.

Bibliography

MANUSCRIPT SOURCES

Battle Monument Association Proceedings, West Point, NY

Julian Shakespeare Carr Papers, Southern Historical Collection, University of North Carolina, Chapel Hill, NC

Confederate Memorial Records, Museum of the Confederacy, Richmond, VA

Devens Statue Papers, American Antiquarian Society, Worcester, MA

Lora Effie Ellyson Scrapbook, Virginia Historical Society, Richmond, VA

Fairmount Park Art Association Archives, Historical Society of Pennsylvania, Philadelphia, PA

Daniel Chester French Papers, Library of Congress, Washington, DC

General Files, National Commission of Fine Arts, National Archives, Washington, DC

Inventory of American Sculpture Files, Smithsonian American Art Museum, Washington, DC

Jefferson Davis Monument Association Minutes, Museum of the Confederacy, Richmond, VA

Frederick MacMonnies Scrapbooks, Archives of American Art, Washington, DC

Meade Memorial Papers, Records of the National Commission of Fine Arts, National Archives, Washington, DC

Miscellaneous Records of the Committee of Fifty, Memorial Hall, Harvard University Archives, Cambridge, MA

Edwin D. Morgan Papers, New York State Library, Albany, NY

Peace Monument Files, Office of the Architect of the Capitol, Washington, DC

Proceedings of the Commissions on the Statues of Generals Logan, Hancock, and Sheridan, National Archives, Washington, DC

Alexander Phimister Proctor Papers, Archives of American Art, Washington, DC

Records of the Albany Soldiers and Sailors Memorial Commission, Albany Institute of History and Art, Albany, NY

Records of the Commission on Memorial to Women of the Civil War, National Archives, Washington, DC

Records of the Grant Memorial Commission, National Archives, Washington, DC

Records of the McClellan Statue Commission, National Archives, Washington, DC

Records of the Sheridan Statue Commission, National Archives, Washington, DC
Soldiers' Memorial Society Records, Andover-Harvard Theological Library, Harvard
    University, Cambridge, MA
John Quincy Adams Ward Papers, Albany Institute of History and Art, Albany, NY
John Quincy Adams Ward Scrapbook, New-York Historical Society, New York, NY

NEWSPAPERS

Army and Navy Journal
Atlanta Constitution
Boston Evening Transcript
Charleston (SC) News
Charleston (SC) News and Courier
Chicago Tribune
Cleveland Morning Leader
Columbia (SC) Register
Daily Tar Heel (University
    of North Carolina)
Daily Texan (University of Texas)
Fauquier (VA) Now
Lewiston (ME) Evening Journal
Meriden (CT) Daily Republican
Middlesex County (NJ) Journal
Nashville Tennessean
National Republican (Washington, DC)
New Orleans Times-Picayune
New York Herald
New York Sun

New York Times
New York Tribune
Ohio State Journal
Philadelphia Press
Pittsburgh Commercial
Pittsburgh Post-Gazette
Pittsburgh Press
Quincy (MA) Patriot
Richmond Dispatch
Richmond Times
Richmond Times-Dispatch
Springfield (MA) Republican
State (Columbia, SC)
Waltham (MA) Free Press
Washington Evening Star
Washington Post
Wilmington Journal
Woonsocket (RI) Patriot and State Register
Worcester (MA) Daily Spy
Worcester (MA) Evening Gazette

MONUMENT INVENTORIES

Baruch, Mildred C., and Ellen J. Beckman. *Civil War Union Monuments.* Washington, DC:
    Daughters of Union Veterans of the Civil War, 1978.
Butler, Douglas J. *North Carolina Civil War Monuments: An Illustrated History.* Jefferson:
    McFarland, 2013.
Civil War Centennial Commission of Tennessee. *Directory of Civil War Monuments and
    Memorials in Tennessee.* Nashville: Civil War Centennial Commission, 1963.
"Civil War Markers and Memorials." In *Encyclopedia of Arkansas.* encyclopediaofarkansas
    .net.
Civil War Monuments in Kentucky. http://www.trailsrus.com/monuments/.
Civil War Monuments in New York State. localhistory.morrisville.edu/sites/cw_monum/.
Civil War Monuments in Ohio. library.cincymuseum.org/cwdetails7help.htm.
"Civil War Monuments Related to Vermont." In *Vermont in the Civil War.* vermontcivilwar
    .org/pw/monu/.
Commemorative Landscapes of North Carolina. docsouth.unc.edu/commland/.
Emerson, Bettie A. C., comp. *Historic Southern Monuments: Representative Memorials of the
    Heroic Dead of the Southern Confederacy.* New York: Neale, 1911.

George, Harold A. *Civil War Monuments of Ohio*. Mansfield, OH: Harold A. George, 2006.

Guitar, Sarah. "Monuments and Memorials in Missouri." *Missouri Historical Review* 19 (July 1925): 555–603.

Hagler, Gould B., Jr. *Georgia's Confederate Monuments*. Macon, GA: Mercer University Press, 2014.

Hillman, Benjamin J. *Monuments to Memories: Virginia Civil War Heritage in Bronze and Stone*. Richmond: Virginia Civil War Commission, 1965.

Inventory of American Sculpture. siris-artinventories.si.edu.

Iowa Civil War Monuments.com. iowacivilwarmonuments.com.

Kansas Civil War Memorials and Monuments. kscwmonuments.com.

Lees, William B., and Frederick P. Gaske. *Recalling Deeds Immortal: Florida Monuments to the Civil War*. Gainesville: University Press of Florida, 2014.

Logan, Charles Russell. *Something So Dim It Must Be Holy: Civil War Commemorative Sculpture in Arkansas, 1886–1934*. Little Rock: Arkansas Historic Preservation Program, 1997.

Maine Civil War Monuments. maine.gov/civilwar/monuments.html.

"Maryland Military Monuments Inventory." veterans.maryland.gov/wp-content/uploads/sites/2/2014/03/Jan-2014-MMM-Inventory.pdf.

May, George, comp. *Michigan Civil War Monuments*. Lansing: Michigan Civil War Centennial Observance Commission, 1965.

McKenney, Frank M. *The Standing Army*. Alpharetta, GA: W. H. Wolfe, 1993.

McMichael, Kelly. *The Civil War Monument Movement in Texas*. Denton: Texas State Historical Association, 2009.

McWhite, Sally Leigh. "Echoes of the Lost Cause: Civil War Reverberations in Mississippi from 1865 to 2001." PhD diss., University of Mississippi, 2003.

Ransom, David F. "Connecticut's Monumental Epoch: A Survey of Civil War Memorials." *Connecticut Historical Society Bulletin* 58, nos. 1–2 (1993): 1–280; 59, nos. 3–4 (1994): 1–289.

Roe, Alfred S. *Monuments, Tablets and Other Memorials Erected in Massachusetts to Commemorate the Services of Her Sons in the War of the Rebellion, 1861–1865*. Boston: Wright and Potter, 1910.

Rose, James A., comp. *Blue Book of the State of Illinois*. Springfield: Phillips Brothers, 1903.

Sedore, Timothy S. *An Illustrated Guide to Virginia's Confederate Monuments*. Carbondale: Southern Illinois University Press, 2011.

Seigler, Robert S. *A Guide to Confederate Monuments in South Carolina: "Passing the Silent Cup."* Columbia: South Carolina Department of Archives and History, 1997.

Soderberg, Susan. *Lest We Forget: A Guide to Confederate Monuments of Maryland*. Shippensburg, PA: White Maine, 1995.

Southern Poverty Law Center. *Whose Heritage? A Report on Public Symbols of the Confederacy*. www.splccenter.org/data-projects/whose-heritage.

Well, Dave. "Monuments and Memorials in Nebraska to Civil War Soldiers." www.civilwarmuseumnc.org/monuments.html.

Westerly Granite Records. Babcock-Smith House Museum. www.babcocksmith.com.

Widener, Ralph W., Jr. *Confederate Monuments: Enduring Symbols of the South and the War Between the States*. Washington, DC: Andromeda, 1982.

Wisconsin's Civil War Memorials. www.suvcw-wi.org/memorials.html.

Adams, Adeline. "War Monuments." *American Magazine of Art* 9 (July 1918): 347–52.

Adams, Henry. *The Education of Henry Adams: An Autobiography.* Boston: Houghton Mifflin, 1918.

Address Delivered May 30, 1910 by John W. Weeks at the Dedication of the Monument to William F. Draper. N.p.: privately printed, 1910.

Address of Hon. Jno. T. Morgan on the Unveiling of the Monuments to the Unknown Dead, Delivered at Winchester, Virginia, June 6th, 1879. Washington, DC: Globe, 1879.

Alumni Hall: Appeal to the Alumni and Friends of Harvard College. Cambridge, MA: John Wilson and Sons, 1866.

Anderson, Archer. *Robert Edward Lee: An Address Delivered at the Dedication of the Monument to General Robert Edward Lee at Richmond, Virginia, May 29, 1890.* Richmond: William Ellis Jones, 1890.

Appendix to History of the Calhoun Monument, Published in 1888. Charleston: n.s., 1898.

Barnard's Lincoln: The Gift of Mr. and Mrs. Charles P. Taft to the City of Cincinnati. Cincinnati: Stewart & Kidd, 1917.

Bartlett, T. H. *About Monuments.* N.p.: n.s., 1883.

Bates, Clement. *The Annotated Revised Statutes of the State of Ohio.* 6th ed. Edited by Charles E. Everett. 3 vols. Cincinnati: W. H. Anderson, 1906.

Beath, Robert B. *History of the Grand Army of the Republic.* New York: Bryan, Taylor, 1889.

Beveridge, Charles, et al., eds. *The Papers of Frederick Law Olmsted.* 9 vols. Baltimore: Johns Hopkins University Press, 1977–2013.

Bleifeld, Stanley. "'The Lone Sailor' and 'The Homecoming.'" In *"Remove Not the Ancient Landmark": Public Monuments and Moral Values,* edited by Donald Martin Reynolds, 207–15. Amsterdam: Gordon and Breach, 1996.

The Blue and the Gray: Statues in Stamped Copper and Bronze. Cleveland: Caxton, 1913.

Bradford, E. H. "Flexion or Bent-Knee Marching." In *Proceedings of the Eighth Meeting of the Association of Military Surgeons of the United States,* 175–83. Columbus: Berlin, 1900.

———. "Science of Walking." *Mind and Body* 15 (September 1908): 225–29.

Brooks, Phillips. *An Address Delivered May 30, 1873, at the Dedication of the Memorial Hall, Andover, Massachusetts.* Andover: Trustees of Memorial Hall, 1873.

Brown, Thomas J., ed. *The Public Art of Civil War Commemoration: A Brief History with Documents.* Boston: Bedford/St. Martin's, 2004.

Bruce, Edward C. *The Century: Its Fruits and Its Festival.* Philadelphia: J. B. Lippincott, 1877.

Burnham, Gordon W. *Proceedings at the Inauguration of the Statue of Daniel Webster.* New York: D. Appleton, 1876.

Cable, George Washington. "The Silent South." *Century* 30 (September 1885): 674–91.

Caffin, Charles H. *American Masters of Sculpture.* New York: Doubleday, Page, 1903.

Ceremonies at the Dedication of the Bigelow Monument, Worcester, Massachusetts, April 19, 1861. Boston: John Wilson and Son, 1861.

Ceremonies at the Dedication of the Soldiers' Monument in Concord, Mass. Concord: Benjamin Tolman, 1867.

Ceremonies at the Dedication of the Soldiers' Monument in West Roxbury, Mass., Sept. 14, 1871. Boston: Hollis and Gunn, 1871.

Chickamauga Memorial Association. *Proceedings at Chattanooga, Tenn., and Crawfish*

Springs, Ga., September 19 and 20, 1889. N.p.: Chattanooga Army of Cumberland Reunion Entertainment Committee, n.d.

Christian, George L. *Sketch of the Origin and Erection of the Confederate Memorial Institute,* 2nd ed. N.p., n.d.

City of Boston. *Report of the Joint Special Committee on the Erection of an Army and Navy Monument.* City Document no. 98, 1870.

Cochran, Thomas B. *Smull's Legislative Hand Book and Manual of the State of Pennsylvania.* Harrisburg: Harrisburg Publishing, 1907.

"Competition for the Selection of an Architect for a Soldiers' Memorial for Allegheny County, Pennsylvania." In *American Competitions,* edited by Adin Benedict Lacey. Philadelphia: T Square Club, 1907.

Complete Speeches and Addresses of Theodore Roosevelt. www.theodore-roosevelt.com /trspeechescomplete.html.

Concklin, Edward, comp. *The Lincoln Memorial, Washington.* Washington, D.C.: U.S. Government Printing Office, 1927.

The Confederate Monument at Charleston, South Carolina: Orations of Gen. M. C. Butler and Gen. B. H. Rutledge at the Unveiling of the Monument in Magnolia Cemetery, November 30th, 1882. Charleston: News and Courier, 1884.

Cowley, Charles. *Reminiscences of James C. Ayer and the Town of Ayer.* 3rd ed. Lowell, MA: Penhallow, 1880.

Cox, Kenyon. "The Sherman Statue." *The Nation* 76 (June 18, 1903): 491–92.

Cram, Ralph Adams. "The Lincoln Memorial, Washington, D.C., Henry Bacon, Architect." *Architectural Record* 53 (June 1923): 478–508.

Croly, Herbert. *The Promise of American Life.* New York: MacMillan, 1914. First published 1909.

Daniel Webster, an Oration, by the Hon. Edward Everett, on the Occasion of the Dedication of the Statue of Mr. Webster, in Boston, September 17th, 1859. New York: H. H. Lloyd, 1859.

Dauphin County Soldiers' Monument Erected at Harrisburg, Pa. N.p., n.d. [1878].

Davis, George W. "The Sanitary Commission — the Red Cross." *American Journal of International Law* 4 (July 1910): 546–66.

"Dead on the Field of Honor." Dedication of the Soldiers' Monument at Gorham, Maine, Thursday, October 18th, 1866. Portland, ME: B. Thurston, 1866.

Dedication of Monument to Confederate Dead of Florida, June 16, 1898. Jacksonville: DaCosta, 1898.

Dedication of the Confederate Monument at Greenwood Cemetery, on Friday, April 10th, 1874, by the Ladies Benevolent Association of Louisiana. New Orleans: James A. Gresham, 1874.

Dedication of the Equestrian Statue of Major-General Charles Devens and of the Monument to the Soldiers of Worcester County in the War for the Union, July 4th, 1906. Worcester, MA: n.s., 1907.

Dedication of the Memorial Hall in Dedham, September 29, 1868. Dedham, MA: John Cox Jr., 1869.

Dedication of the Monument at Andersonville, Georgia, October 23, 1907, in Memory of the Men of Connecticut Who Suffered in Southern Prisons, 1861–1865. Hartford: State of Connecticut, 1908.

Dedication of the Soldiers' Monument at Cherryfield, Maine, July 4, 1874. Portland: Bailey and Noyes, 1874.

Dedication of the Soldiers' Monument, at Peterboro, N.H., on Friday, June 17th, 1870.
Peterborough: Transcript Office, 1870.

Dedication of Tomb of Army of Northern Virginia, Louisiana Division, and Unveiling of Statue of Stonewall Jackson at Metairie Cemetery, New Orleans, May 10, 1881. New Orleans: M. F. Dunn & Bro., 1881.

Description of the Ceremony of Dedication of the Statue of Major-General John Sedgwick, U.S. Volunteers, Colonel Fourth U.S. Cavalry, at West Point, N.Y., October 21, 1868. New York: D. Nostrand, 1869.

Devens, Charles. *An Oration Delivered in Boston, September 17, 1877, at the Dedication of the Soldiers and Sailors' Monument, on Boston Common.* Boston: privately printed, 1877.

Early, Jubal A. "The Campaigns of General Lee." In *Lee the Soldier,* edited by Gary W. Gallagher, 37–73. Lincoln: University of Nebraska Press, 1996.

Emerson, Ralph Waldo. "The Fugitive Slave Law." In *Emerson's Antislavery Writings,* edited by Len Gougeon and Joel Myerson, 73–90. New Haven, CT: Yale University Press, 1995.

The Equestrian Statue of Major General Joseph Hooker, Erected and Dedicated by the Commonwealth of Massachusetts. Boston: Wright & Potter, 1903.

Erection and Dedication of the Soldiers' and Sailors' Monument in the Army and Navy Lot, in Mount Hope Cemetery, Belonging to the City of Boston. City Document no. 80. Boston: City Council, 1867.

Evans, Samuel M., comp. *Allegheny County, Pennsylvania, in the War for the Suppression of the Rebellion, 1861–1865.* Pittsburgh: Board of Managers, Soldiers and Sailors Memorial Hall, 1924.

Evans, Walker. *American Photographs.* New York: Museum of Modern Art, 1938.

Exercises Held at the Dedication of the Soldiers' Monument, Memorial Day, 1882. Easton, MA: n.p., n.d.

Farragut: Mr. Choate's Address, Made at the Request of the Farragut Monument Association, on the Occasion of the Unveiling of the St. Gaudens Statue, May 25, 1881. New York: Evening Post Steam Presses, 1881.

Faulkner, William. *Intruder in the Dust.* New York: Random House, 1948.

First Report of the Free Public Library Commission of Massachusetts. Boston: Wright & Potter, 1891.

Fleming, George Thornton, ed. *Pittsburgh: How to See It: A Complete, Reliable Guide Book.* N.p.: William G. Johnston, 1916.

Flower, B. O. "Saint Gaudens' *Lincoln* as an Example of the Power of Genius." *Arena* 38 (October 1907): 426–28.

Gardner, Alexander. *Gardner's Photographic Sketch Book of the War.* 2 vols. Washington, D.C.: Philip & Solomons, [1866].

Gibbs, Warren, ed. "Franklin County Military Chapter." *Vermont Historical Gazetteer and Biographical Magazine,* ed. Abby Maria Hemenway 2 (1871): 384–454.

Gilder, Richard Watson. "The Farragut Monument." *Scribner's Monthly* 22 (June 1881): 161–67.

Gleason, William J. *History of the Cuyahoga County Soldiers' and Sailors' Monument.* Cleveland: Monument Commissioners, 1894.

Gloria Victis: Unveiling of Confederate Monument, May 2nd, 1903. Baltimore: Guggenheimer, Weil., n.d.

"Grant's Memorial: What Shall It Be?' *North American Review* 141 (September 1885): 276–92.

Hadley, Arthur T. "Military Training of College Students." In *Report of the President, 1914–1915*, 1–20. New Haven, CT: Published by the University, 1915.

Handbook of Information about the Stone Mountain Confederate Memorial. Rpt. in *Shades of Gray: The Changing Focus of Stone Mountain Park*. http://xroads.virginia.edu/~ug97/stone/.

Harrison, Benjamin. "Military Instruction in Schools and Colleges." *Century* 47 (January 1894): 469.

Higginson, Thomas Wentworth. "Regular and Volunteer Officers." *Atlantic Monthly* 14 (September 1864): 348–57.

Higginson, Waldo, and William Robert Ware. "Memorial Hall." In *The Harvard Book*, edited by F. O. Vaille and H. A. Clark, 2:49–72. Cambridge, MA: Welch, Bigelow, 1875.

Hight, John J. *History of the Fifty-Eighth Regiment of Indiana Volunteer Infantry*. Edited by Gilbert R. Stormont. Princeton, NJ: Clarion, 1895.

Hillard, Elias Brewster. *The Last Men of the Revolution*. Edited by Wendell Garrett. Barre, MA: Barre Publishers, 1968.

History of Antietam National Cemetery. Baltimore: John W. Woods, 1869.

History of the Origin and a Description of Memorial Hall of Allegheny County in Honor of the Soldiers, Sailors and Marines of Allegheny County Who Served in Defense of the Union in the War for the Suppression of the Rebellion. Pittsburgh: Memorial Hall Committee, 1910.

The History of Washington Square Arch, New York. New York: Ford and Garnett, 1896.

Holmes, Oliver Wendell. *Speeches by Oliver Wendell Holmes*. Boston: Little, Brown, 1896.

Howe, Henry. *Historical Collections of Ohio*. Columbus: Henry Howe and Son, 1847–91.

[Howells, William Dean.] "Question of Monuments." *Atlantic Monthly* 17 (May 1866): 646–49.

"Human Gait as Illustrated in Shaw Monument." *Boston Medical and Surgical Journal* 158 (January 16, 1908): 100–101.

Huntington, Elijah Baldwin. *Stamford Soldiers' Memorial*. Stamford, CT: Published by the author, 1869.

Inauguration of the Jackson Statue: Introductory Address of Governor Kemper and Oration by Rev. Moses D. Hoge, D.D., Tuesday, October 26, 1875. Richmond: R. F. Walker, 1875.

James, George Francis, ed. *Logan Monument Memorial*. Chicago: University of Chicago Press, 1898.

James, Henry. *The American Scene*. New York and London: Harper and Brothers, 1907.

———. *Hawthorne*. London: MacMillan, 1879.

Johnson, Gerald W. *The Undefeated*. New York: Minton, Balch, 1927.

Kauffman, Samuel Hay. "'Men on Horseback': A Paper on the Equestrian Statuary in Washington, Read before the Columbia Historical Society." N.p., n.s., 1902.

Keim, DeB. Randolph, ed. *Sherman: A Memorial in Art, Oratory and Literature*. Washington, D.C.: U.S. Government Printing Office, 1904.

Kimbell, Charles B. *History of Battery "A," First Illinois Light Artillery Volunteers*. Chicago: Cushing, 1899.

Koehler, S. R. "Our Public Monuments." *Art Review* 1 (November 1886): 8–12.

Kohler, Sue, and Pamela Scott, eds. *Designing the Nation's Capital: The 1901 Plan for Washington, D.C.* Washington, D.C.: U.S. Commission of Fine Arts, 2006.

Larned, Charles W. *History of the Battle Monument at West Point*. West Point, NY: n.s., 1898.

Levering, Joseph F. *Services for the Use of the Grand Army of the Republic*. Boston: Grand Army of the Republic, 1881.

Lincoln Memorial Commission Report. 62nd Cong., 3d sess., Senate Doc. 965, December 5, 1912. Washington, D.C.: U.S. Government Printing Office, 1913.

Logan, John A. *The Volunteer Soldier of America*. Chicago: R. S. Peale, 1887.

Loring, George B. *An Oration, Delivered at Bolton, Massachusetts, December 20, 1866, at the Dedication of the Tablets, Erected in the Town Hall, to Commemorate the Deceased Volunteers of the Town in the War of the Great Rebellion*. Clinton, MA: Clinton Courant, 1867.

———. *An Oration, Delivered at Lexington on the Dedication of the Town and Memorial Hall, April 19, 1871*. Boston: Marvin & Son, 1871.

Matthews, Stanley. *Address to Alumni of Kenyon College, June 23, 1880*. Cincinnati: Robert Clarke, 1880.

McIntyre, Philip Willis, ed. *An Account of the Ceremonies at the Dedication of the Soldiers' Monument, Bridgton, Maine, July 21, 1910*. N.p., n.d.

McNamara, Daniel George. *The History of the Ninth Regiment, Massachusetts Volunteer Infantry*. Boston: E. B. Stillings, 1899.

Mechlin, Leila. "The Proposed Lincoln Memorial." *Century Magazine* 83 (January 1912): 367–76.

Melville, Herman. *Israel Potter: His Fifty Years of Exile*. Edited by Robert S. Levine. New York: Penguin, 2008.

"Memorial Address of Wade Hampton." *Southern Magazine* 13 (August 1873): 229–32.

Minutes of the Fifteenth Annual Convention of the United Daughters of the Confederacy. Opelika, AL: Post, 1909.

Mitchell, Walter. "Harvard's Heroes." *Atlantic Monthly* 12 (September 1863): 385–87.

Monument Avenue Commission Report. Richmond: n.p., 2018.

The Monument to Robert Gould Shaw: Its Inception, Completion and Unveiling, 1865–1897. Boston: Houghton, Mifflin, 1897.

Moody, William Vaughn. "An Ode in Time of Hesitation." *Atlantic Monthly* 85 (May 1900): 593–98.

Moyer, Maude Ross. "The Spinner Memorial." *American Monthly Magazine* 36 (February 1910): 166–68.

Mumford, Lewis. "The Death of the Monument." In *Circle: International Survey of Constructive Art*, edited by J. L. Martin, Ben Nicholson, and Naum Gabo, 237–70. Rpt. New York: Praeger, 1971.

———. *Sticks and Stones: A Study of American Architecture and Civilization*. New York: Boni and Liveright, 1924.

[Norton, Charles Eliot.] "The Harvard and Yale Memorial Buildings." *The Nation* 5 (July 11, 1867): 35.

Ockenden, Ina Marie Porter, ed. *The Confederate Monument on Capitol Hill, Montgomery, Alabama*. Montgomery: Ladies Memorial Association, 1900.

O'Hara, Frank. "Music" (1953). In *Lunch Poems*, 7. San Francisco: City Lights, 1964.

Oliver P. Morton of Indiana: Sketch of His Life and Public Services. Indianapolis: Journal Company, 1876.

An Oration Delivered by General Francis A. Walker at the Soldiers' Monument Dedication in North Brookfield, January 19, 1870. Worcester, MA: Goddard and Nye, 1870.

Oration Pronounced by Col. Charles C. Jones, Jr. on the 31st October, 1878, upon the Occasion of the Unveiling and Dedication of the Confederate Monument, Erected by the Ladies'

Memorial Association of Augusta, in Broad Street, in the City of Augusta, Georgia. N.p.: n.s., 1878.

Perkins, Charles C. "The Victory of Samothrake." *American Art Review* 1 (August 1880): 439–40.

Phillips, Wendell. "Public Opinion." In *Speeches, Lectures, and Letters*, 35–54. Boston: James Redpath, 1863.

Porcher, Frederick A. "A Brief History of the Ladies' Memorial Association of Charleston, S.C., from Its Organization in 1866 to April 1, 1880," edited by Mary A. Sparkman. In *City of Charleston Yearbook, 1944*, 203–15. Charleston: Walker, Evans & Cogswell, 1947.

Power, John Carroll. *Abraham Lincoln: His Life, Public Services, Death and Great Funeral Cortege*. Springfield, IL: Edwin A. Wilson, 1875.

Proceedings at the Centennial Celebration of Concord Fight, April 19, 1875. Concord, MA: Published by the Town, 1876.

Proceedings at the Dedication of the Soldiers' and Sailors' Monument in Providence, to Which Is Appended a List of the Deceased Soldiers and Sailors Whose Names Are Sculpted upon the Monument. Providence, RI: A. Crawford Greene, 1871.

Reichel, William C., ed. *Historical Sketch of Nazareth Hall from 1755 to 1869*. Philadelphia: J. B. Lippincott, 1869.

Reinhart, Joseph R., trans. and ed. *August Willich's Gallant Dutchmen: Civil War Letters from the 32nd Indiana Infantry*. Kent, OH: Kent State University Press, 2006.

Report of Proceedings of the City Council of Boston for the Municipal Year 1889. Boston: Rockwell and Churchill, 1890.

Report of Proceedings of the City Council of Boston for the Municipal Year 1891. Boston: Rockwell and Churchill, 1891.

Report of the Proceedings of the Society of the Army of the Tennessee at the Twenty-Seventh Meeting, Held at Cincinnati, O., and Chattanooga, Tenn., September 16–21, 1895. Cincinnati: F. W. Freeman, 1896.

Reports of the Soldiers' Memorial Society, Presented at the Second Annual Meeting, June 5, 1866. Boston: n.s., 1866.

Report of the Soldiers' Monument Committee, of the City of Fitchburg. N.p., n.d.

Ritual of the Grand Army of the Republic. Philadelphia: Grand Army of the Republic, 1903.

Roll of the 40th National Encampment of the Grand Army of the Republic, Minneapolis, Minnesota, August 16th and 17th, 1906. Philadelphia: Town Printing, 1906.

Rusling, James F. *Mercer County Soldiers' and Sailors' Monument*. Trenton, NJ: n.s., 1910.

Saint-Gaudens, Homer, ed. *The Reminiscences of Augustus Saint-Gaudens*. 2 vols. New York: Century, 1913.

Scrymser, James A. *Personal Reminiscences of James A. Scrymser in Times of Peace and War*. N.p., n.s., 1915.

Sedgwick, Henry Dwight. *Address at the Dedication of the Soldiers' Monument in Stockbridge, Massachusetts, October 17th, 1866*. New York: Baker & Godwin, 1867.

Services at the Dedication of the Memorial Library, Framingham, Mass., February 22, 1873. Boston: Rand, Avery, 1873.

Smith, J. E. A., ed. *The Proceedings at the Dedication of the Soldiers' Monument at Pittsfield, Mass., Sept. 24, 1872, including the Oration of Hon. George W. Curtis*. Pittsfield: Chickering and Axtell, 1872.

Soldiers' Memorial Building, Toledo, Ohio: In Honor and in Memory of Those Who Fought and

Those Who Fell in Defense of Our Country during the War of the Rebellion. Toledo: B. F. Wade, 1886.

The Soldiers' Monument in Cambridge: Proceedings in Relation to the Building and Dedication of the Monument Erected in the Years 1869–1870, by the City Government of Cambridge, Mass., in Honor of Those of Her Soldiers and Sailors Who Died in Defence of the Union of the States, in the War of the Rebellion. Cambridge, MA: John Wilson and Son, 1870.

Soldiers of Oakham, Massachusetts, in the Revolutionary War, the War of 1812, and the Civil War. New Haven, CT: Tuttle, Morehouse, and Taylor, 1914.

The South Carolina Monument Association: Origin, History and Work. Charleston: News and Courier, 1879.

Souvenir: Sherman Statue, Washington, D.C. Washington, D.C.: J. H. Wilson Marriott, 1903.

A Souvenir of the Unveiling of the Richmond Howitzer Monument at Richmond, Virginia, December 13th, 1892. Richmond: J. L. Hill, 1893.

Special Report of the Soldiers' Monument Association, Containing an Account of the Dedicatory Exercises of the Soldiers' Monument at Bridgeport, August 17th, 1876. Bridgeport, CT: Standard Association, 1877.

Speech Delivered by Daniel Webster at Niblo's Saloon in New-York, on the 15th March, 1837. New York: Harper Brothers, 1837.

"Statue of Francis E. Spinner." Committee on the Library, House of Representatives, submitted to Committee of the Whole House, January 24, 1900. Report no. 115, 56th Congress, 1st sess.

Stone, William L. *History of the Saratoga Monument Association.* Albany, NY: Joel Munsell, 1879.

Stow[e], J. M. *Address at the Dedication of a Soldiers' Monument, in Sullivan, July 4th, 1867.* Keene: New-Hampshire Sentinel Job Office, 1867.

Strahan, Edward [Earl Shinn]. *The Masterpieces of the Centennial International Exhibition, Illustrated,* vol. 1, *Fine Art.* Philadelphia: Gebbie and Barrie, n.d.

[Strauch, Adolphus]. *Spring Grove Cemetery: Its History and Improvements.* Cincinnati: Robert Clarke, 1869.

[Sturgis, Russell, Jr.] "Something about Monuments." *The Nation* 1 (August 3, 1865): 155.

Sumner, Charles. "Promises of the Declaration of Independence, and Abraham Lincoln." In *Charles Sumner: His Complete Works,* 20 vols., 12:235–96. Rept. New York: Negro University Press, 1969.

Taft, Lorado. *The History of American Sculpture.* New York: MacMillan, 1903.

———. *Modern Tendencies in Sculpture.* Chicago: University of Chicago Press, 1921.

Thayer, Christopher T. *Address Delivered at the Dedication of Memorial Hall, Lancaster, June 17, 1868.* Boston: Nichols and Noyes, 1868.

Tocqueville, Alexis de. *Democracy in America.* Edited by John C. Spencer. Translated by Henry Reeve. New York: George Adlard, 1839.

The Town of Wayland, in the Civil War of 1861–1865, as Represented in the Army and Navy of the American Union. Boston: Rand, Avery and Frye, 1871.

Tuckerman, Henry T. *Book of the Artists.* New York: Putnam & Son, 1867.

Unveiling Ceremonies of Carroll County's Confederate Monument at Carrollton, Mississippi, December 1, 1905. Carrollton: Conservative, n.d.

Unveiling of the Equestrian Statue of General Philip H. Sheridan, Capitol Park, Albany, New York, October 7, 1916, by the Citizens of Albany and the State of New York. N.p., n.d.

The Unveiling of the Monument to the Confederate Dead of Alexandria, Va.: Speeches of
    Capt. Raleigh T. Daniel, and Gov. Fitzhugh Lee, May 24th, 1889. N.s., n.d.
Unveiling of Ward's Equestrian Statue of Major-General George H. Thomas, Washington,
    November 19, 1879. Cincinnati: Robert Clarke, 1879.
Van Dyke, John C. *Art for Art's Sake.* New York: Charles Scribner's Sons, 1893.
Walker, Kara, James Hannaham, and Ari Marcopoulos. *Go to Hell or Atlanta, Whichever*
    Comes First. London: Victoria Miro Gallery, 2015.
Walker, Kara, and Ari Marcopoulos. *Stone Mountain, Georgia.* N.p.: Études, 2017.
Walker, Katherine C. "American Studios in Rome and Florence." *Harper's New Monthly*
    33 (June 1866): 101–5.
Walton, William. "The Field of Art: Monument to General Grant, in Washington."
    Scribner's Magazine 49 (March 1911): 381–84.
Warren, Robert Penn. *At Heaven's Gate.* New York: Harcourt, Brace, 1943.
Webster, Prentiss, ed. *The Story of the City Hall Commission, Including the Exercises at the*
    Laying of the Corner Stones and the Dedication of the City Hall and Memorial Hall. Lowell,
    MA: Citizen Newspaper, 1894.
White, Claire Nicholas, ed. *Stanford White: Letters to His Family, Including a Selection of*
    Letters to Augustus Saint-Gaudens. New York: Rizzoli, 1997.
Whitney, Frederick Augustus. *An Oration Delivered at the Dedication of the Soldiers'*
    Monument in Evergreen Cemetery, Brighton, Massachusetts. Boston: S. Chism, 1866.
Wilcox, Uthai Vincent. "A Tribute to Peace: The Meade Memorial." *AMA* 18 (April 1927):
    194–98.
Wilkinson, Spenser. *The Brain of an Army: A Popular Account of the German General Staff.*
    New ed. Westminster, Eng.: Archibald Constable, 1895.
Woodward, C. Vann. "The Irony of Southern History." *Journal of Southern History* 19
    (February 1953): 3–19.

SECONDARY SOURCES

Aaslestad, Katherine. "Remembering and Forgetting: The Local and the Nation in
    Hamburg's Commemoration of the Wars of Liberation." *Central European History*
    38, no. 3 (2005): 384–416.
Abramowitz, Sophie, Eva Latterner, and Gillet Rosenblith. "Tools of Displacement."
    Slate Magazine, June 23, 2017. www.slate.com.
Adams, Michael C. C. *Living Hell: The Dark Side of the Civil War.* Baltimore: Johns
    Hopkins University Press, 2014.
Allison, Olivia Evans. "The Seated Philosopher Type in the Sculpture of William Wetmore
    Story, Daniel Chester French, and Augustus Saint-Gaudens." MA thesis, University of
    Delaware, 1989.
Anbinder, Tyler. "Which Poor Man's Fight? Immigrants and the Federal Conscription of
    1863." *Civil War History* 52 (December 2006): 344–72.
Aron, Cindy S. "'To Barter Their Souls for Gold': Female Clerks in Federal Government
    Offices, 1862–1890." *Journal of American History* (March 1981): 835–53.
Atkinson, Rick. *The Long Gray Line: The American Journey of West Point's Class of 1966.*
    Boston: Houghton Mifflin, 1989.
Audoin-Rouzeau, Stéphane, and Annette Becker. *14–18: Understanding the Great War.*
    Trans. Catherine Temerson. New York: Hill and Wang, 2000.

Aurand, Martin. *The Spectator and the Topographical City*. Pittsburgh: University of Pittsburgh Press, 2006.

Austin, Dan. "Grand Army of the Republic Building." *Historic Detroit.org*, 2019. www .historicdetroit.org/building/grand-army-of-the-republic-building/.

Baker, Paul R. *Richard Morris Hunt*. Cambridge, MA: MIT Press, 1980.

Baldwin, Peter C. *Domesticating the Street: The Reform of Public Space in Hartford, 1850–1930*. Columbus: Ohio State University Press, 1999.

Becker, Annette. "Monuments aux morts après la guerre de Sécession et la guerre de 1870–1871: Un legs de la guerre nationale?" *Guerres mondiales et conflits contemporains* 167 (1992): 23–40.

———. *Les monuments aux morts: Patrimoine et mémoire de la Grande Guerre*. Paris: Errance, 1988.

Beetham, Sarah. "From Spray Cans to Minivans: Contesting the Legacy of Confederate Soldier Monuments in the Era of 'Black Lives Matter.'" *Public Art Dialogue* 6, no. 1 (2016): 9–33.

Beetham, Sarah Denver. "Sculpting the Citizen Soldier: Reproduction and National Memory, 1865–1917." PhD diss., University of Delaware, 2014.

Bellion, Wendy. "Performing Iconoclasm." Lecture, Courtauld Institute, June 5, 2015. www.youtube.com/watch?v=IouFJQxRQMo.

Bernd, Candice. "Texas Town Retains Confederate Monument despite Civil Rights Activist's 16 Years of Protest." *Truthout*, August 9, 2015, www.truthout.org.

Blair, William. *Cities of the Dead: Contesting the Memory of the Civil War in the South, 1865–1914*. Chapel Hill: University of North Carolina Press, 2004.

Blanchard, Mary W. "The Soldier and the Aesthete: Homosexuality and Popular Culture in Gilded Age America." *Journal of American Studies* 30 (April 1996): 25–46.

Blatt, Martin H., Thomas J. Brown, and Donald Yacovone, eds. *Hope and Glory: Essays on the Legacy of the 54th Massachusetts Regiment*. Amherst: University of Massachusetts Press, 2001.

Blatt, Martin H. "*Glory*: Hollywood History, Popular Culture, and the Fifty-fourth Massachusetts Regiment." In Blatt, Brown, and Yacovone, *Hope and Glory*, 215–35.

Blight, David W. *Race and Reunion: The Civil War in American Memory*. Cambridge, MA: Harvard University Press, 2001.

Blum, John Morton. *The Republican Roosevelt*. 2nd ed. Cambridge, MA: Harvard University Press, 1977.

Bode, Carl. *The American Lyceum: Town Meeting of the Mind*. New York: Oxford University Press, 1956.

Bodnar, John. *Remaking America: Public Memory, Commemoration, and Patriotism in the Twentieth Century*. Princeton, NJ: Princeton University Press, 1992.

Bogart, Michele H. *Public Sculpture and the Civic Ideal in New York City, 1890–1930*. Chicago: University of Chicago Press, 1989.

Bohan, Ruth L. "The Farragut Monument: A Decade of Art and Politics, 1871–1881." *Records of the Columbia Historical Society, Washington, D.C.* 49 (1973–74): 209–43.

Boime, Albert. *The Unveiling of the National Icons: A Plea for Patriotic Iconoclasm in a Nationalist Era*. Cambridge: Cambridge University Press, 1997.

Bonner, Robert E. *Colors and Blood: Flag Passions of the Confederate South*. Princeton, NJ: Princeton University Press, 2002.

Bostridge, Mark. *Florence Nightingale: The Making of an Icon.* New York: Farrar, Straus and Giroux, 2008.

Breisch, Kenneth A. *Henry Hobson Richardson and the Small Public Library in America: A Typology.* Cambridge, MA: MIT Press, 1997.

Brilliant, Richard. *Gesture and Rank in Roman Art: The Use of Gestures to Denote Status in Roman Sculpture and Coinage.* Memoirs of the Connecticut Academy of Arts and Sciences, vol. 14. New Haven: Connecticut Academy of Arts and Sciences, 1963.

Britton, Rick. "Monumental Questions: Local Statues Are a Lesson in History and a Source of Controversy." *c-ville.* www.c-ville.com. June 17, 2015.

Brown, Mary Ann. "Ohio's Veterans' Memorial Halls." *Past: Pioneer America Society Transactions* 14 (1991): 47–54.

Brown, Thomas J. *Civil War Canon: Sites of Confederate Memory in South Carolina.* Chapel Hill: University of North Carolina Press, 2015.

———. *Dorothea Dix, New England Reformer.* Cambridge, MA: Harvard University Press, 1998.

———. "The Peaceable War Memorial." In *The Civil War in Art and Memory*, edited by Kirk Savage, 245–65. Washington, D.C.: National Gallery of Art, 2016.

———. "Reconstructing Boston: Civic Monuments of the Civil War." In Blatt, Brown, and Yacovone, *Hope and Glory*, 130–55.

Budreau, Lisa M. *Bodies of War: World War I and the Politics of Commemoration in America, 1919–1933.* New York: New York University Press, 2010.

Bullard, F. Lauriston. *Lincoln in Marble and Bronze.* New Brunswick, NJ: Rutgers University Press, 1956.

Bryan, John M. *Creating the South Carolina State House.* Columbia: University of South Carolina Press, 1999.

Burns, Sarah. *Inventing the Modern Artist: Art and Culture in Gilded Age America.* New Haven, CT: Yale University Press, 1996.

Bzdak, Meredith Arms, and Douglas Petersen. *Public Sculpture in New Jersey: Monuments to Collective Identity.* New Brunswick, NJ: Rutgers University Press, 1999.

Carmichael, Peter S. *The War for the Common Soldier: How Men Thought, Fought, and Survived in Civil War Armies.* Chapel Hill: University of North Carolina Press, 2018.

Carney, Court. "The Contested Image of Nathan Bedford Forrest." *Journal of Southern History* 67 (August 2001): 601–30.

Casey, John A., Jr. *New Men: Reconstructing the Image of the Veteran in Late-Nineteenth-Century American Literature and Culture.* New York: Fordham University Press, 2015.

Chambers, Merritt M. *Every Man a Brick! The Status of Military Training in American Universities.* Bloomington, IL: Public School Publishing, 1927.

Chambers, Thomas A. *Memories of War: Visiting Battlegrounds and Bonefields in the Early American Republic.* Ithaca, NY: Cornell University Press, 2012.

Cheney, Ednah Dow. *Life of Christian Daniel Rauch of Berlin, Germany.* Boston: Lee and Shepard, 1893.

Choubard, Alain. *L'histoire des 500 plus beaux monuments aux morts de France.* Paris: Christine Bonneton, 2014.

Clark, Christopher. "The Wars of Liberation in Prussian Memory: Reflections on the Memorialization of War in Early Nineteenth-Century Germany." *Journal of Modern History* 68 (September 1996): 557–61.

Clark, J. P. *Preparing for War: The Emergence of the Modern U.S. Army, 1815–1917*. Cambridge, MA: Harvard University Press, 2017.

Clark, Kenneth. *The Nude: A Study in Ideal Form*. Princeton, NJ: Princeton University Press, 1956.

Coffman, Edward M. *The Old Army: A Portrait of the American Army in Peacetime, 1784–1898*. New York: Oxford University Press, 1986.

———. *The War to End All Wars: The American Military Experience in World War I*. New York: Oxford University Press, 1968.

Cohen, Michael David. *Reconstructing the Campus: Higher Education and the American Civil War*. Charlottesville: University of Virginia Press, 2012.

Cook, Chris. "An Unwanted Monument: The Controversial Liberty Place Obelisk." Blog post. *Lagniappe and Other Essentials*. November 17, 2012. Lagniappenola.wordpress.com.

Cook, Robert. "The Quarrel Forgotten? Toward a Clearer Understanding of Sectional Reconciliation." *Journal of the Civil War Era* 6 (September 2016): 413–36.

Cooper, Jerry. *The Rise of the National Guard: The Evolution of the American Militia, 1865–1920*. Lincoln: University of Nebraska Press, 1997.

Coski, John M. *The Confederate Battle Flag: America's Most Embattled Emblem*. Cambridge, MA: Harvard University Press, 2005.

Cox, Karen L. *Dixie's Daughters: The United Daughters of the Confederacy and the Preservation of Confederate Culture*. Gainesville: University Press of Florida, 2003.

Craven, Wayne. *The Sculptures at Gettysburg*. Conshohocken, PA: Eastern Acorn, 1982.

Crawford, John Stephens. "The Classical Orator in Nineteenth Century American Sculpture." *American Art Journal* 6 (November 1974): 56–72.

Cray, Robert E., Jr. "Commemorating the Prison Ship Dead: Revolutionary Memory and the Politics of Sepulture in the Early Republic, 1776–1808." *William & Mary Quarterly* 56 (1999): 565–90.

Criblez, Adam. *Parading Patriotism: Independence Day Celebrations in the Urban Midwest, 1826–1876*. DeKalb: Northern Illinois University Press, 2015.

Croce, Paul Jerome. "Calming the Screaming Eagle: William James and His Circle Fight Their Civil War Battles." *New England Quarterly* 76 (March 2003): 5–37.

Cunliffe, Marcus. *Soldiers and Civilians: The Martial Spirit in America*. Boston: Little, Brown, 1968.

Dabakis, Melissa. *A Sisterhood of Sculptors: American Artists in Nineteenth-Century Rome*. University Park: Pennsylvania State University Press, 2014.

Dearing, Mary. *Veterans in Politics: The Story of the G.A.R.* Baton Rouge: Louisiana State University Press, 1952.

Dennis, Matthew. *Red, White and Blue Letter Days: An American Calendar*. Ithaca, NY: Cornell University Press, 2002.

DePastino, Todd. *Citizen Hobo: How a Century of Homelessness Shaped America*. Chicago: University of Chicago Press, 2003.

Dickon, Chris. *The Foreign Burial of American War Dead: A History*. Jefferson, NC: McFarland, 2011.

Dimmick, Lauretta. "An Altar Erected to Virtue Itself: Thomas Crawford and His Virginia Washington Monument." *American Art Journal* 23, no. 2 (1991): 4–73.

Doss, Erika. *Memorial Mania: Public Feeling in America*. Chicago: University of Chicago Press, 2010.

―――. "The Process Frame: Vandalism, Removal, Re-siting, Destruction." In
  A Companion to Public Art, edited by Cher Krause Knight and Harriet F. Senie, 403–21.
  Hoboken, NJ: Wiley & Sons, 2016.

Dowling, Linda. *Charles Eliot Norton: The Art of Reform in Nineteenth-Century America.*
  Hanover, NH: University Press of New England, 2007.

Driggs, Sarah Shields, Richard Guy Wilson, and Robert P. Winthrop. *Richmond's
  Monument Avenue.* Chapel Hill: University of North Carolina Press, 2001.

Dryfhout, John H. *The Work of Augustus Saint-Gaudens.* Hanover, NH: University Press
  of New England, 1982.

Easton, Lloyd D. *Hegel's First American Followers: The Ohio Hegelians: John B. Stallo,
  Peter Kaufmann, Moncure Conway, and August Willich, with Key Writings.* Athens: Ohio
  University Press, 1966.

Edgemon, Erin. "Nathan Bedford Forrest Bust Back in Alabama." *al.com*, May 26, 2015.
  https://www.al.com/news/2015/05/nathan_bedford_forrest_bust_ba.html.,

Ellis, Alden C., Jr. *The Massachusetts Andrew Sharpshooters: A Civil War History and Roster.*
  Jefferson, NC: McFarland, 2012.

Emberton, Carole. "'Only Murder Makes Men': Reconsidering the Black Military
  Experience." *Journal of the Civil War Era* 2 (September 2012): 369–93.

Equal Justice Initiative. *Lynching in America: Confronting the Legacy of Racial Terror.* 3rd ed.
  2017. lynchinginamerica.eji.org/report.

Evert, Marilyn, and Vernon Gay. *Discovering Pittsburgh's Sculpture.* Pittsburgh: University
  of Pittsburgh Press, 1983.

Facknitz, Mark. "Getting It Right by Getting It Wrong: Maya Lin's Misreading of Sir
  Edwin Lutyens' Thiepval Memorial." *Crossings* 7 (2004–5): 47–69.

Fahs, Alice. "The Feminized Civil War: Gender, Northern Popular Literature, and the
  Memory of the War, 1861–1900." *Journal of American History* 85 (March 1999): 1461–94.

―――. *The Imagined Civil War: Popular Literature of the North and South, 1861–1865.*
  Chapel Hill: University of North Carolina Press, 2001.

Fairmount Park Art Association. *Sculpture of a City: Philadelphia's Treasures in Bronze and
  Stone.* New York: Walker, 1974.

Faust, Drew Gilpin. *This Republic of Suffering: Death and the American Civil War.* New
  York: Alfred A. Knopf, 2008.

Fellman, Michael. *Citizen Sherman: A Life of William Tecumseh Sherman.* New York:
  Random House, 1995.

Finseth, Ian. *The Civil War Dead and American Modernity.* New York: Oxford University
  Press, 2018.

Fogelson, Robert M. *America's Armories: Architecture, Society, and Public Order.*
  Cambridge, MA: Harvard University Press, 1989.

Follini, Tamara L. "Speaking Monuments: Henry James, Walt Whitman, and the Civil War
  Statues of Augustus Saint-Gaudens." *Journal of American Studies* 48 (February 2014):
  25–49.

Folpe, Emily Kies. *It Happened on Washington Square.* Baltimore: Johns Hopkins
  University Press, 2002.

Foos, Paul. *A Short, Offhand, Killing Affair: Soldiers and Social Conflict during the Mexican-
  American War.* Chapel Hill: University of North Carolina Press, 2002.

Foote, Lorien. *The Gentlemen and the Roughs: Violence, Honor, and Manhood in the Union
  Army.* New York: New York University Press, 2010.

———. "Soldiers." In *A Companion to the U.S. Civil War*, edited by Aaron Sheehan-Dean, 2 vols., 1:114–31. New York: Wiley-Blackwell, 2014.

Foster, Gaines M. *Ghosts of the Confederacy: Defeat, the Lost Cause, and the Emergence of the New South, 1865 to 1913*. New York: Oxford University Press, 1987.

———. "What's Not in a Name: The Naming of the American Civil War." *Journal of the Civil War Era* 8 (September 2018): 416–54.

Fowler, Miriam Rogers. "Giuseppe Moretti: Master Sculptor." *American Art Review* 14 (November–December 2002): 142–49, 175.

Frassanito, William A. *Gettysburg: A Journey in Time*. New York: Charles Scribner's Sons, 1975.

Freeman, David B. *Carved in Stone: The History of Stone Mountain*. Macon, GA: Mercer University Press, 1997.

Frick, Ali. "The Mingled Dust of Both Armies: Yale's Compromised Civil War Memorial." Senior essay, Yale University, 2007.

Fussell, Paul. *The Great War and Modern Memory*. New York: Oxford University Press, 1975.

Gallman, J. Matthew. *Defining Duty in the Civil War: Personal Choice, Popular Culture, and the Union Home Front*. Chapel Hill: University of North Carolina Press, 2015.

Gangewere, Robert J. *Palace of Culture: Andrew Carnegie's Museums and Library in Pittsburgh*. Pittsburgh: University of Pittsburgh Press, 2011.

Giesberg, Judith. *Sex and the Civil War: Soldiers, Pornography, and the Making of American Morality*. Chapel Hill: University of North Carolina Press, 2017.

Giguere, Joy M. "'The Americanized Sphinx': Civil War Commemoration, Jacob Bigelow, and the Sphinx at Mount Auburn Cemetery." *Journal of the Civil War Era* 3 (March 2013): 62–84.

———. *Characteristically American: Memorial Architecture, National Identity, and the Egyptian Revival*. Knoxville: University of Tennessee Press, 2014.

———. "'Young and Littlefield's Folly': Fundraising, Confederate Memorialization, and the Construction of the Jefferson Davis Monument in Fairview, Kentucky, 1907–1924." *Register of the Kentucky Historical Society* 115 (Winter 2017): 39–73.

Glatthaar, Joseph. *General Lee's Army: From Victory to Collapse*. New York: Free Press, 2008.

Goebel, Stefan. *The Great War and Medieval Memory: War, Remembrance and Medievalism in Britain and Germany, 1914–1940*. Cambridge: Cambridge University Press, 2006.

Gold, Susanna W. "Imaging Memory: Re-presentations of the Civil War at the 1876 Centennial Exhibition." PhD diss., University of Pennsylvania, 2004.

Goss, Thomas J. *The War within the Union High Command: Politics and Generalship during the Civil War*. Lawrence: University Press of Kansas, 2003.

Gough, Terrence James. "The Battle of Washington: Soldiers and Businessmen in World War I." PhD diss., University of Virginia, 1997.

Grant, Susan-Mary. "Patriot Graves: American National Identity and the Civil War Dead." *American Nineteenth Century History* 5 (Fall 2004): 74–100.

Greenberg, Amy S. *Manifest Manhood and the Antebellum American Empire*. New York: Cambridge University Press, 2005.

Grimaldi, Anthony Eugene. "The Indiana Soldiers' and Sailors' Monument and Its Dedication: A Study of a Nineteenth Century American Monument and Its Allied Arts of Pageantry." PhD diss., Ohio University, 1982.

Grodzins, Dean. *American Heretic: Theodore Parker and Transcendentalism.* Chapel Hill: University of North Carolina Press, 2002.

Guenter, Scot M. *The American Flag, 1777–1924: Cultural Shifts from Creation to Codification.* Rutherford, NJ: Fairleigh Dickinson University Press, 1990.

Hack, Brian Edward. "American Acropolis: George Grey Barnard's *Monument to Democracy,* 1918–1938." PhD diss., City University of New York, 2007.

Hacker, J. David. "A Census-Based Count of the Civil War Dead." *Civil War History* 57 (December 2011): 307–48.

Hagans, William E. "Saint-Gaudens, Zorn, and the Goddesslike Miss Anderson." *American Art* 16 (Summer 2002): 67–89.

Hagemann, Karen. *Revisiting Prussia's Wars against Napoleon: History, Culture and Memory.* Trans. Pamel Selwyn. New York: Cambridge University Press, 2015.

Hagopian, Patrick. *The Vietnam War in American Memory: Veterans, Memorials, and the Politics of Healing.* Amherst: University of Massachusetts Press, 2009.

Hale, Grace Elizabeth. "Granite Stopped Time: The Stone Mountain Memorial and the Representation of White Southern Identity." *Georgia Historical Quarterly* 82 (Spring 1998): 22–44.

Halttunen, Karen. *Confidence Men and Painted Women: A Study of Middle-Class Culture in America, 1830–1870.* New Haven, CT: Yale University Press, 1982.

Hargrove, June. "The Public Monument." In *The Romantics to Rodin,* edited by Peter Fusco and H. W. Janson, 21–35. Los Angeles: Los Angeles County Museum of Art, 1980.

———. "*Qui vive? France!* Monuments from the Defense to the Revanche." In *Nationalism and French Visual Culture, 1870–1914,* edited by June Hargrove and Neil McWilliam, 55–81. Washington, D.C.: National Gallery of Art, 2005.

Harris, Emily J. "Sons and Soldiers: Deerfield, Massachusetts and the Civil War." *Civil War History* 30 (June 1984): 157–71.

Harrison, Carol E. "Edouard Laboulaye, Liberal and Romantic Catholic." *French History and Civilization* 6 (2015): 149–58.

Harrison, Kathy Georg, comp. *The Location of the Monuments, Markers, and Tablets on Gettysburg Battlefield.* Rev. ed. Gettysburg, PA: Thomas, 2012.

Haskell, Francis, and Nicholas Penny. *Taste and the Antique.* New Haven, CT: Yale University Press, 1981.

Hawes, Kirk. *A Condensed History of Dearborn Park.* Chicago: Chicago Public Library, 1891.

Hawkes, Pamela W. "Our Lady of Victories." *Maine Historical Quarterly* 20 (Fall 1980): 79–99.

Heath, Richard. *The Roxbury Soldiers Monument at Forest Hills Cemetery.* Jamaica Plain, MA: Forest Hills Cemetery, 1993.

Hébel, François, et al. *36,000 cicatrices: Les monuments aux morts de la Grande Guerre.* Paris: Éditions du Patrimoine, Centre des Monuments Nationaux, 2016.

Heuston, Sean. "The Most Famous Thing Robert E. Lee Never Said: Duty, Forgery, and Cultural Amnesia." *Journal of American Studies* 48, no. 4 (2014): 1069–82.

Hicks, John D. "The Organization of the Volunteer Army in 1861 with Special Reference to Minnesota." *Minnesota History Bulletin* 2 (Feb. 1918): 324–68.

Hill, Nancy. "The Lincoln Landscape: The Transformation of Lincoln's Tomb." *Journal of the Abraham Lincoln Association* 27 (Winter 2006): 39–56.

Hobbs, Clarence W. *Lynn and Its Surroundings.* Lynn: Lewis and Winship, 1886.

Hoganson, Kristin L. *Fighting for American Manhood: How Gender Politics Provoked the*

Spanish-American and Philippine-American Wars. New Haven, CT: Yale University Press, 1998.

Hosking, William J. "Lincoln's Tomb: Designs Submitted and Final Selections." *Journal of the Illinois State Historical Society* 50 (Spring 1957): 51–61.

Hsieh, Wayne Wei-siang. "Total War and the American Civil War Reconsidered: The End of an Outdated 'Master Narrative.'" *Journal of the Civil War Era* 1 (September 2011): 394–408.

———. *West Pointers and the Civil War: The Old Army in War and Peace*. Chapel Hill: University of North Carolina Press, 2009.

Hughes, Nathaniel Cheairs, Jr., and Thomas Clayton Ware. *Theodore O'Hara: Poet Soldier of the South*. Knoxville: University of Tennessee Press, 1998.

Hutt, Michael. "Thoughts and Things: Sculpture and the Victorian Nude." In *Exposed: The Victorian Nude*, edited by Alison Smith, 37–49. New York: Watson-Guptill, 2002.

Inglis, K. S. "Entombing Unknown Soldiers: From London and Paris to Baghdad." *History and Memory* 5, no. 2 (1993): 7–31.

———. "The Homecoming: The War Memorial Movement in Cambridge, England." *Journal of Contemporary History* 27 (October 1992): 583–605.

———. "Men, Women, and War Memorials: ANZAC Australia." *Daedalus* 116, no. 4 (1987): 35–59.

———. *Sacred Places: War Memorials in the Australian Landscape*. Melbourne: Miegunyah Press of Melbourne University Press, 1998.

———. "War Memorials: Ten Questions for Historians" and "World War One Memorials in Australia." *Guerres mondiales et conflits contemporains* 167 (1992): 5–21, 51–58.

Jacob, Kathryn Allamong. *Testament to Union: Civil War Monuments in Washington, D.C.* Baltimore: Johns Hopkins University Press, 1998.

Janney, Caroline E. *Burying the Dead but Not the Past: Ladies' Memorial Associations and the Lost Cause*. Chapel Hill: University of North Carolina Press, 2008.

———. *Remembering the Civil War: Reunion and the Limits of Reconciliation*. Chapel Hill: University of North Carolina Press, 2013.

———. "War over a Shrine of Peace: The Appomattox Peace Monument and Retreat from Reconciliation." *Journal of Southern History* 77 (February 2011): 91–120.

Janson, H. W. "The Equestrian Monument from Cangrande della Scala to Peter the Great." In *Sixteen Studies*, 157–88. New York: Harry N. Abrams, 1974.

———. *The Rise and Fall of the Public Monument*. New Orleans: Tulane University, 1976.

Jordan, Brian Matthew. *Marching Home: Union Veterans and Their Unending Civil War*. New York: Liveright, 2014.

Kahn, David M. "The Grant Monument." *Journal of the Society of Architectural Historians* 41 (October 1982): 212–31.

Kammen, Michael. *A Season of Youth: The American Revolution and the Historical Imagination*. New York: Knopf, 1978.

Karamanski, Theodore J. "Memory's Landscape." *Chicago History* 26 (Summer 1997): 54–72.

Kasson, Joy S. *Marble Queens and Captives: Women in Nineteenth-Century American Sculpture*. New Haven, CT: Yale University Press, 1990.

Kazin, Michael. *War against War: The American Fight for Peace, 1914–1918*. New York: Simon and Schuster, 2017.

Keller, Morton. *Affairs of State: Public Life in Late Nineteenth Century America.* Cambridge, MA: Harvard University Press, 1977.

Kelly, Patrick J. *Creating a National Home: Building the Veterans' Welfare State, 1860–1900.* Cambridge, MA: Harvard University Press, 1997.

Kelman, Ari. *A Misplaced Massacre: Struggling over the Memory of Sand Creek.* Cambridge, MA: Harvard University Press, 2013.

Kennedy, David M. *Over Here: The First World War and American Society.* New York: Oxford University Press, 1980.

Khan, Yasmin Sabina. *Enlightening the World: The Creation of the Statue of Liberty.* Ithaca, NY: Cornell University Press, 2010.

King, Alex. *Memorials of the Great War in Britain: The Symbolism and Politics of Remembrance.* Oxford, UK: Berg, 1998.

Kingman, Bradford. *History of Brockton, Plymouth County, Massachusetts, 1656–1894.* Syracuse, NY: D. Mason, 1895.

Kinnee, Lauren. "The Nike of Samothrace: The Next Generation Attalid Victory Monument." *Hey Zeus! The Yale College Journal of Antiquities* 4 (Winter 2002): 38–62.

Kinsel, Amy. "'From These Honored Dead': Gettysburg in American Culture, 1863–1938." PhD diss., Cornell University, 1992.

Kirby, Rachel C. "UNC's Ambiguous Memorial: A Living List of Names." *Names in Brick and Stone: Histories from UNC's Built Landscape.* 2017. unchistory.web.unc.edu /building-narratives/memorial-hall/.

Knox, Joseph T., "Le Général Lee: A Design for the Future." *Virginia Cavalcade* 38 (Autumn 1988): 76–85.

Kowsky, Francis R. *The Best Planned City in the World: Olmsted, Vaux, and the Buffalo Park System.* Amherst: University of Massachusetts Press, 2013.

Kowsky, Francis R. "The Central Park Gateways: Harbingers of French Urbanism Confront the American Landscape Tradition." In *The Architecture of Richard Morris Hunt,* edited by Susan R. Stein, 79–89. Chicago: University of Chicago Press, 1986.

Kresser, Katie Mullis. "Power and Glory: Brahmin Identity and the Shaw Memorial." *American Art* 20 (Fall 2006): 32–57.

Kytle, Ethan J., and Blain Roberts. *Denmark Vesey's Garden: Slavery and Memory in the Cradle of the Confederacy.* New York: New Press, 2018.

Laqueur, Thomas W. *The Work of the Dead: A Cultural History of Mortal Remains.* Princeton, NJ: Princeton University Press, 2015.

Lears, Jackson. *Rebirth of a Nation: The Making of Modern America, 1877–1920.* New York: HarperCollins, 2009.

Lears, T. J. Jackson. *No Place of Grace: Antimodernism and the Transformation of American Culture, 1880–1920.* New York: Pantheon, 1981.

Lemmey, Karen Yvonne. "Henry Kirke Brown and the Development of American Public Sculpture in New York City, 1846–1876." PhD diss., City University of New York, 2005.

Lerner, Adam J. "The Capital City and Mount Rushmore: The Place of Public Monuments in the Political Culture of the Progressive Era and the 1920s." PhD diss., Johns Hopkins University, 2001.

Levin, Kevin M. *Remembering the Battle of the Crater: War as Murder.* Lexington: University Press of Kentucky, 2012.

———. "Trayvon Martin and Civil War Memory." *Civil War Memory* (blog), March 30, 2012. cwmemory.com.

Levine, Neil. "The Romantic Idea of Architectural Legibility: Henri Labrouste and the Neo-Grec." In *The Architecture of the École des Beaux-Arts*, edited by Arthur Drexler, 325–416. New York: Museum of Modern Art, 1977.

Lewis, Alonzo, and James R. Newhall. *History of Lynn*. 2 vols. Lynn, MA: Nichols, 1865–97.

Lin, Maya, et al. *Grounds for Remembering: Monuments, Memorials, Texts*. Berkeley, CA: Doreen B. Townsend Center for the Humanities, 1995.

Linden-Ward, Blanche. *Silent City on a Hill: Landscapes of Memory and Boston's Mount Auburn Cemetery*. Columbus: Ohio State University Press, 1989.

Litwicki, Ellen M. *America's Public Holidays, 1865–1920*. Washington, DC: Smithsonian Institution Press, 2002.

Logan, Albert J. "History of the Eighteenth Regiment, Duquesne Greys, Period 1878 to 1917." *Western Pennsylvania History* 8 (April 1925): 90–97.

Longstreth, Richard, ed. *The Mall in Washington, 1791–1991*. 2nd ed. Washington, DC: National Gallery of Art, 2002.

Lowe, William C. "'A Grand and Patriotic Pilgrimage': The Iowa Civil War Monuments Dedication Tour of 1906." *Annals of Iowa* 69 (Winter 2010): 1–50.

MacLean, Nancy. *Behind the Mask of Chivalry: The Making of the Second Ku Klux Klan*. New York: Oxford University Press, 1994.

Mahon, John K. *History of the Militia and the National Guard*. New York: Macmillan, 1983.

Manning, Chandra. *What This Cruel War Was Over: Soldiers, Slavery, and the Civil War*. New York: Knopf, 2007.

Marchand, C. Roland. *The American Peace Movement and Social Reform, 1898–1918*. Princeton, NJ: Princeton University Press, 1972.

Marks, Arthur S. "The Statue of King George III in New York and the Iconology of Regicide." *American Art Journal* 13 (Summer 1981): 61–82.

Marling, Karal Ann, and John Wetenhall. *Iwo Jima: Monuments, Memories, and the American Hero*. Cambridge, MA: Harvard University Press, 1991.

Marrinan, Michael. *Romantic Paris: Histories of a Cultural Landscape*. Palo Alto, CA: Stanford University Press, 2009.

Marshall, Anne E. *Creating a Confederate Kentucky: The Lost Cause and Civil War Memory in a Border State*. Chapel Hill: University of North Carolina Press, 2010.

McClintock, Megan. "Binding Up the Nation's Wounds: Nationalism, Civil War Pensions, and American Families, 1861–1890." PhD diss., Rutgers University, 1994.

McConnell, Stuart. *Glorious Contentment: The Grand Army of the Republic, 1865–1900*. Chapel Hill: University of North Carolina Press, 1992.

McDaniel, Joyce L. "Caspar Buberl: The Pension Building Civil War Frieze and Other Washington, D.C. Sculpture." *Records of the Columbia Historical Society, Washington, D.C.*, 50 (1980): 309–44.

McDowell, Peggy. "Martin Milmore's Soldiers' and Sailors' Monument on the Boston Common: Formulating Conventionalism in Design and Symbolism." *Journal of American Culture* 11 (Spring 1988): 63–85.

McElya, Micki. *Clinging to Mammy: The Faithful Slave in Twentieth-Century America*. Cambridge, MA: Harvard University Press, 2007.

———. *The Politics of Mourning: Death and Honor in Arlington National Cemetery*. Cambridge, MA: Harvard University Press, 2016.

McGraw, Robert F. "Minutemen of '61: The Pre–Civil War Massachusetts Militia." *Civil War History* 15 (June 1969): 101–15.

McInnis, Maurie D. "Revisiting Cincinnatus: Houdon's *George Washington*." In *Shaping the Body Politic: Art and Political Formation in Early America*, edited by Maurie D. McInnis and Louis P. Nelson, 128–61. Charlottesville: University of Virginia Press, 2011.

McPherson, James M. *For Cause and Comrades: Why Men Fought in the Civil War*. New York: Oxford University Press, 1997.

Mehrota, Ajay K. *Making the Modern American Fiscal State: Law, Politics, and the Rise of Progressive Taxation, 1877–1929*. Cambridge: Cambridge University Press, 2013.

Meixner, Laura L. *French Realist Painting and the Critique of American Society, 1865–1900*. Cambridge: Cambridge University Press, 1995.

Mills, Cynthia. *Beyond Grief: Sculpture and Wonder in the Gilded Age Cemetery*. Washington, DC: Smithsonian Institution Scholarly Press, 2015.

Milne, Gordon. *George William Curtis and the Genteel Tradition*. Bloomington: Indiana University Press, 1956.

Moffatt, Frederick C. *Errant Bronzes: George Grey Barnard's Statues of Abraham Lincoln*. Newark: University of Delaware Press, 1998.

Montagna, Dennis R. "Henry Merwin Shrady's Ulysses S. Grant Memorial in Washington, D.C.: A Study in Iconography, Content, and Patronage." PhD diss., University of Delaware, 1987.

Moriarty, Catherine. "Narrative and the Absent Body: Mechanisms of Meaning in First World War Memorials." PhD diss., Sussex University, 1995.

Mosse, George. *Fallen Soldiers: Reshaping Memory of the World Wars*. New York: Oxford University Press, 1990.

Neely, Mark E., Jr. *The Civil War and the Limits of Destruction*. Cambridge, MA: Harvard University Press, 2010.

Neely, Mark E., Jr., Harold Holzer, and Gabor S. Boritt. *The Confederate Image: Prints of the Lost Cause*. Chapel Hill: University of North Carolina Press, 1987.

Neff, John R. *Honoring the Civil War Dead: Commemoration and the Problem of Reconciliation*. Lawrence: University Press of Kansas, 2005.

Newell, Clayton R., and Charles Shrader. *Of Duty Well and Faithfully Done: A History of the Regular Army in the Civil War*. Lincoln: University of Nebraska Press, 2011.

Nichols, Christopher McKnight. "Education, Expediency, and Democratic Dilemmas in War Time: Inside the Dewey-Bourne Debate." *Journal of the Gilded Age and Progressive Era* 16 (October 2017): 438–55.

North, Michael. *The Final Sculpture: Public Monuments and Modern Poets*. Ithaca, NY: Cornell University Press, 1985.

Noun, Louise Rosenfield. "The Iowa Soldiers' and Sailors' Monument." *Palimpsest* 67 (1986): 80–93.

O'Gorman, James F. "H. H. Richardson and the Civil War Memorial." *Nineteenth Century* 23 (Fall 2003): 3–9.

O'Leary, Cecelia Elizabeth. *To Die For: The Paradox of American Patriotism*. Princeton, NJ: Princeton University Press, 1999.

Painter, Sue Ann, et al. *Architecture in Cincinnati: An Illustrated History of Designing and Building an American City*. Athens: Ohio University Press, 2006.

Paludan, Phillip Shaw. *"A People's Contest": The Union and Civil War, 1861–1865*. 2nd ed. Lawrence: University Press of Kansas, 1996. First published 1988.

Panhorst, Michael. "Devotion, Deception, and the Ladies Memorial Association, 1865–

1898: The Mystery of the Alabama Confederate Monument." *Alabama Review* 65 (July 2012): 163–204.

———. *The Memorial Art and Architecture of Vicksburg National Military Park.* Kent, OH: Kent State University Press, 2014.

Panhorst, Michael Wilson. "Lest We Forget: Monuments and Memorial Sculpture in National Military Parks on Civil War Battlefields, 1861–1917." PhD diss., University of Delaware, 1988.

Pearlman, Michael. *To Make Democracy Safe for America: Patricians and Preparedness in the Progressive Era.* Urbana: University of Illinois Press, 1984.

Peterson, Merrill D. *Lincoln in American Memory.* New York: Oxford University Press, 1994.

Pettegrew, John. *Brutes in Suits: Male Sensibility in America, 1890–1920.* Baltimore: Johns Hopkins University Press, 2007.

Pfanz, Donald C. *Where Valor Proudly Sleeps: A History of Fredericksburg National Cemetery, 1866–1933.* Carbondale: Southern Illinois University Press, 2018.

Piehler, G. Kurt. *Remembering War the American Way.* Washington, D.C.: Smithsonian Institution Press, 1995.

Pitcavage, Mark. "An Equitable Burden: The Decline of State Militias, 1783–1858." PhD diss., Ohio State University, 1995.

Pollack, Barbara. "The Civil War in Art, Then and Now." *Art News* 112 (May 2013): 70–77.

Pollitt, J. J. *Art in the Hellenistic Age.* Cambridge: Cambridge University Press, 1986.

Powell, Lawrence N. "Reinventing Tradition: Liberty Place, Historical Memory, and Silk-Stocking Vigilantism in New Orleans Politics." *Slavery and Abolition* 20, no. 1 (1999): 127–49.

Prost, Antoine. "Monuments to the Dead." In *Realms of Memory: The Construction of the French Past,* edited by Pierre Nora and Lawrence D. Kritzman, translated by Arthur Goldhammer, 3 vols., 2:307–32. New York: Columbia University Press, 1997.

Purcell, Sarah J. *Sealed with Blood: War, Sacrifice, and Memory in Revolutionary America.* Philadelphia: University of Pennsylvania Press, 2002.

Ramage, James A. *Rebel Raider: The Life of John Hunt Morgan.* Lexington: University Press of Kentucky, 1986.

Ramold, Steven J. *Baring the Iron Hand: Discipline in the Union Army.* DeKalb: Northern Illinois University Press, 2010.

Ransby, Barbara. *Making All Black Lives Matter: Reimagining Freedom in the 21st Century.* Berkeley: University of California Press, 2018.

Ransom, David F. *George Keller, Architect.* Hartford, CT: Stowe-Day Foundation, 1978.

Reardon, Carol. *With a Sword in One Hand and Jomini in the Other: The Problem of Military Thought in the Civil War North.* Chapel Hill: University of North Carolina Press, 2012.

Reps, John W. *Monumental Washington: The Planning and Development of the Capital Center.* Princeton, NJ: Princeton University Press, 1967.

Reynolds, Donald. *Masters of American Sculpture: The Figurative Tradition from the American Renaissance to the Millennium.* New York: Abbeville, 1993.

Richman, Michael. "Daniel Chester French and Henry Bacon: Public Sculpture in Collaboration, 1897–1908." *American Art Journal* (Summer 1980): 47–64.

Roe, Alfred S. *The Fifth Regiment Massachusetts Volunteer Infantry in Its Three Tours of Duty.* Boston: Fifth Regiment Veteran Association, 1911.

Roeser, Patricia. "Bunker Hill Monument in Memory and Rhetoric." PhD diss., Arizona State University, 2010.

Rogers, Millard F., Jr. *Randolph Rogers: American Sculptor in Rome*. Amherst: University of Massachusetts Press, 1971.

Rooney, Sierra. "'It's Not about One Statue': Fred Wilson's *E Pluribus Unum*." *Public Art Dialogue* 4, no. 2 (2014): 184–200.

Roper, Laura Wood Roper. *FLO: A Biography of Frederick Law Olmsted*. Baltimore: Johns Hopkins University Press, 1973.

Rosenblum, Charles Loren. "The Architecture of Henry Horbostel: Progressive and Traditional Design in the Beaux-Arts Movement." PhD diss., University of Virginia, 2009.

Rosenburg, R. B. *Living Monuments: Confederate Soldiers Homes in the New South*. Chapel Hill: University of North Carolina Press, 1993.

Ryan, Mary P. *Civic Wars: Democracy and Public Life in the American City during the Nineteenth Century*. Berkeley: University of California Press, 1997.

Samuels, Edward A., and Henry H. Kimball, eds. *Somerville, Past and Present: An Illustrated Historical Souvenir*. Boston: Samuels and Kimball, 1897.

Sandage, Scott. "A Marble House Divided: The Lincoln Memorial, the Civil Rights Movement, and the Politics of Memory, 1939–1963." *Journal of American History* 80 (June 1993): 135–67.

Savage, Kirk. *Monument Wars: Washington, D.C., the National Mall, and the Transformation of the Memorial Landscape*. Berkeley: University of California Press, 2009.

———. *Standing Soldiers, Kneeling Slaves: Race, War, and Monument in Nineteenth-Century America*. Princeton, NJ: Princeton University Press, 1997.

———. "Uncommon Soldiers: Race, Art, and the Shaw Memorial." In Blatt, Brown, and Yacovone, *Hope and Glory*, 156–67.

———. "The Unknowable Dead: The Civil War and the Origins of Modern Commemoration." In *The Civil War in Art and Memory*, edited by Kirk Savage, 81–102. Washington, D.C.: National Gallery of Art, 2016.

———. "Vinnie Ream's *Lincoln* (1871): The Sexual Politics of a Sculptor's Studio." In *American Pantheon: Sculptural and Artistic Decoration of the United States Capitol*, 160–75. Athens: Ohio University Press, 2004.

Scee, Trudy Irene. *The Mount Hope Cemetery of Bangor, Maine: The Complete History*. Charleston, SC: History Press, 2012.

Schantz, Mark S. *Awaiting the Heavenly Country: The Civil War and America's Culture of Death*. Ithaca, NY: Cornell University Press, 2008.

Schiller, Joyce K. "Winged Victory, a Battle Lost: Augustus Saint-Gaudens's Intentions for the Sherman Monument Installation." In *Perspectives on American Sculpture before 1925*, edited by Thayer Tolles, 44–63. New York: Metropolitan Museum of Art, 2003.

Schiller, Joyce Karen. "The Artistic Collaboration of Augustus Saint-Gaudens and Stanford White." PhD diss., Washington University, 1997.

Schneider, Richard H. *Taps: Notes from a Nation's Heart*. New York: William Morrow, 2002.

Schultz, Jane E. *Women at the Front: Hospital Workers in Civil War America*. Chapel Hill: University of North Carolina Press, 2004.

Schwartz, Barry. *Abraham Lincoln and the Forge of National Memory*. Chicago: University of Chicago Press, 2000.

Seelye, John. *Memory's Nation: The Place of Plymouth Rock*. Chapel Hill: University of North Carolina Press, 1998.

Seidler, Jan. M. "A Critical Reappraisal of the Career of William Wetmore Story (1819–1895), American Sculptor and Man of Letters." PhD diss., Boston University, 1985.

Seidule, James Tyrus. "'Treason Is Treason': Civil War Memory at West Point, 1861–1902." *Military History Quarterly* 76 (April 2012): 427–52.

Shaff, Howard, and Audrey Karl Shaff. *Six Wars at a Time*. Sioux Falls, SD: Center for Western Studies, Augustana College, 1985.

Shanken, Andrew M. "Planned Memory: Living Memorials in the United States during World War II." *Art Bulletin* 84 (March 2002): 130–47.

Sharp, Lewis I. *John Quincy Adams Ward: Dean of American Sculpture*. Newark: University of Delaware Press, 1985.

Sherman, Daniel J. "Bodies and Names: The Emergence of Commemoration in Interwar France." *American Historical Review* 103 (April 1998): 443–67.

———. *The Construction of Memory in Interwar France*. Chicago: University of Chicago Press, 1999.

Silber, Nina. *Daughters of the Union: Northern Women Fight the Civil War*. Cambridge, MA: Harvard University Press, 2005.

———. *Gender and the Sectional Conflict*. Chapel Hill: University of North Carolina Press, 2008.

———. "Reunion and Reconciliation, Reviewed and Reconsidered." *Journal of American History* 103 (June 2016): 59–83.

———. *The Romance of Reunion: Northerners and the South, 1865–1900*. Chapel Hill: University of North Carolina Press, 1993.

Simpson, Pamela H. "The Sculpture of Charles Grafly." PhD diss., University of Delaware, 1974.

Simpson, Pamela H., and Donald E. Knaub, eds. *The Sculptor's Clay: Charles Grafly, 1862–1929*. Wichita, KS: Edwin A. Ulrich Museum of Art, Wichita State University, 1996.

Smart, Mary. *A Flight with Fame: The Life and Art of Frederick MacMonnies*. Madison, CT: Sound View, 1996.

Smith, Elise L. "Belle Kinney and the Confederate Women's Monument." *Southern Quarterly* 32 (Summer 1994): 7–31.

Smith, Samuel Francis. *History of Newton, Massachusetts*. Boston: American Logotype, 1880.

Smith, Timothy B. *The Golden Age of Battlefield Preservation: The Decade of the 1890s and the Establishment of America's Five First Military Parks*. Knoxville: University of Tennessee Press, 2008.

Stokes-Casey, Jody. "Richard Lou's *Recovering Memphis*: Conceptual Iconoclasm of the Nathan Bedford Forrest Monument." *Tennessee Historical Quarterly* 75 (Winter 2016): 322–47.

Thomas, Christopher A. *The Lincoln Memorial and American Life*. Princeton, NJ: Princeton University Press, 2002.

Thomas, Christopher Alexander. "The Lincoln Memorial and Its Architect, Henry Bacon (1866–1924)." PhD diss., Yale University, 1990.

Todd, Jan. "Bernarr McFadden: Reformer of the Feminine Form." *Journal of Sport History* 14 (Spring 1987): 61–75.

Tomes, Nancy. *The Gospel of Germs: Men, Women, and the Microbe in American Life.* Cambridge, MA: Harvard University Press, 1998.

Townsend, Kim. *Manhood at Harvard: William James and Others.* New York: W. W. Norton, 1996.

Trail, Susan W. "Remembering Antietam: Commemoration and Preservation of a Civil War Battlefield." PhD diss., University of Maryland, 2005.

Travers, Len. *Celebrating the Fourth: Independence Day and the Rites of Nationalism in the Early Republic.* Amherst: University of Massachusetts Press, 1997.

Trenticosta, Cecelia, and William C. Collins. "Death and Dixie: How the Courthouse Confederate Flag Influences Capital Cases in Louisiana." *Harvard Journal on Racial and Ethnic Justice* 27 (Spring 2011): 125–64.

Trout, Steven. *On the Battlefield of Memory: The First World War and American Remembrance, 1919–1941.* Tuscaloosa, University of Alabama Press, 2010.

Trowbridge, John M. *America's Oldest Civil War Monument: August Bloedner and the 32nd "First German" Indiana Volunteer Infantry Regiment Monument.* N.p., n.s., 2002.

Tyndall, John W., and O. E. Lesh, eds. *Standard History of Adams and Wells Counties, Indiana.* 2 vols. Rpt. Evansville, IN: Unigraphic, 1975.

Underwood, Thomas A. *Allen Tate, Orphan of the South.* Princeton, NJ: Princeton University Press, 2000.

Upton, Dell. *What Can and Can't Be Said: Race, Uplift, and Monument Building in the Contemporary South.* New Haven, CT: Yale University Press, 2015.

Varg, Paul A. *Edward Everett: The Intellectual in the Turmoil of Politics.* Selinsgrove, PA: Susquehanna University Press, 1992.

Viano, Francesca Lidia. *Sentinel: The Unlikely Origins of the Statue of Liberty.* Cambridge, MA: Harvard University Press, 2018.

Waldstreicher, David. *In the Midst of Perpetual Fetes: The Making of American Nationalism, 1776–1820.* Chapel Hill: University of North Carolina Press, 1997.

Wall, Joseph Frazier. *Andrew Carnegie.* 2nd ed. Pittsburgh: University of Pittsburgh Press, 1989.

Walther, Eric H. *William Lowndes Yancey and the Coming of the Civil War.* Chapel Hill: University of North Carolina Press, 2006.

Walton, Jill M. "Northampton Local Monuments: Testaments to an Enduring Historical Legacy." *Historical Journal of Massachusetts* 33 (Winter 2005): 57–82.

Warner, Marina. *Monuments and Maidens: The Allegory of the Female Form.* New York: Atheneum, 1985.

Waugh, Joan C. *U. S. Grant: American Hero, American Myth.* Chapel Hill: University of North Carolina Press, 2009.

Weeks, Jim. *Gettysburg: Memory, Market, and an American Shrine.* Princeton, NJ: Princeton University Press, 2003.

Weitz, Mark A. *More Damning than Slaughter: Desertion in the Confederate Army.* Lincoln: University of Nebraska Press, 2005.

Weller, Allen Stuart. *Lorado Taft: The Chicago Years.* Edited by Robert G. La France and Henry Adams with Stephen P. Thomas. Urbana: University of Illinois Press, 2014.

Wheeler, Frank. "'Our Confederate Dead': The Story behind Savannah's Confederate Monument." *Georgia Historical Quarterly* 82 (Summer 1998): 382–97.

Wheeler, Kenneth H. "Local Autonomy and Civil War Draft Resistance: Holmes County, Ohio." *Civil War History* 45 (June 1999): 147–59.

"Where's Waldo?" *Houghton Library Blog,* November 22, 2013. blogs.law.harvard.edu /houghton/2013/11/22/wheres-waldo/.

White, Richard. *Railroaded: The Transcontinentals and the Making of Modern America.* New York: W. W. Norton, 2011.

———. *The Republic for Which It Stands: The United States during Reconstruction and the Gilded Age, 1865–1896.* New York: Oxford University Press, 2017.

Whites, LeeAnn. "You Can't Change History by Moving a Rock: Gender, Race, and the Cultural Politics of Confederate Memorialization." In *The Memory of the Civil War in American Culture,* edited by Alice Fahs and Joan Waugh, 213–36. Chapel Hill: University of North Carolina Press, 2004.

Wilkinson, Burke. *Uncommon Clay: The Life and Works of Augustus Saint-Gaudens.* San Diego: Harcourt Brace Jovanovich, 1985.

Williams, Brenda W. *Camp Randall Memorial Park: Cultural Landscape Inventory.* Madison: Board of Regents of the University of Wisconsin System, 2011.

Williams, Lewis Waldron II. "Commercially Produced Forms of American Civil War Monuments." MA thesis, University of Illinois, 1948.

Wills, Garry. *Lincoln at Gettysburg: The Words That Remade America.* New York: Simon and Schuster, 1992.

Wilson, Mark. *The Business of Civil War: Military Mobilization and the State, 1861–1865.* Baltimore: Johns Hopkins University Press, 2010.

Winders, Richard Bruce. *Mr. Polk's Army: The American Military Experience in the Mexican War.* College Station: Texas A&M University Press, 1997.

Wingate, Jennifer. *Sculpting Doughboys: Memory, Gender, and Taste in America's World War I Memorials.* Burlington, VT: Ashgate, 2013.

Winock, Michel. "Joan of Arc." In *Realms of Memory: The Construction of the French Past,* edited by Pierre Nora and Lawrence D. Kritzman, translated by Arthur Goldhammer, 3 vols., 3:433–80. New York: Columbia University Press, 1996–98.

Winter, Jay. *Sites of Memory, Sites of Mourning.* Cambridge: Cambridge University Press, 1995.

Woodley, Jenny. "Hashtags and Monuments: Black Lives Matter and America's Racial Memory." Unpublished essay in author's possession, cited with permission.

Wrenn, Tony. *Wilmington, North Carolina: An Architectural and Historical Portrait.* Wilmington: Junior League, 1984.

Wright, Porter C. "The Confederate Monument at Louisa, Virginia." *Louisa County Historical Magazine* 9 (1977): 2–23.

Yockelson, Mitchell. "'Their Memory Will Not Perish': Commemorating the 56th United States Colored Troops." *Gateway Heritage* 22 (Winter 2001–2): 26–31.

Young, Alfred E. *The Shoemaker and the Tea Party: Memory and the American Revolution.* Boston: Beacon, 1999.

Zais, Barrie Emert. "The Struggle for a 20th Century Army: Investigation and Reform of the United States Army after the Spanish-American War, 1898–1903." PhD diss., Duke University, 1981.

Zangrando, Joanna S. "Monumental Bridge Design in Washington, D.C., as a Reflection of American Culture, 1886–1932." PhD diss., George Washington University, 1974.

Index

Page numbers in italics refer to illustrations.

95; Winchester, 83–84, 88, 90. *See also*
Indiana Soldiers and Sailors Monument

Indiana Soldiers and Sailors Monument,
90, 92, 94, 95–96, 118–19, 211, 229, 294–95,
308n83

Inglis, K. S., 11

Iowa, memorials in: Davenport, 57–58;
Des Moines, 105, 158, 198, 318n37;
Jackson Township, 29; Marengo, 309n83;
Waterloo, 73

Ives, Charles, 286

Jackson, Andrew, 4, 37, 131; memorials to,
153

Jackson, Stonewall, 41, 171

—memorials to: Baltimore, 273–75,
322–23n28; Charlottesville, 265–66,
292; Richmond, 135, 206, 323n30; Stone
Mountain, 279, 282

James, Henry, 68–69, 174–75, 220–21

James, William, 100, 103–5

Jarves, James Jackson, 61

Jefferson, Thomas, 3; memorials to, 152, 236

Jeffords, Harrison, 88

Jenney, Edwin S., 98

Joan of Arc, 229; memorial to, 167–68

Johnston, Albert Sidney, 171; memorial to,
135

Johnston, Joseph E., 152, 171

Jones, Charles Colcock, Jr., 200, 203

Jones, Thomas D., 45

Jones, Thomas Goode, 86

Jones, Thomas Hudson, 263

Jones, Wesley, 251

Jordan, David Starr, 125

Julio, Everett B. D., 274

Kansas, memorials in: Paola, 319n45;
Topeka, 73; Wichita, 73

Kauffman, Samuel Hay, 161

Kearney, Belle, 108

Keck, Charles, 76–77

Keller, George, 54, 116, 193–94

Kemper, James L., 135, 155

Kentucky, memorials in: Cynthiana, 78;
Fairview, 265–66; Frankfort, 15, 48,
321n14; Hodgenville, 242, 265; Lexington,

159, 172, 201–3, 202, 322n28; Louisville,
291, 322n28; Morgantown, 310n101;
Owensboro, 90, 91

Kershaw, Jack, 288

King, Martin Luther, Jr., 288

King, Thomas Starr, memorial to, 311n37

Kinney, Belle, 112, 208

Kirstein, Lincoln, 286

Kitchell, John W., 236

Kitson, Samuel, 124, 193, 266

Kitson, Theo Alice Ruggles, 88, 110–11,
116–25

Klir, Joseph, 90

Koehler, Sylvester R., 69

Kolhagen, Frederick, 90, 116

Korean War, memorial to, 285

Kreuzberg Monument, 17

Ku Klux Klan, 278–79, 288–89, 295

Kushner, Tony, 294

labor, 2, 6, 74–76, 177, 182–83, 226, 246–49

Laboulaye, Édouard, 40, 58

Labrouste, Henri, 244

Ladd, Anna Coleman, 254

Ladd, Luther, 73

Ladies' Memorial Associations, 25, 40, 61,
66, 79, 81, 107, 302n25

Lamb, Charles R., 89

Landrieu, Moon, 289

Laqueur, Thomas, 285

Larned, Charles W., 212

Lê, An-My, 295–96

Lea, Luke, 268

Lee, Fitzhugh, 55

Lee, Henry, 102

Lee, Robert E., 25, 125, 133, 171, 179, 207, 209

—memorials to, 7, 294; Baltimore, 273–75,
292, 322–23n28; Charlottesville, 265, 292;
Dallas, 273–74, 274, 292, 323n28; Duke
University, 294; Hall of Fame for Great
Americans, 294; New Orleans, 155, 289–
93, 293, 322n28; Richmond, 155–59, 157,
203, 206, 323n30; Stone Mountain, 275,
277–79, 282; Washington, DC, 271, 294

Lemon, George E., 65

Leutze, Emanuel, 136

Lin, Maya, 285–87

36; Leicester, 38; Lexington, 14, 16, 37; Lowell, 73, 186–87; Lynn, 71, 222; Malden, 98, 120; Manchester, 254; Marlborough, 318n37; Melrose, 73; Milton, 254, 255, 318n37; New Bedford, 321n15; Newburyport, 116–25, *117*; Newton, 20, 27, 41; North Andover, 120; North Attleboro, 308n83; North Brookfield, 28–29, 45; North Reading, 36; Northampton, 36, 38, 303n52; Oakham, 35–36; Petersham, 72–73; Pittsfield, 79–81, *80*, 83–84, 302n25; Plymouth, 303n60; Quincy, 29; Randolph, 307n47; Roxbury, 44–47, *47*, 53; Salem, 83, 254; Sharon, 308n83; Somerville, 21–24, *22*, 220, 309n83; Stockbridge, 31, 222, 303n46; Townsend, 308n83; Waltham, 31–32, 39; Wareham, 309n83; West Roxbury, 45; Whitman, 307n47; Williams College, 303n46, 304n68; Williamsport, 318n37; Woburn, 48, 318n37; Worcester, 43, *44*, 61, 162–64, 170, 188–90, 199, 211. *See also* Bunker Hill Monument; Harvard University; *The Minute Man*; Mount Auburn Cemetery

Mathes, J. Harvey, 323n28

Matthews, Stanley, 132, 137, 142

Matzen, Herman, 94–96

Maury, Matthew Fontaine, memorial to, 315n35, 323n30

McCallum, James, 24

McClellan, Ellen, 149, 172

McClellan, George, 133; memorials to, 148–49, 171, 284

McCrae, John, 254

McFadden, Bernarr, 114

McKenzie, R. Tait, 257, 266

McKim, Charles, 101, 178–79, 212, 216, 236–38, 241, 251–52

McKim, Mead & White, 238–39, 253

McKinley, William, 96

McMillan, James, 176–79. *See also* Senate Park Commission

McNeel Marble Company, 233

McPherson, James, 164; memorials to, 134–37, 142, 158, 174, 284

McQueen, Butterfly, 282

Meachem, George, 39

Mead, Larkin, 40, 58

Meade, George, memorials to, 148, 155, 271–73, *272*

Mechlin, Leila, 250

Meigs, Montgomery, 49, 69–71, 264

Mellon, Richard Beatty, 268

Melville, Herman, 15, 18

Melvin, James C., 218, 220

Melvin Memorial, 218–20, 231

Memorial Day, 9, 25, 31–32, 38, 99–100, 104, 107, 162, 263; monument dedications on, 45, 73, 100, 138, 196, 198, 234–35, 237, 251, 265

memorial halls, 32–38, 55, 63, 68–77

Mercié, Antonin, 156–57, 208

Meredith, James, 287

Merritt, Wesley, 179

Metairie Cemetery (New Orleans), 55, 135

Metropolitan Museum, 220

Mexican War, 3–4, 15, 164; memorials to, 15–16, 37, 78, 136, 229

Michigan, memorials in: Battle Creek, 96; Detroit, 38, 43, 61, 73, 211; Hillsdale College, 88, 96; Houghton, 309n83; Jackson, 96, 118; Monroe, 172; Muskegon, 235–36, 242; Three Rivers, 306n35; Tipton, 78

Miles, Nelson, 177

military cemeteries, 9–10, 19–20, 24–25, 27–28, 49, 56, 261. *See also specific cemeteries*

Military Order of the Loyal Legion, 71, 85, 99, 114–15

militia, 2–3, 21–23, 31, 65–66, 71, 76, 86, 121–22, 124, 129, 177, 195, 234, 251, 262. *See also* Seventh New York Regiment

Miller, Joseph Maxwell, 112

Millet, Francis Davis, 71

Mills, Robert, 15, 299n1

Milmore, Martin, 39–41, 44–48, 53, 61, 83, 116, 119

Minnesota, memorials in: Minneapolis, 265; Stillwater, 307n47

The Minute Man, 59–61, *60*, 66, 118–19

Mississippi, memorials in, 107; Belzoni, 259, 319n46; Carroll County, 86; Jackson, 109;

Johnsville, 273; Syracuse, 98, 118; Utica, 116–17; Walden, 308n83; Yonkers, 83, 90. *See also* Farragut, David G.; George III; Grant, Ulysses S.; Green-Wood Cemetery; Seventh Regiment Memorial; Sheridan, Philip; Sherman, William T.; Statue of Liberty; U.S. Military Academy

New York Peace Society, 221

Niehaus, Charles, 242, 257–58, 284

Nightingale, Florence, memorial to, 110

Nike, 7, 186–87, 189, 208, 210–21, 227, 229, 235, 261–62, 266

Ninth Massachusetts Infantry, 119

Noble, W. Clark, 309n84

Noland, William C., 204–5

North Carolina, memorials in, 107; Charlotte, 291, 323n28; Cumberland County, 86; Durham, 292–94, 323n28; Fayetteville, 99; Hertford, 321n14; Holly Springs, 270; Nash County (Rocky Mount), 87; Raleigh, 90, 112–13, *113*; Reidsville, 322n25, 323n28; Salisbury, 208; University of North Carolina, 125, *126*, 288, 294, 304n86; Wilmington, 49, 265

Norton, Charles Eliot, 34, 99, 239

nudes, 105, 118, 127–28, 207–8, 212, 214–15, 219, 254, 257, 269, 272

obelisks, 15, 38–39. *See also specific monuments*

O'Donovan, William R., 117, 229

Ogden, Horatio Nash, 201

Ogden, William B., 174

O'Hara, Frank, 217

O'Hara, Theodore, 48

Ohio, memorials in: Alliance, 265; Bristol, 20–21, 41; Cincinnati, 41–43, *42*, 73, 119, 236, 246–52, *247*; Cleveland, 45, 90, 92, *93*, *95*, 110; Columbus, 73, 266; Dayton, 73, 268; Elyria, 83; Greenville, 73; Lima, 73; Oberlin College, 303n46; Shelby County (Sidney), 36, 303n52; Springfield, 45; Tiffin, 83; Toledo, 71, *72*; Urbana, 41, 45; Warren, 88

O'Kelley, Stephen J., 119

Olmsted, Frederick Law, 9, 50–51, 53, 189–95, 197–98, 217, 222

Olmsted, Frederick Law, Jr., 178, 236

103rd Ohio Infantry, 92

107th Infantry Regiment, 256

111th New York Infantry, 90

114th Pennsylvania Infantry, 307n43

124th New York Infantry, 88

149th New York Infantry, 98

149th Pennsylvania Infantry, 87

O'Neill, Bucky, memorial to, 170

oratory, 3, 84, 142–53; memorials to, 7, 37, 130, 142–53. *See also specific orators and memorials*

O'Sullivan, Timothy, 132–33

Otis, James, Jr., 37

Pagny, Étienne, 96

Palfrey, John Gorham, 37

Palmer, Erastus Dow, 219

Parker, Theodore, 146, 148; memorial to, 152

Parkman, Francis, memorial to, 218

Parthenon, 241–42, 268

Patterson, John H., memorial to, 268

Paulding, John, 255

Pausch, Edward, 81–83, 88, 116

peace, representations of, 92, 127, 187, 194, 220–31, 263, 266, 268

Peck, George R., 149, 166–67

Pennsylvania, memorials in: Allentown, 119, 226; Bellefonte, 118, 310n104; Bellevue, 268; Ebensburg, 120, 309n83; Canonsburg, 257, 268; Erie County (Girard), 79, 303n60; Girard College, 88, 303n46; Harrisburg, 16, 161–62, 170; Lafayette College, 303n46, 304n68; Lancaster, 304n68; Nazareth Hall, 13–14; New Bloomfield, 98; Norristown, 303n60; Philadelphia, 50, 57, 137, 148–49, 155, 179–80, *181*, 198, 264, 287, 309n83, 313n68, 318n37; Pittsburgh, 29, 74–77, *75*, 77, 105. *See also* Gettysburg

Pension Building (Washington, DC), 69–71, *70*

Perry, Roland Hinton, 226

Pershing, John J., 253, 261; memorial to, 285

Pettengill, Sierra, 295

Phillips, David Graham, 148